# SUITCASE LETTERS

A MEMOIR OF

*travel, adventure and new beginnings*

## JOHN HOWSE

◆ FriesenPress

Suite 300 - 990 Fort St
Victoria, BC, V8V 3K2
Canada

www.friesenpress.com

**Copyright © 2020 by John Howse**
First Edition — 2020

ISBN
978-1-5255-4384-5 (Hardcover)
978-1-5255-4385-2 (Paperback)
978-1-5255-4386-9 (eBook)

*1. BIOGRAPHY & AUTOBIOGRAPHY, PERSONAL MEMOIRS*

Distributed to the trade by The Ingram Book Company

# TABLE OF CONTENTS

101 MONTREAL
(AUG 1955)

102 MONTREAL
(AUG 22 1955)

103 MONTREAL
(SEPT 4)

103 MONTREAL
(SEPT 13 1955)

104 MONTREAL
(SEPT 15 1955)

106 MONTREAL
(SEPT 23 1955)

107 MONTREAL
(SEPT 30 1955)

107 MONTREAL
(OCT 2 1955)

108 MONTREAL
(OCT 12 1955)

110 MONTREAL
(OCT 6 1955)

111 MONTREAL
(OCT 31 1955)

112 MONTREAL
(NOV 7 1955)

113 MONTREAL
(NOV 14 1955)

113 BOSTON MASSACHUSETTS
(NOV 20 1955)

114 MONTREAL
(NOV 22 1955)

115 MONTREAL
(NOV 28 1955)

116 MONTREAL
(DEC 5 1955)

117 MONTREAL
(XMAS 1955)

118 MONTREAL
(JAN 1 1956)

120 MONTREAL
(JAN 1956)

121 MONTREAL
(JAN 1956)

122 MONTREAL
(JAN 15 1956)

123 MONTREAL
(JAN 20 1956)

124 MONTREAL
(JAN 24 1956)

125 MONTREAL
(FEB 1956)

126 MONTREAL
(FEB 14 1956)

128 MONTREAL
(FEB 1956)

130 MONTREAL
(MARCH 7 1956)

131 MONTREAL
(MARCH 1956)

132 MONTREAL
(MARCH 20 1956)

133 MONTREAL
(MARCH 26 1956)

134 MONTREAL
(APRIL 10 1956)

135 MONTREAL
(EASTER MONDAY 1956)

136 MONTREAL
(APRIL 16 1956)

137 MONTREAL
(APRIL 24 1956)

138 MONTREAL
(MAY 5 1956)

138 MONTREAL
(MAY 12)

139 MONTREAL
(MAY 14 1956)

140 MONTREAL
(VICTORIA DAY,MAY 21 1956)

141 QUEBEC CITY
(MAY 28 1956)

142 ROBERVAL P.Q.
(MAY 31 1956)

143 ROBERVAL P.Q.
(JUNE 7 1956)

144  ROBERVAL P.Q.
     (JUNE 17 1956)

146  BLOUGH LAKE P.Q.
     (JUNE 20 1956)

147  BLOUGH LAKE P.Q.
     (JULY 2 1956)

148  LAC JEANNINE P.Q.
     (JULY 4 1956)

149  BLOUGH LAKE P.Q.
     (JULY 1956)

177  BLOUGH LAKE P.Q.
     (JULY 1956) –

178  BLOUGH LAKE P.Q.
     (JULY 1956)

180  LAC JEANNINE P.Q.
     (JULY 12 1956)

181  LAC JEANNINE P.Q.
     (JULY 16 1956)

182  BLOUGH LAKE
     (JULY 1956)

183  BLOUGH LAKE P.Q.
     (AUG 16 1956)

185  BLOUGH LAKE P.Q.
     (AUG 1956)

187  BLOUGH LAKE P.Q.
     (AUG 27 1956)

190  BLOUGH LAKE
     (SEPT 1 1956)

190  BLOUGH LAKE
     (SEPT 3 1956)

192  BLOUGH LAKE P.Q.
     (SEPT 10 1956)

193  BLOUGH LAKE
     (SEPT 16 1956)

195  MONTREAL
     (SEPT 28 1956)

196  MONTREAL
     (OCT 3 1956)

197  MONTREAL
     (THANKSGIVING 1956)

198  MONTREAL
     (OCT 22 1956)

199  MONTREAL
     (OCT 29 1956)

201  MONTREAL
     (OCT 31 1956)

202  MONTREAL
     (NOV 2 1956)

202  MONTREAL
     (NOV 6 1956)

203  MONTREAL
     (NOV 24 1956)

204  MONTREAL
     (DEC 4 1956)

205  MONTREAL
     (DEC 11 1956)

207  MONTREAL
     (JAN 3 1957)

209  MONTREAL
     (JAN 15 1957)

210  MONTREAL
     (JAN 22 1957)

211  MONTREAL
     (JAN 31 1957)

212  BURLINGTON, VERMONT
     (FEB 10 1957)

213  MONTREAL
     (FEB 17 1957)

214  MONTREAL
     (FEB 25 1957)

216  MONTREAL
     (MARCH 19 1957)

217  MONTREAL
     (MARCH 28 1957)

218  MONTREAL
     (APRIL 4 1957)

219  MONTREAL
     (APRIL 10 1957)

220  MONTREAL
     (APRIL 21 1957)

221  MONTREAL
     (APRIL 26 1957)

222  MONTREAL
     (MAY 3 1957)

223 HAMILTON, NEW YORK
(MAY 8 1957)

225 MONTREAL
(MAY 20 1957)

226 MONTREAL
(MAY 21 1957)

227 MONTREAL
(MAY 30 1957)

228 MONTREAL
(JUNE 1957)

229 JEANNINE LAKE P.Q.
(JUNE 17 1957)

231 JEANNINE LAKE P.Q.
(JUNE 28 1957)

232 JEANNINE LAKE P.Q.
(JULY 15 1957)

234 JEANNINE LAKE P.Q.
(JULY 22 1957)

235 JEANNINE LAKE P.Q.
(JULY 31 1957)

236 JEANNINE LAKE P.Q.
(AUG 5 1957)

237 LAC JEANNINE P.Q.
(AUG 15 1957)

238 JEANNINE LAKE P.Q.
(AUG 25 1957)

239 JEANNINE LAKE
(AUG 25 1957)

240 JEANNINE LAKE
(SEPT 6 1957)

242 LAKE JEANNINE P.Q.
(SEPT 13 1957)

243 LAC JEANNINE P.Q.
(SEPT 22 1957)

244 MONTREAL
(SEPT 29 1957)

245 MONTREAL
(OCT 10 1957)

246 MONTREAL
(OCT 19 1957)

247 MONTREAL
(OCT 25 1957)

248 MONTREAL
(NOV 6 1957)

250 MONTREAL
(NOV 16 1957)

251 MONTREAL
(NOV 26 1957)

252 MONTREAL
(DEC 6 1957)

253 MONTREAL
(DEC 11 1957)

254 MONTREAL
(JAN 1958)

255 MONTREAL
(JAN 14 1958)

256 MONTREAL
(JAN 24 1958)

258 MONTREAL
(FEB 5 1958)

259 MONTREAL
(FEB 12 1958)

260 MONTREAL
(FEB 1958)

262 MONTREAL
(FEB 19 1958)

263 WEST 34 ST. NEW YORK
(FEB 24 1958)

265 MONTREAL
(MARCH 2 1958)

266 MONTREAL
(MARCH 11 1958)

267 MONTREAL
(MARCH 18 1958)

268 MONTREAL
(MARCH 27 1958)

269 MONTREAL
(APRIL 2 1958)

271 MONTREAL
(EASTER APRIL 11 1958)

272 MONTREAL
(APRIL 22 1958)

273 JEANNINE LAKE P.Q.
(MAY 11 1958)

# SUITCASE
# LETTERS

# CALGARY
## (MARCH 22 2020)

I left Australia in 1954 and wrote my mother, sister Caroline (Mal) and brothers (Michael, Tony and Denis) weekly for a few years. Mum saved the letters and I first noticed the collection on my first trip back after 14 years on the road. The letters were stuffed into a leather travel bag atop her bedroom wardrobe. A few years later, after her death, the bag had migrated to a back bedroom. Subsequent visits found it progressively on the back verandah, the garage and finally outside under an awning but otherwise exposed to the antipodal elements.

It was then I succumbed to my sister's urgings to reclaim the contents. And so here they are – the adventures of a 19-year-old on the ocean for five weeks to London, hitch-hiking and working in Europe for months, and then Canada. A first job delivering Christmas presents for Simpson's Montreal department store, followed by a resumption of my banking career with the Royal Bank, hurdling university entrance exams, the McGill years in Montreal, the summers working in northern Quebec, playing rugby football for Westmount in New York and Boston, the years as barman-dishwasher at a ladies club on Montreal's grand Sherbrooke Street West. And the kindness of the Bains of Notre Dame de Grace who took in their Australian off-spring for his final all- out effort to get into Medical School without the night job at the ladies club. He didn't make McGill medicine but he got into UBC but that's another tale and it wasn't all such plain sailing after that migration to the West Coast.

It has often struck me whilst reading memoirs that when someone actually recalls his early years, everything seems highly filtered through the matured brain cells of the writer or memoirist. There is little record of what he wrote at that age simply because there was little anyone regarded as keepable, even if it was written. I suppose that's where a mother comes into the picture – she kept these weekly letters so the record is there – with all the politically incorrect observations left unedited. That is especially tender for someone who now is Canadian and so much at home in the world of the politically correct. Just remember that I began under the White Australia Policy – two Wongs in my day were never encouraged to make a White. That all changed but it took time and the Suitcase Letters record calmly shows it didn't happen overnight.

Of course, one doesn't tell all in a family letter. One unconsciously projects a happy face – all is well on the road, wish I could see you all and so on. Otherwise what is the point of being away – you have to imagine you are doing better than had you stayed at home. My father, Beresford Oswald Howse, hit a similar upbeat note in letters from the French front during World War One. Meanwhile one's romances, one's own failings, uncertainties and unmentioned personal disasters emerge somehow, not necessarily in the letters but in fiction, of all things. Another book hopefully will deal with the interplay of the Suitcase Letters and the fiction which, unmailed or read by anyone, accumulated in Calgary just as the letters piled up in Cootamundra N.S.W. And naturally, along with the letters and the fiction, travelled the journalism. Later on, there are stories of OPEC, peacekeeping in Bosnia and Croatia, the Stanley Cup, cowboys and Indians interspersed with letters by now to a wife and five children.

That is the plan now that these Suitcase Letters have been outed from the leather bag and allowed to set the stage. It hasn't been easy. Imagine the stabbing impact of reading Derek Wolcott's "White Egrets" on the struggling memoirist:

--"the bleached regrets/

of an old man's memoirs

--"what? You're going to be superman at seventy-seven?"

"the pitch of paralysed horror/

that his prime is past."

"that peace/

Beyond desires and beyond regrets/

At which I may arrive eventually."

And, as if it is never too late for a reason to quit, Neil Gentzlinger's amusing, almost targeted, literary onslaught on the overcrowded memoir genre. "A moment of silence, please, for the lost art of shutting up," he writes in the Jan 30 2011 NYT Book Review. "There was a time when you had to earn the right to draft a memoir, by accomplishing something noteworthy or by having an extremely unusual experience or being such a brilliant writer that you could turn occurrences into a snapshot of a broader historical moment. Anyone who didn't fit one of those categories was obliged to keep quiet. Unremarkable lives went unremarked upon, the way God intended."

Yes, but....

John Howse

## SOMEWHERE OFF THE VICTORIAN COAST
## (JAN 5 1954)

It was nice having you all down to the boat –terrific feeling as she made off down the harbour. The tow rope broke as the tug was about to cast off. Soon as we cleared the Heads we had "emergency" drill. Entailed going up to "C" deck from our "H" deck home with our life belts donned. Dinner wasn't until 7.30 p.m., just lasted. Went up to the dance (coffee is served in the after lounge) and just listened to the music, all set to participate tonight after I get the rest of my luggage. Pretty tired so hit the cot and didn't stir until the steward brought the early morning brew in around seven. Don't know whether this service will continue as I left no tip.

Colossal out on "B" deck as I write. A beautiful day, the coast line dim on one side (saw all Wollongong and South Coast) and the open Pacific on the other. It's as calm as the Cootamundra swimming pool and all you can feel is the throb of the engines and the constant roll. Soon get used to it. So far so good with the "big spit." Went up to the goldfish pond they call a pool and had a swim. There is a pleasant breeze but the water was cold. Takes me one stroke to cover the length. However you can get wet. All of us in deck chairs now, wearing only trunks so the tan should commence.

No activities organized yet but anytime though we expect to be in the middle of it. For now it's the deck chair. The steward came around last night and peeled off nine telegrams for me! There is quite a bit of talent on board. You'll laugh when I say we got an old Scot in our cabin, pleasant old cow and harmless. Other two are kids traveling with their people. Just got in from the dance and had quite a time. The band is O.K. and women are in excess. A lot get off at Melbourne and the other Australian ports and the London ones get on. Finishing this in my upper bunk. The ventilation is good and the place so steady you'd swear we had stopped.

## OFF SOUTH AUSTRALIA COAST
## (JAN 10 1954)

Had a good day seeing the sights of Melbourne. The city is quieter and prettier than Sydney but of course no harbour shores. Went up to St. Kilda and their "beach" – no surf. Got all my dry cleaning done so that was a break. Then to Princes Park on the Yarra River embankments, the war memorials and city streets. Myer Emporium is a monster. Had a good cool salad there and nearly melted waiting for the Harlem Globetrotters' basketball exhibition. They were late (usually are) and the Sports Department manager was in a great dither, apologizing over the "mike" and racing from phone to phone. Later went to the State Theatre and saw "From Here to Eternity." Colossal. One of the boys here has the book so will get on it.. We strolled around downtown, watched a brawl outside the Australia hotel and ate at Raffles. Then to the wharf. Also in port was the big white , single funneled "Himalaya." Saw her off at 11 p.m. after being abused by an old woman selling warm cool drinks because I felt the bottle before I refused to pay for it.

Departure from Melbourne just as big and pretty as from Sydney with thousands of streamers. Met some New Zealanders at the dance. All play Rugby Union. They didn't even know the difference between League and Union as our Rugby League is not popular over there.

## OFF WESTERN AUSTRALIA COAST
## (JAN 1954)

The Great Australian Bight behind us now as we round Cape Leeuwin and start up the West Coast for Fremantle tomorrow morning. Have had calm seas but today has been dull and rainy. We did our first bit of washing and thought we would lose it at one time with the wind. However it was all there when we collected it before afternoon tea and will start the ironing later tonight. Thriving on the sea air and the appetite is soaring. The food is extra good. There is always a meal not far around the corner. Breakfast is at 7.45 a.m., beef tea and biscuits 11 a.m., lunch 12.30 p.m., afternoon brew 4 p.m., dinner 6.30 p.m. On a day like today all you can do is read, eat and sleep which isn't hard to take. No table tennis balls are available for sale until we are out of customs range tomorrow night as they are in bond. The currency is from tomorrow in Sterling so any surplus (not much) of Australian coin we changed today. A bit "mis" (mean, miserable, lousy) getting 16 shillings for one pound but prices come down a fair bit.

The tan is O.K. now –anyone couldn't miss in the weather we've had up to date, just the swimming and dancing. We're all planning on a holiday at Blackpool when we get to England. One of the stewards had a shot at one of the old ladies today. In a very aloof voice she asked: "Oh, steward, have you any draughts here?" The Cockney went straight to the windows and opened three of them. We all had a fit. He didn't bat an eye.

The crew roped off the bottom deck with nets tonight, a precaution against stowaways when we reach Fremantle. Everyone thought a big storm was abrewing. Adelaide was really a pretty city. Nicely planned, stately buildings, the right size for a city. We left the wharf and hitch-hiked in the thirteen miles to town. The train would have taken 50 minutes. Not a hard place to get to know – we took an electric train to Glenelg which is much the same as Manly. Had a feed, returned to the city and just caught the special steam train back to Outer Harbour where our Otranto was berthed.

INDIAN OCEAN
(JAN 19 1954)

It was extra good to get all the news from you at Fremantle. Had given up but you put Berth 1369 instead of 1359 so I got my mail at sea the following morning. Also a letter from Great Aunt Folo enclosing a one pound note. Fremantle and Perth were very nice , much quieter than Sydney and Melbourne but King's Park and the Swan River very beautiful. Nearly missed the boat coming back . We arrived at 4.45 p.m. and the boat was due to sail at 4 p.m. We had left too early to be told the altered departure hour. Luckily for us the propeller was giving trouble. The gang ways were all up and there was a mad panic when we walked on to the wharf and they let us board via a crew door.

Just now we are putting the major part of the Indian Ocean behind us. Yesterday it was relief to see land in the Cocos Islands group. Peninsular and Orient liners usually drop a gift barrel of food and drink over the side as a break in the islanders' monotonous diet. We had several quick tropical showers as we passed the islands . They came from nowhere and you could see them behind us as we passed. You will all be surprised to hear that I have already met the big boss, the captain. Got back to the cabin a few nights ago and there was the invitation to cocktails at 6.45 p.m. Wore the blue suit. Met all the officers. About 50 to 60 people there. Was talking to some old galah and he turned out to be a serving colonel in the British Army. I wasn't comfortable in the suit as it was hot. All of "H" deck and the New Zealanders on "G" reckon they must put the names in a hat for the captain's cocktail party. I wouldn't think this about it.

My tan now is a brown as the farewell compendium you gave me. Today we had the mixed doubles table tennis. I drew one of the best women as my partner so we won four games to be in the final later. One of the matches we won included the male champion and he almost did his block when he lost. Don Bullivant, the banker friend I left with, was our second victim. In the gent's deck tennis doubles, I was ousted in Round One but have got through O.K. to Round 2 in Deck Quoits. Writing this from the main lounge where there is a programme of recorded music every second afternoon When you don't have the wireless, these are very popular. The service in the lounge is pretty crook; having a lemon squash between dances (English beer is weak, sweet and like treacle) they keep us waiting 30 minutes. The waiter placed my change on the tray, the four pence in four English pennies. Took them up in a flash so we won't be in the hunt in future. I have seen no sign of your Mrs. Thompson. If she looks like a fare-home prospect, I will marry her!

## ARABIAN SEA
### (JAN 25 1954)

Well, Colombo was one of the most colossal days in my life. We got there early and we stood on the rails from 7 a.m. watching the sunrise over the hilly coast line and our first sight of foreign land. A lot of dhows, fishing boats, were out. Once into the harbour, which is a breakwater and full, of foreign ships, we were met by the traders in their flat-bottom row boats, full of polished wood elephants, bowls etc and bunches of bananas and pineapples. They are the greatest bargainers but we knew to leave it all until the ship was nearly going—then prices fall.

Into the wharf by launch and then up through customs. We took a few cigs in and soon swapped them for stamps and a bit of dough. Not many whites around anywhere, everywhere the varied races of Indians, Ceylonese and Malay. They are just in sarongs and no shoes. We left the main street and got a bus to the native quarter. The three of us were the only white trash around so we didn't kick any one out of the way. They are all so friendly and every inch there is a stand or shop of some description, like one continuous row of places selling trinkets, clothes, watch bands, combs, anything cheap and useless. "You buy, master," "All nylon shirt, master," –they hand you a shoddy Jap imitation silk. Bought a reasonably good shirt –he wanted 7 rupees, got it for four. (1 rupee equals one shilling and sixpence Stg). Also bought a pair of strong toeless sandals for 5 rupees. He wanted 8! Then to a cloth pavement shop for 3 yards of cloth for a sarong. A beauty – for 5 rupees sewn. You pretend to walk away and in all be a Jew which suited me. Then into a shop where a sly character asks:"You want to change money?" I knew there would be a market for sterling. "How much you got? " We got two shillings and three pence above the right price per one pound sterling which is O.K. but the fun is meeting them in the back parlour. Met the big boss of one outfit and told him I would bring back gold for him from England but don't worry, we took no chances so all is well.

The food houses were filthy, flies swarming all over the dates, cakes and fruit. The streets are narrow with refuse all over. Everywhere guides tried to fasten themselves to us—we gave in and let one show us a Hindu temple. Had to take our shoes off and leave them outside in the street. I was a bit crooked on this so Gandhi, as we nicknamed him, promptly called one of his mates who I noticed had been following us, and he minded the shoes. Aren't they crafty? The old priest caught us for a rupee and blessed us with a red mark on our foreheads. Got a bit sick of the guide so we gave him two shillings and told him where to go. He thought it a bit "mis" but you soon learn to be tough on this mob, especially the cursed beggars. We had groups of kids younger than you Mal (sister was 13 at the time) running after us, shouting "Please, master," and rubbing their stomachs. Gave one fifty cents (one rupee= 100 cents) but then told them where to go. Also lots of betel-chewing hags around.

The rickshaws are the things that jolt you when you see an old guy wanting to pull you around the city on the hot day it was (we wore our straw hats and shorts), it sure makes you wonder. Just couldn't be in it. They pester you and you tell them where to go. But they, like everyone else, are old sharpies. Then you see an old cart pulled by oxen and led by an old bare-footed Indian, then a 1950 Chevrolet blows its horn -- the old and the new go forward together. The streets are like anthills, bikes, carts, rickshaws, cars, buses, masses of Indians, the occasional yellow-garbed priest. The bars look to be the greatest of dens and from them issue the weird Indian music, like a scene from a harem film. One old guy flashed up beside me and asked me to buy a gold watch which was obviously hot.

So after interesting conversations with everyone we met, from tailors to slouch-hatted policemen, we caught a bus out past the Houses of Parliament and the house of the Governor-General to the famous Hotel Mount Lavinia. Our first glimpse of a palm-treed lined beach. We had our togs and had a slick surf in the warm waters of the Arabian Sea. The waves were small but took you right in and we wallowed in it after the smallness of the ship's pool.

Then we went to the pub and had a fair meal that cost 5.50, or six rupees with the ceaseless tip. A snake charmer wanted to show us his pet cobra, someone else had surfboards for hire; everyone wants to do something for you. The only thing wrong is that you are expected to pay for it. A palmist singled me out and started to read my hand before calmly telling me to put a one pound note in his opened book. I told him to go get himself a job. He got a bit cheeky then but he was small. Then back into town by rail—three classes, we went second. It's hard to get used to seeing no whites about. Made another trip around the streets then queued up to change my dough back into real money. The boat sellers were in full swing and there was more raucous bargaining. They send the goods up by rope in a canvas bag – mostly dust-collectors but no doubt some fine craft. We bought pineapples and coconuts but no food other than at the Mount Lavinia. We didn't need the official warning.

Really a terrific day. Everyone else went on official tours but I think the three of us saw more of it than most. We sailed at 6 p.m. Had a good shower and that was it for the night. Back to boat life with the water sports. First was the Spoon Dive . They scatter spoons around the bottom of the pool. I had everyone beaten with 51 spoons and then Don does 53. I also won four lifebuoy cockfights (you sit in the round buoy and toss the opponent) but I got stoushed in the final. Then there was the fancy Dress dance – Aub did us up with terrific beards and make-up and we looked the part of Indians in our sarongs. And an Indian on board tied our turbans. The tan was handy. Have never seen such colossal costumes. Aub did a stand-up act using the records of Danny Kaye and Jerry Lewis and got three encores. Had me a few dances. The weather is slick and the heat of the cabins is subsiding.

RED SEA, ADEN

(JAN 28 1954)

The Red Sea is not coloured. Did you know that? Well, it was hot today and right now we are heading for the Gulf of Suez. Got to Aden in the early evening and the first glimpse of the Arabian coastline was terrific. Aden is a massive lava rock formation, completely barren and eroded. The pilot boarded here and we sailed around into the breakwater and loaded off into launches. Not far into the quay – a stone landing place. No customs or any currency restrictions since sterling is O.K. but they use the East African shillings of the same value as the Stg shilling. They divide a shilling up into 100 cents. Am collecting the coins of each realm. All the shops were awake for us, even the Post Office offering us sets of stamps. Not the hustle and bustle here of Colombo. The natives seem a little more aggressive and a lot use staffs and walking sticks which makes you feel right at home. As I walked along the main street, I felt a tug at my buttoned hip-wallet pocket. Bashed down and caught an Arab kid a beauty on the wrist. He blew through very smartly down the street. First stop was the Universal Bazaar. You can't imagine the number of watches, cameras, pens, expensive makes all of them; beautiful leather cases, china sets, nylon undies (I'll buy some for you Mal if I come back this way). Of course, there is a fair bit of trash but they had the real thing in Omega SeaMasters for 26 Pounds, all other famous brands with accredited agents, too. Bloke I know bought the gold SeaMaster but I think he's going to sell it when he gets to U.K. Aub bought a camera (23 Pounds). They are 64 Pounds in Aussie. What did I buy? A Hermes Baby Typewriter, a little beaut for 17 Pounds. Am going to learn typing on board and it should be extra good. I went over the machine and all seems to be well. May type the next letter here in the lounge but as the classical music is on, I had better not start up or all the pseudos may get annoyed. Back in Aden after the big purchase had been safely negotiated, we continued down the street, going into every shop. On the verandas they would have their little stalls with cigarette lighters, packs of cards with "52 guaranteed works of art" (a nude on each one).

They don't bargain in the main shops but once we hit the real native quarter it was different. Five kids would rush you all asking for dough so the hand was fastened on the hip. Arabs would dart up offering wrist watches, all looking as poor as crows. They would dive into their pockets and produce five or six shiny new watches. "You buy, Johnnie," "Hullo Johnnie." Everyone calls everyone by that name. These quarters are dirty and the Arabs much taller than the average Ceylonese. We had a look at their coffee and eat houses and saw them gambling and playing dominoes. They have their cafes out in the street, one with a fire in a drum cooking chops. Goats roam at random and blend in with the smell well. We left about 1 a.m. The boat looks terrific coming out to her from the quay, all lit up.

## SUEZ CANAL
## (JAN 30 1954)

Well we made Port Suez and entered the Canal at 7.30 a.m. while I was a Mass. It was the most restless session I've seen with everyone craning their necks to see what was going on outside. The Canal is much the width of the Murrumbidgee and built along the same pattern as the Griffith canals. Being the Royal Mail, we lead the convoy. They allow convoys to run either way. The other ships followed at intervals of about one mile. One side is the desert, sand hills stretch as far as you can see. The other side is tree-lined and some of it is under cultivation. Along this side were the British Army Canal Zone groups, the railway and the tar road. It is single way traffic until we made the Great Bitter Lake where we stopped for three hours to let the convoy from Port Said go down. On the move again, we passed by a lot of of Arabs and fishermen. Mobs of Tommies came to the Canal bank and shouted: "Chuck the women overboard." It was amazing to see the following ships coming around one of the canal bends. They looked as if they were ploughing through the sand. Saw the odd camel and old donkey cart but most of it was sand.

Made Port Said around 9 p.m. Could see the lights for more than one hour but we move so slowly in the Canal. The whole length is 80 miles. Before we went ashore the police boarded by launch. Had to queue up to get the first stamp in my passport. I was a bit crooked as he missed the first page. Once ashore the usual mob of vendors started to yell. This time it was leather goods. Bought a photo album and a kosh. Had a look around all the shops but we were warned not to wander too far off. At one shop the assistant told me to shut up for telling him that a souvenir spoon one of the mob was buying wasn't good silver. I told him where to go ( was a fat wog) and he screamed : "Get out, get out of my shop." I looked outside and saw the big black-coated policeman with a rifle. Shut up, I did. Around the corner at midnight we were in a shop and there was a power failure. Thought it was "on" but no, they soon lit up the place again. With all the hate for the British and the killings, we were on the look out for anything. Came back via a side street and as we passed, little groups would gather. Police everywhere and all armed.

However, am very well as we plunge onwards towards Italy through the Messina Strait, one and one-half miles of sea separating Italy and Sicily. This southern coast of Italy looks beautiful. The mountains are snow-capped and on the small coastal fringes are villages. Weather is cold with a howling wind and a few rain squalls today. Last night we had a real storm. We were in the pictures and half the crowd left to perk over the side. Aub did as well, giving in so reluctantly. We have never stopped roasting him and he is crook again. So far so good for me and I do think a lot bring it on themselves, thinking too much about it. But we haven't done the Bay of Biscay yet. Ah, passed the island of Stromboli about noon. Did you see the film made on it? It was smoking away, and these clouds of steam billowed forth from the lava pouring down the sides of the active volcano crater.

Just in from winning the mixed doubles tennis finals (23-21, 21-14).

MEDITERRANEAN

(FEB 4 1954)

Hope by now the mails have cleared sufficiently to indicate that I am nearly in France. Last night we landed in Naples. It was pretty cold. The harbour is very attractive at night, and with the lights of a massive aircraft carrier and 15 other vessels of the United States Fleet, a blaze of colour.

Through the Customs O.K. and into one of the most impressive buildings. It's the quay block, of shops, a bank, market stalls etc, with a curved, high ceiling. It and many of the other really outstanding structures were put up by Mussolini. The wogs seem to like him up to when he ganged up with Hitler. They are all friendly and many nods and smiles as we sallied down Naples. Walked to downtown. Yank sailors were everywhere but did not impress. About midnight we went into a little café and had the most delicious spaghetti and sauce with sifted cheese and two plates of bread a la Italia. Can they cook spag! Also a bottle of vino (they have it like water only it costs more) but it tasted no better than the sauterne, so attacked a Coke. They are everywhere in Italy.

While we ate, a violin and guitar played. No one could speak English. They played lousy and when they finished, none of us looked up. The violinist got up and poked a brass tray under my nose. Gave him 25 Players cigarettes and Don handed 25 to the guitarist, (A lira is 1760 to the Pound Stg, and here 20 cigs cost 380 lira. One shilling and eight pence for 25 on ship) so they were quite pleased and left us. Can't get over it, one day in Italy, the next in France. Everyone perking (vomiting) now, but as I have to join the church choir if I succumb, am pretty confident.

# MEDITERRANEAN

## (FEB 6 1954)

We docked in Marseilles about 9 a.m. and the bus into town met the ship. It cost 60 francs for the five-mile run through the thickly congested wharf area. The harbour was one of the busiest and extensive we have yet seen. First thing that hit us was the return to civilization. No touts, bum boats –or what they call the natives in boats that come out to the ship—or even buyers for cigarettes. We learnt about the latter before going ashore so weren't inconvenienced by having to carry them around all day. Put off the bus in La Canebiere or Main St. First shop was a radio-TV place but the boss told us that TV had not yet come to Marseilles and it was more or less for display. Two Canadian nurses came in with us so we were smelling perfume for a while. Channel #5 and 10, 22 are some of the varieties but dear, and we ain't worked for a long time.

Mum, you would have enjoyed the main shops—the shoes and clothes looked very smart and high class and much the same prices as Aussie.(960 francs to the Pound Stg). We then walked up town to the cheaper joints, up through the meat and fish markets. The fish market was run by old women in black gowns and shawls almost like nuns. They yell with their coarse old voices and all the time scraping off the fish scales. Just the type for the old hags of the Halles who used to knit away while the guillotine was in action.

Plenty of food around and oranges sold for about Australian nine pence. In one section les demoiselles cooked the most tempting brews. Bought a large slice of a French milk bread, fried with cheese and toms with black olives. About the size of three pieces of our bread. Only 30 francs so lined up again.

All through very few people spoke any English which I didn't expect and it really was surprising just how useful my French came in. Aub, Don and others had no clues on it. They speak terrifically fast but I used all the old, stock phrases and we got by. After a cup of coffee in a bar and some exquisite French pastry, we got a bus to the bottom of the Basilica of Our Lady, a gigantic church on the highest point of the city and from which we could see most of the place. On top of it all was a big statue. All around the walls are bullet marks. It would have been a hornet's nest for snipers . Inside are return thanks engraved into the wall and I even saw two French helmets both with bullets through them. Also medals and ribbons.

In both Naples and Marseilles, the Church is the king-pin and infinitely more powerful than at home. In Naples you would have thought the Pope is King. He was everywhere. Then we went around the Arc de Triumphe, a war memorial, and a few more sights before heading back to the boat. Am looking forward to a lot more of France. The women were conspicuous by their lack of fashion but more of that from Paris. The local businessmen were most dapper. We must have looked pretty foreign as we got a lot of looks.

Nearly finished with the Mediterranean now as we are off the south coast of Spain. Cape San Antonio was the last land we saw as we set a course for Gibraltar.

## TILBURY DOCKS U.K.

### (FEB 11 1954)

Had a most interesting few hours on the Rock of Gibraltar. In there by 9 a.m. but being Sunday and the people of Spanish origin being very Catholic, the shops were closed due to the strict police. We hired a cab for a couple of hours, a Humber Snipe. I hogged the front seat; six of us in it at seven shillings and sixpence each. Really saw all of the island, from trips through the tunnel to getting out and seeing the Spanish frontier guards who were beautifully dressed and "on" themselves and pretty strict. They haven't a chance of getting this off Britain. None of the mob here like Spain.

Well, we are finally here, since 3 a.m. Rose to a fog and the drab buildings of the docks. But it's fining up now and the fog is lifting and for the past half-hour have been watching the London dockies unload the tons of baggage. It's cold but with my supply of new winter garments I am O.K. Bought a beaut pair of leather sheep's wool lined gloves in Gibraltar for 24 shillings. Did all our packing yesterday and our heavy luggage is now in the Customs Hall and we are sitting here waiting and we have another three hours to go because we are the last mob to leave. Only have the typewriter and overnight bag to carry down the plank and then the big inspection begins when we get the rest of our luggage.

This has all been a wonderful experience, these five weeks but am looking forward to doing something and maybe having a good clean job in the fish markets! Everyone here in the midst of goodbyes now so will pass off, have morning tea and should be moving earlier than expected.

# LONDON

## (FEB 15 1954)

Got through Customs with a really pleasant man who passed everything. Then the special boat train to St. Pancreas. You can't imagine the luggage scramble with 400 people and all the bags just thrown off on to a section of the platform. We got down on ours very smartly and rang the Y.M.C.A. Cabbed out there at Tottenham Court and settled down into a double room. It was only 4 p.m. so went into town for a look around and to register at Australia House. It's very smart inside and so big. It's in The Strand. Also saw Trafalgar Square, Piccadilly Circus, Leicester Square, the names so famous to us that it was amazing to find how close to one another they are.

Am finding my way around London very easy and the Underground Railway (the Tube) is colossal. Have a diagram of the change stations and network and all very simple so we haven't missed a trick on it. From Tottenham Court, the next station is Leicester Sq.; change there and next is Piccadilly.

Gets dark early and we had tea at Lyons Corner Store. Serve yourself. Later we watched the Royal Tour of New Zealand on television and to bed, good to be in one after five weeks in a bunk.

Up early Friday and out to St. Paul's to see if there were any jobs at the G.P.O. NO, there weren't. Saw some bomb damage out this way and we had a look at the Bank of England. Visited a pair of labor exchanges but they give you the horrors the way they go on. Out to the other side of the city, Victoria where I had an employment agency to look up. They were extra good and sent me to Allied Traders.

It was a funny old show. Had to go into a typical English manager's office and be grilled. Naturally I have come to London seeking a permanent career. They gave me an exam on simple mathematics which I must have passed for I start Monday in the Cashier's Department at Six Pounds Ten Shillings per week.

Back to Lyon's for tea and saw the play "Cry the Beloved Country," a special performance in St. Martin-of-the-Field Church in Trafalgar Sq.

We now have moved out to the Hotel Hazel Court at Bayswater and will settle in here for one week. Not the Hotel Australia and, hell, don't let anyone say that our way of life is no different to England. Soon as we arrived, we sat down to the TV set and saw the All Blacks versus Scotland in Rugby – a better view than had we been there. More at night and it is amazing. Saw an hour of newsreel and all the Royal pair did the day before. The weather has been fine though misty but not long now until winter is over.

Out staying here is the New Zealand pianist Cora Hall. She took us walking today, from here through Kensington gardens, Hyde Park, Buckingham Palace (saw changing of the guard), Rotten Row and the horse riders down by Big Ben and the Houses of Parliament, across Westminster Bridge to the South Embankment and back by Whitehall Palace and its Horse Guards beautifully turned out with metal hats and white and red plumes. Up "The Mall" which leads straight down to Buckingham Palace, and then No. 10 Downing Street followed by Pall Mall and Nelson's Trafalgar Square.

After a good lunch went over to the Marble Arch at Hyde Park and it is the Domain of London. One old bloke was the best speaker I have seen and only did it to keep people cheered up. Home now to TV.

BAYSWATER LONDON

(FEB 19 1954)

Decided against the job as wages clerk. Instead we fixed up our ration cards, insurance compulsory and got our permit cards to work. Into Forte's, one of London's famous caterers and got a job as a counter assistant.

We are installed where the heart of the world beats, Piccadilly (Rainbow Corner, Shaftsbury Avenue when all your friends wish to call) and we are in training. Having a great time at it and enjoying it a lot. Getting quite a look into the business. We go in at nine this week and wear the typical skull caps, white coats and aprons with a tea towel tucked in at the waist. Felt like a great galah at first but it's O.K. and this afternoon we had our solo serving. It went O.K. and kept them served up. It's mostly coffee, hamburgers and small meals –we'll be learning all week and even get some cooking experience.

From Monday we do the permanent late shift starting at four in the afternoon and finishing a bit after midnight. This will suit us fine as we can get about and see something during the day. Get a day off during the week and every second Sunday so it could be worse. Anyway, we are in the food game and on the house have one main meal and about three snacks at rest periods. Make ourselves milkshakes and ham sandwiches for the latter so we are looking after ourselves .

Wages are only six Pounds a week and we are going into a flatette with Aub next week. He is going colossal, $15 per week which over here is big time. Met him tonight after work and had tea at the Windmill Theatre

All the big theatres are around us here and millions of lights. Walked around them all tonight but we are holding off spending before we see the Continent and rest of England.

The women at work are driving me mad and thank heavens it is only this first week that I have to put up with them. You'd be surprised at the number of older ladies that work. The impact of the war on this country has been terrific. Most of the older people I have spoken with have lost at least one kid in the services and usually have been bombed or blasted out a few times. The way they just go on taking all these restrictions without real complaint – and no one believes that Britain as a world power is finished. "Just let anyone try" seems to be the attitude. They respond to friendliness, just is that you have to speak or smile first.

The most depressing thing we have yet seen is the labour exchange with all the unemployed. One old bloke babbled on about going to Australia. He was lying on the steps.

Finishing this letter off in the staff room. All the women are talking about knocking off dough from the till. They are a hard lot. Seeing some good newsreels on TV and all the snaps of Australia and the Queen.

Love to all, John the Soda Jerk.


## PICCADILLY CIRCUS, LONDON
### (FEB 23 1954)

Writing this at lunch in the staff room. None of the mad women are about except for one who is attempting to entice us to a Red Youth Club. Eating like horses and working the same. Had our first go at night work Saturday and it was terrifically busy. Hundreds of Yanks, a lot of them out of uniform, and as all along the voyage, they aren't liked here. Seem to be a fair few around of enormous black jokers. We are full-time counter boys now and meeting the public in a big way. Even got tipped four and one-half pence last night. The boss thought we did extra well. We did too, on the food. They have now shifted us to Leicester Square, next door to the Empire Theatre, No 2-4, so right in it. The change will be good although it's only another 300 yards down town. The West End and Soho aren't far off.

Now back in our flatette at 10 Queens Gardens Bayswater but the nearest railway is Paddington Station which is also a large steam engine station. This is a very big room with large stove (gas) and gas fire. The furniture is quite nice.

We expect the millionaire Aub to join us sometime this week. It will be one Pound each a week that way. Food prices are generally cheaper so far and the landlady is O.K. We've got it looking like "home" already.

Up above us here are two New Zealander blokes, one a sports journalist who plays Union for a London team and also works at Fortes. The other is a school teacher and makes less than our six Pounds per week. He's always O.K. for a feed in at Fortes.

Funny that you mentioned in your last letter about meeting a kind Scot – well, one of the old nice ladies at work is one and thought I was broke and wanted to lend me one Pound. Didn't accept but it was a warm offer. Can't see us starving now that we're in the food game.

London is a mighty place. So much to see but we are concentrating on doing the sights rather than the high life. Means missing some great shows but I think worth it. On Sunday we went to Regent's Park, one of the large ones here. Beautiful in an English way of green, barren trees and the greyish mist colour that is here for the winter. Also London Zoo with a colossal collection of animals and settings.

The other night a Mrs MacLean , who we met at the hotel, took us out to the best curry I have ever had. She was the wife of the ex-New Zealand High Commissioner and the mother of the pianist I wrote of earlier.

LEICESTER SQUARE, LONDON

(MARCH 3 1954)

Writing in the staff room. We are well in the sway of events here. You should see the crowd that gets around this snack bar. Every type imaginable, the cream of London's barrow boys and their women beauties. The manageress is a beauty and gives me cakes to take home. Also cooks a slick meal for the staff and being Pancake Day she did the honors frying them in butter which over here is sacrilege.

All last night at work we watched the snow falling on Leicester Sq. and it was really beautiful. Not so busy being a Monday night, so all the colonials gathered to my top end of the counter which opens out on to the street. There are trees outside on the square. Right on twelve we blew through and four of us had a snow fight all over the gardens. The snow was about two inches thick.

Later out at the flat, I could see the snow falling on the glass section of our roof from my cot. In the morning all the barren trees were covered with snow to the tiniest branch. After some porridge, bacon and eggs, we went to St Paul's Cathedral. Doesn't look so big from the outside but its enormous dome and wall paintings, memorials to the great all provided a good few hours of interest. You go into the main part and there are the chairs, altar and pews. For one shilling you climb a monstrous staircase to reach the Whispering Gallery from where you look down on to the altar and main body of the church. It is actually inside the dome and you can walk around the circle. An old guy on the other side to us gave a talk on the Cathedral by speaking into the wall. The sound traveled right around to us. Up the most extreme staircase ever and out on to a railed edge around the middle of the dome. Snow everywhere and we had a mighty view of the city. There are a lot of cleared spaces from bomb damage even now. Rather perturbed at the way they had ticket machines here and there for the privilege of entry. Cost us three shillings each by the time we had finished.

Came in early Sunday to mass in a tiny French church off the Strand, not far from the snack bar. Run by French priests and nuns, the sermon in French. Quite a change! Will have to go out to Harringay Stadium and see Billy Graham who is causing a tremendous amount of interest over here. Has he made headlines in Aust. yet? On my mid-week day off went into the Royal Academy of Arts and saw an exhibition of 1500s painting. Van Dyck and Reubens were the important painters.

## BAYSWATER, LONDON
## (MARCH 11 1954)

Last Friday we went out to the Imperial War Museum and found it most interesting particularly the Air Force section with its relics, photos and displays of World War II. Best of all was one of the Battle for Britain Spitfires (it had actually shot down five enemy planes), and the pilot and observer section of a Lancaster Bomber. This is one museum which did not at any stage bore me, also by it powerful collection it brought home the tremendous effort of the civilian population. They had one display where I touched a button and a scene of a bombed-out area lit up and everyone's role was described on a scroll near by.

On Saturday we shopped after a pair of shoes for Aub down the Strand and went to a store run by "Saxone," one of the big names over here. I discovered a room which was fitted out with nets, a set of clubs and golf balls so I had twenty minutes practice.

It was a hectic night at work. Got a bit crooked on the great British public and trust you will all show sympathy to anyone behind a counter. You have no idea how it feels to have about 12 people claiming attention at the same time. Tips are pretty poor and even the Yanks know how many pennies there are to a bob.

Went to High Mass Sunday at Paddington and since it rained settled for Madame Tussauds instead of Windsor Castle. Cost three shillings and nine pence extra for the Chamber of Horrors. The whole lot gave me the horrors and I think it is the most over-rated thing we have struck so far. Afterwards went down to the local inn with the two Kiwis and beat them both at darts, Really surprising – no rush and shove in an English pub. It was like church compared to pubs in Australia but a lot of things are like that here.

Talked one day to an unassuming Canadian student who told me the drum on Canada. Certainly seems a mighty place and he is dropping in again. I have some interesting conversations in slack times but take it from me you have to be careful who you encourage as there are a lot of Lord Montague types over here. Shocking compared to Aust. but then I didn't see all the city night life there.

An industrial chemist off the boat came by and we got him a job here. Anyone we know is always good for a coffee at the counter. Went to the Mitre Inn in Chancery Lane and it was bustling with the legal clientele and afterwards we sat in on a few cases and saw the famous British justice in action. No murder trial although the papers announce one every day.

On our day off we crossed Kensington Gardens (five minutes from the flat) to Albert Memorial which it is fashionable to dislike. But I thought it strangely O.K. Queen Victoria made it for her beloved husband. After that to the Science Museum (boring) and then to Laurence Olivier and Vivian Leigh in "Sleeping Prince" at the Phoenix Theatre. Wonderful. Mum, you would have enjoyed it.

## BAYSWATER, LONDON
## (MARCH 25 1954)

Thanks very (very) much for the birthday present which will come in handier than any present ever I think. Nanna and Aunt also sent me two Pounds so it will all go toward making the tour around a little longer. Feel like moving soon as we have got around London pretty well.

Had a few hours in the British Museum which is close to our old YMCA. The best yet, with old roman, Egyptian , Assyrian, Greek relics which are terrifically interesting when you are actually there seeing them. That night I had to go up to Charing Cross branch to relieve for three hours. Charing Cross Road runs into Leicester Square so it was a bit of a change. Took half an hour to get back looking at all the theatres, bookshops and men's wear stores.

On our day off we caught the Green Line coach from Marble Arch to Windsor. The castle is gigantic and beautifully preserved, not a relic and everything so neat . We saw all through the State apartments, banqueting hall with its table of cedar which sits 150 guests, and sits on a carpet weighing two tons. (A Yank said to the guide: "Well, you know, sir, I find that hard to believe.") The castle's St George's Chapel is the best holy house I've yet seen with its gorgeous stain-glass windows, stone work, arch roof, slender long walls, Royal banners of knights hanging from the sides, cedar choir boxes and simple chairs and an atmosphere of a church not a tourist place like the Abbey and St Paul's. No doubt the old tykes knew how to build churches, this one is 500 years old. The village is quaint by Aussie standards but attractive.

We talked to the locals in one of the pubs where they sat around a fire with massive pints (I settled for a glass as the beer is pretty thick and sweet). They wanted to talk about Australia but one old bloke gave us a few amusing tales of life in the Castle. Across the Bridge over the Thames in which we saw the Etonian boat crews and white swans (which was which?) and then out into the narrow streets of ancient shop fronts mostly selling school goods and wants. One pub, "The Cock Pit," started in 1427!

Next the school itself loomed up. It looked a bit crusty but is 500 years old. The young aristocrats, in their hammer-claw tails, white bow ties and stiff dress shirts, were everywhere, about one thousand in all at the school. Noticed, in their memorial to the old boys killed in the war, there was one private! Back to town by a different way but the 25 miles is mainly settled. At night to the Winter Garden Theatre and Agatha Christie's " Witness for the Prosecution." Mighty.

Just in from the most wonderful spectacle I have ever seen. "Swan Lake" at the Royal Opera House by Sadler's Wells Company. Aub knows the ballerina Eileen Fifield (Aust.) and she presented us with three 19-shilling B stall seats. A colossal place, the only one kept in a regal manner with glorious upholstery, crystal chandeliers and ceiling. We were facing the Royal Box, wot? No royal mob there. It was my first ballet and the grace, skill, poise and beauty of them all had me semi-tranced. Rowena Jackson was the prima – I even enjoyed the male parts. The settings and stage lighting were amazing.

Sunday we all went up to Aub's fellow artist's house at Teddington, one of the scenic River Thames villages which help London's picturesqueness a lot. Eighteen miles out and on the way we saw the light blues of Cambridge University out for a spin. Jack met us and showed us the locks and neat weirs of the upper parts of the river.

Back via The Angler's Arms Pub where we had an ale. A drink before Sunday lunch is a custom here and the country club atmosphere and friendly casualness of pubs over here presents a great case for more adult hours back home. Then to a good feed with Jack's wife and two kids who were all pretty thrilled at having three diggers home. Made sure I said my quota of "fair dinkums" which always goes down well.

One other day we went to Hampton Court and the old Tudor Palace built by Henry VIII amidst glorious grounds and open to the public. Saw all through the palace and it is well preserved. The lawns and acres of park around it make the whole show very attractive indeed. What a life it must have been in those days.

Everywhere here is green and Hyde Park and Kensington Gardens look terrific. Yesterday we walked down to Paddington Green (Polly Perkins) and then around these ancient slum buildings and old arch ways joining streets. The Mersey Canal is nearby and we followed it up a few miles. A lot of barge traffic was on the water, coal mainly. There is a large canal network over here and it is cheap. Even saw a horse-driven barge – an old draft pulling a great barge doesn't seem right in a city except London. Also saw some of the boats that took the British off the beaches at Dunkirk.

Thanks to you all and the birthday gift, we tossed in our jobs and leave at the crack of dawn on an excursion up Liverpool way to see the Grand National. To us that's about 9 a.m. Bought a rucksack so am ready for the road.

## BAYSWATER, LONDON
## (APRIL 6 1954)

Had a great time up north. Started off with the new rucksack and sleeping bag and your 20th birthday present in my hip pocket. We got a train to Barnet, an outer city suburb and on the highway. We are now hitchhikers. Wasn't long before I was mobile and finding the English countryside every bit as nice as expected. On the way up to Liverpool, through the Midlands, and there is not much room between built-up areas. You're no sooner out of a town and you hit a village or city. In between are small meadows or fields, attractively green and hedge fences and the ancient farm houses.

My first stop was Luton (we split up on the road and some drivers don't like picking up two people) and walked around this choir-famous town whilst the traveler for shoes made a quick call. On then through villages and towns, the houses in some places built right on the road so that you almost drive through the front door when you take a sharp bend. Even thatched roofs in the older places and the surprising thing is that they don't look out of place.

Everything is on a small scale with land and not a waste land in the country. You remember the view of those Murrumbidgee cultivated flats when driving into Uncle Angus's place; that's about as near to England as I've seen. Fair amount of crops and the pleasure-loving farmers don't give a hang when the hunt goes through trampling everything down. They enjoy the same social position as the Aust. grazing and country families .

However it doesn't take long to hit the great chimneys, smoke of factories and great heaps of dirt and slag from the coal and iron ore mines. The latter are like hills and pyramids having accumulated over the years.

We had lunch at Leicester and about 8 p.m. I was dropped off at Warrington, one of the great Rugby League cities found up in Lancashire. Caught a double-decker train to Liverpool, and it ran worse than Sydney's. Liverpool is dirty, no life or lighting, all smoke and industry, untidy people. However caught a ferry across the harbour to Birkenhead, and then a bus to Chester where there is a youth hostel. Don was already there – only one shilling and sixpence for a bed and not bad. It was an ex-country home of some ancient.

Chester has an old cathedral; all its shops are of the Tudor style and through the place runs the Roman Wall, a relic of their rule. We walked along it, met two Aussies and knocked about with them in the morning. One had been on the move seven years and had seen 45 countries (??!!) Then into Aintree Racecourse where we saw the mighty Grand National steeple chase. There was a tremendous crowd and I lost two shillings and sixpence on the horse that came in third.

On the way we rode in a truck through the mighty tunnel under the River Mersey. Four lanes of traffic, two slow, two fast fly through with no pedestrians and nearly three miles long. Got a good view, too of the extensive though dirty docks and the liner Empress of Canada which turned over after a fire and was only salvaged from the dock bed a few weeks ago. All this two hundred miles from London.

On Sunday, we went up to Wigan, home of footballer Ken Gee, and at present coached by Eddie Ward. Also home of an English mate whose brother-in-law, after giving us a good feed, packed us into a motor cycle and side-car and drove us around the surrounding country.

Next morning we were off early for the Lakes District, one of the beautiful areas of the U.K. Hitched up through Lancaster to Kendall and then by foot and short rides to Keswick where we slept at the hostel. Get the map out and you'll be able to follow all this a lot better. Cook our own grub as everyone has outfits and sundry cutlery. You should have seen the hunched figure with pack who earlier walked through Preston drinking a bottle of milk.

The country up this way is the prettiest yet and you would be amazed at the stone fences which run along all the roads, make up the meadows, go up hills, down dales. How they did it, the patience and labour, I don't know. Must have been done long before the 44-hour week.

Each time you stay in a hostel, you do a small duty in the morning before they return your membership card. I swept the room out, the boys did the staircase. We walked for miles along side of Rydal, and Grasmere Waters which were the haunt of Wordsworth, the English poet. Very attractive. We then began to do some minor (major to Don and me) mountaineering.

Hellvellyn, the mountain is called and is the third highest peak in England – three miles to the top at 3,100 feet. The top was covered with snow and no sooner had we made the summit, a 60 m.p.h. gale blew across the peak bringing snow and hail. I had no gloves or hat and a cursed ground sheet which I couldn't keep done up. All feeling left my hands and I was so cold that I couldn't have cared less had I laid down and died there. However self-preservation and the thoughts of more Australian summers made me press on with the result that I am here now and none the worse for wear, and really well and thriving (who wouldn't be on five weeks work since Xmas!). We skied down on our boots the first part of the descent which ran into four miles before we were down to the road. Was warm once we left that lousy peak. From it I had seen a frozen lake but as there was a false edge of snow and a fierce wind, I didn't dwell too long looking over the side.

Stopped the night at a pub, a temperance hotel which is common in the country. And we had a colossal afternoon tea with nine teas and a lot of toast, rum-butter, cakes and bread. Not bad for two shillings and three pence. After we hostelled around some of the lakes at Windermere, Derwent Water, Ullswater and most of the others including Bathesswaite.

Next day we climbed a great pass contrary to my resolution of never climbing anything ever again. Had a great view of the winding mountain road . On the top we toured a slate factory. Here in the country slate is used as the chief roofing material. It's an old skill and we watched a guy cutting slabs off a block of it with a hammer and chisel.

We then walked back and got to Keswick. Had a feed (eight pence) and then hitched to Whitehaven where Rod has a sister. I forgot to mention that earlier we went over to Workington to watch the locals defeat Liverpool in a first grade Rugby League match.

Back in Whitehaven, Rod's brother-in-law (handy friend this Rod) drove us 50 miles around the district. The whole coastal strip down to St Bees is fairly well industrial and although they seem to rave about their coastal scenes, you really couldn't compare it to our South Coast. Lake Wastwater was a beautiful sight with its crystal water and attractive feeder streams.

One thing I did observe up here is the method by which mountain snow and springs feed the rivers by their pretty streams. The mountains come to the very edge of the water and loom in the background. Giant screes, which are the steep slopes carved by crumbling rock rolling down, all black due to the amount of granite and slate. Drove along country roads that are like canals with both sides lined with stone fences, farm scenes of chickens and it all looked like one of those sets we used to play with out at Wirrilla. Only a little more peaceful. Also drove around the big atomic energy plant at Bellafield. It produces plutonium used in the Bomb and has giant air purifiers, to ensure radio-activity doesn't get to the population, reaching mysteriously into the sky like a Buck Rogers city. Back to Rod's place in Wigan by midnight.

Another all-day hitch hike got us back to London via Watling Street built by the Romans and made into a highway from the old road. On Saturday we joined a great crowd out at the Oxford-versus-Cambridge University Boat race which was won by Oxford plus Australia. It was a mighty sight to see the eights flash by on the water followed by a horde of river craft and ferries rounding the bend loaded with people. Had afternoon tea with some people off the boat in their beautiful flat a few yards off the race course.

Sunday mass at Paddington and then we went to Petticoat Lane where there is the most famous market in the world. You could buy everything there and you have to be on guard as the mob of London cockneys are pretty sharp. Streets of stalls, auction sales and some good bargains.

SCUNTHORPE, LINCOLNSHIRE

(APRIL 13 1954)

Hitched up as far as Bawtry, 13 miles from Doncaster and made for the Labour Exchange at Scunthorpe. Got a compulsory card and after an interview both got jobs as labourers with United Steel at their Appelby Frodingham works.

Began Sunday 7.30 a.m. and go through to 4.30 p.m. except Saturday but hope to get the overtime there too. Each morning we go to the labor pool and are given work under a foreman. We collected shovels and crowbars and proceeded to shift great heaps of slag and iron which had spilt all over the rail lines. Slag is the molten remainder after iron has been taken from the raw ore. It gets pretty hard once it is left around so the blisters are on their way.

These works are one of Europe's biggest and we worked under an enormous blast furnace. On one side poured molten iron, as bright as the sun; on the other, slag. After the spilt bits have cooled down and solidified, yours truly arrives on the scene. Today we were sent to the melting sheds where the great furnaces heat the mixtures that become steel. That part is done above on massive steel and iron platforms 50 feet from ground level. We were down below all morning cleaning up, shoveling etc. They have their own railway lines and about 10 engines. Did some amateur fettling too.

Over 10,000 men here. Don and myself with an ex-Royal Navy stoker went up top to the "platform" to shovel heaps of rubble down a chute into a railway truck. It is really an unbelievable atmosphere with giant magnetic cranes, blinding blast furnaces, massive mixing machines, steam engines and the roar of industry.

However it is O.K. and, as you might expect, I am going easy. The idea here is, as one old bloke said to me, "Just keep the bell tingling." The foremen are beauties and remind us to do it all in good time and not to try too hard. Pay is only eight pounds weekly but am working into a sound position for overtime.

The people we stay with are O.K. and have TV, beautiful meals and hot baths for three pounds ten shillings so we only save three pounds from our pay but with overtime will have something with which to go on to the Continent after Scotland.

On our day off we hitched to Hull and ferried over the River Humber from New Holland. Made Beverly, a most historic village with an attractive cathedral. Stopped at the George and Dragon pub after there were no lifts out on the road and it was so cold.

## SCUNTHORPE, LINCOLNSHIRE
### (APRIL 21 1954)

Rise 6 a.m. daily, breakfast on bacon and eggs and catch the bus to the works. Have bought a billy or enamel jug with screw-in top lid. They are universal amongst the 10,000 here. And the Mrs. fills it with the brew for coffee. Hot water is supplied. We brew up at nine and three.

Disaster today. You know those old brown duds of mine. Well, I was loading scrap iron the other day and bent down to collect a bit and the seam went from waist to fly. Spent thirty minutes sewing it up last night but today caught the cursed pocket with the shovel and tore the side seam another eighteen inches. Had to staple it up to stay on the job. My army boots have collapsed after ten days at the works.

Most of the week has been shoveling in the shed or shop where iron plus mixtures turns into steel. On Good Friday we were bricklayers' labourers for an extra three pence per hour.

Went to Stations of the Cross that night. Had a great Easter: worked 36 hours, most of them at time-and-a-half. On Saturday we clocked in at 7.30 a.m. and got in 24 hours. Don't think I've gone mad as after you know the run of things, this job is a "steady number." We worked in the plate mills and all night resounded with tons of scrap steel being dropped into empty tubs by an overhead crane. Our job was to straighten evenly up the scrap with giant pincers and leather gloves. Excellent for the muscles but it was on and off. We used to go for it , then rest up. The job finished at 3 p.m. but as we couldn't clock off until 6 p.m., we were forced to sleep in the recreation hut with most of the other dodgers. Some of the lavatories at work are reading-prevention: no seats, just a tiled pit with cement rests for your feet.

In our English home the TV is in full blast and the eight-year-old boy never leaves it from Children's Hour to closing time. Everything the Mrs. says, she "sees on TV." Tonight we watched a play, "Six Characters in Search of an Author," and quite good. In general it's 50:50 but TV is a marvelous thing if you could only have a choice of channel.

Scunthorpe is a great place for soccer and we have been to a few matches. They use the head just as much as the feet. There is a big following over here.

Am looking forward to moving on to Scotland in about three weeks.

SCUNTHORPE, LINCOLNSHIRE

(APRIL 30 1954)

We did a 20-hour shift yesterday but have to admit we finished five hours before clocking off. We rushed the job through, working in brick canal passages under-neath the giant rolling mills where squares of steel are flattened out for use as plates etc. They are water cooled and great heaps of slushy iron filings accumulate. We came in with the shovels, wheelbarrows . One night we worked ramming a mixture into a blast furnace. Very monotonous work but plenty of breaks though my hands got tender. Don't believe any stories of hard-working British labourers.

I'm keeping fit and well and making 12 Pounds weekly (68 hours). Then they told us we were to become shunters on the works railway. They have ninety train engines and railway plant about the same size as the Cootamundra depot. We each reported to an engine and have to rush about coupling trucks, changing points, stoking the engine, breaking vans. Over here the law insists on shunters using a long stick with a hook to couple trucks, so that you are not required to go in between the moving trucks. This is a blessing. The old hands say it was a very dangerous practice and were impressed when I told them of fearless shunters like Ron Hulm at home. There is a definite knack in looping these three links to a hook at the end of a poll. Yes, there sure is. We now bring the ore from the mines which are in the works and take it to the blast furnaces where it is melted down to iron.

Am sorry I can't write about anything but work. Am enjoying the Petrov spy case on the front pages and it is doing a good deal to shake people from their complacency. Look after my army gear please as I shall be needing it in Indo-China soon.

## SCUNTHORPE, LINCOLNSHIRE
### (MAY 11 1954)

Assure you of my safety as far as the molten metals are concerned. Whenever a ladle full passes within 50 yards of us, we stop work for a quarter of an hour. The engine drivers are good blokes and like most people, not over anxious about work so we have frequent "snaps." This keeps me up to date with the newspapers.

These blokes spot you as a foreigner straight away. No one has seen many Australians. Even my Army battle-dress was queried today. Will have it cleaned before my audience with the Buffs.

Our landlord Jack Jones entertained with tales of Dunkirk last night. He was in five major landings and is a typical Britisher of old: all for England, brothers in Australia and argues that the old lion hasn't really had it as a world power. She has really. Over here you get the feeling that you are right in the middle of world affairs and when you see how the voice of Asia looms above the scene, you realize just what it mean to all of us in a few years.

The Jones family still is glued to the TV set. Crept in and watched " The Cisco Kid" today in Children's Hour. You would be surprised at how many people here have TV and the part it plays in the everyday life of a family.

## SCUNTHORPE, LINCOLNSHIRE
### (MAY 11 1954)

Have had a good week and put in 70 hours. I say 70 "put in," I was there at work but don't imagine for a moment that I was madly toiling away. This is how I spent the day;

Sunday: in at 7.30 a.m. and shoveled coal in a drizzle so at the sign of a shower I would retire to the shed and await the passing over. My mate was an ex-South African Line seaman and army paratrooper. As I have recently read "The Red Beret," I got on well with him.

Monday: road around the works on an engine pulling specially weighted trucks, checking the numerous weigh b-ridges. The boss asked me to do an extra shift. Read "War and Peace" for three hours and then back to my shunting.

Now on full scale so earn 27 shillings for eight hours plus an eight shilling production bonus. The latter only applies to those actually concerned in the production of iron (not to labourers or office staff!!). We haul the ladles of slag out from under the blast furnaces and take them to tipping areas where, when cool, the slag becomes rock-like and is used for road making. It's a terrific sight to see those 200 odd tons of molten slag pouring from four ladles which the shunter (i.e. me) tips. At least, I tie them all up and the engine pulls a wire rope which upsets the ladles. The slag rushes out with a great roar, there is terrific heat at it crushes down the hillside on to green grass which is gradually diminishing as industry strides on. In the background was a creek and large clouds of steam flew up in the air as the slag hits the water. I stand well away but at dusk or late, it is really a grand sight and well worth going up in gas for!!! Everywhere you go around the works, you see pots of tea being brewed. They are mad keen and we are the same. The engine drivers are usually munching away on something, or his mates are diving into their pockets for a biscuit. And groups of old cronies are boiling a kettle. There are many hot taps for the "mush-up" as they call it.

Tuesday: just yard work all shift with an old Lincoln guy who has driven engines for 52 years.

Wednesday: another 7.30 a.m. to 10 p.m. day, hauling iron ore from the mines. You have to watch it with 600 tons that you just don't let it run off with the engine.

Next day, the same thing but was sent off by the driver for hourly breaks as he runs a Starting Price bookmaking racket on the side and he had to meet his runners, so didn't want me hovering around taking notes for the police. Locomotive men are everyday one horse punters. There are races in different parts of the country and much betting talk. It gives me a chance to doze off in the little warm cabins; they are scattered all over the works and you can always rely on someone lounging inside them. But the driver is boss. What he says, goes.

Went down town before work Friday and bought new military boots (thirty three shillings) as the newspaper lining on the others wasn't too successful on the hard surface around here. The old girl at the shop gushed: "Ah, everyone begrudges buying working gear." Anyway, they'll be good for hiking.

Saturday, in at 6 a.m. and off at 2 p.m., however we finished the job somewhat before then! Had a good laugh this morning: a crane driver (on rails) and an engine came to one another and neither would give way. They sat there like great fools, both refusing to budge. The respective shunters blew through. They could still be there.

And yes, Mum, we are going to Ireland alright, so rest assured, I shall look up the Foley clan. Fellow Irish workers here say it's "a verra pop-lar naaame." Large number of Scots, Ukrainians and Poles work here. They aren't a bad lot.


LOCH LOMOND, SCOTLAND
(MAY 20 1954)

Feeling very well writing this from an old Scottish clan castle by the bonnie-bonnie banks of Loch Lomond. It's really a beautiful view from the window –the water of the loch, or lake, the green roll of country from the walled castle, and in the background, the Highlands and the peak of Ben Lomond. The weather is sunny and it all lends itself to a wonderful setting.

We left the steel works Saturday with Madan an Indian engineer friend, by 3$^{rd}$ class (bit below Aust. 1$^{st}$ class!) train to York. It is a most historic old place and we had a look over a museum in which there were some well-preserved settings of streets, shops and rooms such as a kitchen, of a few hundred years back. Through the city runs a wall built to keep out marauders and now used to entice tourists. It runs around what used to be the main part of the city but of course York has outgrown it. Walked around it and looked over into the grounds of York Cathedral. Spacious and the old-world atmosphere of serenity with the birds and seats under the trees. Then into the Cathedral. It is all Gothic style and as usual full of regimental colours and memorials to "officers and men" who fell in the Indian War. The whole city seems rather old-fashioned and they look after their ruins more than their new places. I'm inclined to agree with your Graham friend and the need for some bulldozers here. Reckon I've seen more of the old Roman Wall across England than the guy who built it.

Went to Mass at St. Wilfred's Church, which sounds un-Catholic I know but I was mis-directed into a Protestant show and it was High Church and took me five minutes to tell the difference! In the Cathedral there was a confession list that surprised us.

The York Hostel was O.K. and we left about 1.30 p.m. to walk 16 miles before two Aussie girls in an old Austin stopped. We crammed in, tied the packs to the back and set off for Scarborough on the East English Coast. Pulled up at 11.30 p.m. and they went off to bed and breakfast at a pub (14 shillings and sixpence!).

A cop thought I was prowling, flashed me with a torch and after explanations, invited me into the station fire until the girls came back to drive us to a haystack. They dropped us off but a dog flew out and began barking so we moved to a field and slept there. Bit hard and cool but we must be soft. The girls returned at 9.30 a.m. and drove us to industrial Newcastle where we parted. Kept hitching and spent the night at a good hostel at Carlisle, a neat and pretty place just over the border in Scotland.

INVERNESS, SCOTLAND

(MAY 27 1954)

Very fit as I write this in the common room amidst the usual mob of Australians. Have met more on this trip than ever –one of the Yanks said: "Say, what I wanta know is what's left in Australia?" Seems to be hundreds of us, particularly girls.

Made Glasgow and had a good look over the city. Reputedly the "tougher than Chicago," last of the Razor Gangs," "Watch Your Step," place but really seems like any other city and the people there willing to break their necks to help you. Anytime I wanted directions, just looked a bit doubtful and someone would dance up and ask me what I wanted. Mainly an industrial city and we passed the great ship-building works of John Brown etc. who built the Queens Elizabeth and Mary on the Clyde River – they float down to the Firth of Clyde after launching. It's no wider than Suez Canal so a launching must be a grand sight to see. Even went to a museum and art gallery – some villainous-looking Scots V. English relics. Attractive parks and public baths (10 pence including towel and tiny piece of soap). Ordinary bath with a locker and hot and deep but I didn't go for the worn-down back brush.

About 4 p.m. we left for Loch Lomond where I wrote you last. Had the perfect awakening from my bed, looking right out on the lake. We walked around the loch and went to sleep on the bank in the sun after sumptuous meal of two bottles of milk and rich brown bread. Milk is the best food I've discovered. The lakes are surrounded on all sides by hills and Friday we passed further into the Highlands through tiny villages and finally to the hostel at the foot of Ben Nevis (4,410 ft., highest in U.K.) where we saw great snow-covered peaks, mists and gorgeous forests all around. The hostel is right at the foot of the path up the mountain but after the Helvellyn effort, that's as near as I got to it. Fort William is the town on the loch. Typical lake-style scenery but the blow is that the hostel is three miles out in the hills. Luckily the gals in the Austin turned up, put us on the road next morning and after a series of good lifts, we made Inverness. Came up through really fine country, the best part, I think, of the Highlands with the mountains, heather on all sides and by the lake side, the acres and acres of forests running up the hillsides, great firs all under the Government Timber Scheme.

Passed by Loch Ness where the fabulous monster is supposed to be; an old sea serpent with great head and teeth, and seen by responsible and non-commercial viewers. The lake is very deep and our truck driver believed in the monster. Also saw the memorial to John Cobb and the measured mile where he blew up in his speed boat jet at 240 m.p.h. This place is nothing new but a nice River Ness and several bridges. It was so bleak when we arrived that we went out to a movie –Norman Wisdom in "Trouble in Store." He's very funny. Mass at 8.30 a.m. and felt left out of it as everything was answered in Latin by the congregation who appeared very devout.

How are you all? Bit cold? Just nice and warm here and soon it will be shorts weather. Arrived back from Scotland after a pleasant day in Edinburgh. Really a nice city and everywhere the flowers were in full bloom. We went up to the Royal Castle now used as a barracks for a Highland regiment and also housing a detailed museum of ancient uniforms and old, old regalia that turns up all over this country. They are the greatest junk collectors and that is from me – I already have a bag full of it!

The youth hostel was in a pretty, residential area and opposite was an 18-hole putting green ,very popular all over Scotland. We were eating and drinking in the park when the cannons on the castle hill volleyed out to announce the time at 1 p.m. Walked down to Holyrood Palace where the Duke of Hamilton, Scots High Commissioner was in residence. Got as far as the gate. Leaving Edinburgh next day a local cop pulled us up half way up a hill on the outskirts and said we had been house breaking. We laughed and he said it was quite serious. However we talked him out of it and he drove us on five miles. Got down to Rod's place at Wigan by three extra good lifts. A truck driver even bought us tea and an ex-Rugby Union player for England arranged a lift right to Rod's front door. On arrival we found the house in upheaval due to the dog having cancer and facing eminent destruction. They are very fond indeed of their pets.

Back in London this morning we decided to go into see the Queen's return from Scotland. Isn't she mighty! Left me gaping. The Duke must have been elsewhere; he could have been in the front seat but I forgot him. She's terrific. I was in the front row outside Buckingham Palace Gates.

Before that we watched the Grenadier Guards rehearsing for the trooping of the colour. Saw the lot in an hour –the sergeant major, the officer, a major having to get assistance to get his sword out of his scabbard, a captain dressed in black coat and frills with great sword, and the aloof-est of anybody, striding up and down the parade ground.

After the Queen disappeared, we met two other friends and went off to St Martin-of-the-Fields Church in Trafalgar Sq. where we saw the Queen Mother. Again very close and I heard her speak (not to me). Most gracious and she acknowledged stares of tourists, and she was well-preserved in furs whilst the

Queen wore blue at the Palace. Struck me as slightly pathetic -- this beautiful young lady having to be Queen. Saw the film of her Aussie tour –the old country gets better and better and we get quite nostalgic over the bush and beach.

On Sunday night we took a flood-lit tour by bus of the city. All the spots are illuminated and Trafalgar Sq. with its fountains and Nelson Column looks extra good. In fact, with winter over, England seems to have awakened. Or woke up to itself.

CORNWALL

(SUMMER 1954)

Have just had a feed of snags, spuds and brew and feel pretty tired after a long walk. Well, after that day of Royalty, we got off down south. Went through Kent with its gently sloping hills (everywhere is fantastically green after home) and the hop fields with their great network of ropes and poles like a spider's web to support the hop growth. All along the roadside and hop fields are high wind-break hedges right on to the road. Tall poplars, too, so it is all pleasant but almost unreal. Picked up by an old chap in a Humber Snipe who had been to Aust. before he was dragged into business with his father. Really is fabulous what my digger's hat has done for us in the way of lifts. Nearly everyone signals even if they can't stop and four times on this trip they have gone on a few miles to put us on good roads.

Made the hostel at Brighton that night and while waiting for a bus to take us into town, a woman pulled up, shouted at us to get in and took us right into the famous pier and fun centre of this seaside pleasure resort of Sussex. The beach is pebble with no sand but the amusement facilities, sports etc stretch for miles along the sea front. It is one of London's and the South's popular places. They even have a mini-railway up and down the promenade. Wouldn't suit Manly or Bondi but goes mighty here. The pier is a good 150 yards out into water and is a Luna Park and Dance. Millions of lights would make it quite a spectacle at night, (saw it at day!). Also down here and now used by the Council is a palace, formerly the summer resort of the kings and queens a few reigns back. Modeled on Indian design with domes and columns everywhere. I thought it was a fun fair called the Royal Pavilion. Really a wonder that the monarchy isn't finished when you see a relic like that.

Away by mid-day and down through Hampshire to Portsmouth. As it is a Royal Naval depot, it collected a battering during the war. That's still obvious although there are a lot of new buildings. Went down to the docks and looked over Nelson's ship, "H.M.S. Victory," or at least the ship he died on. Ships interest me more than museums so it was worth while. The conditions 1750-1805 must have been torrid especially the crew's quarters although I had to stoop the entire round of the ship and the tallest officer in 1805 Battle of Trafalgar was six ft four and one-half inches.

The Town Hall here was de-roofed and is a grim reminder with its lions of marble like the Bank of New South Wales Sydney Head Office, and the half-down brick walls. The cursed hostel, when we got to Southampton, was booked out by a party of South African kids so it cost us ten shillings, for a bed and lousy breakfast. However in fine spirits down to Southampton Docks where "we're from Australia" got us visitors passes inside the gates. They are surprisingly strict.

Went up and saw the 53,000 -ton liner United States in its berth. Really a beautifully lined ship and the last word in class, so they say as you aren't allowed on. The crew was rolling up dressed as well as the passengers. At quarter to one, with our pass, we went up on top of the new Overseas Terminal and saw the colossal 81,000-ton Queen Mary leave for the U.S.A. Doesn't look so great at first glance but just see that bulk slide out from the dock, pushed by the tugs and you realize that it's every bit four times as big as our SS "Otranto." No gay farewells. An Englishman, seeing his wife and daughter off, explained that "Oh, well we have got used to it, you know: we English don't make a fuss about it things." Still, the distance across to New York is only 3,000 miles and four days odd.

Got some good snaps with the camera you gave me nearly seven years ago but three hours later I found I'd left it in a ditch whilst changing into my boots on the roadway. This was is Salisbury and immediately I got on the road and hitched back 20 miles to a village outside Southampton. There it was, thank God. The gang digging up the road was most amused as I stepped out of the car and produced a camera from the ditch. Don had gone on to Exeter so I just rambled on quite a few miles through most attractive country. Not so built up and more hilly with the reappearance of thatched roofs and stone fence and the farm houses and yards with chooks and haystacks as though they had jumped out of a painting book. At 10 p.m., I lay my bag down in a forest by the roadside and, under the trees, went to sleep. That's my current idea of life. Must have been late sleeping 'cause when I woke, I asked a family passing by what time it was. "Quarter past nine!" Got out on the road and Don was sitting outside of Exeter on the footpath

Through Plymouth and it also full of new buildings after the war. We didn't stop. Our next lift was in a heavily-laden wheat truck with a terrifically friendly driver. Has a motor bike and goes off to France and Holland each year. He jumped at Arnhem, Holland during the war. I am going to make a pilgrimage there! Was walking along the road later when a station wagon stopped and , as we were putting the bags in, the driver said: "Well, you've got 20 miles to make up your mind whether you'll come camping with us for the night." Ended up on Par Beach on the Cornwall Coast in a tent with a great family. He was a dentist, one of the daughters taught Domestic Science, another was only 16 and just right for you Ned, and two boys, 11 and eight, who were the most intelligent kids I have met. It was great to eat that hot meal and Pa insists on Devon apple cider but luckily not the "Farm Brew," which is the same as jungle juice. We camped right on the coast but too cold for a swim.

He drove us to the road next morning. I was determined to get to Land's End which is the furthermost part of England. It rained, blew and got misty but finally made it with a car full of Krauts. Nice people and the day eventually fined up. The peninsular is of rugged rock and green, wind-swept land but its height and seascape are quite appealing despite the number of "1ˢᵗ Houses," "1ˢᵗ Teashop," "First and Last Souvenirs." This hostel is seven miles out of Penzance and three miles from St. Ives. You know: "As I was going to St. Ives, I met a man etc etc." We walked along the coastal path then finally had a swim in the Atlantic and even got a bit sun burnt but Lord, that water was so cold we couldn't breathe, so didn't last more than three minutes. The town or village is typically Cornish – streets narrow and cobbled, and winding , but on the sea front, there are most stylish milk and snack bars. The old man who rowed us across the water for three pence was 76 and looked as fit as Michael. Said his advice was "Don't worry."

Saturday night at the youth hostel. Well, this Ireland is great, only got here Wednesday and already I am a fan of the old green. A good trip up through Devon, Cornwall, Somerset and Gloucester where we passed a night and saw over the old Roman hot baths where a few centuries ago, the officers of the Roman Army wallowed about, perfumed and massaged after wild orgies. Made Shrewsbury that night –up through the county town of Hereford where the famous cattle come from. Nice country and the rain was O.K. too. Used to it now as we got it all next day on our way up to Hollyhead through North Wales. That trip (the team is now four – a Canadian and a Dutchman Wilhelm) was really beautiful. The country is mountainous with jagged peaks, great slopes of rugged land with rock outcrops and timber. Also attractive streams which seem to have a beauty of their own after our dry creeks.

We were in the back of a large lorry and the water kept flowing down the boards towards us -- we built dykes of mud and straw but got a bit wet anyway. However, we got there and aboard the Irish Mail ship which was "The Hibernia," a most modern 4,000 tonner of British Railways. We had our bread and marmite in the lounge, hacked away at the bread whilst fellow passengers wallowed in seven shilling, three-course meals. We got a bunk (21 shillings complete) and rose at 8 a.m. in Dublin. Hitched into the city after two pints of milk for breakfast. However, on arrival had bacon and eggs at a Woolworth's store. The first point of interest was a very interesting look over the "Guinness is good for you" Brewery. It spreads over 65 acres and we saw everything from the barley and hops to the finished brew. Their public relations man was most friendly and after the tour there is the sample room. Later, had lunch on a monument in the main street, O'Connell St., as we couldn't find a park.

Noticed a lot of poverty and ragged dress with an apparent high rate of unemployment but they don't like work much over here and I don't blame them. We left about 3 p.m. Rode forty miles in the Dickie seat of a small roadster and just can't get over how green this place is.

Also so religious, with open air shrines for Our Lady – a statue in a cliff face and a cross on a hill and everyone blessing themselves as they pass the churches. Pity that there is a bit of poverty in such a really beautiful country. We came down by Cork with the people as friendly as anybody I've met. They use little carts with donkeys and Ma does the shopping or Pa and the kids bring the milk in to the Co-Op. Time hasn't altered them too much, life is peaceful and they just take their time. Just out of Cork is the old creeper-covered Blarney Castle where you lean over an 80-feet drop to kiss the Blarney Stone. Then you receive the gift of the gab. I liked this castle much more than the preserved ones.

## GOLDERS GREEN, LONDON
## (JUNE 21 1954)

Told you before what I thought of Ireland's beautiful lake, hill scenery, waterfalls and lots of views and several miles tramping around the high country. Back on the road and the country seems to fall off a bit as we neared Galway country. They do have a great problem over here. Out this way they really are peasants and bitter things have been said against the Catholic Church. However, I think the people themselves know and expect little better.

Everyone wants the other six counties of British Northern Ireland whilst up here in Northern Ireland itself they detest the idea of leaving Britain, all except the Irish Northern Catholics who follow the directions of Eire (Southern Ireland) and who some suggest are traitors

The rain held off until we had gone to sleep under some trees by a stone fence and then it drizzled all night but I couldn't have cared less so awoke about 7.30 a.m. and as the water seeped through, waited for the rain to abate. Ended up getting dressed in it –it poured all day so we cut right through the centre to Dublin. This Irish brown wheat bread must be good for the body as we didn't catch cold and am fit and well as I write. Lost our two mates somewhere.

Next day we went up through Belfast to Dunluce which is a few miles from Port Rush. One old man in an Oxford car stopped without us hailing him, bought us tea and 12 scones, drove us ten miles out of his way and then bought us a packet of biscuits for later. All of our lifts up in the North were good. Dunluce Hostel was a large converted farmhouse of stone and right on the coast. Up here the coast is really nice, cliffs and sandy beaches, coves and big stones. Nearby were the ruins of Dunluce Castle, right on a headland. To avoid the six pence admission we had to scale an obstacle worthy of any commando.

Next morn we went five miles walking along the coast to the amazing Giant's Causeway. Great volcanic rock, formations in regular shapes of five, six and seven sides and thousands of them. They looked as if they had been carved.

Afterwards traffic was mighty slow and we dozed by the road for an hour but in the end we had to take a one shilling and sixpence worth of bus which was bad. However the next lift took us down to Belfast and we had a few hours around the city before sailing for Liverpool 140 miles away in the 9,000-ton "Wester Prince." As we passed down the harbour we saw some of the shipbuilding yards which are the world's largest. We slept on the floor in our sleeping bags and had nine hours afloat. Sea crossing got a bit rough but I didn't toss the voice.

To sum up: Northern Ireland is like England, industrial, progressive, Protestant versus Catholic, and it is very evident.

Two good lifts got us all the way back to London. Am staying out at Golder's Green with some other Australians in their attractively situated flat. It was good to have your three letters, with all the news, at the Bank of New South Wales. Had been looking forward to them.

BRUSSELS

(JULY 7 1954)

Writing this from the capital of Belgium The hostel is most central, very near to the Grand Place which is a square, enclosed by the Town Hall and other buildings of the same design and period, gold laced, pinnacles of iron and architectural frills. It's acknowledged as the city's only preserved block from the old days. The other place of interest was the immense forest (the Wood of Soigne) of tall beech trees, through which the Belgium driver of my large Citroen drove me going by out-of-the-way paths. As we came into Brussels, I repaid him by pushing the car to a petrol station as we had run out of petrol when we hit the main street.

The shops are full of colossal wares and we could have spent a fortune. Bought some rice, sugar and food at a supermarket; something like Coles only 100 times faster, with hit tunes, people yelling the price of fish, din of shoppers and everything from steaks to perfume on sale.

They were giving samples of a Devon-like sausage so lined up a few times.

We went on a long walk and came across the famous statue of the little boy and the gushing fountain spurt (Mannekin-Pis they call it). We adjourned to a bar where no fewer than nine television sets showed Austria beating Paraguay in the World Soccer final. Mighty game and I like to watch it despite the looks of the waitress as we sat without ordering. Tipping is a lousy habit – drones are stationed everywhere from lavatories to bars.

Today went to Mass in the Notre Dame de la Chappelle, around the corner from the hostel. You kneel on the seats and for the reverse, sit down towards the pulpit which was an enormous wood-carved affair in the centre of the church.

The next day we hitched to Paris, ending the day with a walk around Pigalle and Montmartre Hill where all the bright spots are. Man, you should see 'em – the artists painting the beautiful white dome of the Cathedral of the Sacred Heart—the art shops and displays, the cafes that reflect the gayness of life here, on the sidewalks , the colorful street scenes can be watched from the seats of a café. They are bars too but the attitude is one of openness and not the closed glass windows of our Central and Globe Hotels. Really beautiful city and eagerly await the return visit. The hostel is pretty grim –might stay at a pub next time.

Well, from Paris we went to Rheims where there is one of the oldest cathedrals in Europe. You remember the lace work in that church history book, beautiful windows and side altars. Otherwise the town is the centre of the champagne industry. Saw all the vineyards but couldn't afford a sample at 20 shillings per bottle for the good stuff. Wine is very cheap—some about two shillings per quart but I had one glass shouted me by a Frenchman and hated it. Tasted like that stuff we had in Sydney. Enjoying the car trips with the French and Belgiums (sic) very much. They teach me quite a lot and we get on well. From Rheims (we split up in Europe) I hitched all day to the border of Luxembourg.

Just made the hostel, set amidst the steel works. Only a tiny country with a population of 300,000 of which 60,000 live in the city of Luxembourg. They speak a mixture of French and German, both of which are official languages. It was a bit Prussian at the hostel but clean. Our room was under the shadow of a giant railway viaduct.

Well, countries seem to be flying by and today am in the sprawling city of Hamburg up in northern Germany on the pretty River Elbe. Population of 2,000,000 and as a port and industrial centre it took a mighty bashing last war. The hostel is on the main hill, overlooking the harbour-river and as the best and newest hostel I've yet seen, commands a grand view of the shipping and riverside. The city is uncolourful otherwise and the rain doesn't help. Just in from Mass and got wet.

After Brussels we went up to Antwerp, the important port of Belgium. In dock were units of the U.S. fleet and the cruiser "Des Moines" was really the cleanest boat I have ever seen. From there straight to Rotterdam in a sweet* factory van. We ate his supplies whilst we talked half English, half Dutch. This place has the most modern buildings and shopping centre yet seen. The new style is in and the designs are mighty. In 1940 the town was nearly flattened by a German fire bomb raid and in one section all that was left was a wind mill. This now remains as a monument and looked good amidst all the newness.

The Dutch are most polite and helpful and due to immigration keen on Australians. Their hostels are run with thoroughness and neat as pins. Food was cheaper particularly vegetables, milk and fruit which is my diet with " der brot and der margarine." Eating Schwartz brot now –it's the black German bread the P.O.W.'s lived on and it packs a bite.

From Rotterdam to The Hague where I sat in on a session of the Dutch Parliament for half an hour. Belgium, Holland and Luxembourg still have their Queens etc. although they are far from the people who envy the genuineness of the British monarchy. The country is fabulously flat, like Cootamundra's Fisher Park, with canals everywhere. They are used greatly for transport in barges. Fields and farms are small, usually fenceless with canals keeping the dairy stock in. At six pence per quart, I drank a ton of milk .

The Dutch, as the others, dislike the Germans. There was a park with wild deer near the Parliament Building. When I went to take a snap, they came up to me so I think it had been done before. We stopped the night at a little village ten miles from Amsterdam. The locals all wore clogs which they parked outside as they entered their neat houses. People seem to take a great pride in their residences on this side of the world, particularly in country villages. They take life easily and some were even in the native dress of long, black dresses, colorful aprons, knitted scarves and cone-shaped hats with the men in baggy strides and woolen shirts with yellow clogs but I think this was more because of the great fete and carnival on in the city.

Next day we stopped in the city after a day around the canals. They have a great old time with their street music grinders, side shows and vendors of everything imaginable. On Thursday we went out to the Olympic Stadium and standing in a crowd lining one of the boulevards, watched the start of the Tour de France, the greatest cycling event over here. Three thousand odd miles over 21 days, up and down the Pyrenees and French Alps with floats and much advertising, many sponsored by French newspapers. The group of motor police from France to escort them on the highway, got a big hand. The riders are preceded by a convoy of cars.

Got away next morning and to the German border. The country didn't change much up to Bremen except on a larger scale to that of Holland and more woods. All is still nice and green. Bremen is still in the rebuilding stage. They have paid much for the war. Many maimed on the streets but shops and conditions now O.K.

## KOBENHAVN, (COPENHAGEN, DENMARK) (AUG 1954)

Got away from Hamburg after a late night on the city's fabulous Reepeerbahn, Deutschland's answer to Pigalle in Paris. (Forgot to tell that I spent a few hours around Arnhem where the big parachute droppings were on Sept. 17 1944. They have memorials here and there on the spot where the first group touched down. The cemetery is most impressive and British stocks high throughout the area.) The hitchhiking in Germany is very good and made the Danish border in good time with an ex-P.O.W. of Australians in Egypt, World War I. As usual: "prima," "ja, prima,"

Denmark for me hasn't been so hot on the road* but made Kolding. There a chap showed me where to buy bread, then asked me to tea, stop the night, and to cap it, sent up breakfast in the morning. It was colossal. Slept in his daughter's dainty room since she was away at camp. Food is their main industry and they send most of it to England. They don't like the Germans but have good relations with the Soviets.

Made "Wonderful Wonderful Kobenhavn " (Danish spelling) and with two Sussex chaps toured the world famous Carlsberg Breweries which is run as a trust for the arts and research. Turns out some one and one-half million bottles per day and more modern than Guinness but "Just as good for you." They piled the bottles on the table, invited us to come again. Would like to see the Cootamundra 1st and Reserves football teams do a tour around it. As the public relations officer said after giving out all the figures of production -- "and it's a well-guarded secret: the amount consumed on the premises." By the faces of the workers, they did alright for themselves.

The city seems most attractive –stately buildings, great squares. Up here, as in Deutsch, they call the town hall the "Rathaus." This latter is built on a square which is surrounded by the best collection of neon lights I've seen. You know the running lights on a Broadway show. From the "Politiken" newspaper headquarters, they run the news around the top of the building and on all the roof tops are the latest U.S. signs, dispelling somewhat Danny Kaye's Kobenhavn. However, progress, I expect! Tivoli fun grounds are unique for there is an amusement fair that somehow lacks the usual air of "clip joint"* and cheapness. Very fit and well and will ask for the bread shop some more.

KOBENHAVN

(JULY 25 1954)

Your son and brother just in from work, his fifth day at washing dishes. Not a bad job and the food consumption is at an enormous level. Have tried the old brother Michael plan of "big appetite" and now I eat, " all de time," the women cooking me pancakes, making me sandwiches, bowls of this and that in such a way that I am in a happily bloated condition all day, some position I have often wished for whilst hitch-hiking. Get 20 krone (one pound sterling) and all meals. Go in at 11 a.m. and finish at 8 p.m. and if we wish, everyday. The Danish are the most prolific eaters and coffee is brewed all day. Milk, meats, special ice creams and tons of greens and vegetables.

The chef is a 24-year-old English-speaking Dane and a good chap. "John, you look hungry," is his favorite joke. We go to Koffee together and he has brought some Danish books to teach me the tongue. Doesn't appear difficult and nothing to lose. Went home with him the other day at 2 p.m. The wife, a pretty blond as most of them are, brewed coffee and sent us in a stack of pastry and cakes that seemed to disintegrate as soon as they entered my mouth. Then to a modern church (Church of Denmark is equivalent to Church of England), whose walls were of glass, and whole design of the future if ever churches exist that far. The latter to frighten you! I didn't like it as a place of devotion. We returned to the radiogram, went through his collection, mostly English and U.S. Everyone keeps up-to-date with the pops, using Danish words. The house was furnished neatly. They have two kids, Toms and Gedda. He makes about 960 krone per month. After a great meal of the usual smorbrod , we visited the neighbors, also a chef at the place Don works. Same chain. He played the guitar and they sung Danish songs along with English ones. More coffee and his fabulous stamp collection and aquarium of tropical fish which he breeds. Lit up in a dark room, they look quite novel. This chef couldn't speak English but he gave me some beautiful stamps which may have a resale value.

My chef is to look after our social welfare. Moving off from the hostel tomorrow , already six nights overdue, to a student hostel that he found for us. Will stop there a few weeks before moving on to Norway, Sweden and if possible Finland. Have quite a bit to see yet with Italy, Switzerland, Spain and Berlin beckons, too.

Have been looking forward to some mail for a few weeks, It seems years since I was with you all or even heard the news of the day. Mal, you are looking after my things, aren't you. My chess set etc. Will have a ton more when I come home but when you have to carry it around on your back, you don't collect so much junk.

Many German boys come to the hostel and they are fine types. One last night could have been the typical Luftwaffe type. One lived in Berlin and wants to show me around if I get there. They are all ages up to 19 and have in many cases a maturity, no doubt due to the war and political aftermath in Germany. Their English is always reasonably good. I close amidst a din of WOG students having a time.

## KOBENHAVN

(JULY 29 1954)

Only 11 more days of washing dishes ahead. Why I ever complained about your porridge saucepan, ma, and meat dish, I'll never know. However have put on four lbs. since arrival in Kobenhavn and the face getting typically round as I thrive well and truly. Had a steak and a pancake for an in-between snack most nights but now my chef friend has gone to another restaurant and in his place we have a female chef who is typical again of women with a little authority over the male. She irritates me as she always seems to have some trifle to be done and uses pots like a millionaire.

(Forgot to tell you, Ned that at Wimbledon I saw Budge Patty beat a Yank Stewart who looked just like you in everything from play to looks of decision, disgust and shouts of anger. Perhaps the muscles and tan might be different as I haven't seen you for a while but I imagined Stewart as Ned the whole game. On the Centre Court and if you could have seen it, I think you would be a lot keener to make it; besides, there would be free admission for brother John on his 50th world tour.)

Last night spent at a Danish student's house. Met four friends of the chef's brother and we talked and played the radiogramme until late. His family were over in Sweden (just a few miles away) so plenty of room. Bought me rolls, coffee and pastry in bed so I rose at 11 a.m. just in time to get to work. Saturday night went to see "The Hitchhiker," about one who kills everyone who stops. Means that we will be stranded here, I expect, as I found it bad enough on the way across. We are on the island of Zealand here and had to ferry across from Fyn which is joined to the mainland of Europe by a very impressive bridge.

Kobenhavn about one million people and at the moment stacks of tourists everywhere and I mean everywhere! Downtown tonight you could hardly move. My restaurant is around the corner from the main street. Take a tram anywhere for four pence and have a stop at K.A.R.'s door.

KOBENHAVN

(AUG 5 1954)

It was most amusing to read in your letter that on the very day you were snuggly seated at the Roxy watching the happy scenes of Danny Kaye, your third son was tramping the streets in the rain looking for a job. Found one too— by the time you read this will have washed dishes for 22 days straight and have earned enough krone to last six or seven more weeks on the road.

Haven't been doing much except a few walks around the city and the fish markets with the rough old "sacs" as the Danish call the fish ladies. Equivalent of our "bags." We took the chef and his wife to Rita Hayworth in "Regn" (Miss Sadie

Thompson), the picture here in English with Danish sub-titles. They live out in a new suburb of attractive houses and blocks, Sunday to High Mass in a church just off Gammel Kongej where I work. It and the main street are the main shopping streets. Will have to pay the shops a visit soon as the old blue nylon socks have "begun" to hole. For the past 15 days we have had rain but finally we see some sun.

On Sunday night, the chef's Ma and Pa had their 25th wedding anniversary. All the family great greats were there, showing just how long they do live on the food here. One old boy fought in the war of 1890. The chef insisted I show him that guard photo of mine and the old chap got quite excited. Another one I asked "Are you having a good day?" in Danish and for 20 minutes he rambled on, I not understanding one word. Ma and Pa danced the waltz, a few speeches and Great Papa passed out in a chair and had to be led off to the cot. Amidst frowns from Great Mama. They have the radiogramme and most of the latest hits. Peter, Don's chef, lives next door and is a breeder of tropical fish so that his flat resembles Taronga Aquarium. He plays the guitar and entertains well. All the ladies drag out the cigs and watch the clock around for the 20-minute break. I am the only male here and have been "eyeing" mounds of cursed potatoes all afternoon.


EIDJFORD, NORWAY

(AUG 15 1954)

Writing this 80 miles from Bergen after a few days spent coming up the west coast of Norway through the most spectacular scenery. Left Kobenhavn Monday with the wallet nicely reinforced with note. Up to Elsinore Castle, scene of Shakespeare's "Hamlet," before the ferry across to Sweden. The south of Sweden is industrial but as we went further north it changed to hills and pine forests, double storied houses, nothing on a big scale and the time between lifts a few hours. Spent a most comfortable night in a barn –met two Germans and we pitched in the hay. At 9.30 a.m. the farmer (Swedish are supposed to be unfriendly) took us into the kitchen where we had a colossal breakfast. Then on to the road and a Packard Clipper with a most pleasant Norwegian businessman and family. Crossed over into Norway by a large modern bridge which spans the fjord and gives a beautiful view. Drove on to the most really delightful house, furnished and decorated so tastefully and inspired, and a gorgeous sight of the Oslo fjord waters in which they swim. Lunched and looked about his "metal name plate" industry and then he had the gardener drive me to the road in a Russian imported car. An American consular Chev. Station wagon took me into Oslo—the general landscape up here is mighty.

Since I plan to return to Oslo next week, made for Bergen. Another meal with a ski industry man traveling with two mademoiselles from France. Stopped to look through his summer house set up on a hill – all houses are of wood, it being so cheap and a good insulator against the cold. We had a cognac and a meal but only made 30 kilometers more so hired the camping room of a pub, set amongst the treeless lake country and high up.

Very thinly settled around this place – over across the tundra rocky wastes were a herd of reindeer which I got close to. They are run like cattle in this part of Norway and eaten, so Rudolph probably won't make it this Christmas. About 10 p.m. a Kiwi mate landed in and next morning a car stopped with Don and another N.Z. mate from SS "Otranto." The four of us were driven all the way to Bergen by a driver from the Aust. Embassy in Amsterdam.

Fjords were made by the great glacial movements some 16,000 years ago, The road winds over steep mountains, along the sides of gaps and gorges, mountain streams, runaways, giant boulders and waterfalls. One beauty crashed down hundreds of feet into a gorge. We stopped by and walked around the edges, all a bit windy for the drop was sheer and the railing slight. Narrow road through granite hillside, tunnels through granite hillside, wooden snow prevention drive-throughs, barricades to keep the road open. I thought these high parts were like Mt. Kosciuszko, (ed. Australia's highest peak). but the waters and great hills are unique and just the country I like. Bergen (140,000) is Norway's second city and from the hostel on the top of the mountain, we look down on the entire scene, the waters down to the sea, other streams reaching inland behind, just so high that you see over them and further inland.

STOCKHOLM

(LATE SUMMER 1954)

Aboard the "A.F. Chapman," this is the hostel you have read so much about. Really, the best yet, modern and comfortable. We are in a four berth, reading lights and hot showers. The ship, once on the sailing runs, is anchored at the naval station right in the centre of this beautiful city. Came down from Oslo last night.

Today is sunny and walked around the waterways across many bridges, for the city is built on islands, to the stately Town Hall with its great courtyard to the fruit markets. Then saw over the two prominent D.J.'s of Stockholm. One regret is that I haven't a station wagon and a glove-box full of traveller's cheques for the stores are busting with the most luxurious wares. A prosperous country this Sweden, no wars and good trade relations with the world. Unfortunately the Swedes do not come up to the standard of the Norwegians and in a lighter way, the Danes.

But to resume my travels: left Bergen after a really fine time. Had a swim in what turned out to be the local reservoir, a tour over the large sardine factory and then left on a boat for Stavanger, 200 odd miles down the coast. Four of us have been having a ball of a time but the 400 miles down to Oslo took me two and one-half days. Tuesday, many small rides along the coastal road with a thin strip of country for grazing and hay cutting before the rougher stony stuff sets in. They cut as much grass as they can for the snow covers all (up to eight feet) and already it is getting cool up here.

Saw some massive rock formations. The road winds over steep hills; once on top you meet a lake or gorge or a view of a fjord. Passed by the Josing Fjord where early in the war, a British destroyer rescued a party of merchant navy guys from the Germans. There was also an eight-mile-long overhead conveyor line transporting iron ore from the wharf down in the fjord to the inland smelting works. Being a steelworker, I displayed more than the usual interest.

The two N.Z.'s and I met up that night in a little village. Don got a lift further on. Wednesday, rained all day as we hitched on. Wet as hell but morale high. Found a little school 150 miles from Oslo and slept on vaulting-horse mats in the gymnasium and also discovered some hot showers so soaked for 30 minutes.

Every thing looks so snug and secure, neat piles of wood outside, freshly painted houses, the red all-timber barns, the cattle with bells. Then you see a river, with hundreds of logs floating downstream to the big pulping factories for paper export or for cutting. Mostly soft woods. On the logs, where they bunch up, say on a large bend or before they are shot down special by-ways, are macintoshed lumbermen, hooking the logs into the current, pushing them from the banks or joining ten or twenty in a link to hold the remaining hundreds. Thursday was extra good and went quickly on the road with a load of meat. Helped him unload and were rewarded with a nice, large polser (Devon sausage which we ravaged). Eating well but am looking forward to revisiting my friends in Kobenhavn at the restaurant. Enjoyed a long lift into Oslo where the other two had prepared a feed and congenial company.

We began Friday by riding the train to the ski jump where each year they have the championships we see on the newsreels. Gave us a great view of the city. Down then to the Radhus or Town Hall which is fabulous. Finished after the war, it is of the "neo style," brick, great flowing sheeted fountains in front with kids swimming about and no one fussing. Wooden carvings in recesses surround the outside walls and inside it's colossal with great wall murals depicting every phase of Norwegian life, industry, the war and the people. The walls simply are just masses of colour. On then, to Frogner Park, where the life work of sculptor Vigneland has been collected to form the most unique of outdoor exhibitions. His works, both in stone and bronze, reflect his interpretation of life according to sex and it is all most interesting. He shows, by various sculptures, the life cycle from birth to old age and his figures and expressions are amazing. His chief work was a tall vertical work, some 50 feet high, depicting the struggle for life. It shows lots of figures pawing on top of one another for the peak which is gained by the few. It is surrounded by 20 other works, some very big. He took 25 years over it all.

Then to the Kon Tiki raft which sailed across the Pacific with six men. Made of balsa wood and used to prove a theory of where Polynesians came from. Saw also the Viking ships on which our ancestors sailed to England. Big rowing boats and smart lines. Back at the hostel I brewed up a good meal with custard dessert. Met a chap who had hitched from Finland over Lapland and down to Oslo. That's a trip I should like to do some day.

Saturday – didn't get far so settled in a clump of trees off the main road and slept very well. Next morning just made it to the road when a Chev. stopped and got right to Stockholm, 450 kms and I felt so good. Am very well and thriving on the open air. If you ever want to get in touch with me, I am c/o Miss M. Wescott, 54 Clifton gardens, Golder's Green. She sends my mail on from the bank.

# COLOGNE, WEST GERMANY
## (LATE SUMMER 1954)

Came back to Stockholm (hostel) and left after the female warden had disturbed me about midnight to enquire re my using a sleeping bag instead of a sheet. Went to a cafe where you eat as long as you like for four shillings. Not brilliant food but you can imagine the quantity that went down. Thriving on the general diet. First lift of the day was in a large taxi and the Swede took me home to breakfast of sour milk, eggs, cheese and fresh milk. The former I drowned in plum jam so it was appetizing: not rotten milk, just soured. Slept that night under some trees and next day drove with two Aust. navy boys who passed the same naval college exam as I sat for at 13. On their second trip over here and are enjoying life. One tried to catch fish while his mate and I cooked a meal and slept in the sun on a stream bank.

Driven along the sea shore on a fine day from Hamlet's Castle or Helsingor to Kobenhavn. It's a pretty drive, with lots of bathing and boating and beautiful homes.

Friday, got your mail in Kobenhavn and enjoyed all the news. Spent the day eating and calling on our friends at the restaurant. Left next morning and a textile man stopped in a few minutes to take me across (150 miles) Denmark to Kolding, in Jutland, and shouting me a feed.

Spent the night at Flensburg and next day, being Sunday, was hopeless on the road. Eventually was rescued from the elements by the Royal Air Force who took me to their station. Had a meal, much talk and then to the hostel for the night. Monday started off slowly but my luck changed and a luxury bus, returning empty from a tour of Europe, stopped so that for 100 miles I sat in style, with a great observation panel in front of me, to see all. The British again!

Slept the night in a hay stook. There is much wheat in this northern part of Germany. A farmer on a tractor picked me up for a slow 30 miles but then the Gods relented and a cosmetics baron (ex-Panzer Corps) arrived in a sports car and driving gloves. Sped along the great autobahn (built by Hitler to give the Germans work in 1933) the 300 miles or so to Cologne. Almost 70 mph all the way. Everything on the land looks so intensive over here.

Don was already here so we made off on a tour of inspection. The city of 700,000 took a dreadful bombing, worse than London for there are still great broken buildings and heaps of rubble and they work hard here. This is the great industrial area of Germany, the cities of Dusselldorf, Essen, Bonn etc are all concentrated here. In the centre of the city is the Gothic Cathedral whose spire is the tallest in Europe (500 feet). The Rhine River flows through the city as is crossed at many places by fine bridges, all new since the war.

The hostel is on the bank of the river which is picturesque and has green areas preserved.. The hostel is run along prison lines – in the morning we get "Atchung, Atchung," and a great tune played on a 'cello accompanied by song from the warden. However for 10 pence it's a cheap bed. The shops are stacked with Eau de Cologne and of course they have the giant factory here which turns out the scent. Will buy a barrel and deposit it in the station wagon.

This is all in the British Zone. Soldiers and R.A.F. are all over the place but are generally received well by the Germans, more so than the Yanks and the French. The latter are hated.

INTERLAKEN, SWITZERLAND

(SEPT 3 1954)

Had a glorious trip down the Rhine after leaving Cologne Tuesday morning. There was just too much damage from the war still left to make any visit enjoyable. Must be the worst city in Germany, every building seems either half-damaged or erased. Bonn, 20 miles down the river is the capital city of the German Republic. We went on a tour of the Bundeshus, the Parliament House and a beautiful new building with the Lower House sitting beneath an enormous eagle done in gold on the rear wall. Seemed a bit Hitler-like but most German. They love a uniform—the dustman, street cleaners all have theirs and the old men always have their peak hats with braid. The police force is German but soon we will see them all formed up into an army. The guards on Allied bases all over Western Germany are Germans. Also at the House of the President.

Next to Coblentz about 50 miles south and sitting on the joining of the Mosel and Rhine Rivers. Had a long promenade along the banks and hovering above us on the hills was the old castle. At the confluence there is a granite monument called "Deutsches Eck," regarded as a symbol of unity for the past one hundred years and a hope now for the unification of the Western and Russian Zones. Saw also Weindorf, a village kept open for daily wine festivities and much publicity for the wine industry. The latter is very important. The road though is very narrow, just enough for cars and trucks to pass, and for the train tracks. The river runs between big hills on which are grown the grapes for the vino. (This aerogram is made of German paper and is bad to write on) The vineyards are terraced like the rice fields of Japan and completely cover the hillsides in green. The banks, along which the road runs, are lined at nice intervals by little villages. With the sunshine, the busy river traffic of barges, ferry boats and other craft, it was a great day.

Down to Heidelberg that night. Rose at 7 a.m. from my "inner-spring mattress" to walk along the Rhine bank past all the grand old homes of the German upper class, now occupied by fat-faced Yankees. Americans "own" Heidelberg. Suddenly I saw appearing from the mist an enormous castle. I walked up the steep hill and arrived panting in the courtyard of the most fabulous castle you could imagine. Wasn't a soul about the great moat and drawbridge, massive gate, façade and balcony with a superb view of city and river. The front was carved and sculptured with a medieval tower. All surrounded by gardens and the first castle in which I've been really interested.

Later over the border into Basel and off to Berne, the Swiss capital via the quaintest of villages which seem to have ignored the march of time. The shops with their overhanging roofs and colourful setting of wooden beams and wares out in the streets, the farm barn in the centre of the shops with haystack almost on the pavement, the clock tower and arch, under which you drive into the main market square which invariably has a fountain and traditional style house of two of three stories and some shutters. Was picked up in one of these villages by an Australian from Tasmania. He was going down to Venice so joined him and as he can only take one of us, will meet Don there.

Had rather a quick look at this modern city. Having to deal with three languages (Italian, French and German), the government has done a grand job in forming such as settled country. The Swiss landscape is always beautiful, the roads wind about hills and lake sides, this colorful town on the shores of Kimsee: nothing can match it. The railway is totally surrounded by mountains including the majestic Jungfrau (13,633 feet) which I can see from the hostel, its peak and sides covered in shining whiteness glistening but never melting all the year around despite the sunshine we are enjoying at present. My driver decided to ascend it by train tomorrow – four pounds ten shillings but a unique experience to go up by tunneled lifts to the underground restaurante.

Tourism and watches are the main industries. The tourist with dough is hit all the time but Ma, they can't get it if it ain't there to be got. Spent today on the lawns of the lake bank, swimming and getting some sun. The rest is welcome as on the move again early.

The hostel is crowded with a dozen Aust. girls tonight, from all over the place including Jill Croker. She looks well. Had to laugh, we cooked a great meal and as soon as it was over, the 12 women proceeded to write their trip books in a most grim manner. Am not sure of my plans for the future – keep my bed vacant for next summer.

ROME

(SEPT 15 1954)

Arrived in the Eternal City after passing over some remarkable scenery in the Swiss Alps. The pass was efficiently constructed and once, on the down run of the St. Goddard, had 35 hairpin bends. The other was the Sustien Pass: it ran past the glaciers and peaks, the colorful views of gorges and deep drops to mountain valleys. Then you have the Swiss lakes, really wonderful at Lugano, lovely old homes on the banks and terraces upon the hillsides, the streets shaded and typical buildings with square windows, shuttered three or double storied. Into Italy and Lake Como, similar to Lugano. These two are surrounded on all sides by hills, and of course the big tourist resorts. Next stop was Milan –have been camping out quite a bit whilst my driver bunks in the Morris.

Milan is chiefly industrial but its cathedral is the most famous of Gothic still left in Europe. In another church I saw Leonardo da Vinci's "Last Supper," a fresco done on the wall of the Saint Mary of Grace Church. Some of these Italian churches are a mass of fresco work inside-- so different from other countries.

Awakened by rain at 5.30 a.m. so on the road early. Had a great meal in a café: only ordered spaghetti but the girl misunderstood and I couldn't believe the pile of food she placed in front of me.

Stopped at Brescia and Verdona, both full of architectural interest but it was all becoming a bit slow for me so I hitched on alone across to Venice. You gain the outskirts by car and then all vehicles are parked in an enormous garage. The Italian driver (my French again very handy) spun up a road of acute winds and bends to park on the top storey — number 10. From then on it really is all canals and the trip by the Grande Canal at night to the hostel was beautiful with the stately old palaces all flood-lit on the water which laps at the front doorsteps. This main canal is quiet large and runs through the centre of the city. From it branch the narrow waterways, bridged here and there. The traffic is all boat – the "trams" and "buses" are ferries and motor-boats are the taxies.

Gondolas are for general transport by the locals and to row the tourists who sit back on cushioned seats and go by as if they were on the "tubs" in the Luna Park tunnel-of-love. Whilst not in position to have one for an hour, I did ride across a 200-yard waterway between the island, on which was our hostel, and the main island. The main square is an enclosure, one end is the colorful, domed mosaic-worked gold cathedral and the other three sides are of long single unit buildings. Life goes on serenely in this unique place – no traffic noises, busy streets of small shops with chains hanging in the doorway. The square is a hive of activity: one hotel with its tables out in the open was being used as a picture location. I liked Venice with its peaceful waterfront and the whole atmosphere somewhat different from the rest of Europe. It seems to have ignored the March of Time.

Left per giant semi-trailer on which we sunned ourselves and dozed for the countryside was drab. Passed through Padua. You remember the House with the red singlets at the Brother's School. Funnily enough the Communists are quite strong up in these northern areas whiles the Fascists return south of Rome. On from the hostel at Bologna next day and into Florence, a fine old Roman city with many relics of the past beautifully set upon hills. We climbed up one and it was balconied in marble, with a fine view of Tuscany, the province. Leaving Florence we hitched through vineyards and agriculture –all sorts of crops and came to rest somewhere in the middle of nowhere about 5 p.m. I slept under a bridge and very well, too. One thing about Italy is there's always grapes or fruit somewhere so I did quite well. But there were no rides and I spent 22 hours in the same spot. Some children gathered me figs and wrapped them in green leaves before giving them to me. An old peasant lady gave me bread and refused payment, her son showing me his Communist Party card and cursing with me the capitalists who refused to stop.

Finally a French driver took me into Rome and on the way in, whilst he went to eat, I visited the Colisseum for one hour. Tried to imagine myself as a Roman general watching the Christians being eaten by lions. What a fabulous unit ancient Rome was. From here to Saint Peter's. It is an amazing first sight –the great square enclosed in a pincer movement of giant marble columns mounted on top with statues of saints. Didn't go in but will later as shorts are barred and woman must wear long sleeves. It certainly looks a grand sight, this centre of religion. Unfortunately, the next Papal audience is not until Thursday night and I don't think we'll have time for five days here. Some Australians girls went to the audience last night and had all sorts of things blessed.

Am very well, and this spell of good weather is putting a cap on a great time. Met the Canadian who I was with in Ireland by chance and he says I must thrive on this life on the road. Have not yet decided anything definitely about my return. Should be before Xmas. Shall holiday at my summer house in Cootamundra, write some memoirs and then to Canada and the United States to recoup the family fortunes. Yes, Ma, the Happy Wanderer made the hit parade here in August.

## ISLE DE MARGUERITE, CANNES FRANCE
### (SEPT 1954)

This address should be preserved for posterity. Arrived on the Riviera Thursday night and am on a short holiday before my yacht leaves for the Bermudas!!

I did return to the gigantic St Peter's Cathedral before leaving Rome. It's immense inside and beautifully preserved. Such a change from the usual run of decay. Many paintings, side altars but the most impressive is the great "square" and its 24 Grecian pillars and saint statues. That's where you feel the size of it. Before the main altar is an altar sunken into the floor beneath a covered canopy, used solely by the Popes. Could have seen him had I the time. It would have meant an extra two days for an audience with 698 others. Perhaps next time. They have a fabulous library and museum in the Vatican including the ceiling paintings of Michelangelo.

Saw many relics of ancient Rome , something I really enjoyed was the enormous buildings centred in a settlement on the outskirts of the city, put up by Mussolini at the height of his reign and all in white stone, futuristic design. Some are unfinished and now used as an exposition and congress places. Walked about the streets and the colossal railway station with its curved roof and glass, so that you lose that smoky effect of stations.

Left Rome early next morning on large 66-feet-long transport trailer returning empty from a load of 11 cars. Rode on the truck's back along the coast road, an unusual place as it was so loud and I looked back along this empty truck framework. Saw the Leaning Tower of Pisa flood-lit in the night. The country is average coastal up to Genoa. This city stretches along the coast and is the port from which Columbus sailed to America. Here a French couple picked me up in their open sports car. Really the most pleasant day motoring I have had –the weather is glorious and we spun along the Italian Riviera at a nice rate.

Miles of beaches, holiday resorts and fabulous hillside homes sitting above terraced orchards of olive trees and vineyards, an occasional pine and the tree-lined driveways. Beautiful view of the sea from the coastal road –and you drive by the shore the whole time. Some very nice resorts –San Remo, Leria , Imperia. Had a swim on one of the beaches. Nothing like Bondi but water calm as in Ceylon. Ate a picnic lunch and naturally the bottle of vino, fairly weak drop and they do drink a lot of it in Italy and France. Crossed back once again to France and entered on to the hallowed grounds of the real Riviera.

First place was the State of Monaco, an independent principality which lives on the profits of Monte Carlo. Saw the latter but not from the inside although some South Africans and Aust. girls had a flutter of a few hundred francs. Would have been my doom had I entered and would be a Mecca for Brother Ned's gang. You play with a two-shilling minimum. On to Nice –the waterfront lit up in a blaze of colour, the casino in full swing and the hotels, cafes out in the streets doing good trade although the season must close on the 27th, and one should then go to Venice! One of my lifts was an Englishman who lives here and he gave me an amusing tale of the social set-up and annual migration. Cannes at the moment is the place to be—we've had three days of sunshine on this island where the hostel is the former castle of Alex. Dumas"s "The Man in the Iron Mask." Swimming is mighty and a good crowd here.

MADRID SPAIN,

(1954)

Finished my holiday on the Riviera and a slight tan was on its way when we left Monday morning. Hitched all day through the southern wine fields of France and by night made Avignon, home of the earlier Popes. Up early next morning and walking out of town, a van stopped and I rode straight through to Barcelona. Driver was a Dane from Kobenhavn so we got along fine. When you pass into another country, France into Spain, the change isn't a sharp contrast. You notice it long before the border – the Spanish aspect of church bell towers, square houses, long square windows and shutters, dirty pastel shades, some villages all white, the dark skins. Grape harvest is in full swing – all women at work in the fields, the men carrying the baskets of grapes on their heads, dumping them in horse-drawn box carts. They then drive off to the local wine press. About one o'clock everyone retires under the vines for siesta by a bottle of vino for two hours. The border check was thorough as Spain is a police state. Police are everywhere. The soldiers are the rangiest, dirtiest mob imaginable, earning a penny per day. Police and navy are quite immaculate. Made the city at 8 p.m. and went into a bar to ask directions and was given a card to say "a friend of Bar Layetana," handed it in at a hotel or "pension" as they are called, and got a nice room, hot water and full board for ten shillings per day. But the face dropped at the breakfast of coffee and three slices of bread. However that's the Continental breakfast and I supplemented it outside.

Don turned up next night with an American. We saw a lot of the city which like Madrid is a surprise. Both have many tree-lined boulevards, squares and large fountains. As the hub of finance for the country and a lot of South America, there are many banks. In Barcelona, the commercial and residential areas are separated by a hill from the industrial groups on the outskirts. Being a port, it developed from the waterfront: this is where the old city is, a maze of narrow dark streets, dingy shops and laneways packed with cheerful people and goods. The food providers are stocked well with olives, meats, vegetables, grapes and bananas—the wine shops with gigantic casks and the brew at four to six pence per quart. Three of us purchased goat skin carriers because at that price, wine is cheaper than water. Mine holds a quart so that's enough for a meal (??) The church for Mass was dimly lit with a devotional atmosphere of people at prayer and of pointed Gothic with a beautiful cloister yard with a pool of swans and shady trees.

Went down on to the port waterfront. It was alive with ships asailing for South America and Africa but no extra hands wanted. The American boy went off to Mallorca, an island where he says he is just going to dig in for a month. Walked out to the bull ring, an arena like the Colliseum, examined the circle but found no gore stains, only Coco-Cola bottle tops. Also saw the 80,000-seat stadium which is a beauty. The Barcelona Exhibition grounds were alive with color and fountains –they have the periodic exhibition of wares and products from the world. On the hill top there is a great walled jail for anyone who says Franco is no good. Don went on down south from here but I had some misfortune in some money transferred from England not arriving on time in France so have had to curtail my Spanish trip and cut north to the capital. Bit of a blow but it should be in Paris.

The train trip across (hitching was too slow in Spain) was an experience. In my usual class with the peasants, everyone happy and shouting, singing and dressed up for the occasion. The wheels revolved once and the food came out. At lunch time, I was standing for a time in the corridor when a hand started waving. Went into the compartment and had a seat and a sandwich thrust at me. From then on, it was pretty good. Met a senorita who could speak French. She was very fair, a Castilian from Barcelona so the trip was quite interesting for the state of the countryside is pitiable. Wind-racked mountains, worn and torn at for centuries, dust bowls, erosion, dry fields, salt brush vegetation -- rocky and stony, with villages in the centre. Lord knows how they do it, a little simple irrigation on the river flats, hot sun. Half way through, the secret police flashed his badge and everyone dived for their identification papers. They enjoy talking to you and think that you can understand despite my ignorance on the language. But we all got on fine and they are a decent simple bunch. Franco now is building up a middle class so things here are on the way up.

Met at the station by an old English guide who took me to the pension I am installed at. Again in the city and feel this hotel business at 10 shillings per day is the way to go. Meals other than breakfast are good – veggies, meat, fish and fruit, and the room is big with a double bed, two chairs, desk, wardrobe and wash basin. However have lasted for a long time over here, three months and more after Paris, so it's time to halt for a while. Will write from Paris and then again from England to let you know just what I'm going to do. Your mail is being held for me so will catch up on all next week. Love to you all – expect the footy is just about over and the baths* on the way. Mustn't let a winter catch up with me. Don has applied to join the bank for two years in London. Assure you of no similar intention.

## LONDON
## (SEPT 1954)

Back once again in the Big Town and good to get your latest letter. Missed some in-between ones in Spain due to my hasty retreat. Left Madrid on the Saturday night. On the train met an English-speaking lawyer who provided all the details of the regime and many comments. The country changed 100 per cent near San

Sebastian and even resembled Switzerland and at times it was hard to believe that the south and its rocks and dust is the same country and an overnight trip away. The Civil War wrecked a lot but I liked the people I met, friendly and good. Walked over into France at "lunch time." It began to rain but still these coastal villages looked most attractive and colourful. Hitching good despite last week's lousy weather. Rode in a truck to Bordeaux. Next morning a ride with an insurance man who took me home to lunch. What luck and am pleased of that little French I speak. Meal began with beer, olives and sausages, a chop, wine, cheese, then potato, stewed apples, coffee and cognac as the area is the centre of the cognac industry. All was served as separate courses by the poor wife but she rallied well after a few inquiries on the children.

Five minutes back on the road and a couple returning from holidays stopped. Went all the way to Paree, broke the night at Tours, following the Valley of the Loire along small country roads where there is such a difference in the countryside once you move off the main road. Weather had changed and we drove into the capital mid-day Tuesday. Bit of bad luck, my money wasn't there for I had hopes of going wild buying a few things. Result was a hurried exit after two days. Saw the Louvre Gallery and just at night, walked around the town with a Jap who had been there two months and two Britons. Millions of clubs, gals and life but when you "got no money" it's best to head back so Friday off to Le Havre. This is the biggest port and the most completely ruined in the Invasion. Great building schemes are still under way but no suitable ferry from here so hitched up the coast to Dunkirk, scene of the famous evacuation where I evacuated myself on the early morning ferry to Dover. The fogs and mists have already returned down there but it is nice and peaceful.

To London on a tourist bus which had been on the continent for months. Feel that I have had a good time over there and now will begin to work something out as to getting home. Going into town tomorrow to see about a ship. Stopping out with the Australians at the flat in Golder's Green. It's good having a place to come to. Last night to the local show as everyone usually broke on Saturdays. This morning, after Mass, to Petticoat Lane again. Everything for sale and the latest method is to throw Biro pens and cheap cigarette lighters into the crowd and then pawn off all the goods when people are in a good mood. An 18-piece dinner set of the old Chinese willow design (Nanna, I think has some) went for 18 shillings. Would carry well in the rucksack

## LEICESTER SQUARE, LONDON

(OCT 12 1954)

All last week I looked for a job on a ship and saw a few shows. Enjoyed a concert Monday and then Agatha Christie the following night. Met Aub Wednesday—he is still prospering and did a gig at the Hotel Piccadilly for seven pounds. I work 48 hours for that. We saw the film "The Belles of St Trinians," a film about Sister Caroline, Cousin Deirdre and Co. The weather holds but already the fogs and whisperings of what is to follow. Next night with one of the girls to "Intimacy at 8.30," a revue in Piccadilly. Good fun and a bit of glamour. Spent the day going through my junk collection. Friday we had a fire and played poker. I won the princely sum of four shillings which from my half pence, is O.K. Saturday I was to go down to Tilbury Docks to look for a ship but the big dockyard strike is on so not much is doing. Instead my old manageress, who I dropped in to see at Fortes for a meal, talked me into working a little. That's what I'm doing now here at Leicester Square—all my food and a few quid. Serving the same old, habitual bunch. Don has not yet returned from Spain. He has not heard word about the bank but remains keen. I am not so keen to resume my banking career and feel that when I return, it may be the chance to start afresh in something else. Am quite keen on the Dept. of Territories, New Guinea Division, a year's school in Aust. followed by 18 months up there as Patrol Officer. The boss is calling so had better go. Will get a customer to post this. Will let you know when I have something definite about where I'm heading.

## LONDON

(OCT 17 1954)

Am still in London. It would certainly be grand to do the return trip to Australia overland but you'll know by next letter. This week I worked most of the time but my social life included Noel Coward's "Blythe Spirit" which I did enjoy. What a difference the theatre is from the movies and for one shilling and six pence, it's great. The productions are first class, settings and effects the best for the big West End season is the attraction. It was a good parody of séances—the result is everyone wants to have one. Wednesday, I took a few hours off to stand with the crowd in the Mall which is the big avenue leading straight through to the Palace from Trafalgar Sq. Had a good view of the Queen and Duke, Emperor of Ethiopia

Hailie Salassie and coaches full of officials. Most impressive was the Company of Queen's Life Guards on their beautiful horses The route was decked with enormous flags of the two lands and guardsmen in dress uniforms lined the route. The officers look most aristocratic with their swords and jackboots.

Last night took one of the girls to a dance at Australia House. Had fun. Today Sunday Mass in my old blue suit which is tight on me now. Returned to Golder's Green where we had the big Sunday dinner –all put in the dough and it works out well. In the afternoon, walked around Hyde Park and the "blue blood" of shops in Knightsbridge. Harrods is the shop and often visited by the Queen on a buying spree. Tonight we went to Albert Hall and heard Eileen Joyce, the Australian pianist. The first section was Fantasia by Tchaikovsky but the second, a concerto by Rachmaninoff "soothed me" too much that I passed out but revived for the vigorous Overture 1812 about Napoleon's defeat in Russia. The hall is circular, great rows of seats spiraling up to the top where sat yours truly in his bowler and twirling his cane. Excuse me, one of the cooks has just brought me a plate of apple fritters that require my attention.

LONDON

(OCT 25 1954)

The great dock strike is still going strong. Spent first three days of week down there but nothing doing at all. Today's reports show no change. Working 10-4 p.m. at Fortes. Don is back with us but has received a fare home from his people and leaves Nov. 16. I am awaiting some details from the Dept. of Territories but of course remain indefinite on that until I get home. Thursday night we saw "I Am A Camera" at the New Theatre. It was set in Germany before Hitler and I enjoyed it. Friday to "Joan at the Stake" with Ingrid Bergman. It didn't get the expected raves but before it was Act.1 of the ballet "Giselle" which I liked very much. After it all, I was dragged around to the stage door and out SHE came with Roberto—it must be lousy to be mobbed the way she was. Sat. night I saw the best musical revue yet, "The Boy Friend." The period was the 1925's at a French finishing school for young English ladies. Most of the gals, Mum, reminded me of your photo album but we did have a good night there and afterwards a big combined meal – some of the girls are quite talented at informal ballet, act etc but no complaints from the neighbors below. Am just back from Swan & Edgar, the Men's Shop in Piccadilly where I purchased a jumper and shirt.

At the moment, with all this delay and uncertainty, I feel like hopping the next boat to Canada and coming home with a few quid. Very well and have put on weight.

## LONDON
### (NOV 9 1954)

Sorry, Mum, to be so late with this but I wanted to get things finalized before writing you again. The "Largs Bay," which we had both booked to leave on Nov. 5 has been delayed to Nov. 20 so that dashes any Xmas hopes. I have decided that I will now go to Canada and America for I feel that I would have some trouble settling down without seeing them, although I'd love to see you all.

Am very well, an A1 migrant for Canada and I hope to leave this month with Vic Murray, the Canadian boy I knew in Ireland. Met him again last weekend. He has his B.A. and was looking for a job teaching. I think, really, this is the best idea for me. I want to collect as many ideas over there as I can and, with a few quid, get out on my own when I come back—a family business, perhaps. I hope you understand, Mum, when I say I'll do better by leaving the bank. It would be miserable with the way I think now and I'm happy to be my own boss. Just have some faith in your third handsome son who is still the sober, non smoker who left you in January. I'm confidant I'm doing the right thing. However, that's life! Am seeing all the shows before I leave. And tonight just have come in from the House of Commons where I was seated from 3 p.m. listening to the debates. Sir Anthony Eden and all the Conservatives with their feet on the tables, Clem Atlee like a tiny rat and almost viperfish when shot at about his trip to China. Horrible manner, and in the background the old warriors asleep. Not that I blame them for I passed out during one discussion on road safety and had to be awakened by an usher in tails. I enjoyed Eden and his talk on South East Asia. All the members came in from the bar except Winston who so far has avoided me.

Yesterday Aub, Don and I went out to one of Aub's artist friends at his new double storied home in Teddington, on the Thames. It is lovely out there and his wife did the great meal. The autumn colouring of the trees is gorgeous – a gold, brown cover seems to be over all. We walked around to the East Molesey Cricket

Ground where the Australian tour always starts. Also Tag Island, which carries the bounty for anyone who hits the ball there on the full!

LONDON

(NOV 15 1954)

Canada is a "go." Vic and I leave on Nov. 28 from Southampton, for New York. We plan on two days there before going up to his uncle's place near Boston. Am quite thrilled with the idea. From here to Montreal to an aunt and Vic goes on to Winnipeg, his home town, while I begin to dig up new fields in the catering trade. He has been working on the 10-4 p.m. shift at Fortes with us. At the moment, we are the centre of attraction with the premiere and Royal Command Performance of "Beau Brummel" tomorrow at the Empire Theatre next door and the Queen, Duke and "Unhappy Princess" all scheduled. Doubt whether they will dive into this "dive" though. However they will clear the snack bar so that the staff will have a box view of proceedings. Saw Stewart Granger (palid), Jean Simmons (beautiful), Jane Russell (hard), Rudy Vallee, all going in for rehearsals yesterday. Also Anna Neagle.

Last night about 6 p.m. (working back) I served the British Empire ex-champion Jake Tuli. Ah, fame. Tuesday night I went to an exhibition of Diaghilev who organized so much ballet and who did such a lot for it. It is one thing I have discovered a genuine interest for. Wednesday, Rod, who is from Melbourne and on an art scholarship from the Melbourne Art Gallery (also at Fortes!), Aub and a few others had a meal out at the girls in Golder's Green. It was voted that I would organize a séance as I had experience of them with Cousin Vod in Sydney and by now everyone had seen "Blythe Spirit." They all thought it most amusing and me insane until someone's grandfather (deceased) came on the scene. Friday, I took a girl to "Can Can," Cole Porter's new musical. It was fun, set in Paris and showed the can can of Lautrec. The costumes were gay and it kept moving.

Yesterday Rod took me around the Tate Gallery which houses English and foreign paintings. All the artists from Moulin Rouge had worked there and Rod was very informative. Toulouse-Lautrec, Renoir, Cezanne, Picasso, Pizarro, Manet, Van Gogh. The corresponding Victorian era of English art made an amusing comparison. Saw Robert Morley in the comedy "Hippo Dancing." He is really good but an egotist, I thought. Also "Sabrina Affair" with Ron Randall, only fair although he was O.K.

## LONDON

## (NOV 22 1954)

Hope you are not too sore at me leaving the bank without you wanting it but I think you'll understand I have had no intention of returning to it since I left. I've been about enough now to know my real mind and things are easier and seem to unfold once you sense it that way. Wrote and thanked the bank for their past considerations. Doubt if they'll close up over it.

Am at work and the crowd is gathering in Leicester Square. Two and one-half hours still to the big entrée into the flower -splattered Empire Theatre. Down the middle of the street is a fence barricade already holding the mob back. Was talking to a policeman outside before I came in to work – he will have 399 mates to help keep order as the fans go berserk once the stars appear. I've just come from a hour at the National Gallery in Trafalgar Square, only a block away. The Square makes a nice study at night – darkness at 5.30 p.m. with the column of Nelson, the giant lions and fountain, the balcony walls, the cars and red double-decker buses and all the lights. It's cool here now and a mist settles in early. I think London is the one city you could become fond of, in its buildings and atmosphere. If I find uranium, I'll bring you over, Mum, with your daughter and put you in a flat at Knightsbridge for a year.

Most excited about the upcoming sea trip to Canada – the "Italia" is a 22,000-ton liner and from the pamphlets appears quite luxurious. Sail about midday with the boat train at 8 a.m. Sunday week. Vic's parents are trying to tie up a host for us in New York which would be mighty.

We've been closed three hours and the privileged staffs of Fortes, including myself have seen all from the front step, the crowd having been pushed back away from us. All the stars –Elizabeth Taylor, Granger, all I mentioned before, Jack Hawkins, all the furs and tails, glittering necklaces and beautiful hair-styles, dresses, faces, the occasional crank who in his six shillings seat went along as if he was shearing sheep. Then the Queen, Duke and Princess Margaret, looking all as royal and grand as ever. And back to work for me as the crowd began to enjoy our tempting wares and preferred to wait on outside, like patient creditors, for the departures after the performance. By midnight, they still were standing there, faintly visible in the fog which had descended on the Square. Having gorged myself, changed out of my uniform, popped my head out the door, saw the Royal and Not-So-Royal departures, and off home. They put a fence down the middle of the street to keep the 10,000 in control.

Worked back again Tuesday for every "dollar" counts now. Next night, Vic and I took two girls to Her Majesty's Theatre to a show "Tea House of the August Moon." It was a good skit on the American Occupation forces, trying to teach the natives democracy. Please destroy this letter for I shall be liable to indictment if the U.S. security forces ever know I have written that! They have millions of forms to fill in before they allow you in. However I am looking forward to seeing them on home ground as the ones you meet abroad could hardly be a fair average. I hope not.

Friday night all went to the local theatre and saw "Guys and Dolls" which has just finished its West End run. It was very well done and set in the "crap game" area of New York. The numbers were O.K. Last night went along to The Duke of York's and saw "All For Mary." The story was pretty ancient – the old one of the ex-husband meeting up with the present one etc but very well done by a cast of actors including David Tomlinson. All their efforts certainly made it enjoyable.

Just in from a walk around Hyde Park. Stopped at Marble Arch with the soap-box orators for a while. Also passed an hour at the National Gallery. Well, that's my London news. Will write you next from Canada, three thousand miles across the Atlantic which is supposed to be pretty rough at present.

## ATLANTIC OCEAN
### (DECEMBER 1954)

I am on the blue Atlantic, one week out. Running a day late due to the bad weather we struck on two days. Am very well and thriving once again on sea travel. Vic and I are in a 4-berth cabin on the SS "Italia"with a Scot and a Londoner. It's pretty crowded, more so it seems that our SS "Otranto" six-berth but I think it's because we are all on the same second sitting for meals. The latter are good – our steward is always piling on the food for us. Some days there haven't been many in the dining rooms due to the "perks," but we wagered that if one of us went down with sea sickness, he would have to do an item in the ship's concert. That in itself keeps me from getting sick. Each evening at dinner there are strolling musicians.

The days go by with chess, snoozing, talking, "games,"—and four of us go down to the gymnasium each afternoon where I have become fairly proficient at bag punching. The swimming pool is a beauty, modeled on Roman bath lines with great columns supporting an observation walk. It's all in-door and nearly three times the "Otranto" pool. The tourist class accommodation with its four lounges and smoking rooms and ample deck space was a surprise. The official language of the ship is German and not a great many speak English.

Today it is flat and we have sunshine. All are about now but they disappear once we spin about on the ocean. Night life is very gay – dancing and old German-Bavarian nights of music and song. Have never known any race sing as the Germans. On board we use American money so am adjusting myself. They have 100 cents to the dollar which is worth eight shillings and nine pence in Australia, half dollar, quarter dollar, dime and nickel. We haven't been spending much as both much in the same boat, literally and financially. Had a good laugh on deck the other day. An old Yank was speaking to a German and told him and pointed to me, saying I was the typical young American and for me to join them and tell the German all about my home state. I told him New South Wales and he didn't know where that was. These Yanks really are a scream. An old guy in a peak tennis cap just walked up, looked over my shoulder and said: "That's mighty funny writin', son, ain't never seen it like that before."

I'll be getting off at Halifax now due to my American visa not arriving in time and due to the hysteria over war and the Communists, they won't let me near the United States. However I'll get down there later on when I am undoubted as a security risk. Instead, I will take the train right across Nova Scotia, two days to Montreal, and then meet Vic at his aunt's place. I'm stopping there until I get settled and should be earning the mighty dollar soon. Feel that, though it is coming only gradually, I am evolving to something I want to do when I return to Australia. Finished up well in London with a great party.

Have just put Vic on the train for the final stage of his trip home to Winnipeg. He had a great time in New York and at his Boston uncle's place. The latter has sent me an invitation down there as soon as I can make it. Today I got myself a job until Xmas with Simpson's, the big local store as an assistant on a delivery van. Start tomorrow at $36 per week. I also was interviewed by the Royal Bank of Canada and am due to begin there as soon as a reference letter comes from the Bank of New South Wales in Sydney. It should be O.K. for the winter and due to previous experience am on $200 per month.

I leave Vic's aunt's place tomorrow and live with a house of university students here. They have clubs known as a fraternity and they all have their resident houses. We all put in $75 per month and then theoretically there is a rebate for anyone who misses meals. You can see by this that wages and prices are high. A hamburger costs 25 cents, a milk shake 20 cents, other groceries fairly high. The newspapers are enormous at 5 cents and you can get a really good second-hand (2 year-old model) cheap car. Here it is just amazing the number of what we used to call "posh" cars on the street – Chevs, Pontiacs, Plymouths (the Bains have one here), Fords are small cars. A big one would be a Cadillac, Buick etc.

The weather is fine, sunny but temperature is about 15 degrees so it's getting down. We have snow lying around all the time and what an attractive setting it makes for Xmas. In every big store, railway station, church, large buildings, there are the most fantastic Xmas decorations. Moving choirs, singing carols, dolls, clowns actually licking lollypops, toy whales spouting bubbles, fairy queens, the streets decked with holly and berry, recorded music in the background, the mistletoe in each window and in the fronts of the homes the lighted Xmas trees, sparkling gaily with hundreds of coloured lights, and Santa Claus. One hotel, whose rooms make a block face has the design of a Xmas tree in red light shades from a pattern of rooms.

However, nice as it all looks I would swap it all to be back with you down at "Makela". Will be thinking of you all and with you in spirit, more or less. Marion, Vic's aunt said to tell you I was to be their guest over the Xmas season and that she'd look after me.

Merry Xmas and Happy New Year.

# MONTREAL
## (DEC 28 1954)

It made Xmas getting all your letters and cards. I got my delivery van driver to take me downtown Xmas Eve and collected them. I went down to St. James Basilica which is only 300 yards down the street (it is built to scale on St Peter's) and heard midnight mass and went to communion. All done in the most formal tradition by the French-Canadian Cardinal Leger, a little too formal for Xmas , I thought but maybe I just prefer Father O'Connor in Murrumburrah.

We had some very light snow and there was the over-covering all about. At noon I went out to the Bains'. They all had the sort of day we have—the branches of the family all represented. Had a light lunch of cheese, crackers and salami in the lounge room whilst one of the grand children performed ballet and tap dance. The big meal was at 5 p.m. and they had the most enormous turkey I have ever seen, 32 lbs (39 cents per lb). It just dominated the table and what we ate, seven of us, seemed a very small flick off its side. They had a New Zealand nurse who had worked in Samoa, Africa, England and now Montreal, and after the meal another two first year trainee nurses from the hospital. Played Scrabble and informed the party that my sister was an expert. The presents they gave one another included most useful gadgets from plastic hoop-clip aprons, plastic shopping lists with markers on your items, and many others. They get a kick out of any novel idea. I received a tin of biscuits with a note to return for a refill as soon as I had finished them. That will be sooner that they expect at my present rate.

Concluded my delivery work in mild weather although it was usually snowing. It was zero for two days and rose to two degrees, then five and eight degrees. I was cold so have shed any inhibitions about being the outdoor type for the winter. And it lasts until April. All indoors is beautifully heated. Played squash up at McGill indoor courts. They have fabulous sports grounds, all indoor, a gorgeous swimming pools and basketball courts. I liked the squash –it's something the same as handball with racquets. Happy New Year.

## KRT FRATERNITY HOUSE, MONTREAL
### (JAN 4 1955)

Had a big party here at the fraternity house on New Year's Eve. I was saddled with a dreadful blind date but despite this enjoyed myself. She lived seven miles out but luckily one of the other guys had a Pontiac so no taxies. If this hadn't happened, I planned to creep upstairs and go to bed without the chivalry for fares are steep. Otherwise the holiday was pretty quiet except for the biggest fall of snow since 1941 and which wrecked traffic and cost the city $750,000 to cart away. Outside, as I write, are enormous snow ploughs and queues of trucks are carting it off.

Today saw me in a grey suit, reasonably fashionable in full cut and three-buttoned, white shirt, grey nylon socks and overshoes at the Royal Bank of Canada on McGill College St. The office is nice and warm: there are many races of quite attractive girls from the Baltic lands, Poland, the South Americas and some French-speaking Quebeckers. This is useful as I commenced to study French tonight. Everyone at the bank seems pleasant and the system does not seem greatly different from the Bank of New South Wales so it should be a good experience. The Wales sent along that reference. For lunch we have 20-cent tickets from the bank and get a really good meal, three courses, three vegetables and milk. For that price it is almost free food. This allows me a 50-cent rebate daily from my $75 rent at the house. The streets are slippery and footpaths have an inch of ice on them in places. The snow doesn't melt so before the ploughs arrive; it is like walking along a trench in some streets.

My New Year's resolution: "To decide just what I will do."

## MONTREAL
### (JAN 21 1955)

Writing this from the office. The sun shines in my window and outside the temperature is at 15 degrees. Beside me is the 25-storey-high Sun Life Building, one of the biggest in Canada. One good point about the winter is the amount of sunshine we have. Am watching this month slip by as it and February are the chief winter months. So far, except for those early weeks, I've weathered it well. Cousin Vod wrote to say he is coming here in April but will advise him well on the purchase of a thick overcoat and decent shoes. The latter are most expensive.

Saw a movie "On the Waterfront" with Marlon Brando. Ticket cost 60 cents to one dollar. Sunday a walk up the Mountain with two guys. It's a beautiful scene. You walk up by a road, everything is white and the houses are of solid stone. You cross on to a wooden staircase and climb steeply. The skiers crash by, in and out of the trees like demons. At the top the view is a full panorama of the city. There is also a chalet full of wares and provisions. A road is kept clear around the Mountain and horses driven by raccoon-coated drivers draw wooden sleighs full of tourists and children. The sleighs are line with rough bear skins.

You're right about Montreal being the city of banks and churches. The Jews and we are firmly entrenched. The "poor" old Jew is, as everywhere else, wealthy, envied and hated. Have not seen a fire indoors here but with the even indoor heating, I don't miss them. Telephones are hired on a monthly rental of about $5 and that allows as many local calls as desired. It's a private phone company, the Bell Telephone Co. Railways have two lines – Canadian National is the government of Canada and Canadian Pacific is a private company.

MONTREAL

(FEB 1955)

Well, my first pay this afternoon so feel fairly flush with a few bucks in my wallet once again. The work is O.K. at the bank, so close, so warm, so many beautifully dressed assistants but I would find it hard to regard it all seriously and I feel that I made the right decision in coming here and leaving the Wales. My week hasn't been very exciting – did a bit of work on my French, had a game of squash. It feels good to be sporting again. Another walk up the mountain and a grand view of the St Lawrence River as it cuts it way through. No shipping on the water now until the end of March due to the ice. It was a fine sunny day and the snow hard. Many people were skiing and the kids were out on toboggan slides. They have a practice ski-lift and run. Over from this is a frozen lake which was like a scene from Punch or the Pickwick Papers with well-muffled skaters going around and round with apparent ease. Walked on to the massive St. Joseph's Oratory. This is a Catholic Shrine. It is full of burning candles and lamps but otherwise done out well with escalators and a tea shop on the second floor. The local Protestants say that we have to keep on building more to it so that we don't have to pay taxes on it. The eternal brawl is on in this province for it is predominantly French and the minority squeals. Scored a brew of tea from some friends of a friend on the way home.

After Mass Sunday I went around the corner to an art gallery exhibition by a Canadian artist, Fred Varley. It was pretty good, I thought and it is a change to see the outdoors portrayed after the subtleties of the Europeans. At night down to Curly Joe's for that big steak. It really is a meal sitting on a wooden plate by itself. We get a plate of pickles and rye bread with chips. In Australian money it costs 13 shillings but it is six times as big as the Popular Café's steak at home. Monday I met an old girl friend off the ship and took her to lunch but at night could only manage a cup of coffee for her at some dive she thought I should see. Tuesday to the local "Nurses Home" where a bunch of Australians and New Zealanders had gathered. They showed slides of everywhere they had been and it was quite amusing because everyone had seen everything. Nurses make good dough here, so Sister Caroline, just remember.

MONTREAL

(FEB 7 1955)

The big cold snap has lifted – a week of sub-zero and zero temperatures has been enough to make me think of packing my bags and catching the train down to sunny Florida with the rest of Montreal society. It was such a relief to walk out this morning to Mass with the temperature at 30 degrees and no biting cold to sting the ears. Had a fair snowfall last night and today the streets are slushy which is a sign of a mild winter. Everyone here felt the cold and it is unusual for such low temperatures to persist for a week. Princess Margaret drew comments when she didn't present herself to the crowd who waited outside the plane at the airport the other night – can't blame her for not showing herself to fools. They must have nearly froze waiting in the open , at midnight.

The bank continues O.K. and am now assisting on the counter in the savings dept. "Your passport, sar." "Jest a minute, ah'll go get it." The tellers are all women. It's quite pleasant and we go to the Honey Dew next door for coffee twice daily, a good hour at lunch and work itself not at a break-neck speed. My companion at the desk is a 32-year-old ex-merchant naval man who came in after a steady job but feels he will have to toss it if there isn't some change. I have not attempted to disillusion him by saying "There's no change, brother."

I am trying to save from my $174 per month after taxes. Entertainments etc are big money – "The Pyjama Game", a successful Broadway New York musical starts this week but it's $3 for a fair seat. In England we saw the best from reasonable seats for as little as 60-cents. Of course, wages are that much higher here but my sense of values can't put these shows at a 27 shillings touch though I down a steak for 13 shillings without a pang of conscience. Yesterday I played basketball at McGill with the boys from the house. Went on for two hours on the wooden floor in the gym which is bigger than the Cootamundra Drill Hall. It has four basketball courts, ropes and "horses" as we used to have at the Brother's School. Next door is the new swimming pool and about ten squash courts. No bodily contact is allowed in basketball which makes it different from that one Cootamundra Rugby League game I played over at Fisher Park. It's very popular here and I was quite exhausted after the epic and retired for eleven hours sleep.

My old clothing relics are gradually giving up the ghost so will have to begin the buying campaign soon. Am doing my own washing except for the work shirts which cost 20 cents to get done. Each Saturday night the old Chinese laundry man comes. He calls about 8 p.m. with a bag over his shoulder, bringing back the shirts the next Saturday. I counted up to ten for him in Chinese and he was much amused. There is a China Town in the city but more on that when I have been there for a meal.

London seems to be having its share of snow according to personal reports. That is the city I would like you to see for I am sure there is nothing like her in the world. My French progresses, for at work there are several who are French-speaking and some of them usually talk to me in French so the practice is good.


MONTREAL

(FEB 14 1955)

Sitting at my desk in my room on the first floor, in pyjamas after a bath and pleasantly warm despite the predicted low of 10 degrees below tonight and the high for tomorrow is five below. Today a raw wind tore at everything. It's a 10-minute walk from the McGill College branch to the big 1 p.m. meal at the Head Office cafeteria but it's worth every step on the icy pavements. Yesterday it was snowing as I walked down; today at noon there wasn't a cloud with the brilliant sunshine which dazzles as it bounces off the snow but when I left at 5.30 p.m., it was snowing again. I enjoy the snow for it is never the freezing bite that the wind seems to have, and the white stuff is pleasant to see. The back porch is stacked high with it for the winter. The Hit Parade here includes (temperature now three degrees below) "Hearts of Stone," "Let Me Go Lover," "Count Your Blessings" and Nat King Cole's "Teach Me Tonight."

Saturday I played squash with one of the boys but the racquet collapsed after an hour. At night the Bains took me to the Bellevue Casino, one of the best clubs in town i.e. the best floor show. Fabulous décor in black and gold figures, blue lighting and the chorus, fantastic juggling and a Hungarian balancing troupe whose act was amazing. Then we went around to Ben's, the Jewish snack bar whose specialty is the smoked meat sandwich. Sunday to St Patrick's Church which is only two blocks away and English-speaking so it's something now to be able to have the sermon.

Joe, the lawyer-to-be, has given me a wireless and I get some decent stuff occasionally. The set-up the same as Aust., only the CBC is commercial in its ads, and not nearly as good as the ABC. The BBC is the other extreme. Had five sets of squash with David the Londoner at the university courts. He has just begun his accountancy. He's 22 and recently arrived from Brazil where he had four years as the "office boy." He is full of the overseas Englander (NOT the type you see coming off the boat at Sydney and complaining before they make Martin Place) but is really pleasant company. Played Union for Brazil but of course that is not the All Blacks. Squash is as strenuous as tennis – I won't say more because of the Davis Cup rookie in the family.

One of the fraternity house guys was given two front section seats for the big ice hockey game Saturday night. This is the equivalent of a lottery win here for the national sport has a tremendous following. Seats are all sold out for the season. The arena is newly built and seats 15,000 and the 200 ft ice rink is beautifully surfaced and painted. There are six men to a team, well padded and with razor-sharp blades for skates. It is the fastest game imaginable – they literally fly and it's fantastic what they do. Sticks and punches flew at random as the locals, the Montreal Canadiens (Les Habitants) tossed the Boston Bruins 4-0. When the local star here called Maurice "The Rocket" Richard scored his goal (411th in first grade), it was like Roley scoring the try to win the Maher Cup on the whistle. For the brawls, they simply took off their gloves and all-in. When they spot the stars, it's done by tripping with the sticks, crushing against the fence, bashing from behind. It's the big time in sport here.

Sunday we all went to Mass. Usually collect a black Protestant or two to fill a pew. Came "home" for a meal then went to the top of the mountain and had my first ski. Did O.K. but tried nothing fanciful until I started off down the road and began to accelerate towards a sturdy notice board on the side. It read "BEWARE DANGER" so took a slide instead of a crash. Only hurt my dignity. It's so convenient. I skied all the way down the mountain road but the freezing spell had made the snow hard. It was zero up there but kept moving. Do you mind the typed letters? My hands are too big to write small.

## MONTREAL
### (MARCH 1955)

I was thrilled to get all those photos along with my School Leaving Certificate. Mum, you haven't changed a bit and must be the youngest looking 39 year-old— you beat the matrons of Canada. The girl on the spring-board, I thought at first, was one of the American glamour stars out on a tour until I noticed it was my sister. Quelle figure!

All quiet here except for the blow of a tear (four inches) in my overcoat which cost me eight dollars. The labour price is fantastic when it comes to repairs but offset by my winning the $36 pool with one of the typists at the office. We put a buck in each pay day and they draw the names. There are no lotteries but at the moment Irish Sweep Stake tickets on the Grand National are sold everywhere. I attended the event at Aintree Course in morning suit last March. Must admit the wireless (always called "radio" –it's quite a joke when you use the former) is a morgue on Sat. afternoons sans Cyril and Ken.

The bank is O.K. and my new position in the Savings Department more agreeable. I keep my six tellers in check and serve at the inquiry counter. The Boss of Savings is an ex-R.C.A.F. tail-gunner so we shoot the war a lot –I tell him my experiences as a commando with the National Service at Ingleburn Camp!! Why I wanted the Leaving Cert. is because I have put in an application for McGill University. Nothing definite naturally. The point is that although I miss you and the family, I have a feeling that if I got back and had to start again from the bottom in Australia, I'd just be fed up and want to go off again. At the moment, with everyone studying here and urging me to go to McGill I think it is the one chance I have, especially if I can put myself through on the summer work.

Am doing about three solid hours work each night to get back into trim. Am most keen to do Geology which must be a great thing in Australia and Canada with the new discoveries each month. This would fit in with my plan to travel as a gentleman after such experiences I had in France before getting back to England. What actually occurred was that Aub was to send me 30 Pounds to the Bank of France in Paris but it went astray. So I had two shillings left and London far away. I explained my position to the British Consulate at Le Havre after trying for a job on a ship and passing the previous night on the floor of a shanty on a garbage dump. It was raining like Hell. The consul was the starch of England –an old B. – when lo and behold, in walked the typical ex-R.N. officer, overheard my tale of woe, invited me to coffee, said he was appalled at the consul's attitude, and lent me 6,000 francs. Remember, always be nice to the English migrant –you can so easily misunderstand them. And I put the francs back in his account in London before leaving for Canada.

MONTREAL

(MARCH 1955)

Have just finished the weekly sweep of the room and deposited the heap of filth below. The house is a hive of activity on a Saturday morn. The big change has come in the weather. This week has been gorgeous, between 30 and 40 degrees. The streets are running with dirty snow and ice on the pavements thawing merrily. So it looks as if my first Canadian winter is drawing to a finis. However we had a snowfall two days ago and more forecast tonight. At night the temperature drops to well below the freezing point 32 degree and the melting snow becomes slippery ice for the morning's walk to the office. The hill we live on (Peel St) has to be watched and often have the Council men running about with sand and dirt. When all this melts and heaps up, they come and clear it away – the employment must be kept up as the peak in thousands of jobless arrives in three weeks. I always feel quite thankful as I walk past the unemployment office to lunch and see all the men lounging against the wall. It's a good thing there is none of it out there with you.

Am really not interested enough to do accountancy. If I was, I should be doing it by now. Geology, I think, will give me the profession which will allow me an interesting and useful career, a good salary, freedom and work in different parts of the world. The discovery and working of minerals, and above all petroleum and oil, is foremost in most national economies. Look at the way they are searching for oil in Western Aust. and you will see the work of the geologist. Another advantage is that I want the education McGill offers me and the chance to work my way through.

The old mathematics bug-bear has again raised its head and I will have to pass an exam in that and also one of the sciences. Going to see a registrar next week and if it remains as above, I shall be off to the wilds as soon as possible with a satchel of Algebra and chemistry books, to emerge in June for the examinations at a local high school.. If that doesn't come off (i.e. passed) I will take the boat home, build a house on the South Coast and retire.

After London, Montreal seems fairly small and hasn't the interest London has. But I like Montreal and if I stop here, the University is only one hundred yards away. I am pretty settled on this convenience. It gets very muggy and hot in August but I hope to be away for the summers, making the fees and living expenses. It will cost me about $1,200 each year. I am 100 per cent and the weight has soared to 192 lbs. They never use "stones" here. I can't take to the coffee so drink milk most of the meals which with the lunch hour epic, explains my putting on a stone (14 lbs) since arrival. Saturday had the weekly game of squash and then went to the annual Rugby Union meeting with David, the English accountancy student. It was full of Oxford, Cambridge, ex-Public School types, "Jolly Good Show, Rex," etc but a keen core of Union players. For Easter, they go to New York to play against the club there but as it will cost about $50, I won't be going. McGill also has three teams.

Work continuing O.K. Had a pleasant evening with the Bains the other night,. They have a new high fidelity radiogramme and some beautiful records. I do enjoy good music although still have the old hit parade. One is on at present but 1-20 and No. 20 has only begun. Had to go to the steak house for the usual Sunday dinner so missed the remainder after: No. 19 "Gotta Go Get My Baby." 18. "The Ballad of Davy Crockett." 17. "Rock of Love."16. "Unsuspecting Hearts."15. "Teach Me Tonight." 14."Make Yourself Comfortable." 13. "Naughty Lady of Shady Lane." 12."Let the Sun Shine In."

Had a really enjoyable weekend up in the snow. David came up with me by bus after work Friday. All the gear was borrowed. Arrived at Sainte Marguerite and went on five miles to our lodge which was one-half mile off the main road. It was snowing lightly after a good fall and you can see how much was around the house. The hosts were English and the meals over the weekend were mighty. They had a log fire and a large library. The house was similar to one I stopped at in Norway, just the thing for an informal weekender. Hosts had spent a few years in India so that our room was furnished in that fashion. At midnight, there was a crash and in came five Scottish girls. They were a lot of fun and we did have a good time.

Sat. morn and David and I were the only enthusiasts and skied up the road to the Chalet Clochar where there is the big "Chalet" and the ski runs. Practised on the smaller one before making the big ascent.

The country did look beautiful from the top of the hill. I think I should have enjoyed it more had I not descended on skis. However we made it in fine style. The last half was down a straight run. It was thrilling, hurtling down but decided a little more practice was necessary so retired to the smaller hill. The rope tow makes a great difference. Paid 50 cents for 12 rides. Going up the big hill we used a T-bar which is supposed to push you up, pressing on your behind. As we had never seen them before, we blundered into sitting down on them. The Frenchman cursed us but we caught the next O.K. Came back after lunch and attempted "turns" on the down slide.

Sat. night relaxed—a few others came around and they had the pick-up at the house. Everyone else was United Church and as the "hostess" was getting a taxi into the village, everyone turned out for church. I went to Mass at a pretty new church. As we are 60 miles from Montreal, and amongst the Laurentian Mountains, the people were French. Quebec gets French and Frenchier as you go north. The most striking thing inside was the Stations of the Cross, all carved from wood and impressionistic in their portrayal. It was a refreshing change from the usual plaster. The other statues were also of wood. Place was full of skiers as there are good runs in the village. Back to the lodge and after lunch more skiing followed by a visit to the "Chalet." It was a hive of activity with the more sophisticated types who prefer to remain inside all day. Caught the bus back at 9 p.m. so had a long weekend of it.

It only cost us $11 for the accommodation which is pretty reasonable in Canada and being my first break out of the city, well worth it.

Amazing how I've settled into things here and I am pleased you are keen on the way I'm going about the University. Realize that doing "Geology" must be a bit of a shock to you all. I will come out with a B.Sc. but the opportunities seem pretty good in the natural resources line. My plan is to live a full life and not become too much dependent on others for work etc. However I have that examination in algebra, geometry and chemistry to hurdle. Interview with the registrar last week –he was most affable and enthusiastic. I am working on them now at night.

MONTREAL

(MARCH 22 1955)

Here is your third son now to attain manhood. Got your telegram and letters and pleased to have them. Also Nanna and Aunt, Leila, Joan and a few others so the day was rich in greetings. Spent it all rather quietly – I guess when it just creeps up on you like that, you don't notice it and the days are just rolling by. Fifteen months since I was with you all but I do feel a lot surer of myself and pretty confident that all will go O.K. I miss "67" and being with you but now with this chance of going to McGill – and the way it will affect my chances later on – well, I just have to take it and hope you don't change too much in the few years I will be away. Growing up is a painful experience. But am looking forward to September classes and getting down to work with a will. It will be what I make it and there is a lot to offer. You'll recognize me by the Chev. Station wagon and I should be able to tell the good-looking blonde sun-baking on the verandah. I agree that it is best not to disclose anything outside the circle for a lot can happen and I'd look a bit foolish appearing back with my rucksack and little else .

Am waiting on the call from the copper company. I was referred to the M.L.A. and he wrote advising me that he had forwarded my letter on to the right quarters. I won't regret leaving the bank although it was heaven to get such a job for the winter and I am in a decent job there but it's not my line and the incessant ticking, searching for this and that, bits of paper, is a bit OFF. Will inform them soon but in Canada you don't say a word until you have the next job to go to. Six hundred thousand out of work now but from now on it gets better. Am attacking the

Algebra, Geometry and Chemistry with gusto. Have been given all the books so no problems there.

This second day of Spring has begun windy and drizzly. Rained all day, the sloppiness of the last of the snow and this rain made it dreadful on the footpaths until, lo and behold, we had the big snowfall and everything returned to the blanket of white. It was attractive looking out the window at it falling on the trees and street. I have a window with a hole in it, the result of an ice snowball but all here in the house are a little more sober with the exams beginning next month. Reading the "Kon-Tiki Expedition," about the raft that sailed from Peru to Tahiti. Did I tell you I saw it in a museum in Oslo, Norway. Enjoying the book. Another you must read is "The Captain's Table," by R.Gordon (author of "Doctor in the House,"). It's about the passenger ship from England to Australia and so true.

MONTREAL

(APRIL 1955)

From this side, your international footballing son and brother has recently returned from the State of New Hampshire. Drove down the 200 miles on Friday night to Dartmouth College. This is one of the big American colleges – an amazing place which dominates the small town of Hanover, just over the border. Stopped with an accountancy student in his bed-sitting room. Two beds in a room that leads into a sitting room. Very comfortable and just the thing for university life. The grounds are known as the "campus" – with over two thousand resident students, there are the big fraternity houses, some like castles compared to our 3511-Peel St. It is a Liberal Arts College: few work their way through as fees are $900 and on top of that there's the board etc. Met some good guys –Americans are a lot different at home, thank Heavens. College life seems pretty much one big party. They gave us a fine time and beat us 14-0 with that. We are straggly but will improve as the season goes on, I hope.

Sunday I went to the little church on the campus and back to someone's dining hall for breakfast. Got away before lunch and had a pleasant drive amongst the green hills of Vermont, the Spring making the country look very nice. Passed along Lake Champlain, in parts still iced up with great chunks lying on the banks. These towns, St. Albans and Montpelier are attractive little places. Coming back into Montreal, it began to rain as we sped along "Motel Drive," 25 motels together, hundreds of their huts, neon lights and restaurants, invitation to "Drop in at Charcoal Joe's" etc. Some signs are most elaborate affairs and the idea is very popular here in the north.

Tallied up my statistics last night – have done 30,000 miles and touched 20 countries but over here life is much the same as home, so hardly feel on the move right now. David has asked me down to Brazil for a month but will have to miss out on that.

## KRT FRATERNITY HOUSE, MONTREAL (MARCH 1955)

It was good of you all to send the five pounds and have locked it away for a rainy day. A "spin" comes in very handy. Yes, I do find leaving jobs difficult as with the Bank of New South Wales but over here, banking is less the time-honoured institution and more the hard-going business, clamoring to the public like every other business after the mighty dollar.

Thought we had seen the last of winter when last I wrote but with the blizzard over the weekend, the slush and filth are back with a vengeance. The snow becomes covered with a layer of black dust when it has been lying for a time so it destroys the romance of mid-winter whiteness. The city council has a big job cleaning it away and, with the giant machinery and men, it costs them a large amount which has to be voted down. The water is streaming along the streets and sidewalks and my galoshes have sprung leaks.

Today was sunny, and up to 45 degrees. I went across the street in my suit coat for the first time since my arrival. The fashions too are taking a turn for the good and the girls looking most attractive. The material doesn't seem to have that high English quality but the styles are really smart. We have a Jewess who wears a different blouse and ensemble each day and is the envy of all. You'll excuse the above paragraph but it is the result of the conversations at the office and the fact that I am isolated amongst ladies in the Savings department.

I go the library each night to work on the "terrible three," (geometry, algebra and chemistry). Pleased to say I am finding them O.K. and having more success than ever Mr. Nichols had with me. He wrote me a nice letter from Chatswood. Went to Rugby Union practice and I think I made the team to play New York at New York over Easter. As you can imagine, I would be thrilled to make the trip but it will cost a few bucks. However there is a chance we'll get a lift down and then be billeted. Happy Easter.

MONTREAL

(EASTER 1955)

Arrived back per Greyhound Bus from New York this morning after four wonderful days in "God's Own Country." Yes, Mum, that's the land and N.Y. the city. Got away mid-night Friday – five players and a wife who couldn't be left out, in the new Ford. Crossed over into the States about 1.30 a.m. with snow flurries and a beautiful moon-lit night. We sped along the smooth highways, down through the State of New York to Albany where we had the most awful coffee I have ever tasted.

As soon as day broke, it was evident we had entered into a new country. Along the road side were hundreds of new motels, freshly-painted stylish new houses, neat, clean and the ever present snowmobile in the front. The road, by this time the Tartonic Park Highway was a superb cement four-lane way, divided in the middle by a green belt of grass. The fuss Europeans make over the German auto-bahns is now to me, amusing. The countryside was rolling, spacious, a little like Australia, with lots of trees. We sped along at an effortless 65 m.p.h. and reached the city after a pleasant drive along the bank of the North Hudson River on the Henry Hudson Express Highway. On one side the river with its docks and moored ocean-going shipping, on the other the gigantic apartment buildings, Columbia University and the Riverside or Rockefeller Church with its high tower. Then past Grant's Tomb (he was a famous general in the U.S. Civil War) and a sudden sign "To 82$^{nd}$ ST." Off we shot and in a few minutes were eating breakfast on Broadway.

I think a little explanation of the city set-up wouldn't go astray. It is the easiest of cities to get around by virtue of the fact that its Avenues all run north and south and are numbered, 1$^{st}$ to 11$^{th}$. Cutting them at right angles, East to West, are streets, 1 to 84 in Lower New York. It's so much simpler than the names and winding streets. Broadway is the exception – it cuts across the lot, diagonally. This is Manhattan and we are on Long Island. Fifth Avenue runs down the centre.

After breakfast, we drove down Broadway and the open business of Good Friday and the Easter crowds. At the Taft Hotel, we were met by the NY rugby club president who collected David, myself, the driver and his wife who are both Scottish chemists, and took us to his delightful home, 15 miles out in Bronxville.

This wasn't "The Bronx" which is a less classy suburb off to the city's north but a spacious area of large English-style houses and lovely gardens. Host Ed Lee was a lawyer and their house the last thing in good living on a tasteful scale. Grand old English wooden beams held up the roof and ceiling. They bought a big place "because we wanted to have lots of folk come to stay with us." Had a dinner of tuna fish and lobster but was pretty beat.

Then Ed took us to Radio City which is the Rockefeller Centre on Fifth Avenue. We went up the 70 stories of the R.C.A. skyscraper and what a marvelous view of the city by day. Saw the Statue of Liberty in the harbour downtown and the mighty sister buildings. Central Park stretched out. From 850 feet you can see a lot. The wind tears at you and for a moment I felt a little apprehensive of being swirled off into the blue. Underneath this group of buildings is the amazing underground network of shops, bars and everything you can imagine. A reporter once lived there a week without any need to emerge. There are the offices of the Australian Trade Commissioner and across the passage the "Down Under" Bar and Café. Then home for a small welcome party.

Saturday morning broke so fine and sunny, the first really warm day of spring. I joined Pete (7) and Doreene (8) in a game of badminton on the lawn before Sandy (Mrs. Lee) called me to a breakfast of grapefruit, milk, bacon, sausages, muffins, eggs and tomato sauce. {"We just never think of fried eggs without Ketchup.") Couldn't resist the chairs in the sunshine on the lawn but the game was due at 2 p.m. so we packed into the Ford and Ed's station wagon and into Manhattan, under the river by the Brooklyn Battery Tunnel and to the open air stadium in Brooklyn for the game. Around us there were many wire grills with teams of junior baseballers, all shouting, slanging: Italian-Americans, and Puerto Ricans who have U.S. citizenship as a U.S. territory. We were beaten 18-7 by the New York team – they had a few college players from Princeton and Harvard. One guy knows David Hawkins, the Aust. swimmer at Harvard. I took things easy in my way for the conditioning and knowledge of this style of rugby aren't good yet. Drove over the Washington Bridge to the State of New Jersey where there was a party and buffet supper.

We left and came back into town. Naturally no theatre seats for shows were left under $7 so went up the Empire State Building, 102 stories and 1472 feet high. New York at night from that height is certainly a sight. The skyscrapers, some whose windows were lit up to form gigantic Easter crosses, the millions of lights, the glow from Times Square where Broadway meets 42$^{nd}$ Street. We came down, ears popping and walked down to that famous area of movie houses, theatres, amusements, bars and neon signs. I am afraid it leaves good old Piccadilly in the shade. Even David admitted this and he is the typical Englishman (Limey!).

Sunday the others left for Montreal but David and I came in, deposited our bags at Grand Central Station (a maze of underground and the main foyer with its roof showing the positions of the Heavenly bodies). From here to the Easter Parade on Fifth Avenue. St Patrick's Church on the avenue was crowded so heard Mass with the multitude on the steps. Then the stroll down Fifth in the sunshine –this was one of the most impressive events of the trip – hundreds of people, casually strolling down the Avenue, some dressed in the smartest styles and Easter bonnets and hats but no display of bad taste or ostentatiousness. New Yorkers like their parade as it is and it was fun. Wearing the grey Austin Reed jacket, I felt quite spry for an aged of 21 years. St. Patrick's is the most famous of New York's churches and is opposite the Rockefeller Centre. Said a prayer for you all inside.

Had a meal at a Chinese place on 7$^{th}$, a mixture of dishes and a good brew of tea. Then a stroll around Central Park and a sit in the shade to watch a ball game. Down then to the Y.M.C.A. on 47$^{th}$ where we booked in for the night. Clean and showered, we went around to the Waldorf Astoria for a drink before setting off for the artistic community of Greenwich Village. It was quite interesting –there was a difference in the atmosphere but you really have to know these places. Celebrated our night out by going to Louis Armstrong at the Basin Restaurant. He puts on a colossal show and we enjoyed him for quite a while. "There's a place where the people are reet, on Basin Street." You would have to see these Negroes when they really get Hep to the music. They go right back to Africa, I think. Forgot to mention we went to the Museum of Modern Art where the exhibition of photos, "The Story of Mankind" was held. Truly marvellous portrayals of life by the camera.

Up Monday and around the corner from the YMCA to the beautiful United Nations Building. It stands on the East River and we had a most interesting tour of all the Assembly rooms – the General, U.N.E.S.C.O., Trustee and Security Councils. What a wonderful position to have – a representative at the United Nations. After a late lunch we went to the Easter Show at the Radio City theatre. Fabulous extravaganza in the real Hollywood fashion, gorgeous colours and the Rockettes, a chorus of 50 odd girls who were the last thing in precision and everything else. Caught the bus after a little shopping on Fifth Avenue – bought two shirts whilst David purchased $18 worth of long-playing records. This is the way to travel—no more rucksacks, beards and hitch-hiking.

## MONTREAL

## (APRIL 1955)

Am afraid the international footballer was dropped from last week's game at the Federal Capital, Ottawa. However I went along for the drive and watched the boys put up an impressive showing, winning 18-6. Left at 10 Saturday morn and drove the 120 miles in about three hours. Nice drive with the country improving and only an occasional glimpse of snow.

Crossed off the island – Montreal is a 45-mile-long in the middle of the St. Lawrence – over that teeming river by a series of bridges. Saw a gigantic paper pulp factory which brought back memories of Norway and the timber being floated in great masses down a water way of the river – and a machine picking bundles of logs and stacking them.

Into the Province of Ontario – the French influence still strong but this city of Ottawa is mostly English-speaking. Saw parliament's spires and buildings, the perpendicular, tall Peace Tower – all built on the Ottawa River. Crossed over the Ottawa River and back into La Provence de Quebec for the game. The field was beautiful, green and soft. They gave us a reception

After the game (Rugby Union is social if nothing), there was a good party but I like a fool offered to return early so as to allow a married guy and his wife to have my place in a later car. Just as I'd met an interesting girl but that's luck –the boys are still getting in from Ottawa!

Work is fairly busy with Savings Interest being credited, checked, found out, checked again and so on. I manage a pretty good time at the office. The French typiste has been replaced by a beautiful little thing from the Island of Aruba, off the coast of Venezuela in South America. It is a Dutch colony. Over in the library last night, I saw a familiar face and immediately remembered it from Oslo. It was Tim Porteous, a Canadian law student who I had met at the Youth Hostel.

Really is a small world – occasionally at the bank I have an Australian inquiring about travelers cheques and they get a surprise to find a local. Just in from rugby training. We are still indoors although it is quite mild outside. Play basketball and exercises .

On Thursday I begin a job with a Women's Club as young man about the place, helper in the kitchen. I have a trial for one month and get free board and room. This will permit me some saving from my bank salary.

THEMIS CLUB, MONTREAL

(APRIL 30 1955)

Have left my pen at the office, so, Ma, you will have to bear with my typing and remember that the personal touch is there as I am behind the machine. You'll notice the new address — have been most fortunate in getting a part-time job with a rather social Women's Club. I do the odd jobs about the place—changing light globes, a little washing-up, putting the screens on the windows, vacuuming on Saturdays etc. Not too laborious (excuse my North American spelling) and it fits in well with my banking. Creates the balance between the mind and the body : I receive no pay for this but have a nice basement room with affixed lavatory and wash basin, plus all my meals (walk "home" for lunch) which is a good deal for I've said before, living is costly here.

KRT has stopped serving meals and most of the guys have left for summer jobs. Ed, my roommate at the house, goes to sea every summer and has worked his way up to Mate's position. He ran away to sea, went to Japan and China and at twenty-one came back to McGill. He will be in 3$^{rd}$ Year Science next Sept. (the Fall!) and hopes to go into medicine in the following year. You can do either Science or Arts for three years as "Pre Med School," taking the useful subjects –biology, zoology, physiology plus and others such as languages, philosophy. I've read through some of the courses on geology and have to admit they don't seem to have what I want to do, that is, past going to McGill in September. Am still working at the old cronies of chemistry, geometry and algebra that I need to get into McGill on top of my school leaving certificate. Just keep this all within the family and it will pan out.

The bank is a bit hectic these days with the interest still unbalanced and women resigning. I was toiling away yesterday when a note came through from head office for four of us to report down there for audit work. Walked off with visions of knocking on the door, walking behind the counter and saying to the juniors: "I'll count your postage box." However, I was amazed to find that all I had to do was to machine balance the ledgers. This went on to 9.30 p.m. I was preparing to leave when a great hulk came up and ordered a Frenchman and myself to balance a pile of vouchers. The total came to $225 million and the thing was out over $5 million. At ten after ten, I was pretty fed up so just put it on their desk and came home. I had had enough of being an auditor's "Joe Boy."

The district about me on Sherbrooke Street is rather nice – the Art Gallery is across the street, next to the large Chateau Apartments which look like a big castle; there are two old stone "black Protestant" churches, some lovely old homes still clinging on in the face of the city's growth. The change in the weather has been truly amazing. No overcoats, mild even steamy due to the proximity of the St. Lawrence. With the slush, cold and snow, I wasn't so impressed with Montreal but now it's beginning to look really nice, the leaves on the numerous trees, the lawns, parks, even flowers. You know it's Spring, you can feel the change almost overnight. The people are at last shedding their blankets of clothes and the "petites demoiselles" are "tres jollies."

On Sunday one of the boys from the fraternity house called around in his MG. We drove around to Mass and then, hood down, sped out 30 odd miles to the Lake of Two Mountains. It was sunny and man, that stream of shining metal tearing out of the city – every man and his dog seems to have a car but I guess that's the way things are back home almost. We had breakfast at the new drug store out at the Dorval Shopping Centre. This is a new business suburb and at the centre, in the middle of a great parking allotment is the "L-shaped" line of shops. Everything has been centralized to that area which makes it convenient for the out-of-towners for the Big Seven (as they call the largest retail stores) all have their branches out here. The Banque Royale du Canada is also out there. It was a nice drive out along the shores of Lake St. Louis, past many fine homes, yachts and golf clubs. It always amuses me to hear Canadians on the Jewish question – all clubs either are Jewish or non-Semitic. "When they get Jews in a place, it starts to get untidy." Their big yachting club is "The Sir John Reading." Hope my letters are carefully screened before being handed about.

P.S. I have free access to the food at the club for my suppers.

Really a beautiful day here, sunny and just warm enough for the sports coat, check shirt and one of brother Mick's woolen ties that he sent me, and to which I am very attached. After the winter in Canada, spring is the delightful season of the poets—at home there never seemed to be a very great transition. Here the layers of ice, the piles of dirty city snow made black by the choking fumes of thousands of automobiles, have melted. Lawns and parks simply have turned from white to green overnight. McGill campus looks beautiful – the leaves, the football field and the Arts Building covered with creepers (and creeps!) do make a picture.

Have a week off at the club so it allows me the liberty to appreciate nature in the city. Everything else has taken on a fresher glow. My diary, if I kept one, would read:

"Up at 9.15 a.m., breakfast and down Sherbrooke St in the sun to the library. Read two hours and thence to the book store where I order supplies for the summer."

Contrast this to May 1 1954 in the U.K. steelworks :

"Work until 11.30 but sit tight as we will be loading the ore trucks. Leave at 10.45, collect new time card and home to watch mighty football association final West Bromwich Albion versus Prescott on T.V."

I remember that was the first time our English cousins invited us into the T.V. room and Don went to sleep. T.V. is the greatest exaggeration ever; don't bust yourselves trying to get one. The Bains have got everything but they draw the line at T.V. Mrs. B. just rang me and wants a bit of assistance on a wood pile so am going out there this afternoon.

Read an amazing book, "Seven Years in Tibet," worthwhile getting it. It's a paperback and the story of a German mountaineer, caught in India during the war, who escapes through Tibet.

Is sister Caroline ready to be flown out here and presented at the annual Debs. Ball? It's such a joke, anyone in North America "coming out." They've usually been out since 13! As in Sydney, top society centres around the departmental store owners, the Eaton's and Ogilvie's etc. Have a job on Thursday, washing walls and polishing floors for a rich old girl out in the Town of Mount Royal. $1 per hour but these women are notorious to their servants but of course one must respect one's betters

MONTREAL

(MAY 1955)

Read an amazing statement from the "Chicago Tribune": "Australians are slap-happy over anything American and often refer to their country as the 49th state." Surely this is not so when Canadians, their next door neighbours (Montreal is 60 miles from the U.S. border) are insulted if you say they are the same as Americans. At the bank, there is a guy from California. He's O.K. and very amusing for he realizes how the Yanks do act when they go off as tourists.

Can now let you in on a little secret. Cousin Vod is now in England and as I see it, joins me here in about a month. Hasn't mentioned what he plans to do but didn't want anyone to know in case he decided to flip out on a boat to Canada without seeing the family in England. Rather odd but just don't let it filter out. And today a telegram: "Arrived, commence immigration arrangements." I hope sister Caroline is reading and doing O.K .at school. When I send you two off on a cruise I want her to be able to show a clue or two. My dental bill arrived – one filling and the x-ray cost $10 so not too bad. If you see Mr. Gibson, tell him the Montreal dentist was very impressed with my fillings. And have no thoughts on my taking to the whiskies. Although a little more tolerant, I still retain that rather strong feeling re the ale. They do drink whisky neat in the States but not so much here. The Yanks say you spoil two good drinks if you pour water on to it but then when you talk of America, you speak of an immense country of 160 millions, of all different groups, so you can't really generalize too dogmatically. It's just a question of where it fits in—with many people taking life in a hurry, it's neat but I must say all my old gals here at the Themis Club always dilute it.

Another nice Sunday evening with the Bains. They have just got this year's Dodge.


MONTREAL

(MAY 12 1955)

Wonderful being able to hear you so well on the phone Sunday morn. It is certainly amazing to think of our voices floating across the U.S. and from California to Sydney. I heard you so well but was naturally a little disappointed to miss the two Maher Cup footballers. I went of to Mass after I left you and you went to bed so it does seem strange. It was a beautiful day here so in the afternoon I had my first game of tennis for the season. Am afraid the squash hasn't been good for my game and of course it is ages since I played so I didn't reveal the form i.e. what there is of the latter.

This week has been fairly quiet. I worked a little on the School Certificate. By cutting down the outings, I always have something on hand for the big "do's" such as New York and anytime I feel I want a night off, I go around to K.R.T. fraternity house where there is a new line up of chaps for the summer. They are mostly from Queen's University, Kingston Ontario. They have record players etc.

At the club, I am now the 6 p.m.-8 p.m. barman. The manageress (I get along well with her most of the time) is giving me the principles and I served my first "whisky sour" last night. It's a good trade to know – maybe I'll be the cocktail barman at the Albion in Cootamundra one day. Have a large stock on hand -- I do this five nights per week and make up a few hours on Saturdays but always can get away to anything I want. If I decide to go to McGill (i.e. pass) then the job is open for me and would be ideal.

Already the weather is a little warm for my suit so may be forced to purchase a "Palm Beach" tropical next time I go down "South of the Border." Clothes are cheaper in the States –we have a special Quebec tax which puts up our cost of living in this province.

MONTREAL

(MAY 24 1955)

Have just returned from the holiday weekend – we have the Queen's Birthday or Victoria Day – and am back at the club awaiting a guest whose bags I shall carry to the room and with hand extended for a tip, will then be ready for bed.

Really glorious weather. Ray Dho, who sits for his final C.A. this Fall (autumn), collected me in his M.G. after my Saturday morning duties and in brilliant sunshine we flew off the sixty miles to the border and down to Burlington, the largest city in Vermont. Shopped about for a cheap light summer suit but no luck so bought our provisions (it was a return to last year on the road only I kept thinking how well off I was) and drove out to the lake shore. Lake Champlain extends right down from the border. Had a meal and set off across the centre of the state for Hanover where Dartmouth College is. These 13 "original States" as they are called, form the New England section of the United States. These were the original British colonies and include Vermont, New Hampshire, Maine, Rhode Island, Massachusetts, Connecticut etc. It's generally acknowledged that the residents of these states are more likeable. Philadelphia, capital of Pennsylvania is quite a centre of well-born society (not nouveau riche) and is the big joke amongst the Yanks who think the old social aspirations quite a joke. The countryside all through Vermont was as green and luxurious as any I have seen . All along the main drag, it is the same pattern: neat, clean, well-looked-after villages and towns. No fences but lawns, gardens and fresh paint. Civic buildings such as town halls, municipal offices and parks look different. Civic pride must run high.

We spent the night at a fraternity house, thanks to someone who had met me last time. He remembered that I was from Australia so that got us sacks. Spent Sunday swimming in a lake just out of the college. I told you of the mansion fraternity houses, done in the best of colonial style with white pillars and balconies, the village of Hanover set in amongst all the University buildings. The lake water was cold but I started a tan. The Dartmouth Outing Club gave us a hut some three miles out in the scenic bush so we drove out and walked the final three miles. It was a log cabin hacked out of the scrub and we ate the rest of our Swiss cheese, dill pickles , bologna and canned beer. Ray tried to put me off with stories of grizzly bears but I was pretty tired and passed out. Got into Hanover next morn and bought a very nice grey-dark Shetland wool sports jacket, a pair of "stretch" socks and the button-down collar shirt which are very much the style in the U.S. We had to go back the same way and as the roads suits the M.G., didn't waste a lot of time.

Don't get the wrong idea about the United States from what you hear if it is all adverse. I have stopped at lots of small villages, towns, talked to many ordinary people and found them just the same as anywhere else. There are the Wallendbeens of America and the Tom Hickeys too. Most of them are friendly and helpful or otherwise just neutral. You may think that perhaps I tend to say more about the States than I do about Canada. It is because it is of more all-around interest to me. As the greatest country in the world, a massive power of 164,000,000, you must admit it is the place to which all our destinies are tied up. Naturally Canada being so much smaller, economically and politically –although geographically larger – is swamped with influences from south of the border. Our northern frontiers are lined with radar stations built by joint command and dually manned. If there is an attack, it will come over Canada. War here would not be the shock Pearl Harbor was at first although a lot is at stake when there is the "bomb."

Life goes on well in Montreal and I am managing the bar well. It's not too rigorous and usually a good time between drinks.

MONTREAL

(JUNE 2 1955)

Here I am, once again from Montreal, Queen City of North America. I enjoyed your news Mum, certainly is great hearing all the various doings and knowing that, except for a few broken bones in football, all are well. It's really warm here now—such a quick change from bitter to the rather unpleasant mugginess. I can't quite get around to a summer suit which is the style here. Am glad you like Richard Gordon's books. I do have happy memories of Paris although I was a little broke there but that's just one of the things that happen now and then. Note that girl travelers add something from each place they go – piles of bracelets and spoons. I think sometimes that was the reason they went to a place. Really have few souvenirs but have kept a diary since I left and there are quite a few memories in there!

The club is fine and I get on well with the French-Canadian cooks who enjoy helping me with the language. I have become pretty profane as they swear a lot. When a Frenchman swears, he just curses on of the Holy parts of the Church i.e. Tabernacle or Chalice. That to him is the expression. Meanwhile my drink repertoire increases with "Pink Ladies" and "Singapore Slings"—the "lades" are generally congenial though just occasionally I meet the viper, bejeweled, rich and repulsive.

Gave blood yesterday—my first effort since the measles years ago. I doubt if I shall ever qualify for the Gold Giver's medal. The assisting nurse was a Melbourne girl who I had met in Stockholm, Sweden. They do well, nurses so sister Mal, give it some thought. Had an amusing card from Ed, my old fraternity house room mate. He drove out to Vancouver and sent me from San Francisco Calif. a photo of Alcatraz Prison in the Bay with "Wish You Were Here" inscribed across the water.

MONTREAL

(JUNE 28 1955)

It was good to have your letter on returning tonight. Mails between us have been slow. One reason is that Sherbrooke Street runs east and west –I have never used it as such but if you put it on the letter it will save a day at least. The line, of course is the French division in the East.

Friday here was the Fete of St. Jean de Baptiste, De La Salle qui est le patron saint of French Canada. I was happily working at the office (English sector did not close) when the accountant walked up and demanded if I had anything to do. I sensed more work so answered that I was off to lunch, He replied: "Put your coat on and have the day off." I thought he was joking but blew through very sharply. An Australian plumber from Melbourne came around and we stood outside the club and watched the Big Parade of Les Canadiens Francais. It lasted for hours, everyone from M. Duplessis, the provincial Premier (our provincial parliament sits in French) to floats honoring the old French settlers who were first to arrive here.

Ray Dho, the chap who has the M.G., called and asked me up to his father's summer house. Made some swift arrangements re the bar and the vacuum cleaner, and we departed at 8.30 p.m. Friday and arrived at Sainte Alexis (in Quebec there are literally thousands of "Sainte" places) about 11 p.m. It's a 90-mile drive and, both non-smokers, found we were without a light when we left the car and had to stumble blindly on by the path which goes through thick bush around their lake to the house. It was pitch black, just couldn't see one another under a foot away. The uncle and family were there and thought we were thieves. It was here too that my experiences of real French-Canadian life began. French is spoken all the time and although I still don't understand it, I think it only right that no concessions be made for me, for that seems to be the main trouble here –the English-speaking people try to dismiss Quebec as those "French" and rarely take steps towards a better understanding of their people. It is certainly the best way and indeed the only way to get to know them and this is by their language.

In the morn we had a swim in the lake. It was about as half a big again as the two Fisher Parks with thick, tall woods surrounding it on all sides. The wooden house, two stories, sat on the bank with a jetty of pine trunks and "home-made" bridge. Lovely location— sole owners of the lake, so complete privacy. I think Canada has over a million lakes. Many are just owned by people who enjoy the escape during the summer from the city. Naturally with winter everything just freezes although a few are winterized -- the houses, I mean. Rowed back over to the car. I was a lousy row-boater and had us revolving in the centre, not getting very far ahead. We drove around the thickly wooded hills and beautiful lakes with quite a few houses about and occasionally a village. It's always a shock to see gaily-painted houses and shining 1955 Cadillacs in places the size of Wallendbeen. As brother Tony used to say: "Everyone has a quid these days."

Had a look over a trout breeding factory. Here thousands and thousands of fish are bred from eggs to a foot-long and used to stock the surrounding lakes with good sport. Must admit that the most interesting sight here was a pool in which the manager kept all the mal-formed fish. Here I saw two-headed fish, some joined at the waist, others with heads growing out of their stomachs, all sorts of malformations you can't imagine. Forces you to wonder at it all.

We then called on the neighbors. They are very wealthy and have spent over a $100,000 on their summer house. They live here on their lakes, amidst their four little farms between April to November. They have just about everything you could wish to have. Nothing ostentatious for the French differ here. They have one daughter left who I think is pretty keen on Ray. God, that would be the only signal I'd ever need. We stopped on to a good lunch – one of the Molsons came in. They are the big brewing company here but he made no impression as he said nothing. Couldn't understand the French either, I expect.

They have a beautifully terraced hill garden and lawns along their house side of the lake. Returned about 5 p.m. to our place and got cleaned up for a visit to Grand'Mere and Shawinigan Falls, two towns about 30 miles north. Called on his mother and some married sisters before we went to the country night club and had a few dances with nice French girls. Here they come to a "night club" as they would a 50/50 dance at Cootamundra. There is no sophistication at the words "night club."

Sunday I swam across the lake and back without much trouble which pleased me for I despair sometimes at the lack of chances to play sport. The kids all thought me rather a hero – the youngest ran to his mother to say that "L'Australien" was crossing the lake without a boat. Am mad on the swimming. It has been so long since I have gone for a decent distance. Tried to catch a trout but am not an enthusiast in this direction so we ate five of the catch his uncle managed at five in the morn.

The Club is going well and it's nice to be in a position for the occasional free weekend but am caught here for the long one – Dominion Day or Canada Day coming up. Maybe it's just as well.

MONTREAL

(JULY 4 1955)

The weather is really warm but a bit too muggy and it feels it will rain any minute although the sky is cloudless. The long weekend (Dominion of Canada Day) brought great crowds of Americans into the city since today is also their Independence Day and any Montrealers who could escape did. Had to stick around at the club for Friday and Saturday, just to be on hand as there wasn't a lot doing.

Escaped by bus Sat. night to Lachute , 50 miles along the Ottawa road where the Bains collected me in their new Dodge and took me to their lake. Vic Murray came Friday. He has taken a job with the Migration Department and was on his way to Halifax. We all had a grand time. It was just great to shed the city and we almost swam across the lake on our arrival just after midnight. Water was beautiful. It's a fairly long lake but narrows to one-third or a quarter of a mile or more. We went across and back, three-quarters of a mile over-arm in the morn. We felt so fit that later on whilst we were out in the sailing boat of the neighbors that we dived off the side and did another three-quarter mile up the lake. I just wallowed in it. Vic and I took a canoe and with two paddles, flew around the lake. They also have a row boat with an outboard motor which I drove for the first time. Their neighbors (the old guy is a professor at McGill) has two sons so we took the sailing boat out. It was fun for a while but the water was too good not to be swimming in. Am pretty burnt today but trust a tan will result. It is my first real touch of the sun but am still not used to it being summer and July. Had hot dogs on a barbecue in the open and a ton of water melon. These summer homes (nothing glamorous but intensely practical) are just the thing to have when the seaside is not with you. They've told me to come out just when I feel like it. They are very good to me and I do appreciate it. Their daughter Barbara is going to do her Master's Degree at McGill this year.

Am looking forward to seeing Clive "Killer" Caldwell – he was an old hero of mine.

Has been really hot this weekend and have vowed no matter what the position is, I shall never spend the summer in any city again. With the water content and 90 degrees, it is difficult to imagine a winter when your ears freeze and head aches from the cold. I expect my moans are due to the fact that I missed out on the lakes --- the Bains go off too early of a Friday night.

Tuesday night went up to the Chalet on the mountain with Joe. He leaves for Europe in September on a $2000 scholarship for leading the class home in law. Have been giving him a tip or two. The Montreal Symphony Orchestra has begun their open air concerts – they set up a full stand and sell tickets but for my impoverished class, there is the grass so we stretched out and enjoyed two hours of music. Off again Tues. for an operatic series. It's good, this free "culture" –the only time any of us have it.

Back in the Savings Department since Monday. Was rather enjoying loans for the work was at least of some merit and use but now it is the monotony of tick tick, although I have the occasional diversion with the "slip outs" for coffee and les demoiselles. How would you like a French-speaking daughter-in-law? "I t'ink not, eh?" Have no fears. I have taken that old demon brother Michael's advice: "Wait until you are 30."

The relieving manageress at the club and I hit it off well. She is a nice woman with a boy just 16. Has learnt the trade in six years – her husband is an English bank manager but like the black sheep, is never mentioned. She works in an Ottawa boy's school, Ashbury College. Yesterday it was amusing. Someone rang up and asked me what they should give to a group of eight 20-year-olds at a luncheon reception. I advised a whiskey or gin sour (i.e. one and one-half ounces plus lemon, ice etc) but the mother shuddered and said a Punch would be best. I then proceeded to brew up the "Hole-in-One-Punch" from a book in the bar. It went over well but the amusing thing is that it has more "strong stuff" in it than the "sours." However the kids probably had been on it since 16 or 17.

Down to the docks today and looked over three of the smaller ships of the Canadian Navy. I'd never join the navy especially the small ships since I stooped about all the time. Even the ladders couldn't hold my feet. Will stick to the "Italia" and "Otranto" type although some attest that the latter was a bit hard. Not I.

Expect your news tomorrow. Last night went out to see the American chap, Fred and his wife Pat. Sat in the back lawn talking until four this morning. Nice couple –she is an architect and her people come from Oyster Bay, Long Island New York. That's one for a cocktail party.

MONTREAL

(JULY 25 1955)

Really pleased to have your news today after an absence of two weeks. Your third son is thriving and well. Was thrilled to get a call from Jean Caldwell, and went down to the Windsor, the Canadian Pacific-owned hotel. It was grand meeting her (she looked very nice) and Clive and she said she had seen you near Easter and we yarned a lot with me enjoying all the news of home. We had a drink and then they took me out for a steak. They flew off to New York Sunday.

Am still very keen to begin in October and am working on the entrance exam. My first is at the end of the month. It will be a relief to know just what the way is blowing in two months time. Did I mention before I am now keen to do Science since I tossed out the idea of geology. If one shines in the initial three years, there is a chance of going into medical school for four years. Naturally I am not kidding myself too much but I do feel that Medicine if anything is the answer to what I really want to do. And of course Canada at the moment is the place where I have the best chance. My present position at the Themis Club takes care of most of the financial difficulties at really little worry to me for it is most casual. Either way, if things turn out differently, I will have lost nothing by all this ambitious talk. Just shelve these ideas (with the rest of my ramblings) amongst the family and we'll see how things turn out. Does seem to be ironic writing like this but ever since leaving school, the news of anyone studying medicine has left me feeling a little hollow inside.

Tues. night was the concert on the mountain. Again most pleasing although at times I find the people who insist on talking a bit hard to put up with. The weather has been hot – even 90-95 degrees – and Ottawa, Canada's Canberra, sent all her public servants home at 1 p.m. because it got up to 91 degrees. Isn't that the limit although the humidity makes 95 degrees worse than a dry 105 degrees at home?

The big news is that Cousin Vod is due at Quebec City on Saturday. For some strange reason he doesn't want anyone to know his whereabouts so please don't say anything of it. I sponsored him as the migrant is much the same way as my beloved elder brother sent me that dramatic 50 pounds sterling. He arrives as I did, flat broke but luckily it is summer so things will be O.K.

Davis Cup tie here on Sat. and am hoping to see something of it. As I tell Canadians, it will be just an exhibition. The local Davis cup man, Rochon, has just declared: "If I don't get a crack at the Aussies, then I'm through for good." I am having a game Thursday night at the Mount Royal club where the cup is being played. One of the guys is a summer member.

My plumber mate came around Sat. and I fed him soup and toast. He is due off soon on a five months Arctic Radar Station job along the Distant Early Warning Line which is this continent's first line of defence if the Russians decide to have a shot. They say it gives the industrial U.S. cities six hours of warning so old "Ike" should at least have time to get underground. We all seem to like him here. You just don't seem to put him as a Republican but as someone above the party mob brawl which is about what U.S. politics are. Adlai Stevenson, the Democrat, appears with a new date in all the gossip columnists' diaries so I feel he must be through.

Must see "The Dam Busters," on downtown near the bank. It opened this week and Richard Todd appeared. He stopped at the Ritz Carlton, 100 yards down from the Themis. The movie was made on Lake Ullowater –Don and I were there in March 1954. Isn't time going! It's getting near 1 a.m. so will be off to bed, as usual the tangled mass of sheets and pillow. I have not become one single bit tidier than the other three brothers. Is sister Caroline as bad?

MONTREAL

(AUG 2 1955)

The big reunion took place Sunday afternoon with Cousin Vod's arrival on the boat train from Quebec City. Came over on the "Franconia" and is as well as ever. It is amazing how little things have changed and you can imagine the conversation since Sunday. Am just in from coffee and Vod has departed for his abode in our Harlem area. He has a room with Pete, our club janitor from Jamaica, so, really the dye is cast, and we will have our stories to tell. Doesn't seem 19 months since I saw him but being in mail contact does preserve quite a bit. (I hope.)

He hasn't a job as yet but should have something soon as we thought it best, with his law degree, to get something half-respectable like the bank or Sun Life.

He has accused me of a Canadian accent, unjustly I think but I have countered by claiming he has a broad Australian effort. Tomorrow he comes in to do the breakfast and lunch wash-up as temporary measure here. I feel quite superior.

Watched Lew Hoad and Hartwig blast away at the Canadians on Sat. afternoon during the Davis Cup tie. Brother Ned is as lazy as Hoad on the court and the latter's efforts weren't too impressive. Frazer and Cooper certainly looked good, their services, especially Frazer's, were terrific. It was a beautiful day for tennis. Harry Hopman was in fine spirits on the sideline. $1 to get in!

Tuesday we went to a concert and I was able to introduce Vod to Joe Brebant who has just got his law degree and a Sorbonne scholarship. It was a programme of opera extracts and quite pleasant. Meanwhile back at the bank, my job has changed for the better and I am relieving in the Loan Dept. Here instead of mortgages and securities, bills of sale etc., they write notes and have the boss approve a loan. I follow it right through. It has brought me out of the doldrums and given me something to do. Still manage the coffee.

Weather is the worst I have struck. The atmosphere is thick with moisture and it is plain lousy at times. My shirts are soaked as the place is not "air conditioned." One of the big stores has its temp. almost down to zero so it is like walking into an ice-box from the black hole of Calcutta.

Finished my investigation with the old girl who hit the bank with $50 forged endorsements. Went out this morn with a bank investigator, I had dug up all the facts and identified her. She was Jewish and would not admit to anything but due to my friend's "know how," she signed a statement promising to repay and keep it out of court. Naturally no Jew alive gives $50 away for nothing. She was as cunning as a fox and I was no match for her really but my police friend did the trick and it was her alright. Just temptation at the moment, I guess.

My French friend from the bank has been moved. He would come over to the loan dept. and improve my French with some conversation. Am sorry to lose that as the girls are dead losses on the explanatory side. Will close now as Arthur, the club's French-Canadian kitchen man has come in and he always exchanges French with me.

Have just returned from a day's swimming. Went off at 7 a.m. with John and Jane Smola, a Czech couple who have just taken out their Canadian citizenship. I work with Jane, the husband will be a chartered accountant next year. Another refugee, an ex-professor came too, so it was quite cultural as well as being a lot of fun. To escape the city as frequently as possible is everyone's aim. Drove up to Rawdon, 50 miles from Montreal and rather a pretty spot with great outcrops of rapids which could be seen in the river due to the low flow during the summer. Swam most of the day and am thinking of taking it up, should I stop on in Canada. Got a good burn and at last am losing that pale look. It was interesting for they are all longing for the Communists to be pushed out so that they can return and are hoping (although I cannot see it) for events to move at the Geneva Conference. The old professor said he was on the hanging list and escaped the prison with the two wardens assigned to him.

In all, a social weekend. After the vacuuming of my room Sat. morning, I met David Cuthbertson who is a member of the Mount Royal tennis club, and thrashed me 6-2,6-3, 6-3. It was my first game for three years and I was satisfied enough with my form.

That night to a party. Quite a few interesting people –the pursers of the Cunard New York boats, and the C.B.C. Chile programme producer and his French wife. Other odds from the South American republics and a girl from Spain. Naturally I spoke of my two weeks (?) in Barcelona, her native city. Events almost broke up when the discussions concerned "harbours." I said: "Sydney Harbour is generally thought to be one of the most picturesque." Some one replied: "What about Rio, Brazil?" I admitted I had not seen it. The reply came: "Oh, is Rio only second class because down there they speak Portuguese." My final reply: "Yes, that's just it!" Can't stand these complexed nationalities that feel inferior or at least think that you regard them as such. One thing (although I did not have much to do with it) I've always been proud of and thankful for and that is to be of British stock. Also the height is a definite advantage. Don't misunderstand me but wherever I go, I find that although people may dislike the English and their off-shoots, they are afforded some respect. Being third generation Australian does not alter the position of some types.

The entrance exam draws close on Aug. 31, so am doing a little preparation although the weather is dead against study. Plan to take my holidays and swat up for two weeks prior to the exam. You know how hopeless I was at Maths so you can imagine how much of this is new work. However trust things will turn out well, for the bank, although congenial and pleasant, is becoming increasingly tiresome.

MONTREAL

(AUG 15 1955)

Your two migrant sons are prospering in the New World. Vod has spent his first two weeks on the prowl for a job and he begins in the Montreal Trust Co. Monday – on the same salary as myself, with a free meal thrown in so all is well. He had a few odd nights at the club doing dishes. One night we were both at it, hands in the water and at the dish cloths. I thought: "What a successful pair we are." However let us hope that events improve. Vod put an ad in the paper for the "man about the house" position but failed to mention that he was the "male student" with the result that sweet letters from young housewives are rolling in, describing their sunny rooms, smiling infants and like of Australians.

Have been working on the matriculation subjects. There is quite a bit of ground left to cover and with the two jobs, not an awful lot of time. Both the bank and the club are pretty soft jobs –"gold bricks" – so am not tired at all. Happily the heat wave has left us with quite a bit of rain falling this week although now it is steamy again. The new bank job is a lot better and I have managed the usual agreeable hours. Don't get me wrong. I haven't got lazy, just like my comfort.

We visited a friend last night, Alex, from the bank. He has installed himself with the son of the Argentine Australian consul in a $100 per month flat. It is really nice when you compare it to my basement room and Vod's place in the negro section of town. My plumber friend from Melbourne went off to Baffin Island last night, flown in on a five-month contract and will earn sixty pounds per week, free clothes and board. It certainly pays to have a trade. Pete, the old Jamaican janitor here is a strict Seventh Day Adventist so I do his stuff each Saturday. There were great screams when I emerged late at 10 a.m. this morn.

One of the girls at the bank asked me in what language do Vod and I converse. I told her Australian and that he didn't speak English but hoped to learn it here soon. Then another asked me: "how much is the fare to Australia?" I said:"$300."

"Is that by train?" she said. Pretty hopeless, some of these gals.

MONTREAL

(AUG 1955)

Each month I have the week locking the vault after all have finished. It's part of my new job as relieving in the Collections Dept. Isn't too strenuous so have an hour or so to wait around the office. Vod is thriving and just rang to say he was through for the day at 4 p.m. He also has a five day week, likes his work and "the people are agreeable, " and as he gets the big free meal each mid-day, all is going well. We haven't done much since he arrived since I have been putting in a final effort as I have exams in two weeks. Will be disappointed if I don't get in to McGill as it means another year, although the money would be handy.

Weather is lousy. What a summer it has been! The worst I have spent anywhere except for the odd weekends in the country. The two jobs are fine but you do have to limit your activities. Am thinking of the casual way at home in Cootamundra. We go swimming twice a day, strolling across old Fisher Park in the singlet and shorts. Am looking forward to seeing you all and 67 but nothing concrete until the present plans begin to roll.

The Bains have gone down into Maine for their holidays. The Atlantic Coast is very pretty but lower down there have been big hurricanes, with 200 deaths in Connecticut, New York and Pennsylvania. The hurricanes have names just like the planes in the Japanese war. When the last typhoon blew out, the headlines read "Connie Is Dead."

Am following the Davis Cup over coffee. An amazing write-up on Lew Hoad in the Gazette said he gave an "awesome exhibition of power tennis." Let us hope when you open this, that my prediction for a 4-1 Australian victory rings true. They are going to put it on T.V. so should see at least two matches. Both of us would be keen to go south to see it except for the old question. Vic Murray is down at Halifax (where I landed) with the Immigration Dept. Doing well and has just completed a tour with an Australian official, two weeks around eastern Canada, just showing him the country. All expenses but as I met the Australian before, didn't envy Vic. He was the small 5ft 5 inches type public servant, apologies to our local Lands Dept.

MONTREAL

(AUG 22 1955)

This is your old sports announcer Ted Harris broadcasting from North America, on the eve of a great victory, "to the nine million Aussies who bleary-eyed but happy after listening to three days of tennis amongst the clatter of breakfast dishes." What a terrific result. Doubt if anything has thrilled me so much as the way "we" smashed down the Cincinnati crew-cut and the rolly-faced Bill Talbert who predicted last week: "Well, I'll figure on it being 3-0 for us on Saturday so I'll just put in Ham Richardson, we'll be playing for fun on Sunday." For fun, they sure were with the joke on themselves. Vod and I raced off to the nearest tavern to watch. Taverns are all equipped with T.V. so we arranged for the Davis Cup to be shown. My 20-cents tip made up for the small quantity of beer consumed. As Vod quoted George Bernard Shaw: "The liquor debt of my family has been fully paid."

It began at 2.30 p.m. with a really exciting match and you can imagine how fortunes rallied, hopes fell as the scores went up and down. Although it was already 2-0, we must have thought it vital. Vod, after the U.S. won the fourth set, had the look he always has when down two shillings and sixpence at poker. The first set was colossal and we sped through the second, Hartwig was very consistent and served with Lew, on and off like a traffic light. We were thrilled at the final smash—there is something very dramatic in the cut down the side-line which clinches a Davis Cup series.

Have spent the rest of the week hovering over the collections and negotiating two weeks holidays from the bank so that I can do something for the exams. Have Chemistry on Thursday and the other two the following week. My course in the former at Sir George Williams College has ended. It certainly stimulated my interest in Chemistry after the efforts of Bro. Finbar and Mr. Whright.

Weather is beautiful but the writing is on the wall for I have put back the blanket and the breeze off the street window into my basement room is cool tonight. My room, including the self-contained bathroom, would be about the size of your bedroom, Ma. Have an ironing closet, dressing table drawers, a narrow bed, the pedestal and the desk. It's painted cream and on the walls I have maps of Canada and the U.S.A. They are wonderfully useful. My heating pipes are not discretely hidden as they are "en haut" but nevertheless as long as they prove effective in 20 degrees below, they'll do fine by me.

MONTREAL

(SEPT 4)

Am very well and writing this from the bar of the Themis Club. Have just served a Sauterne down in the dining room. There is something depressing in a dining room full of women eating. It's as though they are all scared of speaking to one another or maybe it's because I have had to serve evening snacks in the bar during this last week while the kitchen is being repainted, and I think I have had enough of them. Sure, I get on well but you can imagine how it is with them all changing their minds about peaches and pears just because one old girl demanded one or the other. The boss, who has recently returned from England, is in a foul mood – so foul it is childish and when the long face comes in, I have to cover up to prevent from laughing. Ma, I forbid you to join that wretched affair on Cooper St which is an American idea of women taking over and placing all men as assistant housekeepers. Otherwise events are running smoothly. I did my Chemistry exam and think it was O.K. The algebra and geometry, which I've been teaching myself, will provide a stiffer hurdle. The big hockey season began this week. I think it is weak the way they have so few organized competitions when you think of how many teams –juniors up—play cricket or football in Sydney. Here they prefer to see it on T.V. or make a dollar on Sat. afternoons.

MONTREAL

(SEPT 13 1955)

Came home for lunch hoping I'd hear from you and sure enough, the letter was there. The position is a little tender here at the moment with my waiting for the entrance results, McGill begins next week so perhaps by the time you get this, I will have started.

Weather has turned cool. The sun is shining but there is a nip in the air. Should be nice for about a month "et alors l'hiver." I resumed at the bank yesterday after the break for the exams and was promptly bundled off about a mile along St Catharine St to a branch for relief work. Am back at McGill College today although there seems to be a lull in my activities. During the summer there is a definite regression in banks as far as the clerk work is concerned. Winter brings it to its peak.

Vod is installed in a nice rooming house about 10 minutes from the Themis Club. He has kitchen facilities and we change about between the two "residences."

The chef is a great guy and we often smuggle a meal to Vod when he visits. Must get back into some sports as soon as things settle down. Read where the Montreal star footballer made 201 yards in 20 runs. We both roared when we thought what a decent Rugby League player could do in 20 runs. Sport is good at the big "cash" level but Montreal only has one big team. Minor and junior leagues are very few, non-existent I think. That is why Canadians are so weak at everything except ice hockey.

## MONTREAL
### (SEPT 15 1955)

My big news is that I have been admitted to McGill. Was informed on Monday morning and since then have had the big mad rush. (Elementary Algebra 66, Elementary Geometry 61, Chemistry 61.) Now that the start has been made I feel surer of myself and begin my lectures in Science tomorrow. I know, too, that it is Medicine that I want so here in a few words are my plans. Please all, never refer to me back there as actually being in Medicine. That would be bad form and besides there's one hell of a lot to go before that question comes up.

The "pre-med" course consists of three years (sometimes four) in which you have to cover quite a few subjects pertaining to Biology. Other courses in the classics must also be taken. My first year consists of Physics, Chemistry, Mathematics, English, Botany (half course) and Zoology (half course). These are compulsory for anyone contemplating medicine. Second and third years are different; you take the subjects likely to be of use and dealing with branches of medicine such as genetics etc. In the third year one takes the Medical School entrance examination and if accepted, then the four years of medicine.

Of course, all the above is my idea of events at the moment. It does seem a long way off and a long time before I see you all but let's just see how things turn out for this year and I will be in a position to tell. The breaks so far have been grand. One thing is for sure that I'll be home once I've done something with myself. You must agree that Canada has been a boon to me – am getting the feeling of really fitting in and belonging but at the same time firmly fixed with the idea of eventual return to the homeland.

Maybe you are wondering how I am financing this deal. Well, the two jobs have put me in the position of being able to pay all my first year fees, buy the required books, clothe myself and still have $200 for spending money. Today I left the bank. They were surprised but all very pleased and hoping I do O.K. I think the accountant felt like packing up and coming too. My fees are $375 plus $15 for student's union, athletics etc. Books I can cut down to $30 and by stopping on at the Themis Club, will not have board worries. With the first cool breaths already here, the room and club are beautifully warm. You'll pardon my outburst in my recent letter but was just a bit annoyed to see this "Women's Club" idea spreading to Cootamundra. However I guess it's all pretty harmless! Just don't join!

Rather dramatic in the room right now. The pre-fight broadcast is on from New York. Vod and Vic, who is working for the migration dept. out at Dorval after finishing at Halifax, are stretched out on the cot. The drawls are coming forth and here is one from me despite all the ballyhoo: "Marciano will K.O. Moore." Vod even did the washing up for the Boss. This puts us in fine, a valuable state of affairs.

Today at university we had to write an entry compulsory composition. I hope I didn't damn my chances by my words on Peron. We have been following the over-throw in Argentina. It's certainly stimulating to think that all those countries are on this continent. (Sic!) Alex, at the bank keeps me in touch with Latin America.

In short, Ma and all, it's a tremendous feeling to be on my merry way again. The job here fits in so well as to be in the closest harmony with the course. My mornings are full but the afternoons leave a few hours for a snooze. "To New York and the World Title Fight."

P.S. Thought that as the battle goes on, I might introduce you to McGill. Begun in 1829, it is the premier university of Canada and has the world famous medicine faculty. Lately, most fortunate with enormous grants from local brewing interests and private donors. There is a beautiful new library, an underground tunnel connecting this to the Arts Building, The other faculties have their buildings around the campus. The Science Building is also renewed and has terrific facilities including a cyclotron which is used in atomic physics. (More on this after when the junior is a little more clued up). The new fits in nicely with the old –there is the old chapel and the rest of the administration buildings of creeper, grey stone. The campus is the grounds on which the university is built. There are lots of trees and a fair amount of open space with paths. It's so convenient, five minutes from the Themis so it is almost like living in the fraternity house. The main gates on Sherbrooke St. have a small clock tower, called the Roddick Gates after an eminent surgeon. It's a fine institution as you will see when I send off a few photos.

P.S. Mum, please keep on holding the letters and envelopes. If they get too bulky, put them in the tea chest.

MONTREAL
(SEPT 23 1955)

You're certainly a champ with the letters, Ma. I can just imagine the scene and enjoy knowing what you are all doing. Also the cricket news. Have just come in from the library with the Physics problems but came out on top and so survive another lecture.

Vic came in Friday and he, Vod and I saw "Great Expectations." The McGill Film Society puts on the classics each Fri. night. Gosh, I enjoyed everything about it with the background of the old convict who made his fortune in New South Wales. Canadians love having a shot about our ancestors coming out on the prison boats. I showed a girl the elastic mark from my ankle sock and said it was a birthmark all Australians had, from the chains of their forefathers.

Saturday the big football match and McGill defeated their main rivals in Toronto "Varsity. It was a "turn up" for the books and McGill also won the Rugby Union game. What a mess a good Rugby League team could make of these pie-eaters at North American football. One of the major difference is that there is blocking all the time but would love to see the South Sydney team in action here. Who won the premiership this year?

After it all, we went to dinner at the Bains. They had the professor of engineering from McGill there. He seemed quite interested in Aust. but otherwise was like anyone who puts up buildings.

Was walking through Steinberg's, the giant supermart and bought a box of chocolate biscuits just for old time's sake. I'll never forget those sagas when there was a pound of Scotch fingers in the house! Being warm, well fed and clothed makes the big difference when you haven't got a lot of dough. However I have $5 per week spending money so that's O.K. Buys me 50 small glasses! Played three hours of squash today: cold as hell, 35 degrees.

Raining here tonight and daylight saving time ended Sunday so nightfall is one hour earlier and I keep feeling that winter is pretty close. Getting into stride with the lectures and the hours of my timetable gradually filling up. Have some 15 hours of lectures plus eight hours of Chemistry, Physics and Biology laboratories. The rooms are spread out about the campus in the various departments. Barbara Bain, the girl in the boat picture I sent, (no emotional attachment) is one of the assistants to the Biology professor. She has her B.Sc. and now is going on for her Master's degree. Have seen Vic a lot during the past few weeks. The two of us with Vod have seen quite a piece of the town's night life down east, at the bottom of St Catharine St. The place "jumps" downtown. Brother Ned would be in his element with the hep-cats. Arthur, my French tutor at the Themis Club says" the old place isn't the same since they cleaned her up." Mayor Jean Drapeau spends his time closing down the clubs.

The ladies are streaming back for the winter as summer resorts empty. We have the heat on already although I think a little too soon. I am as snug as a bug down here in the basement. It will take a lot to blast me from this place. On Sunday went up the mountain with David –the colours of the maples are fantastic. Now they are a mixture of brown, gold and flaming red, in beautiful combination. In the Laurentians they say it is as nice now as you could possibly wish. Have some English guests at the Club. One of them is a sparkling 84 and lives in Lacock Abbey where she found the Magna Carta in her garden. They gave her a trip to Canada and the States.

Nothing yet this week from you so will get this off. Have just finished writing out the menu in gigantic script for the big Thanksgiving Dinner on Sunday at the club. It's going to be a colossal feed and Vod is busily getting himself in a position to participate! It's a day (national holiday Monday) to thank God for the prosperity of the nation. I'll be thanking at lunch time.

Vic has left for the U.S. border job so I have been free to get some work started although all the cronies of last winter are back. Had quite a bull session last night.

Everything is going fine although the perils of my first Physics laboratory were experienced this afternoon. They are some job – two straight hours plus Heaven's knows how much more when I begin to write it all up. The rest of the subjects are O.K. although my interest naturally is biggest in Biology. We are studying plant structures as though they were human. Not a great difference, I guess.

Have been swimming up at the gym for a few lengths before I go to the bar. Have put in for some water polo but the guy wanted to know what position. I couldn't think of any position. Am in good condition for a barman. The boss just came down to retrieve her "Montreal Star" newspaper and then said there was a pack of sandwiches left out for me. These have I polished off.

Everyone happy about the Dodgers' first victory in the World Series in 55 years. I got pretty conversant with the terms but my interest now flags until the finals next year. Seeing the Royal Aunt or Princess Royal tomorrow –she is getting the honorary degree.

## MONTREAL
## (OCT 12 1955)

Missed lunch at the Themis Club through having to take someone to lunch and tour the campus. It was a duty show! Finished out last week with a few hours spent in the Physics laboratory. We have to take these intricate measurements and prove all kinds of laws etc. that you come across in elementary Physics. I often think of my efforts at Coota. High and get a kick out of those exams. My partner is an American going through on the Korean Veterans Bill. He's a character and we have shots at one another quite a bit. That's how we got put together in the lab as partners, as he said: "You know, we just about hate one another's guts."

On Sat. Vic and Vod had lunch with me at the Themis. Vic had on his full immigration service uniform and we put on an act in front of one of the girls. Vic asked her how long I had been in the country and said I was to be deported. She answered: "Listen, Mister, I don't know nothing about him." And flew upstairs to the boss. Miss Browning stomped down and found us in hysterics and me with the "Canada Immigration" hat balanced on the back of my head. She thought it a great joke after she had bounced into the room ready to throw Vic out.

In the afternoon we went to the McGill football stadium (capacity 23,000) and saw the McGill Redmen and the University of Western Ontario play a 6-6 draw. After the rules became a little clearer, I like the game and reckon that if things get tough I shall earn my fees by turning out for the seniors! Don't let that out either!! It's a fantastic scene, a North American college football game – with cheer leaders, bands, dancing girls and gymnasts.

Had a few swims last week, too. The pool sure is an asset as is having these free facilities. Rugby Union is on but am a little wary this first year of becoming too involved. Will likely stick with the Westmount team rather than try out for the McGill team. This week and next are going to be hectic. It is fraternity "rushing time" and I have received lists from two houses inviting me to all their functions, The houses are not a bad idea but they do cost the odd "buck" extra and most of the guys in them can afford to throw it around. Main advantage is as I experienced last year living in the KRT house – getting to know a lot of guys. The one I have been asked to join has "houses" all through the United States so it would be useful from that angle for the rule is that "you put your brother up when he visits you!"

The Aust. I met a few weeks back has sent me the news page from the Aust. Information Centre in New York. This should come weekly now. Vod and I enjoy it and it keeps us in touch. However I would dearly like the odd Sunday paper (all sections) and a Coota Herald from you.

Last night had Thanksgiving Dinner with Fred and Pat, the Californian and his wife .He is off with the bank to New York after Xmas and then down to South America. I was really stonkered with the meal – they hacked off this enormous turkey leg and side and I ate the lot with the trimmings of cranberry sauce and vegetables.

It amuses me the way the New York stock market goes down every time Ike gets constipated. He is so good for business and I think O.K. for the nation as a whole. Nixon, who Vod saw him Sydney, doesn't appear too feasible as being the next president. My tip is Earl Warren of the Justice Dept. With my sporting forecasts, I feel fairly well qualified.

MONTREAL

(OCT 6 1955)

Good to have your letter at lunch time. It's now 6 p.m. and am in the bar, quietly sipping a bowl of soup. The appetite is ravenous with the return of the cold weather. Will be back in the overcoat soon. Might even squeeze myself a new one as the one I have is known as a Fall or Spring coat. It went well last winter but I wore quite a bit under it. With the changing in and out of classrooms and buildings, they do get a bashing.

Was to have quite a week with the fraternity parties for new members in full swing but decided I wouldn't join with the job at the club, and also the dough they toss about. Had another bunch of newsletters from the New York consulate this morning. Just as well I didn't return home last Xmas – may have marched off to Malaya with the Australian army if I hadn't felt like settling down. Vod and I meet at the library most nights. It closes at 10 p.m. so we either come down to the Themis or go around to his place for a coffee snack. At the end of Crescent St (the Club sits on the corner of Crescent and Sherbrooke) is the "American Restaurant" which we haunt. It's on the main street St. Catharine.

Joined the Music Club at McGill so feel up with you and your concert going to the Cootamundra Music Club. Have the large Hi-Fi and twice a week at lunch-time, play the concert for an hour. Vod and I have paired to buy a set and records. I had a few records and he has brought some, so precious living is catching up with us.

Mum, if there is something of you that has rubbed off on to me it is: "Turn out the light." I can never leave a room with the radio or the light on but am afraid that otherwise my tidiness is as before. However I still revere my Daks trousers (two pairs) at $26 per pair. And what about Brother Mick, he seems doomed this time to marriage. Where is he going to live? Are brothers Tony and Ned still in the sleepout or is it being renovated for the happy couple.

McGill beaten in the football at Toronto. There was a big derailment of the way home –seven cars off the tracks due to a stalled vacant automobile at a level crossing. No one injured from McGill as their train cars stayed on the line.

Pleased to have your letter at lunch time—a rainy day here but not cold. Have just come downstairs from the kitchen and my meal which is left out of a Monday for nothing is served today. Miss Browning has been putting on the big scene about Princess Margaret's non-engagement. I have been telling her for weeks that it would not come off but she is taking it badly. You know how the English are about their kings and queens.

Had the McGill medical check-up. Was feeling hungry so gave the Red Cross a pint of blood and in return had coffee and biscuits. Met a Finnish nurse who knew all my old haunts in Kobenhavn and Stockholm. Told her about when we were being shown over the famous Carslberg Brewery in Kobenhavn, a group of five Finns joined us. One (no English spoken) came over to me, shook hands and gave me a Finnish 5-marka coin. He was full of smiles; I've never forgotten his face.

People don't vary too much if left alone without the Steelworks shareholders worrying about where the next new lot of arms is going. Every time "Ike" goes to the lavatory, the New York Stock Exchange halts until they hear the result. A little crude but that is how it is.

Also at the Blood Banque was the nicest French girl I have met here. Will be going back to give another pint tomorrow but must take care that I retain some pure blood – don't want to be a full-blooded Canadian!! They give donors a lapel tab:" I'm a Bloody Science man" with the "B" and "Sc" outlined in black to read B.Sc. Get it?

Had a letter from my plumber mate up north who wants me to go down to Mexico with him next summer. He is ONLY making $600 (270 pounds) per month. I wrote back and said my name was Howse, not Rockefeller. He wrote: "Mother Nature can get nasty up in the Arctic Circle. Last night we had a snow blizzard and I awoke to find an inch of snow covering the inside of the hut floor." They are issued with big U.S. Forces sub-zero gear so no worries. May work there next summer.

Kept busy at McGill but am up to date and plugging along fine. Last night to see "To Catch a Thief," with Cary Grant and Grace Kelly. Enjoyed it very much as the background shots are truly fabulous. I swung the bag up so many of those hills and along the coastal road. Vod asked me had I seen much of the scenes. I replied only the big villas, the Beach Club and Grace Kelly. Halloween tonight. I don't know what it means except the kids are asking for dough so will stop in.

## MONTREAL
### (NOV 7 1955)

We seem to have struck regularity with the mails so can look forward to Monday as news day from "67." Now don't get too thrilled about those entrance exam marks. I will have to do a lot better that that now I am in. However conditions have improved. At least I have teachers now. Everything is going fine and already the first tests are on their way. They count if you end up on the margin in the finals next April. I seem to have settled down O.K. and the wheels kept turning.

Vic came in again this weekend and we went to the McGill dance and then to a party at one of the fraternity houses and met the Australian school teacher from Ashbury College, Ottawa, a school for the wealthy in Canada. He says the senior boys stop on up to 19, 20, 21 years. I thought of the train trip to start work in the Bank of New South Wales at Young when I was 15! He is going home for Xmas so if he gets a chance, will call in.

Mrs. Bain has asked Vod and I to Xmas dinner. The shops are beginning to roll up the Xmas displays but I would prefer a brown Xmas any day. Mrs. B's son is in 3rd year engineering and last summer made $1,600 in five months. It will be hard to beat that but the dough is up north where the big radar defence line is being built. Canada has a very sane view on foreign policy, hoping all she can about relations with our neighbor around the North Pole – Russia! The neurological surgeon-in-chief, Dr. Wilder Penfield, of the Montreal Neurological Institute here has just returned from giving lectures to the Russian Academy of Sciences. With China due to have one billion people in a few years, there won't be much sense in U.S. and U.S.S.R. blowing one another up. Had a good weekend on the tips and landed $5. Will keep me for a week.

Congratulations, Mick, on your new job. Seems like a good opportunity and I will be looking forward to hearing how you make out. No doubt it will be a bit strange after all these years but as I went from banking to counter hand in a milk bar, you shouldn't have any trouble walking across the street in accountancy.

Hope you got your birthday wire, Mum. Last year, I sent you one from London which you didn't mention receiving. Also sent Caroline greetings on Sept. 11. It is good to hear if you get them so I can check up if they go astray.

Played squash with David twice so some degree of fitness is on its way. We always play at least three sets – it makes you really jump around and we crash into one another, block and shepherd so the snob value of the game –as Vod says – is lost completely.

Was picked for the rugby team to play in Boston this weekend and will send you a pictorial record – the professor just looked around and said: "I hope everyone is following this." – am in my first lecture of the day and finishing off this letter as he is going over the Calculus test we had last Saturday. We plan to leave Friday afternoon and motoring down through New York State, Vermont and New Hampshire and then into Mass. and once again I meet the Atlantic Ocean. Am hoping Vic will meet us and join up at his border post. Sounds good having pull at the frontier when I think back on the number of border posts I have crossed at all hours in Europe, in drizzling rain, on foot and in plush cars, too.

BOSTON MASSACHUSETTS

(NOV 20 1955)

A note from Cronin's Café in Boston where I sit with Vod, and a Kiwi who made the trip with us. Am awaiting the big Porterhouse steak, a big treat. Feeling pretty tired – motored down all last night and didn't get any sleep. Arrived this morning at seven o'clock and after coffee, made quick visit to Paul Revere's house – he was the guy who rode to warn the American colonists of the arrival of the English fleet. Then to the site of the Boston Tea Party where the Yanks tipped over 30 chests of tea into Boston Harbour. This was the protest over the small tea tax. Then up to Bunker Hill Monument, scene of a famous battle in which the Yanks beat the British. The city is very old in most places there are so many English names and old English-style dwellings. The people have quite a different accent but my impressions of the life down this way must wait until I think things over. At times it is all a little frightening, watching a society like that in America.

This café is just around the corner from the famous Harvard University. We intend seeing over it tomorrow. It has been snowing all day—the match against Mass. Institute of Technology resulted in a 6-0 loss. It snowed the whole time, from start to finish, the flakes were falling. It was quite an experience. I thought I would be cold but kept on the move to retain minimum circulation. The English would play Rugby Union anywhere, anytime. There was an Australian from Sydney on the M.I.T. team.

Writing now on Sunday morning from a luxury fraternity house where Vod and I spent the night. The guys here are most hospitable and the house overlooks the Charles River. The snow last until early this morning and there is still a lot about. The wind is howling but looking out across the campus buildings and the river, it makes a fine scene. They put on a fine party for us last night.


MONTREAL

(NOV 22 1955)

Seems like the old European days are back with me writing from one country and a new one within the next few days. Thought I would finish my description of last weekend. Finished the Boston letter on Sunday morning. Met a lot of students. Noticed the difference in living scales at the fraternity. Ten of us at the KRT House used to battle over two quarts of milk each morning but down there they just put those enormous milk cans on the table, boxes of doughnuts and gallons of coffee. No wonder the Yanks make lousy soldiers. They get it too soft from birth.

Off then to Harvard University. It is the only college in North America that calls its "campus" a "yard." This comes from its start when it was purchased it included a cow yard in 1639. It is now the most respected university in the U.S..

Buildings combine the old and the new gracefully – the residences and houses line the busy Massachusetts Avenue and spread over a large area. The snow had stopped falling but remained on the ground.

We saw a marvelous museum of botany and zoology. Thousands of glass work examples of flowers, of preserved sea and land life, amazing remakes of enormous whales and interesting comparisons of the bones of a man (an Australian aborigine) and an ape, in their crouching positions. Vod retired to the Law School – one of his old Sydney professors had taught there for six years and had told him a lot about it. Not of equal interest to the biologist, the electronic engineer, the accountant and our Kiwi mate who works for Canadian National Railways as a public relations man. We left him and drove along the Atlantic Avenue, through the very old section of the city (over two millions) and by the sea – the Atlantic! The wind was howling and it was getting cold so we stopped off at the teeming, privately-owned railway station for a big meal. We collected Vod at the Law School and drove home. It snowed all the way and although we left at 8 p.m., with the roads a little slippery, we decided to take it easy and got back to Montreal at 11 a.m. Monday, with no mishaps and numerous coffees. There are certainly some hick small towns in the States— are the people narrow and small!!! Took a wrong turn and got to within 141 miles of New York City but the driver would not be in it.

MONTREAL

(NOV 28 1955)

Just in for lunch and pleased to have all the news. Came in with snow on my head as there is a light fall on right now but as it is getting slightly warmer, will most likely be rain when I am ready to return to Chemistry at 2 p.m.Very slippery and I went over on the campus grass this morning. Everyone is into the overshoes for the next six months so no more shoe repairs.

Answered the door last Sat. morn to the owner's representative of the large vacant building next door to the Themis, on Crescent St. He wants me to keep an eye on things for him and the boss is to phone me this afternoon to arrange salary. Even three or four dollars a week could mean a ski outfit for the winter. There are so many convenient places for skiing that it does seem the best winter activity. Play squash twice a week (once on Tuesday, compulsory sports) and the other Sat, afternoon. Took a game off Cuthbertson for the first time since we have been playing together and we must have had at least 200 games since last January. It was like winning the Davis Cup – I have had him down 8-1, 7-0, 8-2 so often (game finishes at 9) and always he has come back so from now on games may be better balanced.

Went to a party Sat. night. All the girls were French and spoke little English so it was quite a test. Came through O.K., the only jolt being from une demoiselle who told me I looked like James Stewart (45). Still I guess it's an improvement on Bob Hope and as well a good honest face. I practiced a stunning farewell before bidding everyone good-night. Am enjoying learning French without too much formal application. Arthur, the houseman comes home about midnight and we have the half-hour lesson. He prowls the streets, goes to movies but is a nice bloke. Am getting the photos of Boston and a few others and will post them off for Xmas. It's not so far off now but never quite the same as it is at home. The decorations are starting to come on and the shopkeepers' predictions "Bigger and better business" this year.

## MONTREAL

## (DEC 5 1955)

What a wow of a time that Cootamundra Batchelor's jump must have been. Enjoyed the tales of the feuding squatter's sons who were cutting up the joint fine. Old cousin David must have looked like a charioteer in the milk cart. It's so long since I have seen him that the span from cantering along the Murrumbidgee flats to the role of amoureuse is difficult to bridge.

Have just shoveled the snow off the steps of the building next door. But am feeling a little anxious as the estate man hasn't returned to strike a bargain in dollars and cents. "I'll rip de joint apart if he don't pay me." Had a fair fall (four inches) yesterday and last night we strolled over to St Joseph's Oratory, you remember, the enormous shrine. The overshoes are on – the homes are a beautiful as any I've seen but I prefer the blue of ocean, and, say, a villa on the Med, to a mansion "in a select area" of a city rat race. It's great fun, one can't deny, being in Montreal city. It's not fast and the pace isn't much quicker than a jet doing a dive. My dive is down Sherbrooke St., every morning at 8.55 a.m.

Am eagerly awaiting Aust. election news. What criminal tactics Prime Minister Menzies uses. Thurs. night myself and 749 others, including Kiwi, went to a debate between one of our political science-economics professors and the leader of the Liberal Progressive Party. The latter is a nice way of saying the Canadian Communist Party and it was on that topic of Communism that they spoke. It's a relief that this is still allowed in Canada. Down South, you'd appear before a Committee for Subversion overnight. Canada differs from the States in that way—there is just that lack of hysteria here. I'm too devoted to the dollars I'll have to earn next summer to have any idealistic student leanings towards the radical.

We recess Dec. 22 until after the New Year. I have one final Botany exam on Jan 7 and then I switch to Zoology, the study of animals and their functions. Please tell Aunt Sylvia there are other medical schools in the world, other people, other lands – the idea that I would "never be allowed" to practise in Australia doesn't exist. If you know how to, then the major part of the battle is over and Ma, you ask any medical man if McGill and Toronto aren't up to scratch. That's all a long way off but the word "never" annoys me. Reminds me of the clock in Hell! Off to the Boston two-step with a chemistry lecture. Will write Friday to make sure of Xmas – How about a letter from all of you? That would be the most cheering Xmas present ever.

MONTREAL

(XMAS 1955)

Just in from Bains at a little after 10 p.m. and Xmas Day just about over, 3 p.m. Boxing Day with you. Really had a pleasant day. Went to midnight Mass from a party, then returned. It was all English but fairly refined and interesting. Enjoyed meeting a graduate of M.I.T. I resumed at 1 a.m. straight from La Cathedrale and all folded soon after. David was there, so as he knew the two girls pretty well, we stopped on, they washing up and myself on the Chesterfield, reading "The Young Lions" which is quite a good novel on the war by Irwin Shaw. Listed to the Xmas programmes but really wasn't tired, so walked home about four. Rose at nine a.m., and listened to the Xmas broadcast. Was quite moved when I heard all the talks of the various Commonwealth nations and was thinking especially of you all. Also helped out upstairs by doing the breakfast wash-up.

A beautiful day, mild after the night's snow and sunny, almost cloudless. Vod came around. Both of us were delighted with your Xmas wire. Hope mine wasn't too great a shock for the Post Office at Murrumburrah. Went out to Bains about 3 p.m. after I had swept the stairs of snow. Certainly feels funny doing that with 95 degrees back home. Talking to a Sydney girl friend this morning and she just couldn't see Xmas this way. Has only been here two months so I guess will get acclimatized. All the girls at the club (i.e. the waitresses etc) came good with presents so now I have a pen, 4 biros, 1 pencil, 2 handkerchiefs, 5 pairs of socks (one of them from the club president), shaving soap and lotion (have rarely used either up to now); from the boss a $4 clothes order at Ogilvy's Department Store. The big news was a $25 bonus from the club. $10 went on Zoology books but it was a grand surprise. I didn't buy any presents as when you ain't got dough, you ain't got it. Collected an extra $4 off the old girls here, too. My sock position was desperate. I told everyone that my present would be Xmas good will spread throughout the year. I am remarkably free from bad moods; I have the odd spasm of anger but generally am my breezy self which helps a lot when you work in with these people. The girls are right down-to-earth and amusing: Arthur, my friend who is in the kitchen, presented me with a packet of stylish soap which must have been made for a duchess, and hardly for the bartender. Am giving Mick the full story of the fare riots – McGill students joined the other universities in protesting bus far hikes.

MONTREAL

(JAN 1 1956)

New Year's Day and almost two years since the Woolloomooloo wharf scene and the big adventure got under way. A year, too, in Canada, one of the most significant in my life, past or to come. This time last year my job with the Royal Bank had just come through, much to my relief. Ever since those few days without a job, I have been a target for "bites"—the haunted look of the unemployed must have remained although from the ovoid features at present, it can't show up too badly. I often think that there is more character in some of the guys that come up and say "Brother, can you spare a dime for a cup of coffee" than in the thousands of well-heeled ants you see scuttling along the main drags of St. Catherine and Sherbrooke Streets. I certainly have nothing to complain of. Am happily settled into my Themis Club, the University, a few books, the gymnasium, records, food and warmth and a few friends including my honourable cousin.

Today it was a beauty, six degrees above zero but sunny and crisp. With a few sweaters under my Harris Tweed sports coat (Vod has a special "Thermo" jacket), we spent two hours strolling up the mountain, watching the skaters and skiers, and using a great slab of snow to complete a few scissors movements up hill. Exercise is the greatest remedy for the cold –what a happy scene it is just above me on the mountain. All the kids on their toboggans with Pop on the back, skiers jumping and flashing in and out of the leafless woods and Beaver Lake, a natural skating rink. The male skaters are a trifle "fairy" – we thought them a bit feminine but perhaps that is due to us not having tried skating. Am buying ski boots soon on my charge account and a crowd of us are going to try to get some skiing regularly. With the Laurentians a $1.50 bus ride away, it is our chance. My God, the week before Xmas was cold – 10, 12, 14, all below zero. A glass of water on my window sill froze in 14 minutes, I wrapped a scarf about my head and am wearing ski mitts on my hands. I often dream of those days at home strolling across Fisher Park in a singlet and bare feet.

Last Monday night we went out to an Australian's place at Dorval for the afternoon, followed by a big turkey dinner and party. It was a pleasant night and both of us enjoyed it. A guy who flew with Peter Howse in New Guinea drove us home. Was Peter one of Dad's cousins? Met a nice couple who were assistant Aust. trade commissioners in New York. I thought the New Zealand Trade Commissioner was a pretty hopeless type – big, red face and seemed to feel that he should have some veneration. I asked him if Edmund Hillary was an Australian. Bob, our host, insisted on reading poems by Henry Lawson and Banjo Patterson, you know, "The Man from Snowy River," etc. He has a fairly broad Australian accent and it floated across the room. You people back there should see a group of Australians who have been away for a few years. A certain nostalgia remains with Bob even after his eight years here. He's married to a Canadian but I am sure he will go back eventually.

In all, it was a happy Xmas. New Year's was quiet –was invited to two parties but I have a fear of New Year's Eve. Have always spent it quietly and dreaded within me the time when everyone goes berserk and whistles etc. Went around to Vod's place and we bloated ourselves with a great meal and walked down to our seat in the American Restaurant for a bit of conversation in much the same style as our nightly visits to George's at Double Bay when I was working down in Sydney.

Am on holidays until the 12$^{th}$ but have a final exam in Botany on Saturday. Would much prefer to regard plant life as a natural phenomena rather than the complicated business of diagramming all those bloody systems that make up the humble tree. Have purchased my zoology books (on the quiet, the manager of the book store gives me everything at cost, this saves me nearly $2 on a $7 book) and am relishing the thought of studying it. I feel that things will have started to roll but always keep in the back of my mind that there is no guarantee of getting into medicine at McGill. It depends on a lot of things which I hope to put right during the next three years.

Caroline and Mick's letters were good to get and I shall reply as soon as I have this exam out of the way. Where did Ned ("Satchmo,") and Tony get to? Tony, typed you two a month ago so you're about due. Ned, have you read the write-up on Louis's tour of Europe. He reckons the cats over there just sit about but appreciate jazz tremendously. The Australian Jazz Quartet was nominated in the top jazz bands played on my "Jazz at Its Best in 1955" programme. I listen every Sat. morn as I clean the basement and my room. Might I renew a request for a few Sunday papers, sports magazines –otherwise I shall warn you to expect the complete North American when I see you or you come and visit me on the lottery proceeds. Have often thought of when I got those "Bluey and Curly" annuals. Poor old artist Guerney is dead now. I am fit and well.

MONTREAL

(JAN 1956)

Have just returned from my nightly visit to the coffee shop. Worked all day on Physics. Now after an hour over the newspapers and a few words with cousin Vod, I am back at the Themis. The midnight to dawn radio show has started. I never seem to miss some section of it. It makes my reading of the Bible a little brighter. I bought one copy of the Good Book. Have never read any of it before, direct, that is. Am not becoming a fanatic so don't worry. It's a pleasant tale.

No letter today and my week has been quiet. Did the big Biology exam Sat. Feel O.K. about it. The professor asked me how I went. I said I was always happy about things as I left an examination room but that the results usually changed my attitude. Physics and Maths are just term papers. Played squash on Sat. afternoon. Often take a set off Cuthbertson now. We've played hundreds of games together. I bought a $15 racquet, an English Slazenger's. David is getting on well and is one guy who will do O.K. later on, I am sure. Have decided not to invest in the big ski outfit this season – no sense in going into the red when I can finish the session free of owing a "red cent." Will just have the odd weekend skiing.

I mentioned that an estate agent called before Xmas and asked me to sweep the front steps of the building next door. I have kept a superficial eye on the place and had despaired of hearing from him. On Sunday he dropped around with $15, promises of more and a key. Have installed myself at a little desk with heat and lamps. It's ideal for study, away from the Themis distractions and right next door.

Building has three stories, ideal dance floor etc so Mr. Howse may be entertaining. Cuthbertson is always joking about "sherry" parties there. He loves his bit of social life and we have shots at one another about it.

Vod sends his regards and is always interested in your news. He is off to New York for a week to see the sights with Meg and Buck who are flying in from Los Angeles for three weeks. Meg and Buck just back from Mexico. The whole of North America is very excited about "Her Grace" Grace Kelly but I shall send you the cattiest extract from Dot Kilgallen whose "guts I hate" to quote a popular saying.

Hit tunes are "Memories Are Made of This," "16 Tons," "Tender Trap," "We'll Have These Moments to Remember," and about a thousand others. Looking at maps today - I am 5,500 miles closer to Moscow than Cootamundra. The basement is a good H-bomb shelter and I almost feel like a Londoner in 1939.

MONTREAL

(JAN 1956)

Just in from the "Riviera," our latest meeting place, over on Stanley Street but we will have to move on as it is starting to attract all the beards, would-be artists and pseudo-intellects. Gives us both the horrors to have that mob around. Otherwise it is O.K. and run by Austrians. We are the only square types who frequent it. Other than the beards etc, the remaining clientele are Germans. Was at the library until 10 p.m. and now nearly 11 so will complete the night with a short spell of Maths. Chemistry went well today i.e. I reckon I passed.

Pleased to note the news of my bag's arrival from London.. Bet you found some skeletons or was everything quite respectable? Was the "billy-can" full of coins? That was a present from my old steel works "mate." He did more work on it than on anything the nationalized steel industry had to offer. And I drank a lot of tea out of it. Mal, you can make a scrap-book out of the posters etc. The big poster is the London railway Tube. My friend Aub's company made them. He also did the rather flattering drawing. Those bangles are from Port Said, Egypt and winner takes all. Let me know if anything else in the bag puzzles and I'll give you the appropriate background. Hell, when you think of being 19 and on the boat, and now almost 22 with the first university year almost over. One birthday as a Fortes counterman, the next as Canadian bank clerk and this one as barman. Seem to have reached the stage where I dread birthdays as much as the "girls" in the

Themis Club. Made $2 this weekend so am "full" at the moment. I will complete the term just nicely on what I have. Have a backlog of $50 odd from taxation but haven't had time to file the return. Am not trying to be the smart guy when I say that Sydney is like a small town after New York and London. Montreal is the same as the "Big Smoke." Will close now as have just been interrupted by the boss to chip ice off the front steps.

MONTREAL

(JAN 15 1956)

Arthur and I have just finished a bowl of tomato soup and a few bread rolls. Yours truly is the dishwasher but the boss doesn't mind the snacking. Pleased to have your letter –I'm a day or two late this week as I had my Physics partner around. He has dropped a bit behind (i.e. further than me) so had to catch up out of my stuff. He's 28, a Korean War veteran, owns a farm in Vermont, not a bad guy but a bit jumpy, or neurotic. Mick, I was thrilled with the book, particularly with the snaps of the country around Gundagai. Have been showing them around and the boss is now very keen to go to Australia as she hates Canada. You know what these Limeys are!! It was nice of you to write Jean Caldwell, Mum, as you probably know, I didn't get around to it although I enjoyed that meal at the Windsor.

It's always a joke to me when I see someone putting on the big act, after the photos I have of one-week-old human embryos. It's an amusing comparison to have the pig and the human side by side at that early stage. This new course has given me quite a kick for we are getting into the various body systems, comparing animals with the ourselves and next week I shall cut a frog in two and "observe the functions." This, I feel, is a start. With my delicate, long, slender musician's fingers and thumbs, I should be able to make quite a mess of the poor old bull-frog. The steel works experience will be handy. I'll never forget the way I used to toss those great planks of iron about with a pair of long-handled pincers. The course professor is a bottler – one you wouldn't mind sitting in for an extra minute after the bell. He's about 55-60, walks about with a microphone attached to his chest. We were discussing the reproductive system (blushes from Caroline) and he said that 20 years ago, students would have closed their notebooks, some even have left the room. Reckon that youth is more knowledgeable about these things today – there was a ripple from the girls. He told us that this was the hour to forget all allusions to storks and cabbage leaves.

MONTREAL

(JAN 20 1956)

Your letter at lunch time, Mum, and enjoyed the array of news you collected. Thanks my old Mal pour la carte sante, you must have guessed your brother had need of a holy card. But when you write again, a little smaller and a few more news for the more I hear from you, the easier it is to trace your growing up. Don't want to meet up with a bunch of strangers at the door when my bony frame drives up in Sonny's taxi. Or maybe it'll be in a pink Cadillac. You can never tell.

Vod arrived in this morning at seven by knocking on my Sherbrooke St. window. Isn't it amusing to think of my having a front on the nicest street in Montreal? He had returned by bus from N.Y. and had a grand time doing Broadway shows, cocktail parties , a visit to Princeton (famous as Yale and Harvard) and Albert Einstein's house, the United Nations (sat in the Security Council). Buck and Meg, installed on Fifth Avenue, certainly gave him a ball of a time. We both have an invitation to a skiing weekend down in Vermont just inside the border of New York and that state. Vod met the judge and so, with luck, we shall be off by Ford (have taken the liberty of inviting an extra with a car). It's only a three or four hour drive but promises to be a pleasant interlude. Will see about some skiing gear but first the obstacle of relief for my club job.

Heavy snow all today. Had to sweep away quite a pile off the steps and it is now up level with my window. It has been extraordinarily mild so far except for the odd day. Expect the cold spell soon but as Mrs. Bain's mother has knitted me a toque and I have ski gloves, winter is O.K. with me. I remember how cold I was on that delivery van 12 months ago; this does seem a change.

Work is going O.K. but no university results yet except for physics which isn't worth reporting, if you know what I mean. I do and it means a bloody lot of work from now on but things are getting along fine and I'm keeping up. Had an interesting lecture on the formation of the brain today. We seem to be learning just enough each day to show us just how much we don't know. It's rather a nice prospect to be before – you can never get it all but there it is, in front of you, for the next 30, 40, 50 days, months or years.

It's midnight and here's "Beth Manly, your Sleepy Time Girl," to be with you until 4.30 a.m. I am usually with her for a while each night until I get fed up and kick the radio off. Hits are "Memories Are Made Of This," "16 Tons," "Tender Trap," and "The Great Pretender." I can capably give off with the lyrics. "Hotter than a heat-wave is my love," sings some hillbilly but I guess he ain't never been down south-west towards Coota.

O.K. Ma, I'm goin' off to bed – have to do some Maths before 9 in the morn.

## MONTREAL

### (JAN 24 1956)

Your letter today and pleased to have all the news. It does seem fantastic every time I read of the hot days and then walk off to a McGill in the snowstorm. Am writing this to the tune of the young German S.S. Guards. They are singing the Horst Wessel song " Die Fahne Hoch" which was one of the NAZI Party anthems from 1933 onwards. Now Hitler is screaming to the crowds of Austrians in Vienna: "Sig Heil," they roar and the massed bands of Germany go into "Deutschland Uber Alles." It is an actual sound track. I think the four Howse brothers would have made excellent storm-troopers if we had been born Krauts. Tell Tony or is it Clancy now ("He's gone adrovin' and we don't know where he are.") to drop me a line when he appears again.

Sunday I went to a reception at the Sheraton (one of Conrad Hilton's) for international students by the Rotary Club. I was the only Australian there and had a long "chat" to the Australian Trade Commissioner, Mr. and Mrs. Steele. He just seemed the ordinary type of Labour Party appointment. Doubt if his job here means more than the odd cocktail party etc and social rounds. Wife watches him like a hawk. Felt at times that I would tell her to go and join the other ladies and to leave him alone so that I could catch up on things. Am going to see him again this week – he says he'll have a few Sydney Morning Heralds by airmail which will be a thrill, only a few days old. You needn't mention my recorded impressions of our national representatives in the large city of Canada – his only knowledge of Cootamundra came from three hours at the railway station. He comes from Melbourne –those two facts didn't help relations.

Had to buy a dissection kit for $6.00 plus new book for another $6. Have the shining scalpel to trim the toes now. Bought a nylon shirt on the charge Saturday.

They are good here and just as soon as I get a little healthier, I shall send over a few. They really don't need ironing and the collars are stiff as boards. I will never be domesticated enough to have an ironed shirt on hand so it is the only thing to do. They always look sharp. Vod has had one since arrival and looks the best-dressed man in town. Played squash twice and beat Cuthbertson 2 games this time. Am in good nick at a steady 185 lbs and a 32-inch waist but my cheeks must measure close to yours Mick. Is there a recent photo of the three Howse brothers?

MONTREAL

(FEB 1956)

Your letter a few minutes ago and it was as usual full of news. We've had the biggest snowfall this winter, about one foot of it. My window is half-hidden from the prying eyes by a great pile of white. Have cleared the steps of my building twice today and am hoping the manager comes around. It's been a long time since that first $15. The machinery and snow removal methods get rid of it very quickly. Snow ploughs run up and down the footpaths so that you walk along the street like Moses going through the sea. The snow builds up on both sides. Still mild, about 25 to 32 degrees above so don't know when winter is going to get here.

You certainly are seeing the latest movies. Charlie Chaplin is banned from the U.S. on account of his "pink" leanings. You just have to be careful what colour tie you wear if you have any ideas of getting into the States. Down in Alabama in the South where the Negroes are mostly, they are trying to force the de-segregation laws which the Congress ordered a while back. Well, a young Negress was enrolled at the State University yesterday as the first black to be admitted and there was a riot. They pelted her with eggs and fruit etc. Well, I guess that is American democracy in action but of course you can't expect the ex-slaves to be accepted overnight although it is nearly 80 years since the abolition of slavery. The South (South Carolina, Tennessee, Kentucky, Georgia, Arkansas, Alabama, Mississippi, and Louisiana) is the most backward area of the U.S. Also the most ill-governed and the poorest. They try to encourage Negroes to migrate to other states and spread out for in some southern states they are 50-50 with the whites. The whites have the property law which says you don't get a vote unless you own so much or pay so much tax. That keeps out poor old Uncle Tom. The Yanks will never be able to say anything against British justice and all this talk of the Rights of Man that goes on in the United Nations is so much rot when you have this on the doorstep.

Have had a quiet week, lots of work to do. Passed the Botany so that is one-half a credit towards the pre-med course. Only another 14 and one-half (possibly 19 and one-half) and they accept you. There is a young Hong Kong Chinese (Tony Lam, 20) who did a few months of first year medicine in Sydney and then came to McGill. Same subjects except that we have to take English literature and plough through the classical works. Played squash last night – nine games, won four.

MONTREAL

(FEB 14 1956)

Just in from coffee with Vod – a night off from my two month plan for the final examinations in April. Your letter this morning. Please excuse the typewriter, know that you, Ma, at least prefer the personal touch of that lousy thick nib but tonight I left it next door in the building where I study. The number of mistakes should be enough evidence of the J.H. touch. Mick should buy a car to commute between the Big Smoke and Coota – one of those "Limey puddle-jumpers" as they are called here in this land of the big ones. You see some fantastic models – I still cannot distinguish between a Ford and a Chev or anything. Guess it is because a car is so far removed from me and things that are far off just don't seem to impress me. I live in the present tense and enjoy it. The record player with its 75 cents per week is my little heresy. Have not made any additions to the collection since the Brubeck classic. Had the family jazz fiend heard of him or is he too deep in the Southern Jazz?

McGill going fine and am very interested in the Zoology – the frog operation was performed successfully and the heart (of the frog) kept up a beautiful beat whilst I slugged away with the scissors and scalpel. Many of the common fundamental considerations apply to man and the frog – that is one of the reasons this sprightly animal is studied in an early Zoo. course. I was thinking of the pleasant hours I used to spend over in Fisher Park, lifting those slabs of mud from the dry dam bed and pouncing upon the families, sealing them in jars and then the holes in the backyard from where they would have vanished next morning. I had better leave this theme as it is beginning to look like the memoirs of a Zoologist rather the start of one.

Heavy snow falls over the weekend and there is a lot about but today was so mild that it fell as a loose watery mass, a few degrees more and it would have been rain. The McGill Winter Carnival goes into full swing on Thursday night with a parade up the mountain to the ice palace, followed by a dance in the chalet on top of the snow-covered hill and skating, several thousand dollars of fireworks etc. Also five queens on the voting list, Friday skiing days, special bus to mountains, a Forum night with the top stars of Canadian vaudeville, ice review and the crowning of the Carnival queen. Saturday, various debating and tugs of war etc, the ice sculpturing and the big finale Carnival Ball in the spacious gym. Man, old McGill really does it – just how many of these activities your son will participate, I will leave to next letter. Am through for the weekend Thursday, the three-hour Chemistry lab having given way to carnival – I don't mind them at all, it's not quite as frightening as it sounds. We have our own drawer of equipment and the book of instructions on each experiment. Nothing so far discovered to shake the world of science except a minor explosion by my next-door lab neighbor.

St. Valentine's Day tomorrow—the big stores feverishly trying to institute a gift tradition. It seems the car business is not big enough. I went out Sat. on my way to squash (Cuth. 7 Howse 1) to buy the Chef one for his wife. She is English so I said I'd get a nice French gift for her. He said if I did that the marriage would be on the rocks in five minutes. She won't learn French (English-Canadian mentality) so as the two kids speak both, they backchat in French – it drives her into a fury. Chef roars in each morning at eight with "Get up. You damn big Australian" in French. He was off this morning so I went through to 9 a.m. which is unusual.

Looking around vaguely for a prospect for the summer. Reckon I may as well stop in town this year as to make sure of the Themis Club as it is pretty necessary for the present until I get a sponsor. Any extra I would earn by going bush for the summer would soon dissipate on returning to the reality of having to pay for full board if I lost the club. Will sound out a few of the local business houses. First year students don't command a very high premium so economics may enforce a return to the $212 per month in the bank. Guess they'd welcome a summer relief man with my international experience.

Love to you all, am off to soak in the bath for an hour, "Goodnight and a good week" says the Valentine programme and that is as good as anything.

MONTREAL

(FEB 1956)

Just finished an essay on the merits and demerits of Huckleberry Finn. Mal, you should read it. It's one of those books like Gulliver's Travels which have been written to take a shot at the world and then made famous as bedtime tales for children. Got your letter today and it was a bright ray as the boss is a bit cantankerous over my failure to register in the bar yesterday. Had worked the previous two Sundays for the two hours so thought it time to call a halt. She'll get over it as it's not that often I bring in the "no overtime rule." You can let the Australian Workers Union (AWU) know that I don't scab for anyone.

No, I didn't throw three coins in that fountain in Rome although I enviously looked at the pile of worthless Italian money on the bottom. Let's hope we can keep up the Limey migration figures so that we don't have pizza shops and hairdressers on every corner telling us how we should have our hair cut like the Yanks. Canadian figures have dropped to hell and the only quota being maintained is the Italian. They have sent a team off to UK to try and get a larger slab of British migration. Must admit that if I was an Englishman with a family and steady English manners, I'd go to Australia. It's a lot different when you are single and don't give so much of a damn for a way of life – anyway you don't have the money for it at this stage and life in Australia seems to me to be that happy mixture of the old world and the new.

A very nice type of Scots woman arrived tonight with a clipped English accent and told me how in 1948 she had lived out in Palm Beach (Sydney) for six months with friends. Over here to visit her son who did medicine in UK at Edinburgh. He left because of the Health Scheme – it's lousy for the doctors no doubt but bloody good for the patients. Britain is very Socialist and out here they are trying to put through a Health Bill. All the Opposition (mostly the medical world, I'm afraid) can muster up is that fine old adage that the individual loves to pay his own way and doesn't want the government interfering with his right to pay his own bills. It's a bit hard to convince most people that it is a bad thing to have the worry of medical bills removed. The way we live here with the last cent going each week on down-payments, on TV sets, electrical appliances and new cars, well, I shouldn't think they'll have a hard time getting the Bill through.

I have today posted off a MacLean's, Canada's own answer to Pix and Life. Also the Spring fashion news from New York which will be fine for the Australian winter, a McGill Daily with 2 articles of interest and the color section from the weekend Montreal Star. It has the article on the average Canadian family and is pretty correct. All in all, it should be an informative day when the package arrives. Feel guilty at times in the sparseness of the material on the adopted homeland that I have sent you – from now there will be an improvement.

How did the marriage rehearsal go, big fellow? Sure you want to go on with it? Remember "for ever and ever" says the big clock. Feeling good tonight, reckon I could toss all except Tony but maybe it's just as well the boast is separated, by an ocean and a week on a plane, from the reality of lying sprawled on my back after three seconds with Ned.

The Carnival went off great guns –I only got to the Thurs. night show. Took a girl from Brussells. Actually it's a small, country town "pres de Brusselles" but we had a good time. She speaks the correct French – Vod and I have bought the French course on records and he has taken the machine to his room for a few months constant indoctrination.

McGill seething of the Alabama incident but if they ask me, I'd say keep out of it. Reckon they are going to give the girl a scholarship here if she wants it. McGill must be the most open and prejudice free university in North America. It's really healthy and I think Canadians are as open on matters like that as anyone. Some of my friends come from Trinidad. Jamaica, Barbados, a colored American from Detroit, about 4 guys from Hong Kong, a guy from Colombia in South America. Somehow when you are all in the same boat, you don't reason in terms of black and white and if that is all I learn here, well I guess it's a start.

Had a letter from Aunt Peg and Richard is coming over from Africa and is taking she and Cousin Christina about in the car. She was presented to Princess Marie Louise and had to courtesy all over the room. She has the old sheepskin from 67 Adams St so that item certainly has a history. Christina loves the school – maybe Mal would like it over there for a few years. "Oh, really John, it is rather late for a cup of tea."

Will retire as I want to be on my feet tomorrow – lectures in eight hours but Tuesday a good day. Had the skin and hair as today's topics. Someone asked would a black man who stopped in a cold climate turn white. The professor nearly had a seizure; evidently the 15,000,000 Negroes down south didn't have the answer. Also I have given up worry of baldness as it appears to be hereditary which means that Mick and Ned will soon catch Tony and I in the race of the bald pates, or the desert heads.

MONTREAL
(MARCH 7 1956)

This week I received two bunches of Sunday papers from you. Pleased to have them but I do think they have gone down the drain in the past two years. Do you remember what the Sunday Herald was like, even the Sunday Sun was respectable? Maybe I caught a bad weekend but I was surprised at how they turn them out now. Only the Racing Section seems to have kept up its standard. We got a good laugh at all the Palm Beach mob with their cravats around their necks but I thought that the Cootamundra Herald was better than the Sunday scandal sheets. God knows why they have to run front page articles on crummy movie stars. Enjoyed the Truth's roasting of the cricket selectors but am afraid to show my Asian and African mates the article on White Australia. I always tactfully support White Australia although it is a touchy subject. A Hong Kong mate says he wishes he had stopped in Sydney now instead of coming over here. He did a year in medicine at Sydney University but his mother has big ideas for him so she brought him an expensive microscope and packed him off to McGill. He prefers the people there and the easier, fuller way of life. Reckons as an Asian he was treated well all the time.

Have the term tests on at the moment so this note written whilst I make the frantic bid at the Mathematics. Chemistry looms whilst English, Zoology have been completed It's a good idea having them now as it stirs you up a bit for the finals. A quiet week – your letter on Saturday. Cold weather seems to have gone, about 30 degrees most of the time but we had snow over the weekend. My job in the building next door has finished so he tossed me a final $15 and that was that!

Vod and Kiwi came over to share my meal –we live within about seven small city blocks of one another and I usually entertain with the meal, and we sit around with the New York Times, our Sunday newspaper. Went and saw "Le Salaire de la Peur" at a French theatre – it has been out quite a while in English as "The Wages of Fear" and is very good. So is "Crin Blanc," another French film which won the Cannes Award.

Had the best mail for a long time yesterday. Was pleased to have all the news and particularly Mal, your letter was the best you have ever written. So neat and mature, you must have hidden yourself away from all the confusion. Was interested in the Reading girl's engagement, more of Australia's land to our friends, the "Limeys." One thing, I guess in coming from Essex U.K., the groom should have a few clues on running the sheep station. Maybe the hand shears will be missed! Fancy old Ned getting off to Queensland for the holidays. I often feel disappointed that I didn't see more of home. It's the same here. I must get off this summer and get the job arranged soon. Maybe it will be the north on the big radar lines which span the Arctic and mid-Canada. Will let you know just what comes up but I must admit the open spaces are calling after 15 months in the city – if there were a few decent swimming facilities in the open it would be a lot better.

No I haven't had any papers but don't worry about sending any more –Jim Steele, the Aust. Trade Commissioner gets them each week and lets me have them. Think the Herald has gone down hill, particularly the Sun-Herald which is almost as bad as some of the New York and London papers. The afternoon "Star" is in the best in Montreal (3 English papers, 1 in morn, 2 afternoon). French gives a wider choice with one up to Star standard. Enjoyed the snap of "Natty Mr. Cole" – they must really go berserk over them out there.

Winter on the move, still windy and around 20 degrees but the sun gets a little warmer and the days longer. Snows still at night occasionally but altogether much milder than the last. Have passed a quiet week with term tests. Wrote English this morning and did O.K. They set us this list of books, and with three lectures per week, that's the course. It's a good idea, I think for me anyway, as it does give me direction in literature. My friend is manager of the book shop so have been able to build a small nucleus for the library.

Still have a fondness for maps and often plan out the routes for "future travels." I was so very near to coming home overland back in London. An Australian friend of ours is in the process of arranging a job in Venezuela with a Yank oil firm. His sole ambition in life is to see every country in the world. Some idea? But not for me. Will get to some work now as I have Tues. afternoon off.

MONTREAL

(MARCH 20 1956)

I got a bit of Spring into me for the first time today. It was sunny and mild with the ice beginning to melt. Right now it's blowing and of course the snow remains up over my window. I open it at night and get a fresh icy blast. However as I am now the owner-wearer of a pair of very smart "Polo" (like a track suit) pyjamas, the cold doesn't touch me. Have that wool rug you gave me for my birthday a few years ago.

St. Patrick's Parade on Sunday – if you ever want to feel sick just watch a Canadian street parade, especially in Quebec. All the Irish and French were out – the convertibles were full of local "would-be wheels" in high hats and doffing them to the amused crowds. It came past my place on Sherbrooke St. but the sight of all those top hats and boiled faces was too much.

Got all your news this morning. Pleased to hear cousin David is in good form. My beard should appear about mid-June. Had the interview with Jim, the Yank from Minnesota who represents United Steel Companies which is one of the State's big steel combines. They have ore holdings about 1,000 miles north from here, up in Quebec's bush. I will be with a geological team, chief functions to be muscle work but as it's 150 miles inland from the port of Seven Islands, no rail and no settlements except our camp. It will be a splendid opportunity to make the $1,000-odd dollars I need and at the same time get some fresh air. I'm longing to stroll around in the open after nearly 18 months in the bowels of the city. Pay is $285 per month, all expenses, air trip up and back etc. Providing I don't take my dice, I should do O.K. I'll never forget the lesson Sid Hobson of Young taught me in how to win on the "bones." The Boss isn't too keen at all on my going but there it is and I feel I can make out on something else. I have to start putting away dough each summer so that if I get the Med. chance, I'll have a year's start on expenses. I'll try and quit work and really make a go of it. The R.C.A. Company want me to quote a price for looking after their building next door – isn't it amusing to think of me negotiating with this electronics giant over a few bucks a month. I will have to under bid a contractor who wants it but if he can go lower than $15 per month, he can have it. Good to know the chess set is on its way. What about asking Frank Walsh to bring my golf sticks over to San Francisco? I could get a mate to bring them over here from the West . Fit and well.

It was really great to have your wire for my 22nd birthday on Thursday. Have to admit it was that which reminded me. Also a letter and two pounds from Nanna and Aunt. And your letter today. Well, I don't, to be quite honest, remember feeling down last letter, as you say. Maybe I was a bit hard on the newspapers!! Poor old Vod missed out on his New York trip. His friends are flying down to the Virgin Isles instead. This is a U.S. island down in the West Indies. However he's over it now and we have a fabulous scheme in hand. Ralph, an Australian guy got back with $4,800 clear after plumbing on the D.E.W. line which is our Distant Early Warning radar line against Russia!!! Just seven and one half months and all that sugar!!

He is off to New York for Easter, back to Detroit to pick up a new Chev, and then he and Vod to San Antonio, Texas. Here he continues on into Mexico and Vod to California to visit Buck and Meg Weiss. I enter the picture with a dashing trip down to meet Ralph in Mexico City (2,500 miles) and then we motor back after a week on the Mexican Pacific coast, meeting Vod at San Antonio, Texas and on to New Orleans, Washington etc. This was all resolved over a few coffees yesterday. Ralph is going anyway so doesn't want any help with the gas. Don't mention anything outside the family yet as no arrangements have been made. I am starting to push on the financial angle. It's certainly a good chance and I would be back in time to start my contract with the mineral exploration company. I got the job O.K. at $285 per month and finalize arrangements next month but am not giving too much thought to anything save the exams.

Spent three hours cutting up the fetal pig this afternoon. They are taken out from the slaughter works—much more interesting than the fish or frog as they are so like us. In fact the one I have is about the size of a new-born child. Admittedly after I have finished with him, he doesn't look much like anything. I ate pork tonight but had to keep washing my hands as I imagined I had formaldehyde on them. This is what we soak our specimens in over the days they are not in use. I will keep my hand in over the summer by slicing up a few grizzly bears.

You are right about my misspelling of library. Was tempted to blame it on North American laziness. There are lots of mis-spellings permitted here. I find I fight them so long and then give it up. One word I shall never use is "NITE" but that is more U.S. than here. Spring has arrived and the four-inch layer of ice is running away but still freezes up at night. I have shed my overshoes and am eagerly awaiting the exams- sure!

MONTREAL

(APRIL 10 1956)

I turn to my weekly epistle. It was quite a thrill to have the wedding invitation for Mick and Jeanette. I keep picking it up and reading the script. Both Vod and I are very impressed but as I said to him:" When you marry a Howse, everything has got to be tip-top, you know." I feel pretty disappointed at not being there.

I have just stoked myself with a bowl of Rice Crispies (Bubble in English), preparatory to a little study in bed. Last night I did five hours of physics and when I hit the pillow I felt as awake as 9.20 a.m. Actually the review is fairly well under way and lectures are tapering off – finishing off with the Zoology lectures on the hormones. They control a lot of the pace of the system also the sex characteristics like the deep voice of Ned and the soft musical twang of Mal. Finish up on cancer Wednesday and a short cut-up of the sheep's eye and we are through. Must take my dissection kit and see if I can make out with a brown grizzly bear during the summer.

Another quiet week. Sat. afternoon went up with David C. and we played squash and swam afterwards. He has 2$^{nd}$ year accountancy exam Wednesday so has the day off. We are meeting for a few sets mid-day tomorrow. Vod and I walked over to L'Oratoire de St. Joseph. It's nice out but as we have been doing all year, we find it good exercise, no matter how cold. One night we strolled out through the cemetery and it was so cold we had to swap hats at intervals. There were many mysterious lights burning on the graves, flickering and glowing in the snow. However the dead don't come out on cold nights.

One of the old girls arrived from Florida, all tanned and so exhausted from the New York train trip that I had to get her a double rye to fix her up. It's amazing how these old girls can spend thousands of dollars sitting around in the sun all year. She was so pleased to see me again and gave me such a greeting that she forgot to tip me for carting the bags up. How I have changed. When I first got here, I used to become very embarrassed if anyone proffered the 25 cents. Now I get sour if they don't, the typical dollar-scrounging North American. Anyway I'm very well and whilst I feel as fit as I have these past 22 years. I don't give much of a damn either way. Mexico is off –too much dough lost in wages.

Your letter this morning provided a welcome relief from my battles with the physics review. Have spent the holiday trying to get things in shape. As always, I have one hell of an amount to do – however I make my first bow on April 19 with English. It's about 11.30 p.m. now, having been doing some Maths, analytic geometry which is a cross between algebra and ordinary geometry. My Hong Kong mate came around and we went through a Zoology paper together. At the moment we are involved with a small piece of work on genetics. This is the study of how the characteristics of Ma and Pa are sent on to the child. It is really a most important subject and we will be doing a lot more on it later.

Spring has arrived. Besides the sunshine, it was welcomed by a wedding at the Themis. Yours Truly officiated as usual, doing the honours with the champagne. We always split a bottle ourselves after it's over but it's cheap stuff really and ruins any study. Was thinking of our big brother. Trust he will be less nervous than this guy was. God knows what they have to be nervous about. All around them are friends but no, they sweat, blush, stumble and stammer. I told the Boss that every wedding I saw at the Themis put me one year further from it. Always have a colossal feed during the festivities. All the delicacies are brought out. Had Vod around Sat. night to put the finishing touches to a pile of sandwiches. There is top co-operation between the Chef and myself. We speak French most of the time and it's very handy when I want to sling a bowl of soup or a meal to a "guest" downstairs.

Good to read that Ned came good with two sixes in cricket. Read in the New York Times that Australia nearly lost to the West Indies. I often think how nice it would be if they played cricket here instead of baseball. Vod and I had a game in the snow with a broom, a few boxes and slabs of ice for a ball. We used to spin it off the ice. It really warmed us up. There is a certain charm in cricket, maybe not when you are field all day and then get run out for 2, but somehow it has a dignity that the raucous baseball will never quite have.

Well, I got more news of the job today. The field manager sent me the list of gear I'd need. The biggest blow was the special Arctic sleeping bag $62.68.

However it does get cold up there although we are only going on the fringe of Labrador. My rucksack will be handy. More of this after the exams. Guns and liquor are forbidden so two evils are out of the way. The only things left are the bears, wild-cats and wolves. God knows what the mails will be like – you may lose track of me for four months. As you can see, I am dead keen. Vod is sorry he missed out now! There are no Eskimos down this far south –they are chiefly on the coast above Hudson and James Bay.

MONTREAL

(APRIL 16 1956)

Pleased to have all your news. Worked pretty well today but with the axe hanging over the head I guess it's about time. Feeling a bit hot –just had five cups of tea. Vod is well and comes around for a meal every Monday night. The club is closed so the girls leave the stack of food out for me. Have them trained – the Boss has decided that I have been so efficient lately that she wants me back for next winter. That is something. I feel that with one year under my belt I can make the adjustments O.K. It's like being in the army. You're all over the place during the first few months "but" soon you find a groove even if behind a tree out of sight.

The old girl I was joking about the tips came to me and asked if I smoked. Well, when you are a barman and people ask you that, it's a packet on the way. I give them to Arthur in the kitchen or sell them to the office. So I said "Yes." She passed over a Ronson lighter which now reposes on my desk. Elegant! I told the Boss (she wanted it!) that I'd have to keep it to flick the cigarette of anyone I took out.

Hope you enjoyed Summer of the 17th Doll. Vod says he has read it and I do remember something about the cane cutters. Look forward to your views on it. My theatre days collapsed on arriving in the New World. The atmosphere wasn't quite right. Had a lot of good times in London sitting on the stools in queues for the good seats at the cheap prices. Often feel I would like to get back into an apartment but then I can't have the lot.

Vod and I just having a battle over the box of biscuits. Have the big pie upstairs but the hands keep diving into the biscuit packet. Start with English on Thursday. Vod is handy with all his background knowledge of English literature but am on my own for the remaining four sciences. We've had a lot to read, beginning with Shakespeare's "Othello." David C. and I read it through Sunday with the dramatic voices. Played squash and swam Sat. afternoon. Met a young law student from Ethiopia. I had seen his Emperor in London and we had quite a yarn. My maps on the wall are very handy for these stray countries. I saw the hills of British Somaliland as we came into the Gulf of Aden on the S.S. "Otranto." It's is right next to Ethiopia.

Hope brother Michael doesn't' drop the ring and that all goes well. Will be thinking of him and her.

MONTREAL

(APRIL 24 1956)

A note that perhaps will make the wedding but I have my doubts. You will detect a certain air of urgency in my style for in three and one-half hours I begin my Chemistry. Have been going like a bomb at it –the first two subjects I feel quite O.K. about – English was a bit long and as in the Leaving Certificate, I didn't finish the last question. However I do think I wrote the best Maths, paper in my career. I have worked fairly frequently at the latter so if the remaining three go as these two, I'll go off in fine form for the summer. Either way it will be good to relax.

Just had your note and good to have all the news. Can't get over Maurie Mac being on town council but I expect he wants to control the taxi license issues. Bet old Russ Flaws is finished. I think, if Maurie can get on, it's time for me to come home and run for mayor. Had a letter card from Chicago from Ralph and another one from Texas – he said he wouldn't give me any details of the trip until after the exams as he knew how keen I was to go.

Yes, it's a bit of a joke my being in Monaco – a bigger one when I remember being caught short of a convenience and climbing behind the big stone fence into a very fine Riviera mansion grounds. Somehow, I feel that my sense of humour is developing along my father's lines. Vod is well and we are planning a small celebration of music, meal and conversation when I am free. I have been a recluse in much the style he was, when the law exams were about in Sydney. I finish the last exam at 5 p.m. Thurs. and begin work at 6 p.m .at a banquet for a bowling club out in the suburbs, Town of Mt. Royal. They wanted a slick barman but I guess it will be just pulling the tops off bottles. 500 cocktails would finish me. One of the girls is working for me but it took three staff changes to get the night off. So it does pay to get on well with one's fellow proletarians.

Guess you'd be having the 7<sup>th</sup> milk shake in the buffet car on your way to the wedding in Sydney. Do enjoy yourselves. My love to Cousin Diana. Is she still with the cosmetics dept? The most fairy-like mixture of male and female, with a skin like Helena Rubinstein. herself, was giving demonstrations in a city store this week. What they do here to squeeze a dollar. Must return to the complex compounds now.

## MONTREAL
## (MAY 5 1956)

A short note to wish you a very happy Mother's Day from your third son, the most remote of your scattered family. Will be thinking of you particularly on Sunday and know you will have a pleasant day. This makes the third time around –since I've started McGill, time just seems to slide by and I'm at something all the time.

. Will write my usual on Monday with general news. Don't worry, Mum, about the bush mail. There's always some way of getting a letter through.

## MONTREAL
## (MAY 12)

Have just spent a few hours on the stack of sports mags and Pix's which arrived this morning. I was really very pleased to get them. Have been reading on the rugby tests, the jockey premiership, in fact all the sporting news I've missed for so long. If you could bung one in the mail each month I'd be happy.

Good to know the wedding went off O.K Have reports from Ned and Caroline but your letter, Ma, is astray this week .Did Mick get my telegram? I sent it the Australia Hotel, 2 days in advance c/o the Starlight Room. Today I got the bill with April 27 instead of April 26, so am hoping that Canadian bungling has not prevented my wishes making the wedding. Am taking a day off – got up at 11 a.m. so am now about to go to the book shop to buy some texts for next Sept. Think I may try and honour in Zoology which would mean three Zoo. courses, 1 Psychology and one organic chemistry for this term

Had the big walk to the Red Indian Reservation on Sunday. We got burnt in the face as the sun was warm. I stacked a pile of sandwiches which were left over from a social afternoon-tea at the club and we ate them on the banks of the St.Lawrence.

Not very impressed with the river scenery around Montreal. Nothing compared to Sydney Harbour or even the charm of the Murrumbidgee.

The Indians live in their own suburb of wooden bungalow houses. It all looks pretty much like a small country town in the outback. Some of the houses were very nice and the wig-wam reposed in the backyard ready for the tourists. There were far too many Coca-Cola signs. Really, this company has done its best to destroy the landscape with its odious advertising. Some of the shops just seemed to be built with "Buvez le coke" or "Drink Coke." Came back to Bain's for the evening meal. We finished off the wood-sawing and had the table tennis etc. Mr B. was ill so I carved. I went off for a nap afterwards saying that I was relieving him in the full sense.

Monday I went cleaning again at the new flat. Same lady as last time. I did everything but she's O.K. A bit tight on the dough, I thought as she worked out my time to the minute. The phone rang and she was off to the Ritz. When I arrived, she had the look of the average housewife. However after the phone call, she disappeared for an hour and emerged looking the essence of the social set. I have never seen such a complete change, literally another person but typical.

MONTREAL

(MAY 14 1956)

Your letter this morning just as I was taking a bath so I relaxed and enjoyed all the news of the wedding, Mick and Jeanette and your doings in Sydney. Feel I've certainly missed a great event but hope to be there at least for Ned's and Mal's. It must have been a wonderful day. Had 130 guests to a wedding here Saturday. As usual, I performed well serving the punch, coffee and champagne. Rather amusing to think of your third son and brother in the white coat and old blue suit trousers whilst 10,000 miles down under his brother starred. You'll be amused too that I polished my black shoes out of deference to M and J's big day.

Monday night went to a French theatre to see a German movie "La fin d'Hitler." It was an authentic study of the last few days of Adolf and very good. Otherwise it's been a quiet week. I go down to the library or shop around for the trip north, buy a paper and return to the bar. Friday had a late meal at Vod's and I was so full that I suggested a walk to the mountain. We did the quick stroll up and down in our true country style. Sunday was a very interesting day – I did the bar from

12-2 p.m. and then we walked down to the docks. One of the crew took us over the "Empress of Scotland," mostly first class. Once you have made the boat trip, it's quite a thrill to walk around reminiscing of old days aboard the "Otranto" and "Italia." Am looking forward to initiating you into all this in your trip to the U.K.

Went up to the Bonsecours Sailors Church. There are many monuments to the old French rule. Don't forget that the French were here for 150 years before the British took over so that the culture is firmly established. I had to ask for direction in French—one old guy didn't understand me, much to my annoyance and Vod's enjoyment. Chinatown is a narrow street full of chattering Chinese, cafes and what look like opium dens. When you step into it, it's just like a street scene from Hong Kong or Shanghai -- the shops with Chinese lettering and the old men on the door-steps. From here we walked up to St. Lawrence Boulevard where there are various shopping centres for Polish, German and largest of all, the Jews. Walked about the Jewish residential area –there are a lot here.

Just had a call about a good job for two and one-half weeks so off I go –at McGill so here's hoping. Am fit and well.


MONTREAL

(VICTORIA DAY, MAY 21 1956)

A problem as to who follows Mum in the order of greeting seems to have arisen within the wide-scattered brotherhood. Where to insert the married couple? Got your letter before we left Sat. afternoon. One of the girls did the bar for me as we had a meal at Bain's before a pleasant drive up with all the family except Grandmother who had gone off to Ottawa. The lake is about 50 miles from Montreal but as I haven't been out of the city since Boston, it really is fine. The water is too cold even for the two hearty Australians but we have kept fit by canoeing, rowing, and walking plus the wood chopping. Arrived around 10 p.m. and went for a walk. All joking about the stars and losing the way and of course we took a wrong turn. This meant a few extra miles until we got back on the right road.

Sunday we canoed the lake's circumference which is some seven miles and in the afternoon rowed Mrs. Bain down to a small store for provisions. We don't seem to have ceased eating at all. Took in some sun whilst I was displaying my "67" form with the axe, as I was in shorts and bare feet. I was as cautious as I used to be with the early morning fire at home.

Today rose at 10.30 and the usual coffee, bacon and eggs etc. Vod and I set off in the canoe and it began to sink. Luckily Joe and Art, two guys I know from McGill, came along in their row boat and prevented us from getting completely soaked in the ice-cold water. Joe, who I roomed with at the fraternity house on arrival has just returned from 7 months in Europe. Studied in Paris on the $2,000 scholarship and had a wonderful trip. Detests the French but reckons the British are great – this is quite a change from the Joe who left last year. Art takes a few courses with me—he is in Arts III next term. We visited them in the boat at their home on the lake just down from the Bains. Art's dad is a doctor in town and they have the big invitations etc. He is a size with hands at least equal in grandeur to mine.

Tuesday dashed down to McGill and clinched a two week job sorting out the gowns and hoods for graduation. Working with a cousin of the West Indian cricket captain W.G. Goddard. He's in commerce and about as keen on work as I am. Actually I have got most of it done so this week should be soft and I will go up to Quebec City either at the weekend or Monday next. Know a recently-married lawyer who can put me up. Spent a fair bit of time around the notice board at McGill which helps to fill in the day – the results are posted as they come out. Made 75 in Maths but that is all so far. Vod sends his regards. He had the in-grown toenail removed by operation but manages to waltz about O.K.

QUEBEC CITY

(MAY 28 1956)

Writing from a pleasant double room (single occupancy!) in the old capital of New France. Caught the Canadien Pacifique from Montreal at 9.15 and in here at 1.15 p.m. Really, the first impression of the city is fantastic. Here is a city of almost 200,000 which seems to have won the battle against time and Americanization. The atmosphere is simply French. After the bustle and crowds of Montreal's cosmopolitan setting, I feel as though I am in a foreign land and for some peculiar reason, I have been carrying my passport in my pocket.

Just across the square is the enormous Chateau Frontenac, the leading hotel in the country and owned by the Canadian Pacific Railway, always just C.P.R. It has numerous turrets and spires, covered with green roofing and dominating the grand view of the St. Lawrence River which appears more as a bay with its ocean liners, tugs, ferries and timber ships. I will post off some cards so that you may have some idea of the scene from the wooden promenade in front of the Chateau. Everyone strolls along it – the only comparison (and lesser at that) I can make is to the confluence of the Mosle and Rhine rivers in Coblentz, Germany. Somehow this local scene seems mightier in its sweeping view, a background of the Laurentian Mountains, the oldest in North America, the steep cliffs and dock areas spread below, and the feeling that the French explorers Champlain, Frontenac and Cartier found these lands over 350 years ago. There are many monuments to the French, particularly Montcalm. One obelisk memorial is to both Wolfe and Montcalm although, despite his victory, the former hasn't fared too well.

The city is of such genuine historic quality, much more so than Boston. Walked past the house in which was signed the capitulation of the French to ourselves in 1759. Tomorrow I will look over the battlefields upon which Wolfe won the day. These are the Plains of Abraham and lead from the top of the hill down to the cliffs up which the British staggered. Went into the Ursuline Convent, one of the oldest schools for girls, founded in 1639. The nuns were chanting beautifully. Quebec has always been tolerant of other beliefs and the English Church of England is full of solid mahogany pews and most startling of all, a Royal Box in which none but those mentioned may sit.

The University is named after a Monsignor Laval, first Bishop of Canada. Next to it is a Jesuit school with tall, ancient buildings surrounding a playground. It could so easily have been Europe. In the Cathedrale, a little girl came and asked for a "sou," a cent. I gave her a nickel and she ran up to the altar rail and thanked Our Lady, forgetting her "merci" to me. Outside in what used to be the market square was a monument to Louis XIV, King of France at this early stage.


ROBERVAL P.Q.

(MAY 31 1956)

Settled in fine at Le Chateau Roberval. Made it here about 8 a.m. yesterday. It was a bit like the army getting settled in but managed a large single room with an enormous bed. I make a point of mentioning large beds because at the Themis my bed is very narrow and it's some luxury to find myself in the double bed, in a room with two dressing tables and a set of oak drawers. Have met four of the other guys who will be in the eight-man team looking after the interests of U.S.

Steel in area 16-D. This area is split up into sections and teams go in to map, search for iron ore and take samples. Right now six of us have taken over the complete house-annex of the Chateau which is just across the street from the dining room.

Met Mr Jim Steel, the boss from Minnesota, and he told me that latest reports indicated that the ice break-up on the more northern lakes was late this year, that we'll be here at least one week. With the life we're leading at the moment, I tried to look disappointed. It's pretty much the same as shipboard routine. I am going to break the ice (not literally) and take a swim in the lake if it gets much warmer.

There is little English spoken and I am very pleased now that I have been picking up French since arrival. Last night we went out and it does make a very great difference if you can bat on in French. People take to you so much more easily. One of our group is from France and Pierre wanted to know where I had learnt as my accent was O.K.!!! This pleased me quite a bit. He's the biggest Frenchman I have ever seen, about an inch taller than myself and powerfully built. More descriptions of the guys as we form into groups. I do know that a dentistry student from Saskatchewan (Mal, the map please—pronounced Sas-kat-chewan, one of the Prairie provinces in the West) is in my gang. My $70 Arctic sleeping bag arrived. It really is a beauty and they say you need it for the nights are cold.

This invasion of Roberval is an annual event by the Cartier Mining Co. There are 45 of us, roaming the town like the invading army. Everyone is dressed for the bush. I bought the enormous boots but not in them yet. My address is c/o Cartier Mining Co., Roberval P.Q. and I'll let you know if it changes as we'll be moving from site to site. Thanks for the chess set and newspaper colour sections.

ROBERVAL P.Q.

(JUNE 7 1956)

Well, still here at the Chateau. Am just about accepted as the local. The ice remains up north although the weather is beautiful here on Lac Roberval. Looking out my window the water seems to have that Mediterranean blue about it. The lake measures 22 miles across and 150 miles of roadwork is required to circumnavigate it. Excuse the scrawl but the boys have taken over the writing room with their bridge. It's very popular in North America. I haven't got past poker yet but plan on keeping it just that. If you're part of a bridge quartet, you can write off most of your time. Besides I prefer chess.

Today Vic (he's from Latvia, had to leave most of the family there) and I played tennis with two of the local mademoiselles. There are more tennis courts in this place than there are in Montreal, I think. Spent the morning talking to one of the local priests down on the "beach" in front of the hotel. What he couldn't say in English, I could say in French so we got along fine. Feel so fit in the bush again. We do the great walks, sometimes after supper (i.e. tea at night). Sunday we strolled 12 miles, six to a little village and had a chocolate, then six back to base. They had an enormous T.V. set in this little café. The place was smaller than Wallendbeen. In Roberval, you just can't help noticing how clean and fresh everything is –most of the houses are painted white, and despite enormous families (12 and 16 are really commonplace), everyone seems well-dressed and healthy. Little corner grocery stores spring up like mushrooms, dotted throughout the town. They're having (I nearly wrote "we're") a clean-up week and the posters admonish all to get busy with the brush, broom and gardening implements. Sunday afternoon, played baseball. Admittedly you bat more often than in cricket but I really can't see what the Sydney "bodgie" boys go wild about. It's O.K. to chatter away at the batsman which makes it a bit raucous. I didn't get any home runs but got off the diamond each time. Bruised a finger during the game. Our medical officers, two final year med. students, have been gingerly pronouncing "no bones broken" after nervous prodding and anxious consultations. Meanwhile I am applying the old Howse natural cure. Don't expect to make the company team for the big game against the local champs tomorrow night.

Ran out to the Indian Reservation the other afternoon, four and one-half miles so am seeing quite a bit of the countryside: attractive with the pine trees, small farms and gentle hills, even the smell of cows was nice. Latest guess, we leave at the end of the week.


ROBERVAL P.Q.

(JUNE 17 1956)

Have an idea that we will be on the move at a moment's notice. There are other companies in town and the great secrets are being withheld from the rank-and-file. This is the latest thaw ever experienced and the "wheels" are looking pretty sad. The land has been explored but our job is to get in and stake the claims before the other guys jump us. These parasites sit around trying to pump information so that they can hop a plane and beat the company men who have completed the exploration.

The weather is so beautiful and I have been enjoying myself so much here that I just don't want to leave and begin the rigors of life in the woods. The rush of McGill, the bar and the study seem a long way off as I doze on the lake front and call for a gin Collins every 15 minutes. I usually take the army hat, sun glasses and a book down to the water after we toss the ball about after breakfast. Yesterday followed the railway line down to the shore for three miles to a sandy beach we had discovered on one of our canoe trips. At the Indian Reservation, the old hunter who had given us a lift out (he insisted we could walk back and wanted the company) showed us the full-blooded Indians who live in government houses. One old guy has his tent – refused the house! There is a restaurant which is the center of reserve life, a large juke box and T.V. sets so the old savage isn't really so backward. He took us home – the fridge was stocked with game and in his garage he had two caged lynx. They are a wild cat, about the size of a medium dog. They growl like a leopard and run about in the bush. He said they usually won't attack, no need to worry. Next day he lent us two canoes for nothing and we paddled around the lake. They are the Indian style and go well once you learn the stroke.

Yesterday morning had the walk but a cool wind prevented swimming. Received a stack of current affairs magazines from Kiwi. He has been moved to Toronto with the C.N.R. Vod is well but Montreal is getting sticky. I'll never forget how muggy it got last summer there in the bank. Last night met my "girl friend" – she collected me in the family car, a '56 Packard, which had the guys on the hotel stairs "doing back-flips," as they say here. Her name – Raymonde LeClerc. Went for a drive to St. Felicien, a very pretty town 18 miles away on a beautiful river site. I get on well with the family. Ma and Pa are "tres gentile." It must be like having the Balt home with my accent. No one speaks English. Will send you some photos of a wiener roast (hot dog) party we had on the beach. Lit a great fire from driftwood and had the dogs with marshmallows in the flames. Six of us – the giant Frenchman and the Latvian – I call him the "mad Balt," myself and three ladies.

BLOUGH LAKE P.Q.

(JUNE 20 1956)

The dreaded march orders came Tuesday and by 9.a.m. next day your handsome son and brother was on a Catalina. We flew down low over our hometown of three weeks and out over the lake. Trip up was two and one-half hours, some 300 miles, the country one mass of lakes and rivers, all so neatly defined. This is due to glacial movements quite a few years back. There weren't any signs of civilization, just miles and miles of northern Quebec. The "Canso," as they call the Catalina here, didn't budge all trip and when we came down low over the pine forests to make the most perfect of landings on the long stretch of water, it was hard to imagine that I was working for a living. The splash curled up against my window and we anchored out from the wharf as there was another plane being unloaded. There were nine passengers so we climbed out on the wings and body to catch the sun. It was pleasant taking in the new surroundings, drifting around like a scene from "The Cruel Sea" film. We taxied into the wharf, cut the motors and out on to the log jetty.

The camp consists of four log cabins, six tents and a military-type lavatory –the latter sits on the hill overlooking the camp and is by far the most precarious undertaking I've taken on this summer. On to more pleasant subjects –the camp area has been cleared of trees and the latter have been used to build the cook-house, radio hut and two storehouses. It's really very neatly carved from the wilderness. Things are done in the American way – we already have the power plant which runs the radio hut and, of all things, two deep freezes. The latter allows us good meat – food is lavish. Tonight I had tomato soup, steak, peas, mashed potatoes, peaches, cake and tea. It's put on the army-style mess tables in tremendous quanti-ties ---the cooks are two affable Frenchmen.

I'm writing this from the radio hut in the midst of a static of pilot reports. "Hullo Blough Lake, can you give me cloud ceiling on Reid Lake, over." They have good old electric light too. Have been fairly busy unloading aircraft most of the day. Great loads are pouring in due to the late start. Have taken off the component parts of a bulldozer—one part weighed 1,000 lbs and we nearly dropped it into the lake as we took it out from the Canso's cargo bay. Spent today, too setting up 50-feet high aluminum radio masts, getting them up by wire cables etc. Weather has been cool – 40 to 45 degrees and I am clad in old golf jacket, army sweater and shirt plus giant boots. There are three helicopters here – the company spends $21,000 per month just to rent them and three pilots. One of the flyers is a Kiwi so had quite a yarn. My French mate couldn't understand his slang and accent!! I was right at home. Our lake is in the middle of pine, hills in the background still have snow on tops.

BLOUGH LAKE P.Q.

(JULY 2 1956)

Rain beating down on the tent as I adjust the hand from shovel to pen. The showers have been fairly regular since arrival but unfortunately today they have lacked length with a result that we have sheltered on the job instead of retiring to the tent and having to be dragged out an hour after the sun has returned. No mail in or out for almost a week –you can expect a few irregularities in the service but not in the writer.

Finished ferrying three complete pre-fabs with my two canoes. Had the Frenchmen working for, or more truthfully, with me. They don't speak English so once again the "fluent command" is useful. Spent two days erecting same – I was straddling the girders with ease. I have never been fond of heights but battled on, convincing myself I should take to flying next year at the McGill Squadron. The third house has been delayed due to missing parts. Just sent a few extras up to one of our northern sites. The pilot sat on a wall panel and it just broke under the strain of his bulk. The two French guys looked horrified but the plane has gone away and I trust there will be no repercussions.

Our chief geologist, Tom Moore, is a southerner from Alabama. He went to McGill. He said he had to give up his southern accent as it was always the big joke in the R.C.A.F. during the war.

This morning I was up at Iron Hill which is one big outcrop of hematite ore. It is black and has sand crystals throughout. One of the boys dynamites it (very safe – I make sure I'm well out of range) and alors, we go in, roll it down the hill and stack it on a tray to be pulled in by a small tractor. My associations with the iron and steel industry are getting deeper –mining, rolling it along in the slag trains and flirting with that molten iron under the Scunthorpe blast furnaces. There are several PhD geologists about. It's been quite interesting gaining small background knowledge of a subject in which I had a fair interest.

Have been taking a few photos and will send them on – it was really beautiful chopping down long fir and spruce trees in the bush this morning. Off the spruce bark you can collect a reasonable chewing gum to keep the mouth moist although that is hardly necessary with the multitude of streams and the daily rainfall. This afternoon Frank and I have been engaged in building the toilet "pit" – 12 ft long, 3 ft wide and 8 ft deep, scheduled so that God help anyone who falls off the seat. The moss that covers the ground is almost a foot thick and the rest so far (i.e. the 18 inches we've completed) has been sandy clay. Frank has just landed in with a packet of raisins. We take it in turns in raiding the cook's storehouse for the added amenities of life. Am fit and well, thriving in the rugged north but miss the newspapers and records. The Frenchmen have a radio but turn it off if anyone but cowboys sing.

LAC JEANNINE P.Q.
(JULY 4 1956)

Settled down once again. Came over in a Norseman from Blough Lake. This is quite a powerful single-engine, top wing monoplane and we skipped off one lake, over the bush for six miles and down to a perfect landing. Had to pitch the tent. The French-Canadian "bushmen" gave us a hand, thank God, as I am hopeless at any constructive bush work. Francois, the chap from France is sharing a 10 ft by 9 ft canvas home for the next little while. It's pretty small as he is bigger than I. Have the stretchers, enormous sleeping bag – I made a bookcase and he a small writing desk – spent an hour forging a stool. Have it topped with a canvas ore sample bag and heavily reinforced at the legs. Result is that whilst the rest of the gang is on their backs, we are happily at the desk. The lamps are very good—the latest Coleman. Also scrounged a torch so that I can read in bed.

It's raining again today but have put in a good afternoon's work. Had two canoes tied together with a 5 H.P. motor and me as driver. It looked a Fijian or Papuan outrigger but we carted parts of pre-fabricated houses up and down the lake sites and didn't sink. Bruce, the Torontonian who is at mining school in Ontario during the winter, came out in the boat and we unloaded a Catalina full of supplies for a survey party. Took five boatloads of supplies to shore. The lake is buzzing with activity. Cartier men number about 25, half of them bushmen. They are good guys, really know the bush. Saw one flee up a tree last night as though he was escaping from a wolf pack—just putting up an aerial for his radio. It's a joke here to say "wireless" instead of "radio." No one knows too much about "torches", they are always "flashlights." The big drilling team from Boyles Brothers is here in force. There are bulldozers crashing out what looks like a new parade ground, outside the tent. The lake is 10 yards away so no excuse for not washing. The water is very cold. Managed a hot bath over at Blough after feeding wood into a boiler all one rainy day. Had returned from a paddling venture to find the mob had used most of the hot water. Even at the Chateau Roberval there seemed to be an aversion to hot baths so I was "pretty mad," that means "very crooked" or, better still in English, "rather annoyed."

Very glad to have your letter but amazed to think you are placing Saskatchewan in Québec. Ma, your son is in Eastern Canada, in French-speaking Quebec whilst Saskatchewan is just 1,200 miles to the West. It is a prairie province, grows lots of wheat. When the tourist map arrives, you will see the magnitude of Quebec. Follow the Saguenay River west from the St. Lawrence and you'll find Lac St. Jean. Alors, 300 miles north, north-east is where your handsome son writes, under canvas which is approaching saturation point, under constant rain. That was like asking someone who had gone to Melbourne "how did you enjoy Queensland?" Bonsoir, maintenant, as you can imagine mail day is quite an event here.

BLOUGH LAKE P.Q.

(JULY 1956)

Pleased to have your letter along with Mal's. The mail service at this end is excellent but can tell you the reason why mine was late last week. When I returned to Blough Lake, I found one of my letters to you on the incoming mail. Someone said I had a letter and that it was – the one I had posted days before from Jeanine Lake! Another delay could be at Sept Isles. It is often fogged-in along the Gulf of the St. Lawrence and only the airway is in touch with the rest of Quebec, no road, no rails.

There has been little activity on my part for the past few days. Rain and a low cloud ceiling have kept us free from planes and one of our Beavers has engine trouble. The temperature didn't go above 60 degrees yesterday. It averages between 60 and 70 degrees and our best day was only 74 degrees. Had quite a laugh at the picture in the Sydney Morning Herald of the Garden Island Dock workers having to withstand "the bitter cold of 44.5 degrees." I wear T-shirt, shorts and army sweater, discarding the latter when the sun comes out. They call this weather "Labrador sunshine," the slight drizzle.

Last night one of the mechanics showed movies on an 8mm colour reel that cost $4.25. It would be quite interesting to know if there was a set anywhere about Coota that you could borrow as there are numerous movie cameras around and the country up here does make a pleasant scene.

Flew over to Manicouagan Lake on Tuesday to deliver the supplies to the troops. It's a fair size and should be on your map. The boys were out in the canoe and had caught some seven pound Northern Pike to supplement the steak and ice cream we flew in. Really these Americans are the limit – no wonder that everyone shudders at the word "trade union." Thank God I wasn't asked to navigate—the country from the air is a great, lonely expanse of forests and lakes, joined up by streams and the plain, split by a range of hills.

Quite at home here. The Kiwi helicopter pilot is joking with someone in the background

And the sound could be coming from the bar of the Coota Hotel. There's a joke here that we can only talk to one another. We nearly had a casualty the other day. Helicopter propellers rotate about 10 feet above the ground. A Boyles Brothers drilling crew was loading the pontoons with ten-foot drill rods and thinking that the chopper had flown off, one of the crew stood up with the rod. Despite the 10 feet clearance, you always seem to stoop way down when those blades are whirling overhead. Well, the rod caught in the blade and by a miracle didn't knock him to the happy hunting grounds. Messed him up a little—they flew him down here and hope to get him to hospital down in Roberval. He's a great hulk with a black beard. And walks around like a brown bear that has caught its paw in a trap and has broken loose. We don't load helicopters here, just send to sites for transporting the geologists about the bush. Did about $10,000 worth of damage.

Went off wood chopping with old Francois, the bushman one afternoon this week. Took the canoe and on the side of the lake, knocked down a dozen big spruces. He was falling them just where they could be easily rolled into the lake. It is the way you cut that determines where the tree will fall. By setting down smaller logs, a man by himself can use them as rollers for much bigger trees. He told me that when he was cutting wood for the paper companies, the men always worked alone, taking strips up the forests, A cord of wood is 8 ft long by 4 ft.

high and 4 ft wide. For this you earn $6. A good man can do two cords per day. Francois tied the logs together, flat on the water and we dragged them back with the outboard motor. We have a motor hand saw which slices the wood up with a minimum of effort.

Was interested in Helen's travels. I remember seeing that same dress on Lambrettas chugging over the Swiss Alps. I always remember coming down into Italy and the twenty "S" bends in a row. I was with a Tasmanian architect in a Morris Minor.

No, there's nothing strange about my doing more Maths. These pre-medical years are designed to give a liberal background. One can specialize but I prefer to battle along, getting a little background so that if and when I begin to study medicine, I will know where I am in relation to the anatomy, the pathology, medical history etc. Personally I expect more from these early years than later on -- against the background of materialism, the cultural background cannot be taken for granted as it is in England and to a lesser extent in Australia. With the majority of students relatively unrestricted as to social and economic position, there are all types at the North American universities – the guy besides me is a graduate but can just write his name (i.e. American). Thus students for professions are required to have had at least three and more often four years university education before beginning their course. I may even take another course in Maths this session—so far it is the only subject I have made a decent mark in!!!

Time is racing. Working on my Physics so should get through this time. Have the radio shack to myself each night. The Duluth guy has donated his radio – the reception is terrific – and we have New York as clear as a bell and tune into the Canadian news. Find their reports on Suez more satisfying than the American news flashes.

*Arc de Triomphe - Marseilles, France*

*'Irish church I went to outside of Killarney' - June '54*

*Heliport, Blough Lake (QC)*

*Early Bush Camp*

*'Fastest ship afloat for Atlantic Crossings - just beat the Queen. We saw them both leave within an hour' USS United States - Southampton June '54*

*Queen Mary Southampton June '54*

*'Familiar Scene in Ireland '54'. 'an Irish Ford'*

*'Scottish Castle - Lived in by Squire! May' 54'*

*'Unique photo, never before attempted of a guard outside the palace!'*

*'memorial to Danish merchant shipping in Kobenhavn - Don. July '54'*

*'Rex Sherlock (NZ) and his helicopter. Blough Lake P.Q Sept 1956'*

*'Many happy days - Don'*

*'Another Victory to the runner-up in the cockfighting - Feb '54 '*

*'Blough Lake from the helicopter'*

*'Roberval base for seaplanes. Stinson in forewater'*

*'Blough Lake 1956'*

*John Howse on left*

*Floatplane (PQ)*

*Bearded John Howse on left*

*'Queens Gardens Bayswater. Feb '54 '*

*'St. Paul's - all about was flattened'*

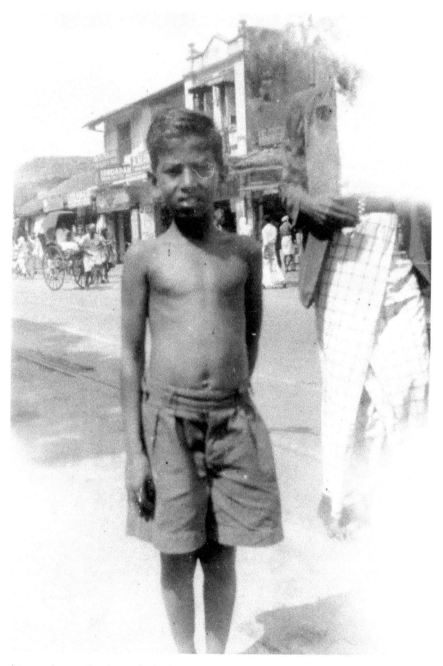

*'Beggar boy, Colombo 22/1/54' Additional note: I gave him a 1/2 and he refused it but followed us about for and hour '*

*'Street scene by your candid photographer - Marseilles France 5/2/54'*

*'Great Bitter lake, Suez Canal - Crowd enjoying sun'*
*Additional note : "the crowd is unusual"*

*'Changing of the Guard'*

*'Youth Hostel Stockholm, Sweden, STF af Chapman Aug '54'*

*'Youth Hostel, Earls Court, London'*

*'A Roman hot bath at Bath, England - June '54 '*

*'Rod, Me, Don - Petticoat Lane London '54'*

*Standing in back row --left to right) : Tony Howse (brother), John Howse (author) with Caroline (sister) in front of him between rows, Michael Howse (brother), Jeanette Howse (wife of MH) and Aunt Doris Foley.*
*Seated: (left to right :Mary Howse (mother of JH and other 2 Howse brothers and sister present); John Pigram (School friend of JH), Great Aunt Adeline Murphy, and Grandmother (Nanna) Mary Foley.*

BLOUGH LAKE P.Q.
(JULY 1956) –

Really a gorgeous day. Have just been swimming and reading all morning but the paradise has been disturbed by the news that we will have two tons of food to unload on a Canso, due in 30 minutes. Pleased to have your letter yesterday. No, I've never read "Gone with the Wind" but will get around to it some day. Will be looking forward to the magazines. Don sent me a pile of papers which arrived last week so am keeping up to date. And the High Commissioner at Ottawa sends me the news sheets each week. I'll always remember the patient wait for Mick to finish the Sydney Morning Herald which he then sat on until he had finished the Coota paper each evening.

Did I tell you that Patricia Chapman is coming to Canada? Got a letter the other day and am going to send her the information on rents etc. Now don't get "blood jealous: Ned. I'll see that she gets home to you O.K. " Have been on the lookout for a note from Tony. You might drop a hint next time you write him.

Life is fine here. I think that for the student who has to earn dough, this job is one of the more agreeable. There are jobs where you can get a bit of experience i.e. psychiatric attendants, lab assistants but they don't pay as much and there is board to pay out. Two of our geologists, both university professors from Missouri, came back here by Beaver this morning. Makes the background more useful when geology is being discussed. Two of their assistants arrived also – both ex-professional hockey players who have free board and no fees down at the Michigan Technical College. Pity I didn't shine a little more at the athletics but thank God McGill doesn't go in for it. They are studying geology and are nice guys.

Went off by myself to climb some rocks in the nearby hills last night after supper about 6 p.m. Took my geologist's wrist hammer and walked and climbed for a few miles. The bush is terrifically dense and of course I lost myself very easily. Had to get up on top of the highest hill and there was the camp about where I was heading but once inside the bush, you just can't see the sky at times. I miss the bush work we were doing over at Jeanine Lake so occasionally go off for a stroll. The night before I canoed around the lake. It is so attractive and quiet. The nearest road ends some 140 miles away. There has really been an amazing airlift to get us all here with the supplies.

Listened in to High Mass with Charlie the cook this morning. It came from Rimouski, which Caroline will show you on the map. I came through it on my way down from Halifax. Sent off a few Maclean's weeklies last week. Let me know if there is any magazine you don't see too often. There are innumerable Sat. Evening Posts, Colliers, Life, Time etc flown in by the company.

Squirrels have invaded the storehouse and are doing more damage than myself amongst the biscuits and walnuts. One of the boys has already shot six. Seems cruel perhaps to you but Canadians say the same about killing kangaroos. Have built a target range and with a .22 do the competitions. Came last this morning despite my long army service but one of our pilots is bringing in some supplies so will get some practice when they arrive.

The girl in the photo comes from Haiti, an independent country down in the Caribbean Sea near the West Indies. It was a French colony years ago but they speak a Creole which is a mixture of Spanish, French and English. We spoke French. She's a nurse at Roberval, studying there and on a tour of sanatoriums. Met her at Roberval. Naturally I didn't say anything about the White Australia Policy.

## BLOUGH LAKE P.Q.
### (JULY 1956)

There hasn't been a plane in for three days due to the shocking weather. Sorted through an enormous stack of mail today and very pleased to have your news, more from Mal. Your letter was as compact as always and such news. I suppose Frank Walsh will have a Yank accent when he gets home from San Francisco. Wasn't it the boxer Tommy Burns who spent a few weeks in the States and changed his accent overnight? Believe it or not, our accent is one big international joke. I get a bit tired of people as they exaggerate it so much. Make us sound as if we all came from Bourke. A law student and a graduate of Oxford asked me about it one night last term. I thought he was having a shot along the usual "descendants of convicts" line and answered: "No, we only speak like that when pie-eating Englishmen are around." Admittedly not a very cultured remark but fairly effective.

Gave me quite a laugh to read of Nick and Rod Holman growing up. I do recall them both and the looks of horror from Rod and cheerful terror from Nick when I used to appear in the cloak from behind the hedge. I do that occasionally still to Rose who does the laundry at the Themis. I appear behind her in the coat and hat. She has to sit down for a minute after the vision. Wrote Miss Browning a long letter this week. She is on holidays so I told her I hoped the goodwill would not have disappeared totally before my return.

When the Big Six arrived it was the typical pageant of the wealthy Americans. The directors of U.S. Steel are about as high as you can go in the business world so everything was laid on. Even the students were racing madly about putting down planks of wood for them to walk over 18 inches of water. One guy, the clerk who I help occasionally, is a permanent staff man. The visitors spent their time fishing and hardly glanced at the camp. When they brought their four fish in, Gerry asked me to carry them up to the veranda for everyone to admire. I told him that it would be better for him to do it as it might mean promotion later on. He caught on fast but I was talking from four years of hustling in the Bank of New South Wales. I remember very plainly setting off for Young with the new shirt and tie from Mick. That was over six years back but squatting on a stool in the radio shack 500 miles north of Montreal in the Canadian bush makes it seem longer.

Take to the air as often as I can, flying around delivering supplies and saying hullo to the mob I met in Roberval. Some sites are just two tents and a canoe. Get over to Jeanine from time to time and I'll be back there soon as they have a ton of work to get through. It's a blow as I have just fixed up everything here. Also, it will be hard work but can adjust to that again. I'm 191 lbs now (i.e. 13 stone 9 lbs). Whilst in Roberval I weighed in at 181 lbs. Must thrive on wet days and no work.

Made a basin of ice cream tonight and am checking it every 30 minutes but it looks as if it will need the night to freeze. Put a tin of peaches aside too – thought everyone would be up but they seem keen on a diet of work and sleep around here. Barrie, the medical student had another patient today -- a third year med. student cut himself with an axe at another camp and couldn't stop it bleeding. Went right to the bone, chipping it and piercing the covering so that Barrie didn't like to handle it other than cleaning the gash. Flying him out tomorrow. He has been jumpy lately as his fiancée wrote asking him that their September wedding be put back indefinitely.

LAC JEANNINE P.Q.

(JULY 12 1956)

The Coleman lamp burns brightly in the pre-fab which is now our bunk-house. Eight bodies recline on stretchers reading a variety if literature beginning at a textbook on geology and ending at one of the lurid periodicals which seem to find their way into any decent mining camp. I've found that my ideas on what students read and discussed to be a little idealistic. Next to me (I am in the corner) snores Francois from France, then Vic the Balt dozing after 10 miles of staking claims. Bruce from Toronto failed previously at McGill now studies at a mining school and at present pores over the textbook. My foreman, Vern, from Sault St. Marie, Ontario – a city at the junction of the Great Lakes of Superior and Huron; Hal is the first year dentistry man and is doing surveying up here. He's from Saskatoon, Sask., your favorite province, Mum. Jack is the chief surveyor. He's an Englishman and goes to Michigan Technical College in the States. Finally Svanti from Finland who is at M.I.T. in Boston. He went through to M.Sc. at McGill and is now doing his doctorate. Add to this the groups of pure blooded Indians and the French-Canadians bush men (les bucherons), the Yanks who fly in and out, and we have quite a mixture.

Geology is in the air. I have the Penguin Dictionary and often throw in the odd term just for the hell of it. Very happy about the cricket Test result. Am getting my weekly news from the Australian Commissioner. Also Wimbledon and the golf. Ned looks the best international prospect in the Howse family unless I stage my contemplated comeback with some success. Am planning on playing football this Fall at McGill.

Last few days have been spent in dragging out samples of hematite which contains the iron. Have to pack it in bags and load the bigger chunks on tractor-drawn sleighs. It's half a mile of bush track and a tortuous ride as it is swampy. The mud is calf-deep and came up over my high boots when I got stuck in it this morning. The bush would be a paradise but is cursed by mosquitoes and black flies which don't allow the slaves any peace to relax on the job. My beard affords some protection but it isn't very substantial at this stage. Read "The Man in the Grey Flannel Suit" between lunch and ce soir – will send it on when the gang is through it as it has caused some excitement amongst the book clubs out here.

The Catalina brought the mail in as we struggled back through the mud of our new road. It was almost knee-deep and in places it was quite an effort to drag the left foot after the right. This isn't the memoirs of a New Guinea veteran—just a trencherman whose rifle was a shovel and whose Bren gun was a mattock. Went out with Doctor Tyler who is a geologist for the United States Steel Corporation. He comes from Wisconsin. Frank, he and myself depart each morning and take a packed lunch plus four digging and cutting implements. His job is to map the area, to find all the large rock outcrops. He spends the day tapping the stones with his geologist's hammer. We scrape the moss, roots, dirt and trees off the top. It's about the toughest job so far and fairly constant.

Yesterday the Sabbath and a holiday. Did the washing and read all day. Figure I get enough exercise during the week. Planes roared in and out shuttling the ore we'd brought down during the week. Was cornered for the odd loading party. The ore goes to Blough Lake where I was at first. The Catalinas take it to Seven Islands for shipment to the laboratories. The big fuss on from tomorrow is due to the scheduled arrival of a few vice-presidents of U.S. Steel Corp. Over here this is as if the Lord had announced his intention of calling in. They are coming from Pittsburgh Penn. I read in Time Magazine that the president of U.S. Steel makes a cool $250,000 per year! There is a steel strike on down south and the Steelworkers' Union is negotiating for a 33-cent per hour raise plus a three year contract. For no more demands, the Corp. wants to make it 15 cents per hour and a guarantee of five years. We get a raise if the other guys do – exploration men don't belong to unions as there aren't any to cover us. Right now it's O.K. without them.

Weather rainy and overcast most of the time. Saw snow which had been dislodged from beneath an uprooted tree a week ago, and today was still on the roadway. Every time the sun comes out, great hordes of mosquitoes and blackflies fly out and worry hell out of us. They should be through by the end of this month according to one of my bushmen mates.

One of the surveyors has just begun to strum on the mandolin and to sing a nasal song of the West.

I got my results from McGill and have been given a supplemental in Physics having failed it as suspected. Am now a second year student having passed the year but will erase the smear on my record on Sept. 13. The rest of the marks were in the sixties but I feel the worst is over and have been working ahead up here so that I expect to negotiate the following year with better results. The financial position will be surer, I think. The club will be there and most certainly application to study will improve. I have been choosing my five courses for next session. Will do Zoology, Chemistry and Calculus – the other two will probably be arts courses as the three years pre-med subjects are supposed to give the general background. As I don't feel enthusiastic about anything else to the extent of becoming "it," I will not attempt to make any second fiddle course.

Looking forward to resuming studies again. I do like the bush but at my age the urge is to get on with the course. I must write to Miss Browning. She kissed me goodbye much to Vod's amusement when I left. Says she will have me back.

Your letter as always Mum gave me the whole picture at home. The letter took six days from Cootamundra to the Canadian bush which is very good. One of the guys got a letter from Toronto postmarked July 10, the same date as yours! Yes, Lake Louise is at Banff in British Columbia (sic) and the hotel is owned by Canadian Pacific. I could have worked there this summer but would prefer the dough up here. It must be one of the most scenic places in the world from reports.

The lake water is still a bit cool. I took the motor boat down to a sandy beach two miles at the end of the lake and submerged with the cake of soap . Am very well. The big Frenchman had to give it up the ghost for an hour on the job last week so the healthy upbringing is paying off.

P.S. The 17-year-old camp dishwasher who doesn't speak English just informed me he was purchasing a 1956 Pontiac. He makes $185 per month clear.


## BLOUGH LAKE

### (JULY 1956)

Feel in particularly high spirits as I sit in the wireless shack and write you once again from Blough Lake. The word was sent on Thursday so I packed into the Beaver and was flown over to help out here at base camp. Must say it came as a breath from the Gods. The work here consists of looking after all the supplies and dispatching the ore out to Duluth Minn. Over at Jeannine, I was digging and blasting the iron out of the hill. Here I am checking it off the small planes and getting it loaded on to the larger Cansos (Catalinas). It involves quite a bit of stevedoring.

Today was sunny and cloudless – such a change and in camp the flies aren't too numerous. Had a swim at lunchtime off the side of the plane. Water is still cool but I guess about as good as it will be. Not exactly in the tropics as the Labrador border is only seventy miles east. Am sharing a tent with two bushmen and Barry Wilson who finishes medicine this year down at Queen's University, Kingston Ontario. He has his first aid post set up here and is going over the stock. A few minutes ago he'd lost the drugs. So we thought the cook had got to them but they turned up. Charlie the French-Can cook is really very good. He told me he was drunk for seven months during last Fall and winter. Being at H.Q. for supplies means we live royally here. There is chicken, steak, stuffed olives, cans and cans of fruit and juice. Discovered the carton of chocolates last night. Also the boxes of assorted biscuits. You remember how I used to be at the latter. I'm still much the same. Get on well with the two other French guys. A very little English is spoken by one of them so the vowels and verbs are flowing. They told me I was from Montreal as my accent is similar. That means I have lost my Parisienne!

Over at the other camp Frank used to annoy them by correcting their slang terms. It was if an Oxonian came to Wallendbeen and started laying down the law about a potato not being a "spud" or a battle not being a "blue." Seems so senseless but the French from France are inclined to a bourgeois snobbishness once they leave their grape fields and boulevards.

Have been feeding wood into the boiler which is surrounded by a pile of rocks so that when they are heated sufficiently, we pour the water and have a steam bath. Have a special log shack which is also used as a wash house.

Doesn't seem right somehow but Barry just walked over to the store house, grabbed three tins of tomato juice and put them in the deep freeze for our supper. Quelle vie! The stamps on this letter depict the Canada Goose. They migrate each winter to Florida and come up north for the reminder. Just like the people.

BLOUGH LAKE P.Q.

(AUG 16 1956)

Roberval Catalina brought your letter yesterday, also one from Nanna so am well up on family doings. I trust by now you have your glasses. Your writing was bigger than usual but all considered you did a fine job.

Beautiful morning at Blough Lake, sunny after the first white frost of summer. The ice in the bucket outside my tent was frozen and getting up reminded me very much of a winter's morning at 67. Old Francis the bushman did the honors with the little stove we have in the tent. Seem to take the central heating for granted out in Canada, so much that winter brings none of that early morning discomfort of cold clothes and bare feet on the floor. The bush life helps one back to reality. I always think that the real pioneers, who came to this country without the bottomless resources of the U.S. Steel Corp. behind them, must have had amazing spirit and strength. A late mail delivery or no ice cream dispatch sends us into fits of pained agony.

Yes, it would be nicer to be going into second year medicine at this stage but the number of people who start off with vague ideas on professions just would render the first year a slaughter yard. Ask John Ward and he will tell you the number of victims at Sydney. I read it in the S.M. Herald only last week. I am hoping to do the impossible and be admitted after my third year in science. I will then have four years to do for my degree. As I've said before, McGill Medical School is one of the leading colleges on this continent so don't be surprised if I have to change over to one equally as good perhaps but without the old reputation. Let's hope there are no more sups but I feel pretty fit and ready to go. With first year out of the way, I have found out quite a bit, even on study methods, note taking, understanding, picking lab partners—all these are a matter of trial and error after five or six years away from anything resembling school.

Another visit from our foreign owners at this weekend – the usual quantities of delicacies are pouring in and I am extracting the standard tax: luxurious canned shrimps, Spanish olives, rock and water melons, Californian grapes etc. They sent in 12 new towels for the last visit – when this trip was announced I had to rescue all the towels as they had all disappeared into kitbags and tents.

Work is slackening off. Am going for a trip to Seven Islands if the next Canso plans a quick return visit. Chief Pilot "Moose" Murdoch arrived at 6.30 this morning much to everyone's annoyance. I'll just go to the airport as the plane will be loaded as quickly as possible. 'Sept Isles" on the map, does Caroline search for all these names? When I get back to 67 I will subject her to an examination on Canada. Will send over a condensed version of a special government Year Book.

Most of the radio from Manhattan deals with the Democratic high jinks down at the convention in Chicago. They are more akin to the Labour Party but in a much more moderate fashion. They try to get through welfare bills and protection against monopoly. The Republican Party, under Ike, represents big business with a capital B. They are for "open slather" – no controls and let the spoils go to biggest and strongest. Ike is a moderate Republican and it is hard to find anyone with a word against him. Somehow there doesn't seem to be a great difference between the two parties. Most people have a dollar or two – the big muddle is foreign affairs. The country and North America have become prosperous through big business but there is always a limit—the giant grows too big and becomes more and more part of the government. Look at Charles Wilson who is Defense Secretary in Washington. He is a former General Motors boss so you can imagine the defense contracts.

Vod is well and is having a cool summer in Montreal. I will look up Joan Meagher's relative on my return if he has left his card at the Themis Club. I hope you have explained to everyone that I am the barman and not the member. Let me know if I am to assume the latter!

Camp is a scene of inactivity – three bodies stretched out on the tables and benches. Just had a morning brew (three cups!)

P.S. This is written with the new style liquid pencil – it is supposed to be erasable.

BLOUGH LAKE P.Q.

(AUG 1956)

Have just docked the plane, loaded it for an early morning trip to avoid having to get up before the appointed hour and am writing this to Tommy Dorsey via some New York station. The visiting directors left this morning after a "very pleasant weekend". No doubt about this group. They were a good bunch, the higher they are, the better. One, a Mr. Nagle, was president of a N.Y. bank. Three were directors of U.S. Steel Corp. including Mr. Spang, president of the Gillette Razor Blade Company. He was a very pleasant old chap—full of jokes about our beards and promises to send up supplies of blades. Mr. Reed, boss of Raw Materials, plus the head of Mineral Exploration, plus president of Cartier Mining itself made up the bunch. The only horror was a youngish up-start who was assistant to one of the directors – he was trying to tell "Moose" Murdoch, one of the best bush pilots and chief of one of our supplying airline companies, the best route to go back. It was quite a joke and we all laughed out loud—he was just the typical upstart and we treated him as such.

Have had three very nice trips this week. On Thursday afternoon I hopped on the Catalina for the 135-mile trip to Sept Isles. "Moose" had me up in the co-pilot's seat and I flew for a while. We were at seven thousand feet and as I took it through a cloud layer, we emerged to a colossal view of the Gulf of the St. Lawrence. The breakers were rolling on the long sandy shore. It was so blue after the lakes and rocks of our area up here. The town of Sept Isles is right on the coast – the railway line comes down from the iron mines of Knob Lake and the ore is shipped right down the river through Montreal and the Great Lakes, Toronto etc. The airport is surprisingly modern with tar runways and large terminal with a four-engine "North Star" T.C.A. (Trans Canada Airlines) outside , three U.S. air force double-engine helicopters and an Avro Anson – the latter is used on our air photography surveys. Loaded up again and off back to Blough via the "scenic route" for my benefit – cliffs, fast rivers, rapids and the forests etc.

Saturday with John, the West Indian pilot on a supply trip to the Manicuagan Lakes. We have a construction company planning a power house dam etc on a 250-ft waterfall. Took the boss out to see the camp of Indians who are doing the preparatory work. I had to do the interpreting as they do not speak English – I've seen this group at three different sites now so am regarded as an old friend. Their site is most scenic – on a lake at the bottom of enormous cliffs. The roar of the waterfall filtered through the trees, not noisy but somehow suggestive of the North. Sometimes here at night I walk outside the tent to listen to the wind and a waterfall which is about a mile to the north.

Sunday went to one of our northern sites with Nick, the English pilot in the Beaver. We flew high most of the way -- I navigated with a large scale map, just a matter of lake shapes and only a 30-mile trip. The giant clouds kept rolling across the sky at us. Old Nick would just swerve around them. On the ground you never seem to think of clouds like that. Up at 7,000 feet there is quite a view. On the return trip we had the radio message for us to go to Jeanine to take the "big shots" fishing. They were in the midst of a colossal meal and in we trooped. They thought it quite a joke when I reappeared on the scene – I said I was following the ice-cream and special meals around. Had an hour with the old mob before boarding the Beaver for the return trip with the non-fishermen of the group.

Outside the tourist activities I have been doing a little Physics, a bit of reading and of course the supplies are ever on the move. Events are beginning to slacken here and from now on the boys will be moving out especially the guys at American universities. I will be at Blough Lake to about the 25th Sept. Feel I deserve a short holiday in New York after four months in the bush. The extra days up here will pay for the long weekend of four days down there. My expense account, run along the lines of my Bank of New South Wales days, will take care of the fare.

Temperature at 42 degrees all day. Four of the geologists were on a camp 20 miles south of us today and it snowed all morning. We expect regular falls throughout September. Had hail today and rain in showers but the sky is clear and beautiful tonight. The moon is shining right across the lake. It's almost full and the beam begins on the other side of the water and ripples up to the beach just outside the window of the radio shack. The Beaver is tied up at the wharf; its wings are lit up by the reflection.

The Kiwi brought the helicopter down this weekend. He's had an amazing career and was with the Royal Navy fleet air arm, flying off the "HMS Glory" aircraft carrier. Says they had a brutal job in Korea, strafing anything that moved from groups of women and children to little villages and farms but at the same time, one little group he sprayed with fire blew up! They had been all loaded with ammo. His report is so different to what you get from the Yanks – fighting and stemming the flow of communism etc. I guess both sides of the fence are valid.

BLOUGH LAKE P.Q.

(AUG 27 1956)

Pleased to have our letter on Saturday's plane. The boss took his two kids out on it, thank God, as they had spent the rainy days playing rockets with matches and the petrol dump just outside the door. Have quite a collection of drums and varieties of fuels – there are different types for the aircraft, the helicopters, stoves and generators. The Canso brings 700 gallons in its wing tanks and we drain it off into drums on the jetty.

Did I ever tell you that I had packed my rucksack for the trek home overland from London? See in my old notebook that I had scheduled Athens. Well, it never came off but I would like very much to visit the Aegean and the Middle East. Maybe when you, Mal and I do our junket around the world before your visit to my palatial estate on the West Coast. As soon as I get down to Montreal, I will see if I can get "Holiday" off to you each month. Remember Miss Browning giving me an article on London out of it to read. Each Sunday the New York Times has an enormous travel section. Montreal has the big afternoon Star weekend edition but Sunday isn't complete without the Times.

Spent the afternoon on my Physics. Break up the study with loading supply trips and brews at the cookhouse with Charlie. The PhD. geologist hasn't decided what day he will hand over the supplemental paper. We are all going over to one of the pre-fabs to sit under strict supervision. It has cost me nine pounds for this blunder. Never again. Has begun to rain. A lone Canada Goose just flew over, honking its way north, regardless of the oncoming winter. It should be on its way south, I have put the 7-cent stamp on to illustrate. It was a big bird and very fast, the first we have seen this summer. Temp. 51 degrees. I am still in shorts but the change will be soon.

Friday went into the bush with Dan Bradley, Prof. of Geology at University of Missouri, down at Colombia Missouri. He is doing the map of all the rock outcrops and minerals. At 34, he is well up in this field. He did one year at Harvard before his 30 missions dropping supplies to the French underground and returned to Boston to complete his B.Sc. and PhD later on. He is brought up just for the summer recess. The Kiwi pilot dropped us off on a clearing about 15 miles from Blough Lake. A moose track ran clearly across the patch into the trees. The patch itself was just big enough for the helicopter to take off from. We walked through the bush, me counting our steps, he doing the notes and keeping us on path with a magnetic compass. Up here a compass is way off due to the relative proximity of the North Pole and the iron deposits underneath us. The bush is just the same – we walked until we came to a line of cliffs, about 90 to 100 feet high and sheer in places. Dan thought they were the nicest rocks he had seen all summer. He explained his work as we went along so it was quite interesting.

This section of cliff has a three foot overhand so as it had begun to rain we made a fire and proceeded to eat our bully beef sandwiches. It was beautifully dry and I said to Dan: "What would you prefer to drink, water from the pool over there or a can of Molson's beer." Just for a joke, he said: "I'll take a beer." But it was my joke as one of the pilots had given me two cans last week and I had packed them away. I have never known anyone enjoy that beer as he did. He just sat back on the rock, smoking a cigar and talked for two hours.

This country has never been touched except for our little venture so we were wondering if the Indians ever camped under the cliffs. The rain didn't stop so we had to go on. Followed the cliff line around, waded through streams and small lakes, walked miles up and down hills, across bogs. We were lost most of the time but finally made the end of the lake around 6 p.m. The helicopter appeared through the mist just as we began to feel cold. To cap it all we had to wade into the lake to get on to the pontoons and into the cabin. But the chopper moved and I slid into the water up to my waist, I was so wet anyway it didn't really matter and I had enjoyed the day so much. That night two guys had to sleep out so they lit a big fire and made a shanty. They reckoned it was the best night they had spent despite the rain.

Kiwi took me on a 15-mile hop to one of our sites Sat. morning. On the way back I had a shot at flying the helicopter. Quite a thrill. Took some photos from the air. Sent Tony some I took with my old 620 Brownie. They are still the best and clearest I have seen taken up here. The winder isn't too hot and the lens has to be shaken into position but still it's a long time since the birthday you gave it to me, Ma!

Barry the med. student left to write a sup in surgery last Friday. This puts me O.C. of storehouse, a rather dubious position now that I am "sick" of all the "goodies." Ice cream isn't even a specialty now. The cost of this operation must run well into the millions but I guess tax pays most of it – either give it to the government or spend it. However from all accounts, I should always be assured of a reasonable summer job. Have cooled off the New York visit. When it comes to hard figures, it's like tossing dough out the window. I could go berserk with some of the plays down there but my calendar from McGill arrived today to say that lectures begin Sept. 27 and experience tells me that to be there on time means better seats, better lab partners and less time lost.

Bonsoir maintenant, je vais prendre une tasse de café.

p.s. I'm the only "anglais" left in the tent now.

BLOUGH LAKE

(SEPT 1 1956)

Mal, you'll be 14 in just ten days so as there is a plane on its way from Seven Islands, I had better get my best wishes away on it. A very happy birthday, my old Gunga, and as I said last year, I'll be looking forward to the time when I'll be there pinching my share of birthday cake. You won't be the little girl running about the house in those yellow pyjamas, possibly somewhat more careful of what is showing and what isn't. The cheque is just a little start for your coat. When you settle just what you want, you can find a good one I hope, I'll arrange for the balance to be paid. Suggest you send this cheque back to me and I'll send it back in Australian money from Montreal. After the banks take their cut there is little left and I know a much cheaper exchange transaction.

I am just about to commence the final effort on the Physics which will be on Sat. morning. Over in one of the pre-fabs at Jeanine Lake. Won't it be strange, flying to an exam? The gangs of students are starting to roll home now. Bill Kneller, who was the American geologist I met in Roberval left yesterday. He has been selected for 18 months work down Antarctica but as his wife is threatening him if he goes, is in a bit of a fix. Will get this to the mail drop.

BLOUGH LAKE

(SEPT 3 1956)

A Norseman single-engine plane just flew in from Fort Chimo, up on Ungava Bay, to refuel and was planning on continuing to Roberval. Well, that log boom in Roberval, which was in one of the pictures I sent you, broke and flooded Lac St. Jean with logs making a landing at night pretty precarious. A Canso is coming out of its way to pick up the passengers who are anxious to get to Roberval tonight so we'll have an outward mail. Sent off Mal's birthday letter via Seven Islands but this one will probably beat it to you as there is that delay. Just in case, Happy Birthday, my old girl friend.

Got your letter and wondering how does John Stratton get along on his new sheep station. Marrying a cocky's daughter doesn't make you a farmer overnight. Guess he could feed the sheep cut-rate flour from his dad's flour mill at Coota. As you say my hair was a bit scrappy – I had it lopped for the bush but am pleased to say that right now am wearing it in the best Australian fashion, falling down over my forehead. We received the promised razors from Mr. Spang, the Gillette Razor Company president. I haven't shaved since I left Roberval.

The boys take regular movies and I was starring last night, bringing in a boom of logs on the lake with the canoe and old Francis the bushman. The pilots take turns at displaying their hoarded films, mostly home scenes and shots of the life around these parts. Everyone gets quite cheered up when Gerry shows pictures of his wife and their beautiful home – she is a "colossal sort."

A black bear appeared on the scene shortly after your letter arrived. It looked quite enormous as it lumbered down the hill and raked around the garbage pit before taking fright at the twenty resident tourists. They usually don't attack but all the same I admit to avoiding the outdoor lavatory after dark and as I am always last out of the radio shack, make sure, with my flashlight, that friend bear wasn't lurking in the shadows. Bears are renowned up here for wrecking tents and storehouses in their search for food. They harass a camp, getting bolder all the time until there's a missing place at the table for breakfast next morning. Yesterday Mr. Bear came down, bent over, raking amongst the refuse of a week's camp pile. It looked like a scene from Taronga Park Zoo, and with the crowd everywhere, it just ate on. I slid up and took two pictures with the .620 so hope I got close enough. Then they shot him. This rather disappointed me as the whole thing was just slaughter but the argument is as above. I skinned the head section as they wanted to preserve the trophy. It was the best zoological lab I have ever had. It weighed 200 lbs (not big for a bear, just a one-year-old). Had bear meat pie for morning tea today and I'll flood you with poses beside the skin. Also took a shot of a squirrel with my .620 before someone took a shot with a .22

Our group has been joined by two guys from Newfoundland. This was the final province to join Confederation only nine years ago. They fish on the banks of Newfoundland and the Coast of Labrador. Accents are Irish and almost Australian. An engineer from Minnesota is up taking soundings of the depth of the lake bottom. He was in Japan after the war and saw a lot of our British Commonwealth Occupation Forces men.

Am having a lot of fun in our recently acquired 10 H.P. outboard motor canoe. Previously engines had only one-third of the power so there is a fair bit of power in this one. All set for the Physics sup over at Jeanine Lake on Sat. morning. Will take a Beaver over. That is just the advantage of working for a big company. Last two days were pretty slack so have logged a few hours on the books.

BLOUGH LAKE P.Q.

(SEPT 10 1956)

To the tune of "That's What the Good Book Says" from C.B.S. New York, I am attempting the weekly news sheet at my corner of the radio shack. The pilots are filling in their logs and cash sheets. They are an agreeable lot. Have them well trained to bring in a newspaper anytime they strike civilization.

Pleased to have your letter on Wednesday. The snow at Cootamundra amazed me – especially banked up around the garage. Expecting some here anytime now. One of the pilots reported flying through it early last week. The ice is getting thicker and "oftener" (the latter a local acquisition). Once it starts to form on the smaller lakes, we'll be off in a flash. The greater mass of people will be off by the 19th leaving myself with three or four other students and the bushmen plus the boss. Am due to register Sept. 25 and lectures begin 27th. May see this job right to the end; alternatively an escape through Sept Isles on the 24th.

The life here is superb. With the physics supplemental completed yesterday (I am fearfully apprehensive as always on that subject) and the general slack preceding the big final clean-up, there is lots of spare time for one's "personal affairs." The books and news come in regularly from Vod who is fit and well as ever. Spent this afternoon driving the 10 H.P. outboard for Bill, an engineer from U.S. Steel up here to estimate the amount of water on Blough and Jeanine Lakes. He is one of the best types of American –straight-forward, and full of anecdotes on the U.S. way of life. Comes from Minnesota. We went up the river two miles and nearly ended in the water over very small rapids. The boat stalled just as we were caught in the current pouring over the rocks. And he had to jump off on to a large slab of granite and hold us as I got the motor jumping. Water is icy and even wind is cold but it was really very pretty crawling up the current. I like this Canadian bush and reckon I'll be seeing quite a bit more of it.

The Beaver took me to the exam at 7.30 a.m. There was a thick fog over Jeanine. We couldn't see the lake at all but it was well worth the sight, flying above a fog with nothing in view except the rolling masses of vapor and the early morning sun creeping through. What a world exists up there. Suddenly we found a hole and went through it and there was the lake and the examination pre-fab! On the way back to Blough, John, the West Indian pilot decided he wanted to see how it looked above the scattered lining. It was different again this time, the blur of green (we were at 7,000 feet) and great mountains and balls of fluff with the Manicouagan Lakes beneath us.

Public opinion over Suez as usual is lukewarm over here. Nothing ever seems to blast the Canadian out of his indifference except a remark about his similarity to the American. Now that the Menzies Mission has failed, it looks as if the Egyptians have won their little game. What else can we do? The U.S. will not permit force just as the U.K. would not allow open intervention in Indo-China and China. With TV on its way to ruin the healthy Australian outlook and pastimes, you'll be deluged with T.V. jackets, snacks, chairs, glasses etc

BLOUGH LAKE

(SEPT 16 1956)

Your letter on Wednesday and you were right back to form, Mum, with all the news and fine print. Spent a quiet day— read "Lady Chatterley's Lover" this morning. You people who grew up in the Twenties had a hectic time. I was thinking about the First World War and the years after. Please see that Dad's letters from the trenches are kept. I was very silly to take them from the security of their drawer. Maybe later on I would like you to send them over. They were in the bottom of the chest of drawers in the spare room. What I would like you to send over is that old photo album of mine. It should be lying around somewhere.

This afternoon I went for a stroll in the bush, sat on a rock and a very small red squirrel came right up beside me. It kept coming back and finally climbed up a spruce tree and chattered away at me. Yesterday went rock climbing with Jerry. The view from an outcrop nearby is very good, the camp amidst the forest and you can see the lakes and down, 15 miles away is a range of high hills. They are already snow-capped again. Came across five spruce hens or partridges. They are bigger than bantams, almost the size of an ordinary hen. Make colossal meat. They were so wild; they must have thought we were trees as we crept up to within a few feet. Jerry took some movie shots whilst I relied on the .620 old faithful.

Not too much activity around the camp. Plane loads of guys leave every Wednesday, all looking forward to getting amongst the wine, women and song again. I am departing one week via Sept Isles and Quebec City which should get me there in time for registration etc. which closes at 4 p.m. If I miss it, they fine me $5. I could go on up here a few days later but for some things I like to be on time. We've had several very light snowfalls over the weekend, temperature down to 26 degrees and the ice didn't melt back until late this afternoon. The lake itself freezes three feet thick in November. It is dangerous from early October onwards to when we came in this summer. During the winter, DC3s bring supplies in, landing on the ice with skis.

Was delighted to get a bunch of magazines and papers this week. Noticed Publisher Pinkie has changed the lettering at the masthead of the Cootamundra Daily Herald. I was most indignant when I saw "Denis Howse" was not prominent as carrier boy. Was just about to let fly at the editor with a dictionary by my side but decided it might be a bit like President Harry Truman – when a reporter blasted his daughter's singing and he (the president) lashed out. Down in the States the circus is in full swing. What a time they have with these conventions with everyone scrambling to get the guy elected who will best look after their interests, be it a munitions factory or a drug store. If you can get hold of this week's "Life" you will see what I mean.

So long now from the bush. Will write when I am safely installed at the Themis in a week. It has been a wonderful summer and I'll always have a job with this company any summer I like.

P.S. The cook has been drunk for five days on flavoring essences. He's very jovial and still cooks well. We've had two days of snow and rain. The country now is like a scene of the woods in "Wind in the Willows." Roof tops all white—what a change two inches of snow makes. It should melt later on today. Yesterday the camp chief and 'self went off in the snow for a stroll in the hills with guns and rock hammers. He is a most experienced bush worker so it amused me very much when, after telling me he had never been lost in the bush, we suddenly came across our tracks in the snow. At that we decided to follow them back to camp as neither of us had a clue where we were and it was freezing cold through the rubber boots and bare hands.

Sitting in on my first lecture in the Calculus – the usual shuffle of names is going on so will get a few lines off to you. Quite a thrill to lie back and with a clear record. Passed the Physics. Vod had sent me the wire in the bush saying that I had failed. They had put only the marks of the people who had written in Montreal on the board. When I asked to register in Physics again, the girl said: "Why do it again, you passed it." What sheer joy it was, just as I had decided to carry on with it all for a whole year. The Calculus lecture got down to business forcing me to leave this until now at 10 p.m.

Had a good trip down after flying down to Sept Isles in one of the small Beavers. Followed a river all the way and crossed a range of white hills which were the ones formed the far background to Blough Lake all summer. Nick, the English chap was the pilot. Landed on floats at Rapide Lake where a taxi waited. It was rather annoying to me, the way a taxi emerges 10 miles out in the bush to meet the men who have been working for months in the bush. It cost $5 to get into Seven Islands. Met up with one of the helicopter gang and had a reasonably restrained night. I was dead sure I wasn't going to dissipate my dough in the best traditions of the north.

Stopped the night at a very modern hotel. This place is a mining boom port, smaller than Coota, it has three nightclubs, enormous supermart and all the other trappings. I caught a plane down to Quebec City, called in at the Anglo-Canadian Pulp Co., where a friend is doing well as assistant to the secretary. This company is owned by the Daily Mirror of London. Couldn't get a T.C.A. connection so came on by train. Arrived at 8 p.m. and received a warm welcome from everyone at the club. The boss got me a meal and I felt it was somehow a lot nicer than going off to look for the $10 per week room. It's good to be back in the old room, nicely cleaned and freshly floored; the bushes outside the window seal me off from Sherbrooke St. It was luxurious to read the paper in the bath again.

Down to the bookstore and began to accumulate the year's fare. The woman from the club still lets me in at cost price which has already saved me $5. Trust by now the mails have cleared up and you are getting the letters on time. I didn't miss up in the bush once from you so the service was really good.

P.S. Weather is really gorgeous. Had snow in the bush for the past two weeks but down here it is almost hot. Am just getting over the irritable stage – crowds and noise after four months away.

MONTREAL

(OCT 3 1956)

Settled in to the Club and lectures once more. Pleased to have your letter at noon. The glasses have certainly made a difference to your writing. Notice you now get in 26 lines to your page! Why can't you imagine someone not shaving for over three months? Besides the economy, think of the time and wasted effort. I only shave here because of my required respectability – the bearded barman wouldn't go down too well. I can imagine the T.V. parties in Sydney in Pelaco sports shirts and scarves all lapping up the American trash which no doubt will find its way down there. At Vod's place they have two enormous sets. All the girls at the Club have them so I should think the party fad which I see in MacRobertson's Chocolate advertisements, will end fairly soon.

Vod is well. I read him all the news as he called in for lunch. He hears regularly from Aunt Peg and both she and Christina are well. Peg had the trip to France and looked up Uncle Vock's grave on the coast. Vod has new job, ( modern day manny) so he minds the children at night in exchange for room and board. There are three of them, 14, 11 (the boys) and Julie, aged 4. The house is very big—two cars, radiogram , piano etc. Vod is capable of using the middle one only.

Lectures are on regularly now. My five courses this year are Zoology, Mathematics, Physiology, Chemistry and Anthropology. In Zoology, will be studying the development of animals right up the line. Around Xmas we are issued with a preserved cat about which we will have to know a lot. Mathematics involves the calculus – it's a branch of mathematics that is generally helpful; Chemistry will consist of the living or organic compounds.

Anthropology is the study of man and his cultures and settlements all over the world from the time he first appeared on earth to the present. In Physiology, it's the body functions and reactions. The text book is a horrifying affair of one thousand pages. Cost 76/6 Aust. If I can get a reasonable average this year and follow up well the next, I should be able to make medicine. My subjects should give me a reasonable background for those final four years.

Had a letter from Don Bullivant, the guy I left Australia with in 1954.He is doing very well in the bank over in Perth W.A. Wants to get married and has asked me to be his best man. How about catching a wealthy squatter, Ma, and pawning your son (3rd) out of hock for two months? Don says he is in line for the Security Clerk position over there.

MONTREAL

(THANKSGIVING 1956)

Have just walked down from the Biology Building after a physiology lecture. Monday was Thanksgiving Day, a North American tradition which to the native means an enormous turkey and family get-together. The Bains had me out Friday night to partake of a monstrous bird which dominated the table like Mick used to dominate reading the daily newspapers. They went off to the country home for the weekend. Mr. Bain had quite a serious accident, nearly died after a bad smash. He dozed off in a tunnel but I am sure it was not due to similar accident causes.

Sat. night I went over to Vod's place. The family was off for the weekend leaving him in charge of the two boys. He has them playing chess but really children here are impossible. It is due to many things but more to the place they are given by the parents—right at the center of doings. Vod says the guy before him was kicked out because he hit the children occasionally—he swears that a similar end may come his way. We played through the folk's record collection – a Hi-fi set and another they never use, plus two giant TVs. Then we had an enormous snack and watched the late "oldie" movie at 11:30 p.m. starring Charles Boyer and Marlene Dietrich. One TV set is in the kitchen, presumably so that the children will eat their meals there.

Monday Vod took his monsters to Cinerama. If you ever see it, there is a Swiss couple who visit Dartmouth College in New Hampshire and eat at a Tudor style restaurant. That is where I ate when I was down on the football trip. I told Vod I didn't want to see the show as I had been to all the places!!!

No news from any of the three brothers for quite some time. Looking through the windows of the library I can see the gigantic frame of the Queen Elizabeth Hotel which is destined to become the largest pub in the British Commonwealth. When I arrived they had just begun scraping the dirt for the foundations and I, in my naïveté, tried for a job there. Luckily I didn't get it or I might still be there.

Pleased to hear that Tony got a trip to Tamworth. Where does he work when they are not on strike? Good luck to them, good conditions have to be fought for somehow. Hope Ned's knee is O.K. -- with luck I'll be able to re-set it for him in ten years.

Walked up the mountain Monday. Gorgeous scene – the maples are in their full range of colours—red, purple, orange, yellow and brown. The whole hill is just one big patch. The Fall is a very apt way of describing autumn –already bare limbs and branches are appearing and there is a continual parachute of leaves . There are a lot of trees on the campus here – out on the green field, the more energetic types are playing touch football. I have had to give up Rugby due to the bar but one can't have it all ways. Playing squash with Cuthbertson tonight.

P.S. We have the furnaces going now, recognition that winter is well on its way. Nights are cold.

MONTREAL

(OCT 22 1956)

Your letter took just five days to get here! Sorry to hear that the Cootamundra Show has been abandoned. A friend has just brought a load of Vod's gear to the club. I will guard it here until his return in six months from his big Canadian North adventure. He leaves Tuesday. You will have an interest now in America's front line defences. He has bequeathed me his library for the winter and I have the record player back. Our collection is gradually increasing. The people out in Outrement are very sorry to see him go—the children are miniature horrors. The woman gave him a Val-Pak! I still have the blue one I left Australia with but as I have had no permanent moves in the past two years, haven't used it in a long time.

Friday night I went to the University Film Club and saw an old German film. Its story was of a mine disaster and the morale of it was that miners of all countries were buddies. The Germans helped the French who were trapped. Also called in at the annual meeting of the Cosmopolitan Club. A friend, Goddard, who I helped with the graduation gowns, is secretary and roped me in as a new member.

Went out to TV last night chez Vod at Outrement and we walked back and had a spaghetti down town around 2 a.m. The town was still very much alive. This afternoon I called in on Joe Brebant who had the year over in Paris. Had a very interesting afternoon amongst his impressions of the countries I had touched in light manner "years ago." He does his final year law exams in June. We are going to see "War and Peace" on Friday night. I read the book when I was a steel worker in England, a lot of it during those night shifts, crouched behind coke bags. Don't remember too much of it but I was determined that I would finish it. Noticed in the Sydney Morning Herald at the Trade Commissioner's Office that direct link by telephone has been made between Canada and Australia.

MONTREAL

(OCT 29 1956)

May I announce that I have an addition to the family – a pause for tea as Ma faints. No, just a kitten which I've had for the past week. In the comparative anatomy course this year, we are given beautifully preserved cats to study in detail. I thought I would like this little fellow for a comparison. Everyone thinks I am going to complete the Frankenstein experiments upon the animal but he is really the most affectionate cat. Only 6 weeks old. I have him trained to enter the toilet to his box. Wakes me at 7 every morning and in general makes me lose more time than I can afford. Every time I sit down at the desk he races up my trousers and starts madly chewing at the pen or pawing me. I let him out the window by a series of stairs made from stacks of books but he seems to prefer the warmth of the basement to the increasingly chilly Montreal Fall weather.

Vod went off Tuesday in fine spirits by train to Mont Joli. The company has an airfield there so he will be waiting up on the south shore of the St Lawrence until they get a request for a store man. Is making slightly more than I was so he should be in good wealth when he returns.

Wednesday night I went to the Australian film "A Town Called Alice." I enjoyed it a lot, mostly because there were the Australians and the shots of the Territory in it. Isn't it amazing that none of us have ever been up there? What an enormous country we have and how small is our Group Nine. Football League area. I often kick myself for not having stirred myself into seeing such places as the Darwin, the West, Queensland and Tasmania. I've learnt a hell of a lot more on Australia since coming away. One of my ideals is to see it all on my return.

You haven't mentioned the Olympic Games. What a tragedy it would be if there wasn't a Howse at the first "Down Under" Olympics. Ned, you old "live-wire," you must be going. What I'd give to jump on the B.O.A.C. plane and see them

($1770.00 fare) ! Your letter Sat. Did you say potatoes two shillings and two pence a lb. They are 10 cents here. Who is making the dough? Now I see that cartoon in the S. Morning Herald with the old girl buying the spud and the greengrocer saying: "Five lbs of potatoes! Who do you think you are, Lady Docker?" I keep up to date at the Trade Office.

Thursday to a public lecture given by Dr. Julian Huxley who has one of the greatest brains now in use. He spoke of the evolution of mankind ("The Possibilities of the Human Mind") and glued together many of the facts we get in our Biology lectures but which require additional thought to fit. One of the Themis Club ladies said she thought his lecture failed because he had no charm. That is typical of our members here!!

Evolution is taught in some American junior schools. I went with an American girl from New York State. Made the dash up the crowded hall at 8.30 p.m. after being held up by drinks at the Themis. She held a seat for me in the sixth row. It was my night to be "at home" for the front doorbell but I felt that missing Huxley for a few old girls here a little too much.

Then Miss B. was waiting on my return, presumably to abuse, but she ended up in good frame when I said the lecture didn't "get out" until 11 p.m.. Of course, some old girl told her it finished at 9.30 p.m. so we had quite a laugh about it today. I am afraid that I am a little past the stage of having to be in and out on request. One must live, however and acknowledge the restraints necessary to permit continuance of my rather happy position at the Themis. Friday a luncheon date at a pleasant French restaurant. At night to "War and Peace." It is a long picture but Audrey Hepburn is refreshingly young and vivacious. The battles scenes are done extremely well. The story is simple for the book was a fairly involved affair around simple themes. Miss Ekberg looks like a street woman as usual—the American accents jar at the court of the Russian czar but as they say here: "They got the dough—so?"

Saturday I studied and the same today except for a visit to a coffee house to read the papers and to see our hero Elvis Presley on the Ed Sullivan Show. No wonder youth is a torrent of juvenile delinquents when young man such as Monsieur Presley is allowed to hold court over the nation's and the world's "teens."

Have been waiting for your letter before writing this week – trust it will be here within the hour. It's pouring outside. I've just come up Sherbrooke St. from the campus and the hair is slicked down for a change with the rain. Had a Calculus lecture at 9 a.m., followed by a conference in Anthropology. Have now to write 3,000 words on one of the South Pacific cultures i.e. Maori, Papuan, Fiji, Samoa etc. Will get into some reading at the library and begin writing next month. I don't know a lot about it right now. Last night I was working well and had three cups of coffee here at the club at 11 p.m. Result: I did (tried to do) Calculus problems up to 2 a.m. and read on to 3 a.m.

Sat. night to a party. All English so didn't enjoy it particularly. I can't stand the middle class English. The worker or the aristocrat but not the center, at least the younger ones. Not a thing in common – met a girl who was assistant purser on the "S.S. Otranto" the trip after mine. She made five trips to Australia. She was quite pleasant and I went back to her apartment for coffee after it. The memory of those snobbish bank and insurance clerks is still with me. I do not remember feeling more out of place in my life before and begin to understand why Vod retired from the Sydney scene whilst he was over in London.

Sunday to Cuthbertson's. He threw a sherry party at mid-day. It was rather a happy show with a very decent chap there who had come through law at Oxford and now leads the province in Accountancy 4th Year. Another "Limey" had spent his years in the oil industry of the Middle East and has now returned to McGill and is in first year Geology.

A long letter from Vod. He is at a base camp on the Fox Peninsula and will shortly be stationed at Coral Harbour on Melville Island, North West Territories. A good map should illustrate. He's a clerk with about as much work as I had. Gets all the news via BBC and Radio Moscow. There is a tribe of Eskimos around the camp and many husky dogs etc. Nothing much else. I have a lot to do this year. You have no idea what comes into these subjects. Organic Chemistry (of living matter) is a maze of formulae. However it is good to be amongst it and am battling on although I may have to leave off the job as I know I will have a lot more next term after Christmas.

P.S. Lots of Australian news coming through now with the Olympics on in Melbourne.

MONTREAL

(NOV 2 1956)

A few words to wish you a very happy birthday from your third and faraway son. I went off to physiology lecture at 9 a.m. and came straight back so that I am settled with a cup of tea. The cat is always clawing away at my pen and trying to get in on the tea but I have settled it now by putting him out under the bushes.

Weather is very mild, almost a record for the first day of November. The wind, rain and snow-slush are pretty close but so far not one miserable day. I am still in the nylon shirt and sport coat. Have not worn my grey suit for almost a year which just shows you what a social lion I am. But to illustrate a point, I have an invitation on my desk for the Newman Ball. This is the Catholic club on the campus. Tickets are $15 double but $10 for students. Add the ritual of taxis and hire of dress clothes and you can see what I mean.

Monday to a very interesting lecture on cancer by Doctor Huxley who gave it just for the McGill lot. Working well – the summer was really ideal as it kept me in touch with things and I had lots of time to do some devoirs.


MONTREAL

(NOV 6 1956)

What a week it has been on the international scene! Have been expecting post cards from L/CLP Howse D.B. with B.C.O.F. Egypt on the stamp. Supporting old Anthony Eden as best I can without joining up. Canada still has no draft but is certainly playing a star role down at the United Nations in N.Y.

The broadcasts of proceedings have been on for hours, Sat. night Dr. Walker was introduced as the Hon. Delegate from Austria. His accent seemed very familiar and the announcer apologized and said it was the Hon. Delegate from Australia. Feel very sorry for the Hungarians but if the U.S. goes in, it's No. III, "for sure" as they say here. Miss Browning comes down to give me her views quite often.

On Friday the Red Cross gave me a very smart badge to commemorate the third bottle I have allowed since my arrival. As usual met an Australian nurse from Innisfail Qld. I had to dash over to the library to check its location. It's up near Cairns. That night at the Themis I served one of Montreal's famous neuro-surgeons a glass of tomato juice. He is Dr. Cone, who with Dr. Wilder Penfield runs the Montreal Neurological Institute, a leading brain research centre. Had quite a conversation with a fellow blood donor whose father also had been a doctor at the M.N.I. She had had worked there for the summer and seen a lot of brain operations. At McGill in Physiology we are at present at the opposite end of things – the nervous system at this lowly level already seems amazingly complicated. God knows how many times more complicated it gets.

Saturday to squash after a few hours in the library. Studied Sat night and on Sunday afternoon went around to Cuthbertson's girl's house. He is quite keen on Louise and we had tea. A really pleasant, large apartment done out with refinement and taste a l'anglaise. I sipped tea from the Royal Doulton and tried not to pick my nose. She is a good five yeas older than he is and her father, who wasn't there, is the Air Vice Marshall.

Tonight to Dr. Huxley's final lecture. It is certainly inspiring to know that such men exist and are doing so much. He headed U.N.E.S.C.O. after the war.

MONTREAL

(NOV 24 1956)

Your letter a little late this week. Just listening to the final newscast from the C.B.C. Hope old Eden hasn't had the axe. What a shocking affair it will be if we have to leave without finishing the job. America's role is really difficult to understand. She seems to be idly watching her only real allies England and France go down the drain. The boss here threatens to fly back to the U.K. if it gets any worse. I am remaining cool and taking cheer in the news that our Defence Minister stated this week that Canada is best served by a voluntary army – that is good for votes and also for cold-footers like myself. Hungary is certainly a tragic affair. I think it has done the West some good in its attitude to Russian Communism.

Last night I took Judith, an American girl to the ballet. It was the Canadian National Corps who have really done very well in New York, Europe and here. "Giselle," which I saw in London and "Offenbach in the Underworld" comprised the programme. "Giselle" is a very old ballet—it has been danced continuously for 100 years and I think a most pleasing performance. It is good to be occasionally reminded that there do exist expressions and feelings above the regard for the current 1957 model cars. Monday night is "Swan Lake." I will never forget the Sadler's Wells version but it's nice to support the locals. As the poor student, I get $3.25 seats for $1.50 so from the first balcony the view is unrestricted. They are really a good ballet from all accounts.

At the moment the cat is sitting on the above lines, chewing at the pen, after a neat trip across one of the prize records. I have him trained, just in time as he selected the assistant chef's bed on his first excursion out into the basement.

Have a lot to do this year. An amazing pile seems to accumulate each week and I can see one of the reasons why the rest of the world regards us as automatons and not of the leisurely cultured class. It is a good life. I never seem to have a minute for anything but study, serving drinks, doing dishes, looking after the cat, reading, playing squash, swimming and entertainments. As I rush down Sherbrooke St I feel sometimes that the North American rush has me firmly held but then there is always the summer when, as you know, my rate very often drops to zero.

First really cold night and day. Will be looking out for those promised gloves from Ned. Am getting soft – rather my blood is altering down to Canadian thinness and I am feeling the cold. I was thinking today that I would soon get into my winter top-coat. Only a winter ago, I didn't change at all. Vod is well and having a colossal time work-wise. He is in with the decent Englishmen, a little different to the Manitoban and Saskatchewan hillbillies and has a little hut with a stove which he runs himself. Just imagine – minus 30 degrees right now and Vod in his hut amidst the blizzards.

MONTREAL

(DEC 4 1956)

Your letter yesterday in the Olympic aerogramme. Pleased to have the news. It's back to the winter schedule here. The snow has settled down on top of everything and the wind tears at your insides – hands and ears tingle and I begin to wish myself down south, Melbourne would just about do it. The Australians have done well—sorry about Mal's spill off the "grid" –imagined the speed of her bike down hill. I haven't ridden a bike since I left home so probably couldn't make the block.

David Cuthbertson, the English chap who arrived here with me just two years ago, has announced his engagement to the Air Vice Marshall's daughter. I am to be best man but much as I would enjoy doing it for him, am afraid the summer's work will give me the necessary excuse to evade the prohibitive cost of renting an outfit, the horror of a speech and having to be responsible for the ring etc. She's

Catholic; he's nothing and not changing. We had drinks at the Ritz lounge Sat. night to celebrate – I've been having quite a few digs at him. Still, in two years, he is 3$^{rd}$ in his class, does his intermediate accountancy next year and will be doomed in June. He's about the first friend of mine who has ever got married. I mean of my age so that it's a bit of a jolt to know that my generation is passing. When I return to the fold with my ten cats, you'll see what I mean. My current edition is at present racing around the floor after one of my black model carbon molecules. It spends hours playing and annoying me. I fear that the experiment on its brain will have to be put forward a few weeks.

Went down to the ballet Monday week night, saw "Swan Lake," enjoyed it although it didn't exactly eclipse the time I saw it before. It was a pleasant evening , I took the American girl. The rest of the week only broken with squash and a meeting of the Historical Society. I served a drink to Prof. Hill from Christchurch N.Z. and his wife who is a Yank but speaks with an Aust-Kiwi accent. It's peculiar but before I even talked to her, I could see that she was from down there – most likely the dress.

Sat. night to the Girls' Residence to pass a quiet evening with a few records. Sunday, the walk up the mountain. Almost forgot to mention a night out with Ralph Harris, the Australian who leaves soon and has promised to call in at Coota en route to Melbourne and give you a report on your third son. Thursday I served 47 drinks which wasn't a bad effort. This will amuse you; two ladies went up on the same night to the boss to tell her what a "pleasant" young barman she had up in the lounges. There is a NO tip rule so I suppose the pleasantness must be genuine – however I don't do too badly.

MONTREAL

(DEC 11 1956)

The cat gave me the usual frenzied greeting upon my return at 10 a.m. from a Physiology term test. I relented and cooked him some pork after the cook and chef had talked me out of giving him raw meat. My argument was that he had eaten raw meat up 'til the day I got him and that as he wasn't a Canadian citizen could probably do O.K. on the uncooked stuff. Wild animals are treated better than the out-of-work over here.

The test wasn't too bad. Illustrated how much there is to do over the Xmas holidays which begin Dec. 22. I will have one fairly important ordeal to return to i.e. the Chemistry exam. Spent three hours yesterday preparing for the lab period – really quite interesting once you decide to get the necessary background material before attempting the experiment. The guy who usually comes across to my lab position to combine the two scientific approaches nearly blew us up yesterday – I looked around and there he was standing in the center of the lab waving the test tube full of blazing benzene. We had been supposed to heat it gently with acid – it reminded me of the Olympic Torch. The experiment was a success – the heat helped things along.

News from Vod. He is well and settled in at his base at Coral Harbour on Melville Island or Peninsula up in the North West Territories, District of Keewatin. Caroline, the map? Ralph Harris, who knows us both well, left last night on a T.C.A. North Star –headline the paper he took on the plane: "66 Missing in T.C.A. North Star." He is getting off at Calgary, Banff and then catching the Orient Line to Sydney from Vancouver. He's a decent guy so look after him when he gets there. He has met Miss Browning etc so should fill in any gaps I have left from my 160 odd letters.

My 2nd anniversary here at the weekend. I read Ralph my old 1954 diary of the arrival and search for a job. It's a little different these days. One of the chief geologists called last week and asked me would I like to go back with them next summer. May have a job as a chemist analyzing the ore samples! Bit of a change from the job last year but it was nice to have the call and I'll drop out this week to discuss such minor arrangements as dough. I can't stand discussing wages – they give you a fair deal and I reckon the $300 with the pleasant summer life and conveniences is fine. One thing is that I don't have to hustle around during the exams – I can shelve it and concentrate on the more vital aspects of next term.

Played in the Province of Quebec "C" grade squash championships last week. Surprisingly won my first round against a reasonably rated player. In the second round I met the champ – it was the equivalent of meeting Lew Hoad in the 2nd round at Wimbledon. He beat me in three sets (the other went to 5 sets), told me to get more playing experience. I enjoy squash. It is tremendously fast at times and a bit like basketball for energy requirements. He was a second year law student and won the title.

Enjoyed the news of the Picnic Race Club and good to imagine Cousin David, Ross Last and Joe Manning on the committee. Give my regards to them. Some action should ensure with their replacement of the elders on the committee.

Clock is around 11.30 a.m. so I had better toss the meal down and race down to the Chemistry lecture followed by three hours cutting up an interesting little fellow called a mud-puppy. He is a nice medium between a fish and a lizard. I described him at lunch with his gills and lungs – old Arthur the houseman became ill. Mrs. Bain asked me to Xmas again so I thought I'd prefer that to an invite to the New York girl's place which means a little involvement.

P.S. Everything full of Xmas here – streets of lights and music emerging from the rooftops. Enormous circus displays of mechanical monkeys and ringmasters. You'll have to see this place one day.

MONTREAL

(JAN 3 1957)

Very pleased to have your letter as it's been (or seems to have been) quite a time since your Xmas card. The strike may have held it up – the Canadian Pacific (which runs in opposition to the government's Canadian National Railway) firemen are on strike. The bosses say they don't need firemen on shunting work in the yards and the Brotherhood of Firemen say they do. Quite a panic with the big conferences, even Prime Minister St. Laurent is in there with a few suggestions. Over a 100 U.S. railways plus C.N.R. agreed to keep the shunters on so that's it's almost equal to a railway strike at home, only there's half the service left. Well, I'm just a pedestrian and am free of the nightmares of the daily commute, in and out.

Weather here milder after a spell of 10-15 degrees below zero after Xmas. Sorry my card was late but as you said, you knew it was somewhere along the way. I also sent a little present that I thought might have been useful for the pre-Xmas season but apparently our louts at the Post Office (not louts really but pleasantly hopeless) seem to have slipped as I sent it at least four days before the card. Also, Mal, your note today and I'm going to write you a good letter once I remove the half course in Organic Chemistry which falls on Thursday and for which I have been preparing all day and at spasmodic periods during the holiday season. It is an important exam so I am treating it with reverence – have at last reached the stage of enjoying the Chemistry which is a good thing to get to. You can be quite at sea with it until you spend a few days getting it organized and it then seems to crystallize out into some comprehensible order.

I did enjoy both your descriptions of Xmas Day. It seems as though it goes on just the same except for the brilliant bowling performances on the lawn aren't so common and with Mick's absence, there certainly must have been food left over. Maybe one of these days you might break tradition and experience a white Xmas.

Spent a quiet New Year's Eve. I can never get that spirited midnight feeling so declined a party or two and put my name on the baby-sitting list. Went off to a young couple –he had been in the air force so the two old veterans had a yarn over two beers whilst the young wife became a little agitated. They finally got away and returned at 3 a.m., quite fit and sober. Didn't catch sight of the baby but as I was having one of my constant snacks, head a cry so turned the TV down and muttered "Quiet" and all went well. Driven back to the Themis and made $6, at $1 per hour. Was thinking it's such an agreeable way to make a buck, that next year, I might form a little company and do it three nights a week or four maybe. The Themis, of course is still satisfactory but having to be on deck most nights, or at least in, has its drawbacks from a purely time point of view. I think I could work better if I felt completely on my own but when I think of the meals, and Miss Browning's departure at the end of the month, I don't do anything rash.

Saw "Giant" on Sat. night with Joe Brebant who becomes the lawyer in May. It is a long but quite an interesting movie from many points of view. James Dean appears much to the local teen-agers' delight. There is a Jimmy Dean cult here that seriously believes he will be resurrected before very soon. He is supposed to be the teenager's ideal conception of his/her mixed-up self. Rock Hudson and Liz Taylor are quite good and despite several gooey love scenes which I suppose Michael and Caroline would enjoy (when Liz and Rock are nursing their twins !!!!!) There is a fine satire on Texas and her people which could in parts be very close to the bone, if applied to the Australian grazing set-up. I've heard you say it and it is even more obvious today, of the drought-broken bums who became the big socialite graziers once it rained and wool went on the boom. This is one of the themes of "Giant" when oil is found on the cattle ranches and pretty soon everyone has a buck, a fur and red hair. I think you'll enjoy it. Remember too that Miss Taylor is supposed to come from the State of Maryland which even to an extent now is considered "social" in comparison to Texas and the rest of the U.S.A., except for Princess Grace's hometown in Philly, PA.

I went to a party given by a physiotherapist and her husband. The latter spent his youth –he's 28 now – looking for oil in the Middle East and is now at McGill in first year geology. So I am not the only grey hair in the class. Well, it was weak as parties go but if you look hard for a while, you can usually find someone reasonably pleasant and foolish enough to want to talk to you.

Had a pleasant surprise the other night. Realized that I would be 23 in March instead of 24 which I had thought for the past nine months I would be. Must have lost count some where. However I felt quite spry for a week or so.

MONTREAL

(JAN 15 1957)

I have just staggered in from the library—the cold is fantastic at 18 below and just ten minutes is enough to make anyone with any sense begin considering a change of climate. The snow is all very wonderful but as I never have the dough to go skiing, it just doesn't weigh up. I am beginning to mellow as the basement sends its warm air circulating around my crimsoned cheeks and nose. California, down in L.A. seem about the logical place to enroll next providing I can finance it. It's been so long since I've laid in some decent, hot, sunshine – yes, it's either the skis or the swimming trunks and the West Coast. The Univ. of Southern California is a very good school. Most of the U.S. medical research seems to be coming from out there. Envy you that 102 degrees but then I guess you'd like to be over here in the snow.

Heard from Vod on Sat. Says he had five Husky puppies that he was going to use for his own dog team but during a very heavy snowstorm he struggled out, guided by an Eskimo to the generator hut where he kept them, about 100 yards from his shack. He left the Eskimo to close the door. He didn't, so that when the storm stopped 24 hours later, the boss found the shack floor and generator nearly ruined by a great pile of snow. Says it was lucky they didn't all freeze to death. His dogs were all banished to a nearby Eskimo village. Reckons he's in the market for a polar bear which is less trouble.

I went out to see the U.S. Steel crowd last week and can have the job back with a $40 per month hike but haven't got enough Chemistry courses as that lab job was for a 3rd year student. However with my "experience" and seniority shouldn't have to overly exert myself. Other alternative is the north which I will have to get cracking on before the boom ceases. One thing about my present position is that I won't lose much time after classes end as they begin paying May 21 and work doesn't even look like beginning before May 30 and also it's out of mind and settled this way.

Saw Douglas Bader's story "Reach for the Sky." Quite enjoyable. Someone left McGill thirty $600 scholarships each year until eternity for needy students of merit. I have only to qualify for the latter two worlds.

P.S. The cat is perched on the shoulder watching every movement of the pen.

MONTREAL

(JAN 22 1957)

Pleased to hear you are all well but am annoyed no Xmas parcel has emerged from the local Post Office panic. It is now over two months since I sent Mal her present. Will leave it for a few weeks and make inquiries. Having our own little heat wave now – 39 degrees above. It felt so warm that I had to unbutton the overcoat and it left me dried out after a morning spent in the stuffy, over-heated lecture rooms. This afternoon I spent three hours distilling in the chemistry lab. Worked like hell the whole time. At the end prepared a brew which should (if I can distill it correctly) give me a fair yield of pure alcohol. It is presently simmering in the lab so there might possibly be a party next week.

Sat. resumed squash with Cuthbertson who had to dart off after the game to select the crockery for the new adventure. That night to a dance up at the gym with a very good orchestra. The visitors came down on a social weekend from Laval University, Quebec City. Trying to get some amiability with our French brothers. There was a combined art show which the Gov-Gen Mr. Massey opened, tours etc and a mayoral reception for all the law and arts student who think that by playing politics at University, they will be sure, of course to get elected later on . They are right, of course. The dance was pleasant. Ned would have been in his element for a few of the dances that I refused to even try—they really rock'n roll up there when the cats start digging in.

The cat visited Miss Browning's room which presented her with yet another excuse to moan. Really there is a limit to what any man can take despite the fact that I have diagnosed her main trouble. I am now expected to do the washing up each night as well as the bar and am seriously tempted to quit, studying hard and getting most of my fees on bursary and scholarship.

Vod is well and still surviving on Southampton Island. Says they shot his four dogs. It was either him or the dogs. It's minus-50 outside but 70 above indoors so no worries. He has the London Times daily from England by air mail so that the weekly plane brings the news in a batch.

MONTREAL

(JAN 31 1957)

Your letter this week. The cold weather is through and at 10 above it feels like spring. We have an amateur long range forecaster who has predicted the big cold spell mid-February. He's been most accurate up to date. Was delighted to hear that Ralph has arrived in – knew you'd like him and I expect he had quite a few stories to tell.

Well, the backbone of the week has been broken with three full afternoons spent in the laboratory. Nearly went berserk Monday – we were working in pairs. I was with Cecil Jones, a 6ft 4 inch Negro from Kentucky and each time I bent the glass tubing for our chemistry experiment apparatus, he broke it, attempting to fit into the pattern. This went on for four attempts – the fifth time I took over and by acting like the neuro-surgeon got the cursed thing into place. Cecil is an extremely nice fellow –quiet spoken and fairly clever. I also prefer a States Negro to a West Indian –the latter are O.K. and there are quite a number at McGill. I think (pronounced Cee-sill) is the first Negro who I have felt unconsciously on level terms with. Usually you try so hard to show how broadminded and unprejudiced you are that you fail in getting through. To cap it, our alcohol boiled over. As he said: "It sure was a bloody lab." That is one word I have taught him.

We're on to mammalian anatomy now. This last term is concerned chiefly with the cat. There is an extraordinary number of bones, muscles, veins, arteries to learn but it is all quite interesting and gives a good background to the future human anatomy. My own "muss" is quite large and beginning to object to examination. I fear I will have to use him for home study dissection. I jokingly mentioned this to Arthur who spends most of his free time playing with the cat, and he was quite shocked. It is quite enjoyable to be greeted each night and noon by my friend who is at the moment playing with a pencil, making noise and about to be clipped.

Physiology lab all this afternoon – the cursed string gave way at the crucial point of an experiment on the muscle and nerve of a frog but my partner and self are gradually getting there with a lot of cursing. The nerve was performing perfectly but suddenly went dead for no apparent reason. I trust next week will bring better days but we are gradually clueing up on the pitfalls. My courses seem to be complimentary to one another. The Maths is hard but I am working at it.

Out at Bain's for Monday night. It was very funny. They had just bought their first TV. That is an amazing thing for everyone has TV. I asked Mrs. B. why she weakened. She confided that as her mother wasn't getting out so much, she had bought it for her. Later Grannie came over to me and whispered: "Heaven's knows why they bought this machine. None of them like TV." She is a very fit 81 like Nanna.

## BURLINGTON, VERMONT
(FEB 10 1957)

Doubtless a surprise to see the States aerogramme in the old tin box amongst the leaves from the hedge. No news of you this week so held off writing but decided I'd write off a few lines whilst the guy I'm stopping with takes a shower. Came down by bus last night with Judy. She is stopping out at a women's residence on the University of Vermont campus with a friend from Connecticut. I have been billeted with the boyfriend who has a modest apartment. His name, Lloyd Perry, from near Jersey City New Jersey and in 2nd year Electrical Engineering at U.V. The uni is spread out amongst the town buildings; the effect is rather spacious compared to McGill. The red brick and white pillars are everywhere. Had snow today. The enrollment is 3,000 students from all over the States. The most amazing social facilities are here in spacious lounges, shops, automats, eat joints etc. Giant fraternities loom up all over the place, Yanks are popping in and out and a Hi-Fi set is booming as the blades are getting ready for the Sat. night outing. We are all off to the local movie house and maybe a party after it. Feel young again, in this atmosphere.

Burlington is the capital of Vermont and is a city of 30,000, with one in ten a college student. The local businesses are developed along college lines. Writing this now in a coffee bar after a chicken lunch. The dough is flowing out like water. Went back to the apartment after the movie for a bit of music. Met a son of a McGill doctor from New Hampshire who spends his summers climbing mountains and winters skiing. He failed last year here so took on the instructor's job at Stowe which is the best skiing area in the East and not far from Burlington. We talked quiet a lot about their required two years in the services, Australia and the life over here. They all have a great life and joke about how everyone thinks of them as the capitalists. One big joke here is to accuse anyone of being a bit "pink" or a "Commie." Catching the bus at 8 p.m. The juke box etc is hardly conducive to writing impressions of the States.

MONTREAL

(FEB 17 1957)

It's already a week since I penned that rather scrappier than usual note off from Burlington. The cat has just settled down to a steady snooze so I should be undisturbed. Home O.K. to a very busy week of labs and lectures. Cut up my cat a little more- did all his leg muscles and stomach muscles. Some fantastic names – thank God the human ones are pretty much the same. Physiology went well. Performed the operation on the turtle and had to cut the bottom of his covering (plastron) off and then expose his heart – then the hooks into top and bottom parts (where the blood arrives and departs) and strings to levers so that we could measure rates and times etc. Well, he finally gave up and died so had to hack up another. Luckily this one performed better so that I now have three sheets of varnished records about which I have to write some reasonably sensible remarks before next Wednesday, explaining why and how etc.

Have a physiology exam Tuesday for which I have spent most of the week preparing except for Sat. afternoon when I won my first set (ever) from Cuthbertson at squash. The score 3-2. I have won the occasional game but never a set so it was quite a mark. The other piece of history is that, this week one of our lady club members was appointed manager to a large branch of the Bank of Montreal. This is the first time in Canadian banking history. Banks are full of women over here.

Bought two records down in the States –they cost $4 there but up here $5 plus 25 cents tax. Won't enrage Ned ("cool Ned") by telling you the rather somber titles. I dreamt Ned was over here last night and the week before I was with Tony somewhere.

Miss Browning off at the end of the month. Everyone much alarmed as she has done the club a lot of good in all directions. Generally I've got on O.K. with her but we've had our "off" days I must admit that I have periods when I could gladly toss the dishes on the floor. During the Xmas break I read a book in which a guy was temporarily washing dishes and said: "Why, the hell, do those fat pigs have to eat so much, so often?" Well, that about sums it up. However when I realize that the meals and room and closeness to McGill are on the "taken for granted" basis, it doesn't seem so bad. The bar is slack enough, so I can get a little reading in there.

Our McGill Winter Carnival later this week – they've built a $4,000 palace of ice blocks, enormous, like an office block.

We have a wedding here at the club Sat. For the first time since I've been here, it is an open bar so that the place should be a shambles. Even on the limited quota, a few always succeed in knocking themselves off. I had to be on guard last event. Everyone got a little gay and wanted to throw confetti at the bride. Since I have to clean up, I went around the whole crowd informing them that this was expressively (sic) forbidden within the club. There is quite often someone I know at these affairs, usually from McGill.

Very mild weather in the 30s, just below freezing so that is certainly pleasant. Spring is on the way but we'll have more snow and wind yet.

Back to the nervous system.

## MONTREAL

## (FEB 25 1957)

It is raining, quite mild but when it hits the ground or sidewalk the ice forms. Spent a precarious ten minutes skating along to my Maths lecture this morning. The lecturer didn't make it until 9.15. The class had walked off in relief except for the five other stalwarts who remained to do problems for the hour. I never feel quite that sure of my mathematics that I can breeze off whenever the opportunity presents itself. The trucks and machines are out spreading sand so that the city won't be sued for broken hips. Winter brings an amazing array of machinery out on the streets – giant tractor-like combines chew up piles of snow, diesels clear the sidewalks and workmen are hard at it with the old shovel into the truck. Old Pete has sprinkled the front steps with salt several times so that none of our members should land up in the gutter of Sherbrooke St.

It has been a gay weekend. I swear my last as the big push has got under way from 9 a.m. today. Starting Thursday night, we had the night on Mount Royal with an amazing fireworks display. We watched it walking up the wooden staircase and with its multi colours against the starry background with Montreal spread out beneath, it made an unusually effective scene. The dance later was full of the usual rock'n roll which to me is still sheer nightmare. There was a tremendous crowd in the Chalet so it didn't matter too much. The campus was full of very clever ice sculptures. Some were quite artistic and cleverly packed out of ice and snow The Ice Palace dominates all –in fact it rivals the library.

Friday was Forum Night, held in the Montreal Forum or stadium where the local "Canadiens" hockey team has its H.Q. McGill defeated L'Universite de Montreal in the inter-collegiate game 4-0. It is a very fast game –the Canadian style is rough as bags according to European standards. This was followed by the graceful McGill co-eds who put on quite a show – a few professionals then dazzled around on skates. It was my introduction to an ice show. The climax came with the crowning of the carnival queen, an attractive beauty called Carol. Also has Miss Canada and M. Jean Beliveau, the star Montreal Canadiens hockey player as attractions.

Sat. the big wedding at the club – up and down the stairs with chairs, plates etc then three sets of squash with David C. and back to the bar after the nuptials. All the young folk succeeded in making pigs of themselves on the free grog. The barman dispensed the potent measures – sent the chef down 8 ounces of Scotch and the pastry chef 6 ounces of gin with my compliments. When I descended to the kitchen I found I had nearly scuttled them. Fortunately Miss B. didn't notice the strategy. I remained soberly aloof, stopping only to evict the best man from behind my bar. I had left the table for 15 seconds to replenish my ice supply and returned to find him installed with the bottle of Scotch poised over several glasses. That is one way of allowing a shambles to come about.

After doing the dishes, I rallied, collected Judy, met David and Louise at the Ritz and had a night out dancing there. Very amusing South American girl succeeded in diverting our attention from our respective partners (i.e. she was the floor show). It was a bit like one of those movies of a swank night club with young and old taking themselves pretty seriously. However we had a most pleasant evening. The Ritz is only a block from the Themis Club so I trust the doorman in his field marshal's coat doesn't see me as a threat to his clientele. In Canada, it's just the dough that counts. Really: where else could the barman of one club dance at the reputedly "best" place in town?

Well, as I said it's work, work until May.

MONTREAL

(MARCH 19 1957)

The regular feature of Monday (your letter) seems to have stopped so that I get it any day up to the following Tuesday. Mine must be just as irregular so that from tonight I shall make each Wednesday the letter day and trust you will do likewise.

Have just returned from the Museum where I went with Miss Bancroft to view "The Story of Man," a photographic chronicle of man all over the world. I think I described it in my letter from New York City nearly two years ago. It is an enjoyable exhibit and the camera is at its most usefulness rather than being the mere recorder of faces of killers and new born babes.

Spent this afternoon in the Physiology Lab. Most amusing time as had to do tests of dog's blood by drawing it up a tube and depositing and mixing it with other solutions. Accidentally took a mouthful and the guy next to me couldn't get it up his tube because he had the horrors, after seeing my effort. Still, it didn't bother me too much. We worked then with a solution of mixed, crushed-up brain. Another experiment was blood tests of our own blood, drawing it off through tiny tubes and seeing how fast it took to clot. Then we had to count blood cells under a microscope so it was quite a satisfying afternoon's work. They are tiny, about four and a half million cells to half a centimeter of blood. You take a sample, put it in a ruled rack and count the squares to get an average count. Then, multiply by a mysterious figure and you have it.

Tuesday is always cat anatomy day – working patiently on the head. Always think of Mal's operation when we do the eye and its muscles and big nerve. I presented Mary, one of the waitresses here at the club, with an eye and told her it was from an old man. She was petrified. On Monday finished the Chemistry lab for the year. This is early but there were some urgent repairs needed for the lab –thank Heavens.

Spent Saturday morn, after the usual vacuuming, amongst the skulls in the museum and then I defeated Cuthbertson 4 sets to 2 in crushing style which wasn't a bad effort as my head was still a bit sore. A couple of days before, I had felt so fit that I hopped or jumped as I ran up to the kitchen from my room and hit the pipes in the basement roof. Thanks to the Howse constitution I was able to resume in ten or fifteen minutes but had an enormous egg on the head. It's fine now. Finished up that evening at the Women's residence for a quiet evening. Sunday worked three hours at the bar and then to Bain's for a meal.

A roll of Aust. Posts and People arrived today. Am just removing myself to the bath to read in comfort for an hour or two.

MONTREAL

(MARCH 28 1957)

I was thrilled to get your birthday telegram on Friday morn. Spent a quiet 23rd birthday. At lunch time the chef arrived singing "Happy Birthday" with the cake. Charlie had performed the feat of making a chocolate cat and there was a bottle of Coke tied with a red ribbon and "Best Wishes from the Management." Cuthbertson is like you – he never forgets a birthday. The news traveled so I got the "shout" to the pictures (a $1 bill). Mrs Mannock had me up for a drink. She really is a pleasant person to be associated with here at the club. She has spent eight years in Italy, heading United Nations Refugees etc and before that was with the British Army (in action!). Says this is a trip before she returns to "don the shawl."

No, I haven't as yet cut up my cat. It is at present gorging on the meat and milk. Has grown tremendously and all very keen on it. There was quite a battle when I left for the weekend over who was to officially be in charge. I give it little mental exercises each night by lining up eight shoes and putting a small ball in one of them. It goes through the line – as Ed Roach said when he saw it, the impressive thing is the eight shoes. He knew me when I got to Canada and says that "bloody migrants" with their shoes, radios and record-players are the end.

The week topped today by the laboratory exam in Chemistry which I hope was O.K. The next is comparative anatomy – four of us had the specimens sent up and have been working on the "parts" all Saturday. I squeezed in the squash game during the lunch hour break, 3-2 in Cuthbertson's favor. Wednesday spent with the piece of rabbit's intestine which we hooked to a recording point and took measurements of the contractions which went on all afternoon despite the fact that it was just a piece of flesh. We tossed in drugs to record the effect etc.

Vod is well and he will be down in May. Had some photos developed for him and he looks fit and in his element against a backdrop of Eskimos, snow and fur skins. Thanks for the bunch of magazines this week. Will save them on my "after the exams" stack which I have in the corner of the room. Weather is springy now –what a change. The sun is nearly warm, 37 above and the streets are dry. You do notice the change of seasons and welcome it.

The medical acceptances are out this week so the excitement is quite intense. I will put in my application in December and trust I will be lucky enough. There are 1,200 applicants for the 104 seats each year – they take you either after the third or fourth year (i.e. B.Sc) and then the four years of straight medicine. McGill has the leading school in Canada and apparently is in the top five on this continent. There are many American applicants – 33 per cent are Yanks in medicine here. Must get down to my Anthropology paper on the Balinese.

MONTREAL

(APRIL 4 1957)

Well, your letter finally came in a day or so ago. I was wondering whether I should fly down for a weekend to check things out. The exams are almost upon me. Have Comparative Anatomy next Thursday. Have to answer 60 sets of questions in a room full of dissected animals. Am bringing my lab cat back to the Themis tonight so the stench should blend well with the room. It is the same colour as my live friend and the girls will have the horrors when I tell them I have finally sliced up the club pet. The lab is worth 30 per cent of the final mark so it is really quite important.

Physiology went well with satisfactory experiments with a series of frogs, each with different parts of their nervous systems damaged. They were still hopping about without their heads etc. I think the girls were hopping just as much although it isn't exactly the pleasantest thing I have seen – an old bullfrog jumping about with half his head and brain cut out. However science marches on and perhaps the applications to human beings won't be so drastic. I enjoy this course although it is one of the more difficult to get through. Zoology lab consisted of a trip through our museum where we had to do comparisons with skeletons of men, apes, cows, horse, wolves, tiger skulls, whales (enormous). One whale tusk was nine feet long, as big as an elephant's. Have just handed in my term paper on the formation of the higher animals from the bony fish we eat each Friday. It took me quite a time to complete.

The movie "Smiley" was written up in Time, using complete Australian slang. There were quite a few letters written in, asking whether it was any good as few people understood the "lingo." The film editor quipped: "Not real grouse but fair dinkum." Why they send pictures like that out of the country, I don't know. How was it? You didn't comment. Haven't been to a show here for a long time. Sunday night I went out to dinner at Louise's, David's fiancée. She has the attractive (most) sister just back from Europe. The Air Vice Marshal sent the girls and son, who is a C.A. through McGill. An Australian couple from Sydney was there. He said I looked the typical Riverina country type and asked what Sydney school I had attended. This was most amusing to me but satisfying to be reassured that the American way of life hasn't claimed me. However I sometimes have my doubts as they were telling me about Australia for ten minutes before I stopped them and informed that I was a Cootamundra bloke!

Mick, a letter after the exams but am thrilled at the prospects of becoming an uncle. Raining tonight, snow storm this morn. The weather is crazy. Elvis Presley was in the capital last night. All the teenies and oldsters were happy. Has Ned started his sideburns for Elvis yet? Am feeling wonderfully well.

MONTREAL

(APRIL 10 1957)

Came up to Cuthbertson's this morning to assist in the removal of some furniture for their apartment. They bought a few chairs from some neighbors and I have landed myself with a $15 pair of Attenhofer skis. They sell at $70 so it was quite a bargain and will make the winter a lot healthier if I can start some skiing next season. I am late writing this week as the anatomy exam was yesterday. It was quite good and I think I did O.K. – 120 questions on the nerves, arteries and veins of quite a few animals. I knew the cat pretty well –had the preserved specimen in my room for a few nights. The next big event is Calculus on April 25; from there it is Physiology and Anthropology on the 30th, Chemistry May 2 and six days later Zoology.

Judy has asked me down to Hamilton N.Y. which is a university town made up mostly of Colgate University, a fairly prominent uni in the East. Her mother drives up for her so it will be quite pleasant to have a few days off after the battles of the next few weeks. That part of New York State is quite attractive and we may work in a visit to a place they have in New Hampshire. Anyway, right now it's the exams that are mainly on my mind.

## MONTREAL
(APRIL 21 1957)

The storm is brewing above us. It is very warm, about 70 degrees I should think which is almost as good as 100 after the winter. Had the wild snow storm last week so this current tropical storm illustrates the range of our weather. All the old ladies are back from Florida and like the wild Canada Geese, have completed their annual migration. They now have a few months of very fine Canadian Spring days until they commence their complaints about the heat of mid-summer. They are nicely "tanned," like old pieces of leather. A tan looks fine on a Sydney or Californian belle of 17 but on one of this tribe appears utterly decadent. It is a crime the way they spend thousands of dollars sitting, sunning their tails in luxurious hotels.

The week passed quickly with industrious attacks upon chemistry, physiology reviews. Am currently engaged in drawing my Calculus up to scratch. It is a pull but trust I will have it in acceptable and passable condition by exam time. The Comparative Anatomy results were favorable – I made somewhere in the early 70s which places me in an agreeable position for the final written Zoology on May 6. I have six full days to prepare for that battle as all rest over by May 2.

Had the final Physiology lab Wednesday. Had to do touch and sense tests, sticking needles, cold and hot shafts etc and mapping out the areas of skin which replied. It's a nuisance having to supply the big lab report at this stage but it has to be done. Had the final lecture Thursday.

It was really Spring weather and I dropped in at the Cathedral. They had the usual side altar decorated. The church is a replica of St Peter's Rome but at present looks as though it was a relic of Hiroshima as restorations are being carried out. Have to work tomorrow. It's around this time that work begins to pall but Mrs. Mannock is much preferable to Miss B. Had the day out at Pointe Claire, 12 miles out along the shores of the Lake St Louis where Miss B. is living with friends. The latter had two of the most agreeable children, really the best brought-up children I have observed on this continent of rude brats.

Vod is well and enjoying his rather interesting life in the far North. Did Caroline find Southampton Island at the top of Hudson Bay? I was down at the Hudson Bay Co. with Vod's polar bear skin to get it cured – was taken around the skin room filled with beaver , mink, otter, raccoon, lynx skins. Was annoyed at the Sydney Truth's inaccuracy in the item about my following him to Canada. At least the trail-blazer might be mentioned first although it was possibly inserted by one of Vod's friends of Double Bay.

MONTREAL
(APRIL 26 1957)

Writing in the bar –had the Calculus exam yesterday and I think I have passed it. If I have, I feel I have reached my apex as far as Mathematics is concerned. Have three more days to work on the next two – Physiology and Anthropology.

The weather is really beautiful now, almost worth the long winter. I think the Spring here is the release from heavy coats, overshoes and groaning ears. Am looking forward to getting away for a few days to Judy's place. I'll come back and work on the graduation business at McGill like last year and then scoot up North. Will be off to the same lake where I was last summer but am trusting my seniority will mean slightly less rigorous work than digging holes in that Arctic till which must be even harder that Coota's Flat oval in summer. However it will be good to be out in the open once again. I think this university-country compromise almost ideal. I thought the Cartier connection best to keep as you have to sign on for five months in the Arctic. However I may still do it as it is a fascinating area. I often wonder why Tony doesn't strike off for the Northern Territory or some of those mining boom areas in Queensland. There are piles of dollars or pounds to be made. How's Ned the public servant?

The buffet here last night but as everyone had stuffed themselves over Easter, only 26 appeared. It was glorious for me as I was on duty until 10 p.m. At quarter to 10, one old girl ordered five Scotch and sodas. I wasn't concentrating too well after the three hours of Maths. Really, I didn't have enough time for that paper – I always tend to do that first time around.

The cat is thriving. At the moment it spends most of its time looking for a mate. It is quite at home under the bushes outside the window. Arthur, the houseman went off to a wedding and seems to have been mislead by his seven brothers down in Sudbury Ont., as he hasn't reappeared. My scheduled bridesmaid for David's wedding is Mary-Jane Ferrier who is his sister-in-law to be. She is most attractive, just back from Europe and very pleasant. Too bad I will be gone but David has some insane faith that I will be around. He says he will drag Point St. Charles (this is a Redfern-type area) for a replacement at the last moment.

MONTREAL

(MAY 3 1957)

Days and exams have been running by without record as I battle the efforts of examiners to unseat me. Here in the bar all is quiet. Mrs. Mannock has just poured a drink to help me on my way. She is extremely pleasant. I announced that I was taking off a few days and would be returning prior to departure for the bush. She doesn't let the small events worry her unlike the predecessor. I can return in the fall should I so desire. I expect I will although if I step into Third Year, I will have to do pretty well in order to be accepted into Medicine the following year. The competition is stifling and I feel the job does have some effect upon my studies. I can't complain: it has been marvelous but the gap out of each night is considerable. However the additional $600 living expenses would be more than considerable. That would render me destitute at present.

Chemistry this afternoon – I think I made it as it was a fair paper. Anthropology also was O.K. but unfortunately physiology was a brute and I have very strong doubts. I didn't finish it, made shocking blunders and in general was way off form. However I shall know by the end of the month. Zoology remains, May 8$^{th}$ so that I have five good days to prepare my knowledge of the hearts, lungs and legs etc of a variety of animals. Having the anatomy up my sleeve makes it better.

Cuthbertson is in his home, apartment not very far from here. He is amazing in the way in which he has scouted around buying the furniture and moving etc. Getting married must be the greatest nightmare. I didn't think he would get there at times but June 14 is the date. He is doing very well with the accountancy and does his Intermediate this summer. I think he will probably win the provincial medal. Vod is well and says the last six months in Arctic have been as pleasant as any he has experienced. Contemplates remaining in the north for a while. He is certainly doing well – seems to have the monthly raise and is meeting a variety of interesting people. The north is most fascinating with the great frozen expanses, the Eskimos, the trips to Baffin Island and Victoria Island. We are planning the re-union during the summer.

The girls at the club sit in front of the TV set. Only Miss Johnstone, who is getting on for 80, ignores it. The others are transfixed. I have just returned from adjusting the screen. Has Coota TV yet? I hope not as it will be a shame when the children swap their tennis and swimming for a measly old Disneyland movie or some sloppy revue. Went around to Pat Chapman's apartment on Sunday night for supper. There were four other Australian girls there. It was fine meeting them all. One was from Perth and three from Adelaide.

P.S. Could you start sending off the magazines to Cartier Mining, c/o Northern Wings, Seven Islands P.Q. Please tie them securely as they get bashed about.

HAMILTON, NEW YORK
(MAY 8 1957)

Well folks, a few lines from the old U.S.A. before I sink into the double bed (it's a good three times the size of my sack at the Themis Club). It is a most pleasant bed and my room is used by the good Dr. Bancroft as a study. The walls are lined with books and there are desks and lights in profusion—an improvement definitely on my facilities in Montreal.

We left on Thursday morning. Mrs. Bancroft drove up and I took her and Judy to dinner at a small French restaurant. She is over sixty –the two daughters coming along late. She was the professor of Botany and met the Dr. who is professor of Economics. We left Montreal at 10.30 a.m. in the Buick, out past the Indian Reservation and just after we had crossed the St. Lawrence, the tyre blew out. As I cannot even drive these machines, the adventure into tyre changing appeared somewhat formidable so with the air of an old hand, I hitched a ride back to the Reservation garage (they don't do so badly, these Indians) and returned with the half-breed mechanic who had the business over in ten minutes for $2.

The drive down was most enjoyable. For my benefit, they took the road down over and through the Adirondack Mountains. The lakes and hills are really a welcome sight après l'hiver a Montreal. Stopped off at the faculty Camp on Lake Saranac which is where Robert Louis Stevenson lived for some time. I remember reading "Captains Courageous", for the Intermediate Exam I think it was. Its hero was the rich boy who spent his summer rowing in the Adirondacks. Whiteface

Mountain is the highest peak in the district; around 5,000 feet. At its foot is Lake Placid which is a well-known resort area.

The country is rugged—pines, birch and lakes but the roads make motoring a delight. The only time it would compare to driving in Australia was a three mile stretch of road repairs. It got a bit bumpy like our Junee road. Came down through Utica which is an industrial city of 120,000. The hills became smaller but the countryside around this small town of Hamilton is decidedly pleasant—I expect that any barren expanse is pleasant after the winter in the basement and the hectic events of the past month. The hills have been left from the glacial retreats which covered the continent four times in the past million years. They aren't as old as the old Quebec rock, over 1,750 millions of years, as old as central Australian deposits.

What strikes me about a small town like this one is the neatness and general appearance of the houses. They are all two and three storied and shining and fresh. Everyone seems to have a buck although as Judy says, a lot have the mortgages. However they live a pretty decent style of life – green, mown lawns, automobiles and a few Cokes every day.

Colgate University has about 1,200 students who all wear the same type of dress and act just like the "all American" boys one sees in Life Magazine. They are a bit like children to talk with but are generally agreeable – fees are about $800 plus expenses $1,000 or so that it is a school catering to the more select i.e. wealthy of the American populace. The facilities are fantastic – they explain why they don't turn out a really good student in anything comparable to an English University. At the moment, the 18-hole golf course is being built, also a luxury dorm –the faculty is poor but the students are rich. It is primarily a liberal arts and science center with no professional faculties but it is allegedly one of the better American universities. I am really in no position to judge but most of the students seem to have had it too good for too long. Maybe I have washed too many dishes – it's grand to have finished. Back to Montreal next week.

Dear Mal, I was so pleased to have your letter and snaps when I got back to the Themis Club. The parcel of old picture albums and Dad's First World War letters was awaiting me. I sent you a card from the States asking why you had not written but I think your last letter was well done and contained a more mature outlook than you have expressed before. What fun it is to have snaps of you, Mum and Ned –all looking so well.

You appear to have realized that it is necessary to go further than the Intermediate at school. I am pleased to hear that you have begun to study diligently for that important post. Well, it's up to you and I am more than sure you can do it. What subjects are you taking? I trust you take a little more care with your spelling than when you write to me. Just careless slips such as "there" for "they're" can mean quite a difference. One little point I always try to remember is to read over what I write in an examination after I have finished the paper.

Of course I'll shout you a pair of snow shoes. I remember how cool the nights were when I used to study for the Leaving Certificate, wrapped in my old dressing gown with a blanket around my legs and looking forward to a brew with Mum and a few biscuits we had hidden. Just go down and book them up and send me the bill by airmail or tell me "how much."

I was very interested to hear your paintings turned out well. Do you feel you could handle a set of oil paints or would you still require a bit more practice on the patterns? Judy, I am sure would send you a set if you write me. They are cheaper in the States than in Canada. I did enjoy myself at her home. It's a long time since I have been in that type of atmosphere. We went for a few drives in the country, did some walks and at night played the records and some chess. Each morning I'd get up about ten and go downstairs to an enormous breakfast. After the washing up (I'm a professional, remember, at that), she'd play the piano. She can play beautifully but doesn't get much of a chance to play at McGill. She is in 3$^{rd}$ year, one year ahead of me and is 20 years. I was looking through her scrapbooks. They have an interesting time at school but spend so much time on extra activities such as school dances, dating boys, social work and summer work that little is left for brain work.

Try to remember that, Mal, and don't try to rush things. Dances and dates aren't really important at your age –it is much more important to develop a good healthy body and by sound study, an equally healthy and full mind. If you would like me to, I will send you a book which will tell you and illustrate just what are the essential differences in men and women. Many times you get the wrong idea of things like sex at school. You needn't discuss my letters if you don't wish –just let them be between you and I but I know you show everything to Mum.

P.S. Join the library. Have you read "David Copperfield?"

## MONTREAL

### (MAY 21 1957)

Your letter this morning. Sorry I sounded a bit off after the Physiology. The results came out very early. I crept up the four flights of stairs and found my name on the pass list –my good lab mark must have pulled me through as I felt I wrote a lousy paper. The rest should be out this week. They are posted on boards just above the room I am working in here with the gowns and hoods. All under control and now have a few days grace until the rush begins.

Went out to the Cartier Mining Co office and they think it will be two weeks before we are on the move. The ice is still thick up north and the weather still cold. That will suit me. They began paying today. There is a chance I may have to do a bit of map work out there in the office so am hoping it will not clash with the position here at the club.

Haven't done too much of note since my return from the States. Weather here is pleasant, sunny with green bursting out everywhere. I strolled up the mountain and across to the Oratory on Sunday. This season puts Montreal at its best. The Westmount mansions are attractive, old stone and built-up gardens.

Yesterday was the Queen's Birthday holiday. One of my old girls was leaving for England so I bundled her stuff into the cab and received $3 for my pains. In the afternoon walked for a mile down Sherbrooke St. to the Show Mart where there was an international trade exhibition. Japan has a large exhibit of clothes, cameras, sports goods etc. The Australian Government was not represented. That old fool Steele probably didn't have the energy to arrange anything.

Saw Joe Brebant Sat night. We were going to a show but such a shocking variety at present that we decided to play a bit of music and talk. He had that year scholarship in Paris and takes his Bar examination next month. Has the $7,300 job awaiting him but says that he is so used to the idea of being poor that it doesn't mean much. Reckons he has spent so much time doing it all that it is the least he would settle for. My policy is not to consider the money angle. If I did, I should still be working in London.

In a bus today, I saw a woman give her seat to a Negro woman with a child. Just where South Africa is going, God only knows but they can't win with their apartheid. In the States, they have finally got right around and now the South Africans ignore all the progress. That is one country I would not migrate to though I should like to visit.

P.S. Off to my third job now.

MONTREAL

(MAY 30 1957)

Well, I'm going into 3rd year when I return in September. The results are out and whilst I continue along, I do not star in anything. It might be an idea if I did – am seeing the secretary of the Faculty of Medicine and getting I trust, some advice on next year's courses. It will be a most important year and I wonder if I should return here to the club. Anthropology was my best.

Weather very warm and I am itching to get the call into the wild. The convocation was a very colourful affair. The Lower Field on Sherbrooke Street was delightfully green and surrounded by the trees of the campus. They had the stands for friends, parents etc and in the centre sat a thousand odd graduates in their coloured hoods. Jerry, the white Jamaican and I had personally outfitted each of them! It was a beautiful day – the university band was out. Had the big rush after it all, getting the gowns back. They are somewhat sorted now. We have the radio and a coffee machine outside the door but I shall be happy to jump into the train and be on my way north despite the extra money I am making whilst on this job.

Expected Vod down next week but had the wire saying that he had been delayed. I retrieved his polar bear skin from the Hudson Bay Co. It is cured and cleaned and is enormous. Makes a fine rug but I will store it for him as it doesn't look as if I'll see him before I head North. Mrs. Mannock, the club boss, just popped in and announced that she had resigned. I am not surprised as I have noticed the change in her enthusiasm for the job. The whole show is not "her cup of tea" as she puts it. Miss Browning nearly ended up insane – it's all these bloody old women that finish people. It doesn't affect me that way, purely a matter of too much time out of my study time.

Last night went out to Dorval for a dinner party given by a Mrs. Cusack who is a daughter of the woman the Air Vice Marshal is marrying. He is a widower. Everyone, except your son who forgot, brought a present for Cuthbertson as Louise has been collecting in the loot from kitchen tea affairs. The show was in their honor and the main course was spaghetti and a meat sauce, served with a very fine red wine. I cannot remember enjoying the taste of wine as much before. Perhaps I shall become a fan and drink myself silly on imported Australian Penfold's. Mary Jane, Louise's most attractive younger sister and my scheduled bridesmaid was there. Also Mrs. Cuthbertson, David's mother, who has arrived from Rio de Janeiro for the big day. She is like you, Mum, puts all the young ones to shame and is really very pleasant. Her first trip to North America but is bearing up under the new life, her only son's marriage etc. She likes Canada tres bien and is going on to the U.K. and Kenya providing Mr. C. can give up his job in Brazil. He is the accountant. David was down in Rio for four years and speaks Portuguese. It is the only country in South America where Spanish is not spoken.

MONTREAL

(JUNE 1957)

I had better orientate to the Syracuse N.Y. Greyhound Bus Station where I have just landed after a day and two nights in Hamilton at Judith's home. The ice, when I left Montreal, looked as though it was going to stay for a good week so the Cartier Mining boss O.K.'d four days off. It was so warm here and we played badminton on a full court we marked out on their back lawn. However the peace was shattered yesterday with the call to arms and I am to catch the 8 a.m. plane North from Montreal tomorrow for Seven Islands.

The attendant had just brought me the milk shake –my bus goes in 15 minutes for Montreal.

(Resumed several days later)

On Wednesday Helen and David Lindsay called and I met them for lunch in the Windsor Hotel. The job with the graduation gowns at McGill had finished so I was able to take them for a stroll around part of the city. I enjoyed the news of you and the district. They don't seem to have changed since my school holidays at Cronulla and both looked fit and well. On return to the club found the sleeping body in my bed. It was Vod! It was tremendous seeing him again. He is heavier built than I am and looks so well. Likes the Arctic, brought back Eskimo carvings for me. Had the sessions over coffee etc Sends his regards to you all. He left on Monday by C.P.R. train for Winnipeg. He's going to stop with Vic Murray for a few days and then on to Edmonton and a possible job with the Hudson Bay Co. on a barge traveling up the Mackenzie River to the Arctic Ocean.

Friday night a dinner etc for Cuthbertson given by myself and six others at the Royal St. Laurent Yacht Club. (Excuse me from now on as it is 4 a.m. Have just finished packing after our respective voyages into the North and West.) We went on to a few clubs as this was his so-called Buck's Party. Saturday his mother gave a dinner around at David's apartment. She showed movies of their new Rio home, beautifully situated high on a hill overlooking the city. I ran the projector successfully for the first time. We went on to the Ritz for dancing –party was the Air Vice Marshal and scheduled new wife, Mrs. C and David Ferrier (brother of the bride) and the four principals in Friday's drama which I will now miss. The floor show is usually a competent single songstress and this time she came from Spain and did the exotic castanet dances and flitted amongst us with the microphone. She ended her act by presenting her bouquet of roses to our table so we all had to don the red roses – the barman at the Themis has been living it up!

I seem to have accumulated the usual mountain of junk. Arthur and I have just stacked it in the storage room. I will most likely come back in the Fall. Use this address: c/o Cartier Mining Company, Janine Lake, c/o Northern Wings, Seven Islands, P.Q. Canada. Northern Wings (Les Ailes du Nord) is the bush air firm which transports most of us and our supplies. They meet us at Seven Islands with the flying boats. Will write more often when I'm settled in the bush.

JEANNINE LAKE P.Q.

(JUNE 17 1957)

Once again in the bush after that all-night packing spree and a brief visit to Cuthbertson to confirm my departure and tidings that I definitely wouldn't be his best man. Taxi to Dorval and met Don Ferrara, the chief geologist. We flew up via Quebec City, over the St Lawrence Rive all the way. The plane was a four-engine

North Star, Trans Canada Airlines, a government concern. Had the luscious meal on board and arrived at Sept Isles about 1 p.m. Checked in at the hotel and suddenly was whisked off on the first plane to go in. Nick, who I played chess with last summer, was the pilot. I flew for a solid hour. It was a good lesson and I picked up a lot of flying hints. The planes usually have only the one set of controls but somehow this one was left with both sets. Had four of the guys in the back as anxious passengers but they didn't realize I hadn't done much flying before. When we arrived I "allowed" Nick to land. Some of the crew from last year are here again – the development of the camp has been tremendous with huts and storehouses, roads, test processing plant, mine etc. As it was just bush when I came in, the change is remarkable.

My job is Labour Foreman!! I have eight labourers, a bulldozer, and a jeep at my disposal. Anything needed around the camp is given to me to do so I put the men of the job and spend the day walking around inspecting! Have them building a 100 ft-long. wharf out into the lake at the moment – the gang is made up of two French-Canadians and six Newfoundlanders. All are most agreeable and they seem to know what has to be done. I have finally learnt to drive, on the worst roads imaginable. Perhaps the highway in a car will be too much for the jeep-hardened veteran. My work also includes running the planes in and out, putting on flights and loading and unloading. The best thing about it is that I am free to walk around as I please and as long as the others keep reasonably busy, I run my part of the show O.K.

The weather for the past three days has prevented any planes from arriving. At the moment, without a proper wharf, we unload them in the middle of the lake on to a wooden raft built over 45-gallon gasoline drums, with a 10 H.P. motor for power. How would soft old Ned be on an 800 lb barrel of mill bolts? The first week is always tough but due to my exalted position, not as tough as last year .Two medical students live in the radio shack with an Irish operator. We play chess every night and with electricity have the facilities for reading etc. Having the discussions with Al and Jocko who are studying at Queen's University, Kingston Ont. One (Jocko) is the college football star and we had the football out today, kicking, and passing those enormous throws. Am not shaving for the summer so the beard is shaping up. Left the shaving gear in Montreal.

Getting on the small Beaver plane at Seven Islands, my old Parker 51, which I had carried and guarded constantly for three and one-half years, slipped out of my shirt pocket and gurgled to the bottom of the lake!

Judy has gone off to a girl's camp at Oakland which is on the coast of Maine. The children over here are sent off to summer camps where they are taught to be nice American kids etc. She runs the swimming division – how I can't say as I think Caroline would beat her over 50 yards but she seems to enjoy it as a summer job. Am expecting the early morn planes so will close off at 11.15 p.m. –your letter should be on it.

P.S. The Montreal Gazette reported David C.'s wedding and that Mr. John Howse was best man!

JEANNINE LAKE P.Q.

(JUNE 28 1957)

It is a misty grey day and depending on one's athletic attitude, either depressing or cheerful. For me it is the latter – I have put my gang to work, given one student the day off and sent my bulldozer man to level off an uneven piece of ground behind the storehouse. He is making $600 per month, nearly twice the amount I am receiving. The consolations of salary aren't so grand after all but for a bum, I'm happy.

No planes will be flying today so with luck I shall be off the hook. Things have changed this year. I have quite a lot to look after; it is more interesting as I am in the picture of all that is going on. Yesterday I installed the fire fighting equipment which is a series of gas, portable pumps which are placed on the side of the lake. Beside each pump is a 1000 feet of hose which is easily joined with the 100 feet on the pump. Each day I take the jeep out along a bumpy, hole-ridden road to Shirley Lake and pump the camp water supply. It is a daily ritual for it is so tranquille out there without the Beaver at work.

One of the advantages of controlling the waterfront is placing myself on the planes for hops over to the sites. We have an airstrip being constructed eight miles to the west. They have struck muskeg which is swamp and the bulldozers are bogging down every second day.

Two miles from the cleared strip is the luxury lodge, $300,000 worth in the middle of nowhere. What a shocking waste it seems – that immense sum for a bunch of American visitors, most of who would enjoy the chance to live a little "bushy." The camp here has the usual number of workers who have been on the big jobs throughout the country. Tales are spun of the Arctic and the D.E.W. line where Vod worked, the mines of Yellowknife, the Yukon, Labrador and Saskatchewan. The North here is the West of the 19th Century U.S. The Yanks have taken over much of the Canadian venture as there is little else for them to dig up down south.

Last night I went canoeing with Al. He is the ardent fisherman. Fishing still bores me, a memory of Cronulla days of forced enthusiasm on those school holidays. I left him at an outlet and just drifted off down the lake reading a novel by Graham Greene, "The Power and the Glory." He is the Catholic author. I picked Al up later. The mosquitoes have just arrived so strolls through the bush are now off as a pleasure. We were in one of those low-bottomed canoes and as Al stepped on to the wharf, I reached for the log and it tipped me into the water. It was damn cold and I emerged with the boots full and made a dash for the tent, completely soaked.

We are off-loading the large Cansos in the middle of the lake. Hell, the weights are crushing at times but the gang is willing, providing the direction is there. They tend to treat the planes like a heavy truck. Had one exciting moment when an 800lb tin of mill bolts balanced precariously on the side of the hatch and the raft. Fortunately, we had a rope around it – otherwise it would have plopped to the bottom, as my fountain pen.

Yesterday I made an unofficial visit to Blough Lake to see the old camp. It looked so peaceful yet deserted. The bears have got into the food store room and made a two-foot deep brew of flour, sugar, bottled food etc on the floor. I will have a cleaning party over soon before it begins to stink.

A card from Vod with a flaming oil fire scene. He didn't get the Hudson Bay job and is now in Edmonton Alberta. He is fit and well. Papers always welcome up here.

JEANNINE LAKE P.Q.

(JULY 15 1957)

Have set the lads at work on a log cabin, cutting survey lines, breaking rock and filling oil drums. The master retires to his tent which is rapidly becoming another 1336 Sherbrooke St. Jim Wellington ("Duke"), a 5th year medical student has moved in. That makes 3 medics. There are tremendous battles over patients and an axe cut assumes the importance of brain surgery. It makes the conversation a lot healthier and I am obtaining some background to the medical arts. No one knows very much but it usually provides an agreeable atmosphere and when I do emerge, the relics of last year are not so distant.

This 3rd Year will have to be a lot better. My results for the past two years have not been good and as I intend applying to the medical faculty in December for entrance Sept. '58, this year will have to be a beauty! I think I can do it but may have to give up the Themis around Xmas. Medical fees are $700 per year. At present I am paying $450 but once you're in, you can borrow very easily from all sorts of student funds. All sorts of opportunities are cropping up as far as future summer jobs are concerned. I was over visiting the construction job at Barbel Lake and the boss there was talking about all their far northern construction. He says he could easily get me a summer's work as a foreman which would mean the trip to the Arctic and quite a bit more loot. The Arctic, since Vod's experience, has a fascination for me so that I should see it before settling into the four more years at McGill.

Life here is as pleasant as anywhere. I canoe often at night after supper. Yesterday I swam out to the loading raft. The water is still cold but I can't see it getting much warmer. I went flat out the whole way. We have a well-equipped laboratory here. Last night I did an iron test. This is the type of chemistry I will be performing next year so that I am going to get all the experience I can. Familiarity with procedures and accuracy have to be attained – the McGill system has the student remain in the lab until the results are correct so that I am trying to avoid spending the hours in the Chem lab each evening.

Had a letter from Ralph Harris who is selling Coleman heaters. They are used throughout North America especially in the north. All lamps, stoves, ovens are made by them. He says sales are O.K. He was the man for the job as he had used Colemans for ten months on the D.E.W. line. Another letter from the Themis Club – my boss has left, saying the old women would have her as insane as Miss Browning if she remained any longer.

I have now in addition to seven labourers, two carpenters and two mechanics. The latter earned $195 last week – 96 hours!! I think that is why they have been handed over to me.

Have nearly finished the new dock – shortage of wood has held us up. Have had a nice log cabin built, just like the hut on the tobacco tins.

JEANNINE LAKE P.Q.

(JULY 22 1957)

The summer is racing onwards and days flick by and I seem to have lost my hold on time. Rose at 5 to 5 this morning as the Canso roared over the camp. The sun was rising over the hills with that dawn glow which is soothing to the early upheaval. No gas in the raft engine despite my orders yesterday. My Newfoundland gang says that to get annoyed on Monday morning is to warrant anger all the week. Well, on that count, it's going to be some week. They are a happy bunch, full of jokes and playful as kittens but maddening at times. There has been an agreeable spell of five fine days which has me down to the shorts and boots, plus the tan which for Canada is quite rare. Have swum in the lake quite a bit more than any of the locals – the blood, I fear, is thinning.

Some "set back" news from McGill. I will have to do the supplemental in Maths. Began working on it last night. I took it this year as a course to interest me but fell by the wayside. However with the important 3$^{rd}$ Year and the possibility of a reasonably free turn at the studies, I think I should hit my stride O.K. Marks are not everything and as I am enjoying this life of wintering in Montreal and summering in the North, the effort always seems justified.

The mill is processing iron ore from the rocks I cleared last year. The amount of iron found has proved a paying proposition so that the big mill will be installed and a powder concentrate shipped out by rail. This means a large scale development. It has been interesting watching the growth of this area. As the labour foreman, I am up with most of the camp's doings. Under my control are the helicopter, Beaver, Cessna 3-passenger plane, a Fordson tractor, 3 motor boats and a D-6. I have a pleasant domain, most of the time things run very smoothly. I am gradually training the Newfoundlanders (I am one of the few who can understand their Gaelic accent) to play a more independent role. They respond tremendously to a little responsibility. Bob, who can't read and has to get someone to write his letters, has just come into my tent, and beaming informs me that he has repaired the outboard engine. I had to do the trial run and have shown my gratitude by giving him an overtime job, preparing for tomorrow's Canso which has a load of fuel oil. We pump it from the wing tanks into 45 gallon drums. I remember how I used to experience horror at Tony's work at AMPOL. Well, I toss a gas drum about with ease. With heavy work, half the battle is knowing a little and the other half is native strength.

Have not shaved since leaving Hamilton N.Y. I think the result will be quite impressive by the end of the summer although I doubt the beard will last too long. Some of the beards here are pretty much the real thing but as old Francis says of one of the medic's efforts: "Jim could count the hairs of his beard, with a telescope." Francis is 61 and still going strong with the bush work. His youngest son is 11 years old and he has 14 children with the eldest 37. This isn't fantastic by French-Canadian standards. We speak all the time in French. I also have the four painters who speak a mixture of French and Italian. They come to me for every little thing.

The nights have become cooler. Summer is already half done. I am still waiting for it to begin. Am very well and fit and putting on weight.

JEANNINE LAKE P.Q.
(JULY 31 1957)

A rollicking Saturday night as the still of the bush closes in and I am alone at my desk in the warehouse. A warm night and I sit in my daily work attire – boots and shorts. The boss has been away for a few days so the mice have played. This summer has been much drier than last year. Al, the med student who has two supplementals early next month, has just fallen asleep over his notes, propped up on the bed.

We have the weekly show in the kitchen, mostly antique westerns which go over with a thud. Canadians seem pretty passive about the lousy shows and I miss the raucous comments which would come from Australian mob. Had a card from Vod. He got over to Edmonton, missed out on the Hudson Bay venture, went over to Jasper and then on to Banff and Vancouver with an Australian in a car. At Lake Louise he met some Australian girls we knew in Montreal and he should be back in Edmonton now arranging another northern venture.

Yesterday and again this evening I was up in the helicopter. A large construction firm, which is preparing a site for the power station on the Harte Jaune River, has its camp here. As I arrange the flight schedules, I have ample opportunity to include myself in trips. The pilot is the ex-Korean War jet pilot from Ohio who is also the law student at Ohio State law School. The camp is a few hundred yards from a surging 50-foot-high waterfall which is to be harnessed for hydro power.

Later Nick (the Beaver pilot) and self flew down along the river to Three Hundred Foot Falls, a beautiful white mass of foaming water. It is a pleasant relief to see a river going somewhere after the miles and miles of lakes and still trees. I like this country but am looking forward to the north-western scenery. I guess the bush life has become part of me and the years ahead will have to be split in two as they are now with McGill first and the sojourn in the bush a happy second.

Listening to a Boston radio programme – rather amusing to have the moderate city flavours coming in from the hills, so clear at this late hour. The new boss comes from Sudbury Ont. He is agreeable; no one seems to be mean and lousy these days. We have had a visit from Cyrus Eaton Jnr., whose father owns half of the world. Also a Guy Perini who owns a baseball team. Also the president (God to the permanent staff) said to me: "Good to see you again –you seem to be putting on the beef."

## JEANNINE LAKE P.Q.
### (AUG 5 1957)

Two days of rain ended this morning, with a fine sunny morn broken later on by rain showers. The Catalina has just departed leaving a load of delicacies on the wharf for Barbel Lodge, where the visiting toffs now stay. They are piled (the delicacies not the bosses) on the wharf and I fear will be pilfered. We usually knock a small tax off such items as canned lobster, choc biscuits and salted peanuts. Every conceivable food item has been flown in for the opening of the Lodge – it will be a dry affair. I think they realize that if they start drinking, we/everyone else will.

The camp boss and 2 I.C. left for Montreal two days ago so we enjoy the peace. It all seems to run itself when everyone does their job. It is a fine experience for I can get perspective – little decisions pop up all the time. A typical day would be similar to this morning's events – up at 6.30 a.m. for the breakfast of whole wheat biscuits, eggs, omelet plus bacon, coffee and toast. At 7 a.m. I put the gang to work cutting and clearing the drive from the dock to the camp area. Read for an hour on the works of Dr. Osler who was a famous man in North American medicine. Send off a few planes, talk with the painters, visit Oscar the cook at the drill crew's place for morning tea, unload and dispatch the goods to all the sites.

Last night took the Cessna and flew up the Harte Jaune River to 200 Foot Falls. They are a grand sight from the air. This river joins the Manicouagan Lakes.

Upstream is the camp, just a quarter of a mile from the 50 feet straight drop falls. It is the typical Canadian scene – tents, streams, falls, rapids, pine trees and rocks. It was such a pleasant little after-supper trip. The Biro pen leaked through my back pocket so until the storekeeper looks the other way, you will please excuse the pencil. As soon as I have a spare $200, I am going to get my pilot's license. I often do the flying on these short trips although of course, no landings or take-offs. There are sound flying courses in Montreal and with the familiarity of this bush flying; it should not be too difficult. This is certainly the air age.

Had better get down to the wharf and see how many of my stevedores are sitting on their tails.

LAC JEANNINE P.Q.

(AUG 15 1957)

Am in my warehouse office after sipping tea down at the drilling crew's cookhouse. Have dispatched everyone off for the day and am awaiting the arrival of the Seven Islands plane with the med students to assist in the stevedoring. Your letters have arrived each week and as usual enjoyed your news and had the complete picture of all the doings. Francis, the old bushman, is always interested in you all so I read him your letter in French. He was quite delighted. Most amused at your having the black girl to do the dishes. It read like a colonial wife's letter. Did you thrash her? I remember asking someone (I think it was in Ruth Bassingthwaite's kitchen) :"Why are you black?" She slapped me. The football scene at Fisher Park must get quite nostalgic. Mick and Tony are out and now Ned, too! I had better return to restore the family colours.

The weather is cool –the tan is blotchy and I am wearing a T-shirt and that old red sleeveless wool jumper that had seen its best days when Agnes Maloney gave it to me. Most of the old relics are still with me including that beige cardigan I bought with my first pay in Young nine years ago. The garde de feu (fire warden) who speaks no English just presented me with a carving of a moose which is really very well done. He is a young chap who has done nothing all summer as fires have been scarce. He works for the Dept. of Forests and wants to switch over to us as he will be through at the end of the month. Speaking French has been a great help all summer, especially now that the stores are under lock and key. I still have a loophole for my supplies of juice and chocolate biscuits and cheese.

Juice is a big factor in the meals here. I drink tremendous quantities but hardly see it during the winter.

Yesterday I went off with the boss to look over the airfield which the Tower Company (one of the giant construction firms in Canada) is pushing through. Eventually it will have a 5,000 ft. runway – at the moment about one-half is complete. It is a 24-hour job with enormous scrapers, excavators, bulldozers (D6's and D8's), all digging, clearing. Muskeg is all around. This is a glue-like swamp. It is strange to stand out there with the grey black hills covered with drizzling rain and to imagine the change that the airfield's completion will bring. Had lunch and called in at Barbel Lodge which is now finished and looking like a dream from a Technicolor sequence. The lost pilot who sights it will think he has finally reached Heaven. The day before I was with Jim Steel who is the "big boss" and the other local guy at Blough Lake, seeing how much we can salvage from this place we started at, just one year or so ago. It is all to be let go. It is an ideal place so it's a pity. Am very well.

## JEANNINE LAKE P.Q.
### (AUG 25 1957)

Writing this at the heliport. Have just assisted the pilot and engineer in removing the blades. Russ, from Ohio, hit some drill trays with his tail prop –this busted the shaft from the engine. One slip like that means a long list of checks to make sure nothing else was broken. The blades are 18 ft. long and weigh 90 lbs each. They are made of birch and balsa covered with lacquer. This machine is a "J" Bell model and costs $65,000 odd. We hire it at $9,600 per month plus a $100 per flying hour over 80 hours. They are operated by Spartan Helicopters who are the second largest operators of "eggbeaters" in the world.

The pilot who arrived in last week is a Canadian from Ontario. He worked as a clerk with Australian National Airways for seven months in Melbourne and did not like Australia because no one ate anything but "steak 'n eggs" and everything was behind ten years. Well, despite those opinions which appear a bit one-sided, we get along fine. His name is Harry Dale and I seem to associate that with a poem "Harry Dale, the drover, comes riding home again." I think he was leading his pack horse across a flooded creek and was drowned!!

Pleased to have your letter dated Aug. 12. How is my sister with the mumps? That is one thing she won't have to worry more about. Vod wrote from Fairbanks Alaska where he is installed in a big hotel at a staff conference. He is still based up at Cambridge Bay and asked for news of you all.

One of the pilots here is mad on my Australian Army hat so Ned, can you send him over a size 7 1/8th with a pugaree. Also mate, whilst you are on the job, would you take out a sub to the "Bulletin" for me. It costs two pounds thirteen shillings and sixpence for a year within the remnants of the British Empire. I'll send you the money for both on my return to Montreal. You could send the hat to Nick Capron, Bush Pilot, c/o Northern Wings, Seven Islands P.Q. The Bulletin should go to me at the Themis Club. It seems to be the only Australian mag not full of ridiculous photos of Sydney "bodgies" and American jazz stars. I will send it on to Vod and would like you to get it off as soon as you are able.

Life here is pretty slack. They work pretty hard at the pilot mill but now that the planes only arrive once a day and our camps are folding, travail diminishes. Play lots of chess, drink tea and read. We have begun to ship concentrate out in 325-lb drums. They are damned difficult to handle as firstly the feet, and secondly the plane, have to be guarded.

The last of the black flies are making a final effort on my flesh. We had snow a few days back and it is clinging to the blue hills 15 miles to the south.

JEANNINE LAKE

(AUG 25 1957)

Already the nights are colder and the days shortening. Shirts are back and I don't feel that we have had any summer at all. Probably a Cootamundra January would stun me as much as a Montreal mid-January would jolt you. Am seated in my section of a warehouse. It is quite peaceful and the Coleman stove is gently heating. Amusing to think of Ralph Harris selling Colemans in Melbourne. A note from Vod who has settled back in the Arctic at Cambridge Bay H.Q. for the Western D.E.W. Line He has a big job and a 1,000-mile stretch of territory to cover, ranging east and west and over 12 radar stations. He does his trips in U.S. Air force planes; say he had some fun with a group of Australians in Edmonton. He had on his issued U.S. Air Force jacket (U.S.A.F. and a great pair of wings on its back) and pretended he was a strategic air command pilot. He sounds in tremendous form.

Life here is fine. The bosses returned yesterday but the work was on schedule despite our sleeping and playing chess, swimming and reading. My slaves keep going as the master sips the coffee. The mill results have proved that healthy iron percentages are contained in the deposits. The open-cut mine is operating where I did the rock scraping and blasting last year. So far they have put through the tests but now the fully-sized mill is scheduled. The iron is joined with oxygen in a black crystal which is called "hematite." Great layers and folds run throughout the rock bed of this whole northern Quebec area. Here we have drilled over 60,000 feet of samples in several places to ensure there is enough of the hematite in this locale to warrant the millions of dollars that are going into it.

The rock contains, besides the hematite, many other minerals and elements which are of no value so that is the reason for building the mill which separates the iron oxide from the crushed ore. I look after the dispatch from the docks but there is a road and railway on the way so the ore concentrate will be freighted to a harbour to be built at Shelter Bay on the St. Lawrence. The ore ships then take it through Montreal and the Great Lakes to Chicago for the smelters in Pittsburgh and area.

I have been down to the Falls where the power station is being surveyed. We are "sans" the helicopter as every 300 hours the engine has to be taken down and checked. Had a letter from one of the Themis Club members. She said I "was greatly missed." I mellow as the summer progresses and the difficulty of finding an additional $700 presents itself .I will be off at the end of the month for Montreal – my supplemental exam is set for Sept.3 and they have given me time off so shall fly back on Sept 4 for the extra 20 days work. Fare is $40 but I have a lift down. Boss says that I may return for the winter – I have doubts on that, certainly.

## JEANNINE LAKE

### (SEPT 6 1957)

Your letters plus papers were here to greet the prodigal son after his sudden junket to Montreal. How really happy I am to be back here should not be difficult to understand. I am in my summer element once again and it is pleasantly tempered with the knowledge that I shall be back at McGill in three weeks. Met the new boss –one of the main reasons for hopping down there was to check that the Themis was O.K. for another year – at first she appeared to be the absolute nightmare, rather a common quality after the two English women but I've come across "odd-balls" (as they say out here) often enough to know that the still tongue and active head can surmount most obstacles. The Themis of course is very necessary and I am out this year to erase the previous two years' mediocrity. I shall have to if I'm to be accepted at McGill where the applicants amount to 1,200 for the 100 odd seats in the medical school. However with Nanna and Aunt praying on my side, I should get there. Actually when I do, I will feel a lot more settled.

I was pleased that the Asian 'flu hadn't laid you down. I can imagine Ned sneaking off to the bed for a few days off. We are supposed to have it in the Fall and everyone will have the 8 shots, I guess. Mick, of course, owes me a letter. You might, Big Brother, wire me the results when the baby is born. Am getting quite excited over the prospects of a nephew or niece.

Come to think of it, I might leave that flying license a while yet. Unfortunately, my flying instructor has been shifted and his successor – well, I'll leave him alone until he learns a little more, by himself. Drove an Oldsmobile around all this morning whilst waiting for the plane. Went out to the Indian reservation where les sauvages live in small wooden square houses and have a most attractive school and church. They are the old Iroquois tribe but don't do so much scalping, except the odd tourist. The driving practice on the Jeep in the bush has been most useful.

I met a Limey who worked out on the Mary Kathleen uranium mine in Queensland. He said there was good money being made but the conditions were lousy – too much dust and too many Italians. He didn't do too well here anyway so blew through on a week's leave to visit his dying mother and never returned.

My ears are still ringing from the noise of the Catalina which is not quite the T.C.A. standard in comfort. On the way up, our purchasing agent Homer Wilson flew most of the time. He's a docile looking chap but flew the Super Forts over Germany in the daylight bombing raids. Naturally that will bring a healthy scoff from the Australian Air Force vets! From Montreal it was really a gorgeous trip. We rode just above the clouds the whole trip and the scenery was unbelievable. Great masses of fluffy whites and greys, wisps of vapor and enormous cloud "banks" which made the trip like a voyage through a deep valley. Have you ever flown, Mum? Well, next time you are off to Sydney, I'll shout you a ride on A.N.A. –that is, if you promise not to want to get your private flying license.

LAKE JEANNINE P.Q.

(SEPT 13 1957)

Friday the 13th , my lucky day -- fresh from beating the chemist at chess. We play each evening and usually end up about even. He is Yugoslavian, in 4th Year at McGill and honoring in Chemistry. Should soon have some news about my nephew or niece. The rain has held up the mail for a few days but I have been working very hard receiving 80 tons of ore which the company kindly consented to put through our mill for another company, eighty miles north of Jeannine. Every bag weighs over a hundred lbs and they arrive all day loaded upon two "Otters," three "Beavers" and a Canso. Around the end of the day, the bags get very heavy. The flight engineer aboard IHD (Item How Dog), a Canso, is an Australian, a Jim Diors from Rose Bay.

My successor arrived. He is over forty and must be on a good salary. I've been taking him around on the job. We begin joining up the airfield, Lodge and Jeannine by good roads next week. He has the experience as he did a lot of work on the Knob Lake rail road. This runs to an iron ore mine in Labrador. The permanent staff is gradually taking over from the summer crew as the whole show is now on a year-round basis. However there's always going to be a job if I'm hard up in the following summers.

A note from Vod who says he is leaving Cambridge Bay and going down to work in Calgary, a bustling oil centre in Alberta. My friend, the dog, just entered and is softly groaning on the mattress. It will be an enormous animal and seems to double itself each week. It knows that I am in the warehouse and scratches the door until I admit.

Great excitement over the DC-4 landing on the new airfield this week. This means that there will be no delays beginning work in the summers and thus the paid holidays are finished. They carry about the same payload as a Catalina. The camp is full of aircrew now with the airlift of ore. The captain or chief pilot for a Toronto airline has 14,000 hours as a pilot. The general manager, "Tiny" Lefevre, is an enormous hulk who is almost the size of Farouk! They are all returning to Toronto tomorrow.

We had another visit from the U.S. Steel Corporation directors. They arrived on the DC-3 and toured around. Amongst them was the general manager of the Bank of Montreal, so things may soon be officially rolling. I think that results from all the mill tests have been excellent and that this operation will be put on the map soon. Out of here on the 24th and lectures start the 26th.

LAC JEANNINE P.Q.

(SEPT 22 1957)

Writing this from the tent. The Themis sent on your letter. I am due for the dentist as it is over two years since the last check-up. Fees are exorbitant but inevitable. Have one to come out but no trouble. May go to the University clinic where Vod and Cuthbertson went. Glad you enjoyed the Maclean's I sent – it is Canada's effort against the mags from south of the border.

Overcast and no planes. Yesterday I took the Cessna 180 and went off into the north for 75 miles to Mt. Wright which is the highest point in this area. We will have a camp and drilling programme there next summer. Obtained some flying time –the Cessna is much smaller than the Beaver. The trees, especially the birch are a brilliant gold of yellowish brown. Whole hills are enormous patches of color and the remaining country is sprinkled with clumps of brightness amidst the evergreen pines and fir. The Fall is early up here but is the most attractive of the seasons, for it is like a final splurge of warmth as the winter prepares. Today I had the helicopter take me to the Hart Jaune River. We landed at an old drill site with the clouds dark and low, the wind rising. It was rather a strange thought to know that in a few days I should be out of this country. It seemed impossible, standing on that deserted site. Brought back some drill hose. Joe, the pilot from Boston, demonstrated a safety exercise called the "auto rotation." We went up to 1,000 feet with the blades whirling above us. He cut the engine and we fell down rapidly, catching the power back before we hit the water. It is a useful angle in case of an engine failure. Play chess with him – he is a quiet type of the pilot class.

Weather has been mild but as soon as the rain goes, the coolness will return. I'm off tomorrow. Will have a day in Seven Islands and catch the T.C.A. to Montréal. Must shave before I face the old girls at the Themis.

It would certainly be good fun to get back to Australia next summer. Just for a quip I inquired at B.O.A.C. and the return fare was $1,800. Ship would take too long. I was sitting in the tent last Sunday with the stove warming my back, reading the papers. The rain was pouring down and it reminded me very much of a wet winter's afternoon at 67 but Mick wasn't sitting on the Herald whilst he read the local rag.

MONTREAL

(SEPT 29 1957)

Thank you for the good news about my nephew Christopher. I trust the next one (possibly Ned's) is announced before it is celebrating its first birthday.

Settled back in business here at the Themis Club. Some excitement at lunch time. I was settling down to the meal when I saw the Chef dashing upstairs and heard the boss yelling "fire!" I put the fork down, raced upstairs and found everyone throwing water into the manager's room which was a maze of choking smoke. They didn't seem to be making much impression so we called the city fire brigade. The switchboard girl at first thought I was joking but the smell of the smoke decided my case. Had to round up all the ladies and get them down stairs. The three brigades arriver after the frantic dash up Sherbrooke Street. They were tremendously efficient. The waterproofing was laid out over the kitchen which was directly below the bedroom, the fire was put out, the blazing bed and floor extinguished, everything mopped up and swept. Causes are unknown but I suspect the doze with the cigarette but naturally despite the pumping, I am remaining quiet. I was very amused –one of the French members was in her petticoat and wanted me to take the jewelry box down, then was embarrassed after speaking for two minutes.

Have quite a good year ahead and will try and make it an all-out winner. Am doing Histology which is the study of all the different tissues, embryology (study of the early development of animals before they are born like chickens in eggs and one-month-old "dead" babies!), Quantitative Analysis which boils down to six hours in the Chemistry lab, a course in Logic (philosophy) and Human Developmental Psychology. Am beginning well—the Blacker Library of Zoological and Botanical Science is open to 3rd Year students and is a refuge as only a handful use it, the remainder preferring the Central Station atmosphere of the undergraduate library. My other course is in Ecology which is an extremely interesting subject that deals with the life and environment of animals, their spread and distribution throughout the world. The professors seem O.K. Except in the latter course, and in Histology, the class is large.

Vod is in Calgary and getting a job there. Seems well and I've just sent some of his junk out there. I am left with the polar bear skin! Calgary is a modern city and riding the oil and natural gas boom. I am O.K. for dough once again but God knows where it will come from next year if I get into medicine. However money has and will be the least of my worries so far. No Maths this year although the Logic is modern symbolic logic and requires the mathematical approach.

Judith is back into 4th Year. I've met Themis Club members twice when I've been out with her. She had the summer at a girl's camp in Maine and was pretty fed up with it all. The Asian 'flu seems to have arrived here like the scheduled movie – the Girl's College has a big list of patients but so far so good. It's like the weather in conversation here.

Little Rock, Arkansas still holds the headlines – I have a good friend Cecil Jones from Kentucky who is also applying this year. He's the Negro but really a fine fellow and intelligent. I should have said "and" and not "but."

MONTREAL

(OCT 10 1957)

I leave the Club bar sharply at eight each evening now. Instead of being trapped with the dishes until all hours. It gives me a good start for the night and I avoid the noise and personal disturbances of people leaving and finishing work. Being admitted to the Blacker Library indeed makes a difference. It is really is a refuge and peaceful as well as uncrowded.

Feeling very pleased with myself tonight but solely because I am my normal myself again. Sunday I felt lousy, and after work retired to bed. Had a temperature, aches, chest, weak etc. Monday went to lectures but retired to bed again in the afternoon. Tuesday got dressed but remained in the room until the work at night. Felt better yesterday and went off to McGill – today all back to normal after what would appear to be my first attack of 'flu or anything since I am capable of remembering. I think the measles in Young back in 1950 was my last setback. It seems tremendous to be fit again. There is no inducement to remaining in bed when you are on your own. I can see Ned lying low for a few days with you and Mal as nurses in attendance.

I wrote Vod telling him about Uncle Bill's death from lung cancer. He wanted to know what surgery was available for that type of cancer. W.D.& H.O. Wills certainly must enjoy the thought of all those cancerous lungs and throats. It will take more that bribed parties of chemists to persuade me that smoking isn't one of the most harmful habits. Dr. Julian Huxley, the famous biologist spoke here of cigarettes as "cancerettes" – the thought of the tobacco company shareholders getting dividends off people who burnt up about 70 cents a day is enough to keep me off them.

Great excitement for the second time in a week – the young cat-burglar was seen standing in the doorway of one of the old ladies' rooms. Luckily she had departed for the weekend but the next occupant saw him and he escaped through the third storey window. The police arrived at 1.30 a.m. and searched the club. I heard the voices but thought it was the boss showing the friend about – it was the great policeman!!

The Queen arrives in Ottawa on Saturday but won't be visiting the Metropolis of Canada. The capital is in the midst of a bit of a fling – I had a trip there one Saturday for a football match. The Rugby team is at McGill but I can't practise with the job so don't get a chance for a game. Beginning squash tomorrow with Cuthbertson who is off work to study for his Intermediate Accountancy. I think he has a good chance for a medal as he leads his class.

MONTREAL

(OCT 19 1957)

Pleased to have your Oct. 7 letter. It was quite legible despite the "no glasses." Just read yesterday in the Montreal Star's "Australian Newsletter" that the drought was becoming rather serious out there. You had better sell the sheep on the Jindalee property but hold on to our Tamworth holdings.

I went off with Judy to the symphony concert Wednesday night. Have the season ticket and the seats almost at the conductor's feet. Enjoyable programme of Brahms, finished off by going to a party given by an Israeli chap (Odded Frankel) who was with me at Roberval last year and whose photo you have amongst the ones I sent home. It was a wine party. I guess you'd call it a "plonk show." Guy had a guitar so there were songs and later on dancing to the "pick-up."

Friday night to the Film Society show "Odd Man Out." I am a member and this was an excellent showing starring James Mason in a story of a killing in a hold-up in N. Ireland. So different to the trash that continues to circulate through the movie shows here. There is the odd good film but they are rare. Last Sunday we went out to Fort Chambly which is a pleasant small town an hour by bus from Montreal. The trees were nothing but supreme colour – red, gold and deep brown.

Warm spell continues – the lull before the storm. The Fort was a garrison for an early British regiment and is neatly preserved by the federal government. In the dungeons you get really a most attractive view of the rapids and river – almost a temptation to be locked up for a week.

Cuthbertson finished his four Intermediate exams yesterday. Is giving the cocktail party to celebrate Sat night. I go around there when I feel like it. It does feel good to be the bachelor and I have promised to be the perennial baby sitter when their baby arrives next April.

All my laboratories commence next week. This will mean an additional ten hours work per week but I am looking forward to getting started. Have my application form for medicine but have all sorts of photos, recommendations etc to be gathered up. Getting in is one of the most involved businesses but am just going to go ahead and post the application trusting for the best. Maybe you'd better keep those Masses going until mid-June when they let us know

P.S. It feels tremendous to be fit.

P.S. I have added another kitten.

MONTREAL

(OCT 25 1957)

Both your letters arrived Monday and I was most pleased to get such an avalanche of news. You still don't seem to have understood my position here which I have tried to explain over the past few years. I agree, this delay in getting down to basic medicine is annoying in some respects but it is the system in North America and the reason why I am not already delivering babies etc –as the bright young Sydney boys you seem to have the information on. One thing I might add here is that should you have any doubts on Canadian medicine, you might enquire of McGill University Medical College's standing. I know it is difficult for Australians to recognize the fact that there are other universities than Sydney, Melbourne etc.

At the moment I am more the natural historian and zoologist than medical student. Applications run to 1,200 odd for little over 100 seats. My current standing isn't so good but with a better year on the way I have hopes of getting in. The equivalent, chronologically, would be 3$^{rd}$ Year Australia. I enclose an article on medical education in Canada but as for delivering babies etc, they are quite a few years off!!

Today went up to the Histology lab. My partner Jerry wanted to go through a few tissue slides that we didn't get done last Monday. This is comparative histology similar to comparative anatomy last year but all done under the microscope instead of the hacking with scalpels. He is a 4th year Science student and brilliant. He should have no difficulty in being admitted next September.

Saw Kath Pigram this week. She looked very well and I enjoyed talking with her as she is such a pleasant person and wore the suit and hat which is good to see after the mucky campus styles of long socks, rubber shoes and check shirts. Have been meaning to give Patricia Chapman a call but really I've been busy since the return from the bush and intend remaining that way. I escape the Themis sharply at 8 each evening to the library and so avoid pottering about over late dishes which kept me back 30-40 minutes last session. Am awaiting the storm.

Old Mrs. Ferguson (Mrs. B's mother) is still in hospital and having a bad time of it although she's dead keen to be on her way home. Barbara Bain obtained her M.Sc. and today in the lab I was looking at a smear of blood which had been stained so as to show the structure, and on the "glassed-in" slide was written "Prepared by B.Bain." She is 25. Murray, Mrs. B's son, has his degree in Engineering Physics but I doubt if he'll shoot any rockets to the moon for some time yet as he has just become engaged. What a tremendous event "Sputnik" has been – the greatest thing in our lifetime but of course I missed the gay Twenties and the Charleston. The satellite was due over Montreal tonight at 6.15 p.m. but the sky was very hazy and the only thing I could see was a giant "SHELL" sign.

Had a note from Vic Murray who I came over with from London. He is in Toronto and has teamed up again with Maitland-Carter, the West Australian engineer who was with us on the "Italia" for that historic trip across the N. Atlantic to the New World. How's my nephew? And his old man!

MONTREAL

(NOV 6 1957)

Have just sent your birthday cable off by immediate dispatch so it should be on its way across the Pacific within an hour. Thought of you on the 4th and then remembered that was Pop's birthday so of course waited until the last moment.

Last week went to the concert by a well-known Belgian conductor Andre Cluytens. My suit had turned up after it had been sent by the cleaners to the bush as they were tired of holding it. Wore it for the first time in six months. I must have put on weight since my London days. I may apply the great legacy from Uncle Bill to a new suit. Vod had mentioned the possibility of a legacy several years ago so that news of it came as no surprise. After the legal crew has cut off its share I doubt if any will remain for the more needy relations.

Friday night a revival of "A Night at the Opera" at the Film Society – the Marx Bros. do not belong in the new age but they were screams. Cuthbertson and I played squash the night before – he won 4-2 with his wife looking on which prevented my explosive outbursts. She is getting progressively larger and he is becoming more like an old hen, clucking about.

Saturday a quiet evening at Royal Victoria College (the Girl's Residence) after a day in the library. Spent Sunday afternoon down in the Municipal Library. The work piles up each day so that I am on the job keeping up to date. The Chemistry lab began Thurs. and Friday afternoons which means an extra six hours weighing meticulously small amounts of long-named chemical compounds, then heating, cooling, mixing with acids, judging the correct colour change etc. Present experiment is a computation of the amount of iron in a compound. If you don't get it right the first time then a repeat is necessary.

Had a visit to the dentist today. I didn't like the idea of trailing up to the students in the hospital and spending hour after hour in the chair whilst a professor and some imbecile discussed methods of attack. I will probably have a heart attack at the bill as this dentist is on Drummond St., the center for medical and dental treatments. I have six fillings and one wisdom tooth to come out. The Gibson fillings from Cootamundra have lasted the distance well.

Have been out to the Bains where Mrs. B's mother is making a slow recovery from the bowel operation. She is 81 yrs. Was around at Patricia Chapman's and they gave me a tremendous meal. I went after work after fasting. Kath Pigram was also there. She is working at the Hat Shop further out along Sherbrooke St. It really is strange the manner in which three separate Cootamundra identities have arrived in Montreal.

MONTREAL

(NOV 16 1957)

Pleased as always to have your letter dated the 9th and that the cable arrived on time. It's raining here tonight; the boss has gone to her country home so things should be quiet until 7.30 p.m. when I commence the dishes. Have been on the offensive lately re the latter and each evening, I quit precisely at eight, leaving mountains of unwashed dishes to greet the day staff. The bar has been busy so since the return I have enforced the no-overtime rule. I think I have won a "Gandhi" victory in that a student is to be hired to do them from next week. I don't mind helping out on occasions but they do become the leeches when you do the right thing and unfortunately there are never questions on dish-washing in the final examinations.

It feels good to have the old nib once again. I could almost be on the bank ledgers again. Yesterday I decided to stop using ball point pens as they invariably leak and at the best of times, make a mess on paper such as these Canadian aerogrammes which, as an example product of one of the world's great pulp producers, is pretty "crook."

Sunday I spent working on Symbolic Logic as the test was given 9 a.m. Monday. Also in the Histology Lab, four hours of cell life of muscles and nervous tissue, broken for coffee at the "Greasy Spoon," a small eatery just down form the Biology Building but off the campus. As a test I went straight to the library but found I was so ravenous that I had to retire to Mother Themis Club. The girls had left four eggs and bacon out for me so I had the great dish of "scrambled" and several brews. The club is closed Mondays – the time factor after cooking, washing-up etc doesn't differ too much from my regular hours at the bar so I was humble and more cautious for a few days.

Tuesday a Psychology test which I wrote chiefly from my knowledge of Physiology rather than any theoretical nonsense absorbed this year. I still say a good crack on the tail works wonders but more on that as my nephew grows older. I have told Cuthbertson that when I come to baby sit, I shall experiment on his child. He is in fine form –Louise is an experienced hostess and they entertained an old friend, the director of Imperial Tobacco, on Sat night. I have yet to have a meal there. He has eaten twice here recently – I expect he is a bit cautious of the Themis/bush standards I am used to in meals.

Tues. night I studied. Wednesday afternoon a guy who is doing Pharmacy at the Universite de Montreal took me on a tour of the new campus. It is a tremendous place and will eventually become an enormous influence on eastern Canada. It is much more mature than McGill as it is a graduate university. I took Judy to the concert – Mahler, Elgar and that William Tell Overture which precedes Mickey Mouse on T.V. Quite a pleasant programme.

Thurs squash with Cuthbertson who trounced me 5-1. I took the first game but collapsed for the last three. I always enjoy the weekly outing. Last night to a Swedish movie "Torment" at the Film Society. It was certainly a suspenseful effort without the glamour and sex of the usual American offering. Worked at the library all day today. Yes, I am at the dentist every week. He teaches at the McGill clinic where Cuthbertson has his teeth done. I said it was just the difference between us but if the bill is high, the joke will be on the other foot.

MONTREAL

(NOV 26 1957)

Midnight. At last the end of the ball point pen era. I purchased the Parker 51 Saturday.—a silver top this time!

Just in from the ballet – the National Canadian Group. Saw "The Nutcracker Suite"—very colourful and able choreography plus very excellent stage scenes and dress made it a pleasing effort and one which I thought Caroline would particularly have enjoyed. The group seems to mature rapidly and is here for two weeks. We are off again Thursday night to the full "Swan Lake" – Wednesday night, the concert, this means quite a week.

Your letter announcing the first hot day. Am beginning to envy you. Tonight by the Ritz Hotel thermometer the temperature was 17 above. This is cold as it has been mild up until this evening. I have the heavy overcoat out and the scarf – will bring the toque into action soon. Tried to read "Island in the Sun" during the summer but got bored – the scenery would be agreeable, I'll agree.

Thirteen pounds for a radio is what you'd pay here. Ralph Harris left me his new one and I passed the old one on to the Australian girls. I had rescued it from the KRT Fraternity garbage dump and it has played faithfully ever since.

Last Sunday went around to David's place for dinner. There is none of this poor young couple's nonsense with him although he hasn't a cracker. They have got together a most attractive apartment. Louise, being older, is a tremendous hostess. We played squash Sat – 3-0, 0-3, 1-0 to him. I had him to lunch here and showed him photos of what his child looks like at the moment. They (the photos) were in my Zoology texts and I had to sort them out from those of a pig.

Spent the week fairly quietly except for Wednesday night when the new boss went to the ballet and left me to cope with 65 girls at a reunion. Finished 9.30 p.m., after a busy night. However the deal was that I miss the nightmare on Thursday as I go to the ballet. She is usually quite agreeable but is not well.

Friday night Judy rang and said there was a lecture on Australian literature to be given by an Australian at the Canadian Humanities Club. The speaker was a Professor Hope of the National University at Canberra (where I should like to work one day) and his talk was on the history and development of Australian literature. He was really critical but with a reason for as he said: "There is too much of the Waltzing Matilda, tucker box, the slip rails and gum trees in our writing." Why the hell they push Australian slang beats me. It only opens us to ridicule and no one understands it save expatriates like myself. I almost went up to meet him but there were too many women of the "cultural" type around.

MONTREAL

(DEC 6 1957)

Your letter at lunch time – the bush fires must be bad as I have heard the odd radio report and news items have appeared occasionally. This is something for the usual reports never go past the tennis championships.

A lousy Chemistry lab this afternoon. Last week my iron analysis was accepted but this week an ore analysis was rejected so I have to do it over. I enter the lab at 3 p.m. and raise the eyes at ten to six for the sprint up Sherbrooke Street. It is really a solid course and important as an illustration of techniques past the elementary stage. The air is full of fumes and bubbling bowls of chemicals are everywhere. Care is so important because any errors made may not be noticed until two weeks later with the result that you are that much behind.

Friday went to a recital by Swiss pianist Kurt Engel who was back for four encores. A good evening. Saturday I went to bed and read some of the African short stories of Hemingway. Sunday out to Jerry Berstein's place to study histology on this microscope which he borrows. The exam is Tuesday week and is important as the pre-medical students are like a pack of hungry wolves clamoring for the 110 seats.

The tissues are placed between glass plates and are very thin slices of all the different body organs. Many are taken from embryos so you might see a long leg bone all at once or an eye or a stomach. There are different cells in the various organs and they are stained with dyes which stain only a particular type so that you can study them. I will most likely purchase the microscope as soon as I am admitted – they can cost $375.

Mrs. Berstein returned to cook the pizza for us. She runs a fur business and they have a richly furnished home. I am going out again Sunday. When I left about 9 p.m., the first snowfall was in progress. The street lights, the light flakes, the few inches of snow already on the ground, the wind driving it in eddies low on the footpaths –well, it just felt pretty good to be alive and in it.

This week has been socially slow except that last night I saw Miss Browning and we had the big conversation. She couldn't stand England so came back to Canada and is taking me out for bar-B-Q chicken next week. I was out at Bains Monday night. Mrs. B's mother is back on her feet and looks well. They have asked me for Xmas, so has Cuthbertson's wife and another girl I know in my psychology. Meanwhile I'm off to Judy's for four days so it will be a pleasant break. We are studying Freud which puts a peculiar slant on this. Don't be overly impressed with all the "ologies"—they aren't that mysterious.

My two cats are two nuisances and do not allow me much peace when I am writing.

MONTREAL

(DEC 11 1957)

Xmas arrives each year so suddenly for me that it is only the shock of realizing (that the Australian mail deadline is upon me) that springs me into action. Once again the happy season to be spent away, my fourth now. It has been snowing all this week and windy – the department stores have great decorated scenes climbing up their outside walls; there is music filtering through the busy streets as though the angels were on high. Radio is catching on and the tunes are replacing formal Xmas carols.

I have yet to think much about it except to wish you all at home a happy day. I'll be off Sunday on the Greyhound with Judy and will down in the States for 4 days. Have been busy this week as my Histology exam is upon us Tuesday morning and there is quite a lot to know.

MONTREAL

(JAN 1958)

One degree below zero as I walked back from the library this afternoon. Before I left this morning a water pipe burst in my room. This put nearly an inch of water on the floor but as everyone said, it was a good thing for the floor! I always have the window, which is at street level, slightly open – the 5 below here last night was too much for the pipe but I slept warmly.

Your Xmas greetings arrived – I suggest you post them around the 10th next time as I enjoy the card etc. before the Xmas Day. Trust my letter made it to, you but I also posted fairly late. Xmas at Judith's went off quietly and pleasantly – she got up for the dinner but wasn't feeling too well all the time I was there. I prudently did not catch it so returned (a day late). The boss left the kitchen full of dishes for me to do but otherwise there was no scene. The one thing I would do most to prevent is a scene with the women who run these clubs. This one is Canadian, strange in her ways, but managed to see that the club gave me a bonus of $76 which was an improvement on the $20 expected.

New Year's Eve I worked until 8 p.m. and then took a taxi to the Heather Curling Club where I assisted the barman and washed dishes at $2 per hour. Finished at 4.30 a.m. but I prefer to see the New Year in that way especially when one sees the wrecks about—all trying hard to enjoy themselves. The trouble with most of them was that they reached a peak where they were having a good time but with the next drink, knocked themselves too far. The barman kept sending me out complimentary rye and gingers from the Social Committee head. He was an agreeable chap who took me down to the curling rink and informed me on the game of curling. It is like bowling except that stones are slid down ice rinks. The stones weigh 56 lbs and the rink temperature is 26 odd degrees. There wasn't much to do until nearly 1 a.m. As usual, the group of wizened-up characters in the kitchen who took everything, including several gins-on-the-house in their stride.

I passed my Histology Lab and now write the exam next Friday. Also have Psychology and Logic term tests coming up.

Had a day's skiing with David C. up at the St. Marguerite slopes. I fell into a frozen creek and soaked my leg. It was very cold later on and my shirt froze stiff!! It was nearly three years since my other skiing trip north and I missed the practice in between. He came 2$^{nd}$ in Quebec Intermediate Accountancy exam.

MONTREAL

(JAN 14 1958)

The Histology went off O.K. and today we begin Embryology or the study of the development of the Egg and I. Dr. Berrill is the professor. He has written several books dealing with marine animal life, sex and development. Tall, grey-headed and lean – it looks as though it will be an interesting half-course. I have Psychology on Friday and Logic on Monday – both term examinations but they are requiring some effort as the energies have been concentrated on the Histology.

Winter is holding off. It is around 32 degrees, the freezing point which is tropical for this time of the year. Had one short spell of zero weather but at present I have the window open – the cats are out of my way in the yard so all is relatively peaceful.

The new Conservative government seems to be holding the fort O.K. but the Liberals are in the midst of electing a new leader with the departure of Uncle Louis St. Laurent. Ex-P.M. Lester Pearson is the outright favourite with the Nobel Prize and general popularity. I would not be surprised if he leads the Liberals back in. A new election will be held sometime next year as the Conservatives do not have an outright majority over the Libs and Socialists. No evidence of any Labour Party but Social Credit leads a few of the Western provinces. Unions have some power but are not in the class when compared to the Australian unions. Anyway with a fair level of prosperity, most of the people don't see any differences between Cons and Libs. So they voted for a change more than a platform last time. Voting is not compulsory.

Province of Quebec is headed by M. Duplessis who is the Almighty premier. His Union Nationale has a large majority throughout the ignorant French-Canadian backwoods farmers whose electorates are kept on area rather than population. Thus Montreal with nearly two millions does not have the big say in matters political. Politics are generally corrupt, bribes and kickbacks are everywhere. Contractors receive enormous building contracts if they support the party. It's almost like Spain but not a police state. The Church has considerable power – Cardinal Leger blasts the night clubs occasionally. The police are pretty hopeless because their chiefs are always being chased off by graft scandals. The English-speaking minority controls business so they have a much greater power proportionately to the French who fill all the municipal and provincial service jobs.

I, like most Canadians (English) take little interest in political affairs. There doesn't seem to be any major issue at stake especially when at the Club I am on three good meals per day. What is name of Uncle Bill's solicitors? Please print!

MONTREAL

(JAN 24 1958)

I hope by this time you have returned to 67 and that our sister has joined the fold of Intermediate Certificate holders. Am anxiously awaiting the results and hope she does it. I remember hearing about the Leaving at Double Bay and my elation at that humble pass. Was your trip to the coast in the nature of a semi-holiday? I trust this was the case and that you had some respite from the children. If not, and I shall be interested to hear, then any more offers at one dollar and sixty cents per day for minding kids I'll gladly take up in cash from here! I feel quite "guilty" when I think of you putting in eight to ten hours with children and my $1 tip last Sat for screwing a thermometer on the wall for one of the old girls.

Have been on the go since Xmas with three exams – all out of the way in a variety of manners. Chemistry went well this week and resulted in two of my experiments being accepted. This is a very useful course – it has taught me more than just chemistry; that there is a definite discipline implied in ferreting out the percentage of a substance. There are no approximations, no slips allowed and my usual "that will do" methods are curbed. Embryology laboratory has commenced with the microscopes and slides of early life.

Surprised that Vod is returning with Aunt Peg but suggest you do not take it too seriously. He is working for an oil exploration company in Calgary and has plans for a trip to the Yukon where the search for the golden ooze has just begun. I have an interview Thursday with the personnel officer of Montreal Engineering—they are the designers of the Cartier Mining power stations near Jeanine Lake and I supplied their camps and knew some of the chief designers quite well. One of them, an Englishman said he would be pleased to help me on my search for a job this summer. I am trying to get up to Aklavik in the North West Territories which is Canada's northernmost town and situated near the mouth of the Mackenzie River. It would really be an excellent opportunity to see the country as it is 3,000 miles from Montreal i.e. about the same as going from Melbourne up to Broome W.A. It would be a chance also to see Vod as I would fly to Calgary and on to Edmonton and from there the long trip north. Enough, more if I find the job.

Monday night to Bains for the meal –went skating with Barbara who has the position in the Hospital Blood Research Laboratory. Bought new skates and did O.K. I had played squash and swam at lunch time so that it made rather a sporting day. The skaters were playing tag and races up and down the open air rink. I took it easy, fell only twice.

Wednesday to the Symphony with Joe Brebant – did I mention he topped the provincial Bar exams. It was a good programme – main piece as the Beethoven 7th Symphony. The guy next to me stood up and "boo" "booo"-ed loudly when the conductor Igor Markevitch came on to take his applause. I would not venture a reason why.

Last night to the McGill Film Society and saw the Italian movie produced by de Sica who uses untrained actors and ordinary scenes direct from life. It was entertaining but concerned old age and the frustrations of poverty and old age together, topics on which I am reasonably well versed.

Judy is still ill but the recovery is slowly taking place and she should be back this week. In reply, the wog was mononucleosis, which is a condition of the blood in which there is an increase in the white blood cells, the monocytes. It is infectious and brings fever, swelling under the arm pits etc. It leaves you pretty weak for a while and due to its communicability, it is best not to get too close!

Well, I'm going up to the library to read the Limey news and periodicals which the library puts out on the shelves each week. Am very well and the winter isn't too bad except my overcoat is beginning to sound the death rattle, Had the tooth out – a wisdom and it was so evenly done that I had to ask had he really got it. He asked had I been out to coffee whilst he was crow-barring – the crater is enormous but gave me no trouble, No bill as yet!!

MONTREAL

(FEB 5 1958)

I have enclosed the review of "Summer of the Seventeenth Doll" from Time Magazine. It was one of the more favorable. In N.Y. they apparently panned it. The newspaper clip is from the N.Y. Daily News which is something like the Daily Mirror and Sun in Sydney – not to be taken too seriously. In fact Time is only two steps ahead but due to its mass circulation is read. Again the slang provides difficulty – why can't they realize that we speak an altered language in Australia and arrange explanations of a few of the terms, as suggested in the Daily News.

I was out to dinner with the Bains tonight. Barbara and I went skating (not skiing) after the enormous meal. Not a fall which is something. Watched T.V. from Hollywood Direct – a play in which the main character was an Alan Merrewether from Sydney. He turned out to be only interested in the American girl as a means to getting a visa so that he could remain to work in the States. It was quite authentic – accent and dress, even the moustache had an Australian air and of course the inevitable "Let's give it a burl" and "She's a beaut, isn't she?"

My cat, just in the window and now settled, watching me intently, with wet paws drying
on my paper. He goes outside to watch the traffic in the snow which is a foot deep. The boss's cat was taken which relieves me of the care of two monsters. I am quite attached to this fellow –he's clean.

Played squash during the break between morning lectures and embryology. Defeated an English guy 5-0. He had been skiing for the weekend so he was in poor shape for the Lew Hoad of Canadian squash. I spend Sat and Sunday quietly in my winter home on Sherbrooke St. The Chemistry was a bit behind and required attention.

Judy is back but taking it easy. I have been getting her up to date on the subjects we both take. She has three Maths courses but I am of little use in that field. Cuthbertson is all in a flap over the new $250 washing machine plus spin dryer. Why the hell they can't do the diapers by hand for a start—but apartment life, says David, is difficult and I guess the Canadian woman is so gadget, appliance reliant that machines are 'musts' in every household. Marriage over here is one thing after the other but he seems to enjoy it. All the events, duties and bother which really horrify me are what he thrives on but are for me a constant reminder that I remain, your fond but single son, and brother.

MONTREAL

(FEB 12 1958)

I have been looking forward to hearing what arrangements have been made re schooling for Caroline. Your weekly news should arrive tomorrow but as the lull in the bar trade exists now, I'll begin. The past few days have been cool – below zero at night and 2 above on the way to my nine o'clock lectures. The sky remains blue and the snow is crisp to walk on – no slush. Two heavy falls preceded this cold spell – the giant snow ploughs have been feeding tons of it into trucks which dump the white mess into heated drains where it melts and runs back into the St. Lawrence.

The pre-election promises have begun to reappear. Pearson, new Liberal chief, said that university government scholarships and decreased taxation were high on his list if elected. The Conservatives are collecting themselves – they haven't yet quite recovered from their surprise victory last May but it was a bare margin and that is the reason for dissolving Parliament this year.

Unemployment has hit a new peak – a lot of it is seasonal due to the weather. Montreal Port is iced in from December through to April so there are a lot out of work down in dockland. Other outside activities are curtailed – the business people won't admit too much but it looks liker a minor recession which may not recover for a year or at least until a war breaks out. There was quite some relief when the Korean War arrived – down in the States they are beginning to panic a little but old Eisenhower says that things will be O.K. I wonder but hope the boom lasts a few years yet.

Played squash Sat and Monday but with zero and below weather I didn't feel too much like the skating although I tried to get someone interested on my visit to the Bains. I bought the bulky NY Times and in Australian style, spent the afternoon with the papers.

Cec Jones, the Kentucky man who enters medical school in September came around for supper. I raid the 'fridge before they lock it and we have a good meal along with the Jack Benny Show. He returned to study for an exam the following day but as I had spent such a restful afternoon, I decided to walk down town to a movie —'The Quiet American" – quite fair although the shock on facing the blizzard raging up St. Catherine Street after two hours sipping cool drinks in Indo-China, was hard to take. I am still very keen to travel.

The Winter Carnival here in two weeks. I am planning on a long weekend in New York City. It would be a chance to get some work done in the Museum of Natural History which would be most useful this year. "Doll" is still struggling – I hope it lasts until the 22$^{nd}$.

A card from Vod who is till in the West 'where things are best.' I was down at the Trade Office last week and read the previous week's Sydney Morning Heralds and sent them on to Calgary. The typiste is French-Canadian and I speak in French, to the annoyance I think of a very English girl who does something or other there and is also agreeable. They served me coffee. I did not pay my respects to the Commissioner as I did not have any dried fruits to sell.

Will end now. The brew is on and the tea is especially imported from England for one of the ladies – little does she know.

## MONTREAL

### (FEB 1958)

Brought your letter up to the bar so that I will be replying between the whiskey sours and straight ryes. Thought I would like to add these thoughts to the other letter I wrote because I, too, was a little put out at the way Aunt Peg has written you re Caroline's schooling. Naturally I wouldn't say anything to Vod as he is far above these affairs as always. I think as we both know Peg is most likely to get excited when she has had a few sherries. The outbursts flow – perhaps she's a bit lonely in London and as part of the night's loneliness, decided she'd write off with the tales of Spain. As you say, it was her who started the Rose Bay Convent School idea – what can she mean – (other than the "sheddies" as Pop used to say) when she asks about the cash. With the way the three boys have seen the home through, along with yourself even more, I can't see that anyone could possibly expect them to pack Caroline off to school any more that anyone in their own senses would suggest you submit yourself to the horror of a job in David Jones department store every day and a cheap apartment in Sydney. With fares etc, just the nightmare of it all sounds so preposterous that I would just forget Peg's letter.

Naturally you won't but will continue to worry or at least wonder what I think about Mal's visit to the Sydney convent.

Quite honestly I know you have had your heart set on this idea for a long time but surely now, with the thought of the fantastic expense, you will see what I am going to suggest has its points. Mal herself is intelligent enough to realize the position –what good would it do in the long run if she had one year away at boarding school if the entire financial strain for months to come. The only help in life is self help and the worst crime is self pity. Certainly people do small things for you and one is appreciative but on the whole, it is self-help that gets the job over with. Mal should realize that Cootamundra is a very small place and if she is to rise above what Peg calls the "locals" (and Mum, I'm sure you know what I mean because you feel that way yourself) she should plan to help herself. It is not a question of snobbishness – I think more of the Coota townspeople that I do of the local graziers and wheat cockies.

The nuns at Coota should see her safely through the Intermediate Exam this year. I am sure if she applies herself she will do much better that her ignorant third brother who escaped with 4 B's. She should then enroll at the High School for the Leaving Certificate. It is essential and from here she should really begin to work at her lessons. I have been trying to interest her along these lines – surely you could get her to see my point of view but I know that it is not as easy as that for it took me four years and a world tour to shake me up. Also, my good friend Vod has been of great moral assistance.

If she went to the high school I would be able to help out somewhat with a few $ for new tunics and clothes but there are the summer holidays when a smart kid like Mal could work at Meagher's or somewhere in town, saving the wages for the school year. I would not suggest this if I was not doing it myself. If she can see that the Leaving Certificate plus government scholarship would provide her with so much more in life than a year with a lot of wealthy young ladies (or relatives of wealthy people). I am so sure of this – that it is the right course to take, with a little inspired self confidence. Mick could talk to her and discuss these ideas.

Of course there is some sacrifice –she would not spend the school holidays sitting in the sun at the baths – my girlfriend Judy, despite the fact her father and mother are University professors, has worked at something every summer since she as 13!! In the United States, all the children buy their own clothes after 14 to quite a surprising extent. If this is so in the most powerful world power, surely it would suffice in Australia. However she should not be made to do it unless she really wants it. Nursing at Prince Alfred Hospital in Sydney would be rather good for her. Perhaps I could use her later in my clinic.

Well, that's how I feel, If you present the idea and the encouragement and add a little help, then I will do like wise. I have quite a long pull yet but I am sure that Caroline could get along by pretty similar means.

P.S. What is the position of my insurance policies? How much would one year at Rose Bay cost? Did Aunt Joyce leave any provision for it? Write me about these things and we'll see what can be done.


## MONTREAL
### (FEB 19 1958)

Two letters from you during the week and one from our young boarding school heroine Caroline. I was tremendously pleased with the outcome of your hectic week and how everyone chipped in and sent her off. I think it a lot better than the public school and the time table should make all the difference..

Montreal has had the heaviest snowfall this winter. For the past three days, the howling wind has whipped up a storm that has tossed the City into a rattled state. Fifteen inches of snow is a lot in an island city where there are too many cars for too few roads. The temp. has been down to one degree below zero and the gale-like winds fling the snowdrifts about. The walk to the biological building is about my limit. I stagger in with a red face and ears just ready to freeze. My window in the club room has a foot and one-half of packed snow blocking out the light. On the window ledge yesterday there was a six-inch mound of snow inside which had blown in through the minute air hole I have left open to balance the effects of the nearby oil furnace.

Today it rose to 14 degrees and the wind dropped. It was almost summer-like. Sunday the Bains took me up north to their summer cottage. Snow was up to five feet deep so we skied in – they used snowshoes, Barbara and self on skis. It was really a most pleasant trip through the woods, across snow, white and unmarked. We crossed the frozen lake with the wind howling down the frozen valley. I felt like Edmund Hilliary. It was 10 above zero and inside the house after we lit a fire it rose to 20 above. Had tea and sandwiches, then the return trip. Carried on for quite a while on the skis but as the car did not appear, returned to find it snowbound.

Finally got it rolling. The Canadian country scene in wonderful in winter especially on skis and with warm clothing. I felt quite at home in it. My ski harness was troublesome and my hands kept freezing to the metal when I managed to balance myself precariously on the skis which threatened most of the time to sink in the soft snow. However I settled them after a few halts and the hands gradually and a little painfully resumed their proper functions. It was a small taste of what those Antarctic expeditions must go through daily under worse conditions.

Vod was down at Banff for their winter carnival. I had intended going to N.Y. but they have had the blizzards which make everything more unorganized than even Montreal which has the best snow removal facilities of any place. The roads here are packed with enormous snow blowers, ploughs and trucks.

Haven't done much about the summer job position. Will probably end up back with Cartier Mining as the money is reasonable and the life pretty agreeable. This session seems to be flying by. An Australian art exhibition across the street at the Musee des Beaux Artes. Must drop in on it. I agree that Rita Hayworth would be an unfortunate choice for "Doll." Pay a weekly visit to the consulate for the Sydney Morning Heralds.

WEST 34 ST. NEW YORK

(FEB 24 1958)

An overcast morning in New York City. I am just about to plough up the eight blocks and across to 4th Avenue with my luggage. Leave Grand Central Station tonight and arrive in Montreal just on nine for my first class of the week. It has been a good change. I came down Thursday night on the Hudson Delaware Line. The Hudson River was frozen and it is a most unspectacular journey, similar to the Cootamundra-Sydney run only there is no water stop at Demondrille. Spent the day at the Museum of Natural History. It is a tremendous collection of animals set in their natural surroundings, of rocks and plants, displays on the cycles of nature which provide the oxygen and salts for life. The quiet was at times shattered by long crocodiles of undisciplined school children who were part of the Education Dept's extension program. The museum is on 81st St. just across from the Central Park. The park, as well as most of the sidewalks, is covered with snow. N.Y. had a very heavy fall early this week and doesn't have the removal facilities we are accustomed to in Montreal.

This Sloane House is just west of 8ᵗʰ Avenue and on the same street as the Empire State. Yesterday I strolled about – bought a few records and books. The Rockefeller Centre is certainly impressive—the sunken gardens have been turned into an ice rink ad it was crowded with smartly-clad skaters. One elderly chap was putting on a show for the young girls. He was most agile and dressed a la New Yorker. The city itself I like very much. There is movement and a maturity reminiscent of London, spliced with Sydney. The streets are full of trucks, people pushing garments on long wooden trolleys, Yellow Cabs and Irish-looking police. There seems to be a fair bit of new construction –skyscrapers are not really as enormous to the viewer as the long run up the side by the movie cameras would indicate. They are big when you stand at the foot on the sidewalk and sheepishly bend back the neck but they fit into the skyline and don't seem at all the monsters they are thought to be.

Met Joe Brebant who is at the Park Sheraton for a week. We had lunch at Times Square and spent a few hours at the Metropolitan Museum on 5ᵗʰ Avenue at Central Park. I would imagine that the apartment houses we pass on the side of 5ᵗʰ Avenue opposite the park were the homes of the wealthy and old, established New Yorkers. They had that $600 per month atmosphere.

I left it late re theatre tickets so had to sit in the costly stalls for Eugene O'Neil's "Long Day's Journey into Night." This was a drama of the Irish-Catholic migrant making good in the States. I enjoyed it very much and was engrossed for 4 hours! Frederic March and his wife starred. He is a superb actor and carried off what seems to me now, some very difficult scenes. There were just a few times when it dragged. I certainly enjoy theatre and a sound drama on Broadway must be difficult to beat. Joe had been to "The Threepenny Opera" down in Greenwich Village and we met after our shows for a meal. Called in at the Metrapole and listened to a collection of Negroes blast themselves and the excited patrons into Kingdom Come with "When the Saints Come Marching Home." They were standing at the back of the bar on a level above the drinkers. Had a beer which in the States means I drank a solution of weak tea and salt strained through wheat. I guess even Ned could take a couple without feeling high.

I'm going up to the Museum after depositing the bags at the railway. More from cold Montreal.

Your letter was here last week with all the news. It is raining in Montreal! The slush is inches deep and the wet snow and slippery surfaces make walking heavy going .How I would like a nice dry sunny climate for a change.. Imagine, a super market comes to Cootamundra. It must have put a few people out of work but do the big country customers use it? They're more used to handing over a list and having it filled before they take off for the station. All the grocery clerks over here do is stamp prices and stack the goods – a cashier collects the dough and throws the groceries into a large bag.

I was very shocked at lunch time today. Called the Cartier Mining office re a job and the latest news was that one of the field geologists had died the day before of leukemia or cancer of the blood. I was talking to him just three weeks ago. Apparently they took a blood tests when he felt he had the 'flu but had no temperature. The verdict was three weeks but it took him in ten days. He was a doctor of science from McGill, ex-R.C.A.F. Hurricane pilot in U.K. and 36 years old. He was my direct boss for that first summer. I think I mentioned that last summer's boss, Ross Clare, was killed just before Xmas . Being killed is passable – he was an extremely nice chap but losing the two key men at this early stage has jolted everyone. As you know, jobs here are not as plentiful this year but I think I will be O.K. with Cartier again.

The big walk-out on Thursday. The six universities in the province (three major ones are U. of Montreal, Laval U. of Quebec City and McGill) have voted for a strike. Just one day so far but a nuisance as I am trying to finish my Chemistry lab assignments. I guess I can't be a scab although they are only playing at trade unions for the day! The professors are behind it unofficially for more financial assistance for education—this "rotting province" as the McGill Daily describes Quebec. The federal government has the money but under the provincial rights as defined in the British North America Act, cannot give it unless the provinces accept. Quebec under Premier Duplessis the Dictator refuses and as the English-speaking business interests cannot afford to lose his support, they do not come out against him. The English press is for him – tied in with this is the fact that those same interests control the Board of Governors of McGill -- people like the MacDonalds (tobacco), Molsons (beer) and Redpaths and McConnels (sugar refiners). It is ironical that beer and tobacco plus lousy teeth keep McGill on the financial status. More as the strike grows to riots and anarchy rules for a change. The Duplessis government relies on the ignorant farm vote which is kept powerful by having electoral areas based on size and not population.

I am fit and well but exams are getting close.

MONTREAL

(MARCH 11 1958)

A sunny, windy day with the temperature just low enough to keep the inches of ice on the sidewalks solid enough to walk on. Pleased to have your news last week, also heard from our sister in Goulburn

The work is piling up here and final exams loom. Should get rid of the Chemistry lab in two weeks so that will save six hours a week. Have had a good run of experiments of late. Missed last Thursday due to the one day strike by all university students – it was 97 per cent effective in Montreal. One student turned up for the Principal's (Dr Cyril James) Economics lecture. I served him (Cyril, not the student!) at the club last week.

Saw "A Walk in the Sun" at the McGill Film Society. It was a very good movie and had to be withdrawn from circulation before the recruiting figures in the States dropped too low. Pity they don't show it around, most realistic. I took a Gail McEachern who I may have mentioned before. Her father Donald was a neurologist and biochemist, one of the founders of the Montreal Neurological Institute with Dr. Penfield, and professor here in Montreal before his sudden death at 49, right at his peak. They live on the campus. I go often to listen to the records etc and we go over our psychology lectures as she is in the Human Psychological Development course I am taking. Her mother comes as well. She is on the editorial desk of the Montreal Star, a fact I learnt from Gail after I had blasted the Star as a rag. I still read the S.M. Heralds regularly from the airmail editions at the Trade Office. I have not met the new commissioner yet but I trust he is more able representative that his predecessor.

Mrs.Bain's mother had the heart attack but is O.K. although in bed for a month. I was out last week. The Bains are the most non-demanding of people and very good to me. I attempted to buy them a dozen roses (i.e. for the ailing

Mrs. Ferguson) but imagine my horror when the girl said:" The $8 or $12 ones, sir?" I said: "Ferget it, lady. I was jokin."

Nothing definite about the summer yet but Cartier will be O.K., I am sure. A letter from Nanna and Aunt today – Nanna's thoughts and writing are as good as ever. Sunday night to Judge and Mrs. Smith who entertained an Indian from New Delhi and an Australian from Cootamundra under the United Nations Club.

MONTREAL

(MARCH 18 1958)

All Quiet on the Liquor Front. Enjoyed your news yesterday with the cricket scores and social doings. Spring has sprung here but only after the heaviest fall of snow this winter. Fifteen inches threw the city's finance department into a spin but it is melting rapidly. The slush is deep and the streets almost Venetian but dry times are just around the corner and I'll be shedding the "rubbers" (galoshes). The holes in the shoes last comfortably all winter as you just never venture outside without the overshoes.

Excitement mounting over the election called for 31st March. The Liberals held office for 23 years so the change last May and the dissolution by the Conservatives in order to try for a larger majority has given Canadians a greatly increased interest in politics. John Diefenbaker, Prime Minister, seems to have rallied the country whilst Liberal Opposition Leader Lester Pearson hasn't been able to star in domestic matters. As you know, he won the Nobel Prize.

The big issue is of course the recession and 550,000 presently unemployed. If this doesn't pick up in the Spring, it will be a shambles. Quite a few students are having difficulty in the job search. I called Jim Steele, the big boss at Cartier Mining, several times but only spoke to him yesterday. He says the job is there but will give me details at the end of this month. The previous summer they called me prior to Christmas so the difference is noticeable.

I was out at the Bains last night. Mrs. Ferguson is O.K. again and has a very nimble brain at 82. I gave them "Voss" by Patrick White (Australian) for Christmas and she had just finished it so provided me with an analysis of the plot and characters. Murray Bain is getting married in the summer. Mrs. Bain dropped the bombshell by telling me that I could live out there next year and just as long as I want to, when I go into medicine. They all seem very keen to have me on. I will have to think about it. It would be fantastic not having to work at night. She reasons I would have a chance at a full university year away from work and Mr. Bain admits he will have to do the lifting if I don't come. Well, I shall ponder the decision and let you know what I have decided – independence would be OK as Murray certainly had a free rein but it has been a long time since I have lived in a home so there would have to be an adjustment.

Thanks for the birthday wishes. When I see the 19-yr-old types around me I shudder to think of my age but 24 isn't quite the end of the road yet it is my fifth birthday away and the years have flown although it does seem a long, long time since I have seen you all. If Uncle Bill's legacy was one thousand pounds each I'd be excited as I would like to return for a summer once I have got myself into medicine. I guess I will have to settle for a quick trip down to Mexico City after the exams.

MONTREAL

(MARCH 27 1958)

The lounges are quiet so the barman, after completing his three-course evening meal, begins his weekly letter as the water boils for tea. I still drink a fair bit although the tea is lousy over here. Coffee is good and I drink a fair bit of that too.

Am in good form as on Monday I completed my analysis of brass and the course was finished on a good note as I was very close to the exact figure. Have the final April 16 and finish the year May 5.

Very pleased you got down to Goulburn. Caroline wrote how pleased really thrilled she was to see you. Will be keen to hear how the cricket final goes. Poor people, you must be looking forward to winter. Spring is really here –the streets are dry and the keener ones like myself have shed our overcoats. In Canada you have three top coats – Spring, Winter and Fall. I use the sports coat in Spring and Fall.

Excuse the stains on this note paper but the teapot spurted brew all over the place. Sunny and warm today. Psychology lecturer failed to show so Gail provided coffee on the terrace. At 12 I played squash—each week this English guy and myself battle it out. This week he wins 3-2. Last Wednesday I did 4-1. Returned to Miss Gail's where lunch in the sun, the first outside meal of the season. Her brother John, who finishes at a boarding school in Vermont this year, is home on Easter vacation. He is coming to McGill next year and is 18, but the school is an advanced progressive outfit so that his preparation should be adequate.

Last Sat night to the Ritz with David and Louise to see D. receive the Governor-General's medal for 2$^{nd}$ in the intermediate accountancy examinations. He sat in the front and left us back in the slums with the other relatives. Both of us were bored until his name was announced. All the other C.A's received their certificates. Has that big brother of mine qualified yet? An afternoon tea was served then as six o'clock approached, Cinderella ran up Sherbrooke St. and his grey suit changed into a white jacket. I must say I was very pleased to get my birthday wire –you, Nanna and Ned remembered. To the dishes, will finish later.

Have not seen Patricia Chapman and Kath Pigram for a long time. Will see them this week as Kath departs for U.K. soon. One of the Australian girls has the badly broken leg. I advised them to go skiing to catch the Canadian winter and this is the result. I visited her yesterday. She looks fitter than I have ever seen her and states that being in hospital in Canada is like living in a luxury home or hotel.

I'm going to do some Embryology as it is 9.30 p.m. and I left the track to read something on Mexico.

MONTREAL

(APRIL 2 1958)

Your letter yesterday –congratulations on the cricket win, Ned. The big news in Canada is the landslide Progressive Conservative vote which puts 'Mike' Pearson and his Liberals out for another four years. I liked Diefenbaker's campaigning and also wanted to see him back with an increased majority –a P.C. was elected in my riding for whom I had duly voted. The complaint now is that the P.C.'s have too great a majority. Last Monday I was at Bains for election night – we watched the election reports on TV. They had a fantastic coverage and TV images from B.C. and the Prairies kept floating in. It all seemed to me that the whole business was devoted to telling us something two or three hours before we would find out under less ardent work by the C.B.C. Radio.

Jim Steele, of Quebec-Cartier is being a bit evasive about the job this year. It was O.K. a month ago but I have had that odd feeling which comes when I'm dealing with someone who talks better at the end of a phone . He is supposed to call this week. Saw "Bridge on the River Kwai" last night with Cec Jones. It was very good. "Guinness is good for you." The scenery of Ceylon is magnificent – when you see it, there is a scene of the Mount Lavinia Hotel where I spent a few hours for lunch, a swim on the beach and tea on the terrace.

Everything came back minutely and I became quite excited. Cec was a wireless-operator in the U.S. Air Force in the Far East just at the end of the war and had flown everywhere in Asia, even down to Melbourne. I must admit I am very keen to go to the East so possibly could do a year in Tropical Medicine in Australia after I finish here. Don't get too hopeful of my being accepted without a B.Sc. into Medicine. I won't know until June.

I am due to go to an address at 4 p.m. by some English doctor of Zoology who is doing research on population movements in the sea. My squash partner failed to appear. I returned, after a fairly fruitless effort chasing around by myself, to have lunch with Gail. She had another girl also – very sweet young blonde who had 18 months in Switzerland at a finishing school and spent last summer in France. I remember serving her at the Themis Club so it was quite fun! Her brother is off as a chauffeur for two ex-Russian Royals who are doing a Grand Tour this summer.

I met an Australian on the street yesterday. He had youth hostel badges plastered all over his jacket which was something I never got around to doing, I am grateful to say. He is a fitter-and-turner, on the unemployment of $17 per week. Jobs are darn scarce but I am not too worried as something usually turns up. The exams seem to be more important at the moment. I am working well as I have some free afternoons and with Easter on its way, should be in a more reasonable position to face them. Tonight, I am going to the Symphony. I have been very pleased with my subscription ticket. There is only one remaining concert after tonight.—the Beethoven Chorale Symphony with a Montreal singer, Maureen Forrester to sing.

Had supper with Kath Pigram last Sunday night. She is fine. Patricia Chapman arrived in from the Laurentians. It continues to amaze me that three Coota people are in Montreal. I disgraced myself by saying that Parker St. went straight out to the mill and out by Des Stratton's home. Kath went to London on Sunday. You might call Mrs. Pigram to tell I have seen her daughter. David and Louise had their 5lb 3 oz daughter but both well. I mentioned what we Howses all weighed in the nines and tens. David was worried.

Easter passed by with a crowd of people in for drinks on Sunday. Going to their church services is merely a social jaunt before retiring to the big meal at the Themis. There is a most attractive old stone church (I cannot spell which branch of the numerous religious groups that exist side by side on this continent) opposite the club. It is open on Sundays only and it is most fashionable but no one looks poor or in need of prayer in their finery and cars. Miss Browning used to say that she had never seen a humble person come out of it on a Sunday. She called this week and we had a drink at the New Carlton. She was quite embarrassed as a group of men kept looking at us. She is on her way to work for C.P.R. at Banff. Good job. My position is still uncertain – Cartier are dickering a bit but I will have to know "yes or non" pretty soon. I hope it comes through – jobs are scarce and it is so wonderfully simple to head for the bush with a swag of old clothes. The life is healthy and I arrive back in the city keen and fit.

My cat was killed Friday night crossing Sherbrooke Street. He used to wander off, through my window each night.

I did not make medicine from third year. The only people they took were three honours biochemistry students so I will be back to do my final year of the B.Sc. in Zoology and Chemistry and, of course, apply again. I should make it then – I'll also apply to Vancouver and other places. McGill is difficult to crack – as I have hinted at before. This year has been O.K. and I am reasonably ready for Chemistry and Embryology Lab next week.

A letter from Vod who remains in Calgary. He is well. Jill Horne seems to be lasting some time as Ned's girl friend. Maybe that is why he didn't visit me out here last summer!!

I went up to see the Cuthbertson baby on Sunday. They live just ten minutes away from the Themis. The Air Vice Marshal was there and he had donated the bottle of champagne for the occasion. He is a very nice old chap and has just married Doreen Day, up until recently the chief of Eaton's fashion department and the store's European buyer etc. I was out at their place on Good Friday, a modern bungalow style with the latest in household materials. Carpets were yellow. Poor David had mud on his shoes and almost caused a calamity. I don't understand the reasons for having these light rugs and then expecting everyone to wipe the last spot of dust off their shoes. It is like entering a Hindu temple.

Saw "Paris Holiday" Sunday night with Gail. It was fair but I enjoy Bob Hope and Fernandel was quite amusing, Mrs. McEachern had left the meal in the oven for us – chicken, fresh fruit salad etc.

The club manager is in hospital, recovering from the gall bladder operation. Mrs. Mannock is back in the saddle and the place seems to be running itself. Activities at the university are slowing up – courses are gradually closing and the search for a seat at the library is the same as looking for the golden boomerang. I do most of my work here at the club but at times, the raucous voices and demands are excessive.

What is Tony's new job in Newcastle? Or is he still pleasantly mysterious as always? Pleased to hear that my nephew is getting along fine. How is his poppa? I trust in condition.

## MONTREAL
### (APRIL 22 1958)

Pleased to have your letter today. I am in the middle of the annual fiasco—the final exams. Chemistry and Embryology laboratories last week and at 9 a.m. tomorrow, Logic. I was owed a few hours by one of the Themis girls so am not working tonight. David and Louise have gone to a show and Sarah (Sally) is sleeping peacefully under the careful eye of Uncle John. She is about three and one-half weeks and beginning to look like a human form.

No, I took everything about not being admitted to medicine this year in stride. Really, I did not expect it this year but as the optimist put in the application. Most of the guys I know here were rejected III year and accepted IV, after the degree. I regret it in one way as most of my acquaintances at McGill were IVth year students but with luck I shall be on my way next year. Just remember that getting in is the big thing over here. In Australia, you're in with less trouble. Here once in, you work hard and they get you through. I will also apply to England during the summer. The set-up is good in Montreal, having the Bains etc and my summer job which has now been finalized. I am off almost as soon as the exams finish –decided that I had better take it whilst it was still there instead of going off on my scheduled Mexican venture. Things have not picked up to any great extent yet – I will be working in the same place as the mine foreman. That sounds pretty important but the mine is just a hole in the hill of iron rock. Whatever I am officially, I usually gravitate to the radio-room where chess and coffee with the first aid men (med students) goes on most of the day. They gave me a $50 per month raise but took it back by charging me $1.50 per day board so I am up $5. However I know quite a few Canadian students without jobs – but to many of them it is all just extra spending money.

How is my nephew? Tell Mick and Jeanette I will write in May, also to Ned and Mal. I hope Ned sent the army slouch hat as I have to face that pilot early next month. He is Nick Capron, c/- Northern Wings, Seven Island P.Q., size 7 and 3/8ths. Tell me the cost etc but I would like to know that it was en route as one's "word" should not be broken in the North country. Also as my flying instructor, he warrants some little courtesy.

Have just checked my charge – she is fine and breathing. David failed an accountancy test last term at his McGill night courses. It was a shock after 2nd prize in the province. I told him it was the ability to spring back that counts. Vod says he always took the legal maximum of failures.

### JEANNINE LAKE P.Q.

#### (MAY 11 1958)

Sorry I'm late. Had the busiest time of my life getting rid of the exams, Themis affairs, the packing was chaos. Left everything at the Themis in the baggage room. Psychology did not go well under the circumstances – the rest, I don't know. Anyway next year's another year and with no night job, it will be fine.

Took Gail to lunch at a French restaurant on Monday –they have a special for business people. It was very splendid and we enjoyed ourselves. She had her last exam Tuesday so no great frolic on Monday night. I didn't go to bed – threw everything into boxes and bags, cleaned the room and took a bath around 5.30 a.m. Caught the plane up from Dorval, a Viscount, four turbo prop engines, two blonde pert hostesses and dumb-looking pilots. Spent the night at Seven Islands in a $6 per night hotel, with steak, chef's salad etc in the dining room which has wide windows full of the Atlantic and the Bay of Seven Islands. The sea is fairly subdued in the Gulf area.

Caught an Otter aircraft up Wednesday. They are a single-engine, famous Canadian-designed plane which has done an enormous amount towards opening the North. I think they are used by the United Nations in Egypt and by the Yanks and British in Antarctica.

Attended the weekly staff meeting of section heads on arrival. It was most flattering and surprising. The supervisor stated that he had my record of past services, had wanted a guy who would sack people at will, and had been waiting for three weeks for me to arrive to take over road construction!!! I now have an army of machines and men at work on the frightening task of making a road which is to link the airport to Jeanine Lake. At present I am based at Jeannine Lake with only the camp chief above me. I have lived two summers previously with him so all is fine. At seven, off we go. Seven trucks, a mechanical drag-line shovel, a loader, D-6, D-8 (both Caterpillars), several labourers – the mud and the slush, plus rain and snow make it tough going. The trucks tear the surface to pieces as it is laid down and the rain and ice turn the lousy "gravel" into a great mud pie. I have the Cats working at drains with the trucks dumping load after load on the surface. Two days of rain already has washed part of it away but on we go. Thank God for my French. They are a tough bunch but my leading hand knows his stuff (I hope) so I am lying low for a few days and really being reasonably easy. The job has to be done – I will let you know if I make it O.K.

The slush is 18 inches to two feet deep. It takes 45 minutes to get on the job by the "slush buggy" which jolts its way through anything imaginable. You take a shaking both ways. Have walked miles looking at the job—the lakes are attractive.

More soon. Happy Mother's Day. I'll be thinking of you.

JEANNINE LAKE P.Q.

(MAY 24 1958)

Well, rocking alone in the old rocking chair – thinking of you with all of your brood out of the way at last. When we started to leave, it didn't take long for all five to be on their way. I think the move to Sydney will do Ned good. Must write him that if he is unhappy with the new job, he should change whilst he's at his peak. The ice is beginning to disappear and the lakes are turning blue. I got flaming red in four hours without my shirt and peeled, despite the two feet of snow and ice still in the woods. Spent the day on the road – the muck and slush provide a constant battle. It seems that as soon as you have a piece of sound road made, it begins to crackup under the strain of the trucks and tractors hauling dirt for the next piece. Today's effort was over a swamp – the dirt just keeps sinking and we keep piling it.

Yesterday a few inches of snow fell. This meant no work which sends all the hourly-paid workers into the blues and people like myself have to look sorry. I don't feel too much pain for them. They usually make more than I do each week except when the bad weather cuts into their hours. I spent a pleasant day reading and writing a few letters. The Australian Trade Office is sending me Sydney Heralds – I would enjoy any magazines you could rake up.

News from Montreal has put a premium on building an airstrip big enough to accommodate Douglas C-3's. I have been named foreman of the night shift. It begins at 8 p.m. and lasts until 6 a.m. Have only had one shift – it is a big change and I enjoy the highlights of sunset, stars appearing and the dawn. Otherwise I get fairly tired and bored. Surprised a Cat (tractor) driver asleep at the controls. This is my main job, to keep things rolling. Most of the machine operators know their jobs well but are prone to slack up when under no supervision. I keep moving as I am also prone to curl up. We have the "lunch" around an oil fire at midnight. Plenty of coffee keeps me on the ball until breakfast and then the free day. As soon as we get rolling, it should be fine as I am always the late bird of the camp.

Yes, the Cuthbertsons will miss their babysitter. I had a fair bit of experience with Mal so have no qualms about young children. She bawled the last time I was there but got her back to sleep so soundly that they had to disturb her for feeding, a lousy idea I think but convenient for the parents.

Two English guys over in Jeannine Lake. They are making a roll to take back to a sterling area country to go to university. Also to avoid the U.K. National Service. Very keen on Australia or New Zealand. I visit each week to attend the weekly operations staff meeting. More important – I have a hot shower and a yarn with old Francis Turbis, of Pentecote on the St Lawrence North Shore, my friend of Blough Lake and last year.

I have mentioned the Lodge, the luxurious mansion built to entertain the top brass. The chef had me to lunch one day last week. It is supposed to be out of bounds but I am temporary staff so have not yet the fear which lies in many hearts. Walked the three and one-half miles over there the other day. He put on a splendid afternoon tea. You would certainly enjoy the place but I don't mention going even to Jim, my boss as he is permanent and so law-abiding

LAKE JEANNINE P.Q.

(JUNE 3 1958)

It felt so good to wake up from the slumbers of the night shift worker to a letter from Gail Mc., announcing that I had passed everything. Had second classes in Embryology, Ecology, Philosophy and thirds in Chemistry and Psychology. It really is a relief not to have supplementals. Just as well, too, for the job this summer is quite big compared with anything else I have had to handle. Last night began at 7 p.m. with eight trucks, three tractors, the shovel etc. The big project is to have a DC-3 strip available for June 15$^{th}$. Can you imagine a great mass of jello with two feet of black soil on top? That is what we are working with – the shovel scoops up a cubic yard (that is a mass of earth one yard long, wide and high). It is dumped into the trucks and carted to the other end of the strip where it is flung off and pushed towards the lake by tractors.

Have had some trouble with the people here. Got rid of a tractor operator (who was hired at the request of a friend of the president) and now it looks as though the shovel man will have to go. He is always on the whinge and these French-Canadians are like sheep – one begins and the rest follow. My new boss is a much older man with experience in Peru, the Arctic etc. He has given me all the authority I want so I walk around with a stack of "blue chips" in my pocket in case things go amiss. The all-round experience in the organization of this job is really quite interesting. The boss goes off for a few days and I am left to cope with forty men. The French is most useful – without it I would be in a fix.

A beautiful day – very cold last night and I kept the engine of the power wagon (Dodge) running. I use it every night; the boss has it for the day. It has the heater. My lead hand is an English chap out to make money. He is good company and we play chess on the off-duty hours. Sunday night it rained – I had to knock everyone off. They are paid on the hours they work so again there was a little bit of moaning. I am on a modest salary and usually earn a lot less than the workers.

Have put on most of the stone I lost last winter. Still undecided about the Bains' offer of a free place top stay for my last academic year. It seems peculiar that I am undecided but as you can imagine after the years of independent existence, going into a dependent arrangement will have its difficult moments. It does solve the problem of work and money. I will make a little on the side with odd jobs and naturally I will do all I can for the Bains. The main thing is to get into medicine.

I will not know until March but am going ahead with applications everywhere. It seems incredible that I have got through three years and if things hold, I shall have a degree this year.

I begin work each evening at 7. It is light until 10.30 –the sunsets are delightful, miles of red ribbon. At midnight the meal in the kitchen – enormous sandwiches and hot coffee. Time passes up until 3.30 a.m. There is the usual crop of problems, break downs, loafers, gas, bogged trucks, bad holes in the road. Have the night mechanic to handle minor troubles. The dawn is always happily received as then I can at least see what one is doing, Am short of lights.

LAKE JEANNINE P.Q.

(JUNE 23 1958)

Five in the morn, in the kitchen. Have played chess since 2 a.m. with Clive. We have a fifty cent wager and tonight I am ahead ten games. The night shift was rained out at midnight. Have had the week of fine weather and the airstrip is coming along O.K. Today an aircraft with the Premier of the Province Monsieur Duplessis is supposed to land. I doubt very much if it will make it.

Please excuse my lateness in writing this week. It is difficult to be regular whilst on night work. I seem to spend the day sleeping but wake often with the noise. I quite enjoy the work itself, especially when the weather is fine and it is possible to see a little progress. Have been trying my hand at driving a D-6 Caterpillar -- as I have three tractors on the job each evening, I should learn a little of what they are capable of doing.

The mud is incredible. Tonight I had two mud-pumps installed on the side of the strip. They have chugged away all night but it oozes on. I got stuck and couldn't move my feet, fell over in the slime, much to everyone's delight. Have no lights but it's really only dark from 11.30 p.m. to 4 a.m.

The Boss was in Montreal for four days. Had to cope with everything. There are 50-odd people here. It grows daily. Another Limey arrived to run the radio. He is from Newcastle. I have been there in my vague way.

Fancy old Ned tossing off the school fees for Mal – what has happened to Uncle Bill's legacy? Enjoy the news of our young nephew Christopher. Am writing to his parents this week. I will look forward to any magazines you send. Really, I cannot see any sense in you going off to live in Sydney. It must be lonely in the house with all of us away now but I can't imagine the city would be any better. You have all the friends in the Coota district.

The Boss is quite hopeless. He panics and after a few grogs, gives the blurred, vague orders. I think he is incapable – changes with the weather. Tells me to be tougher with everyone. I respond by firing a driver off the night shift but he goes soft. It is difficult but I am doing O.K. and have the reason for being here.

Saw "The Sun Also Rises," with Ava Gardiner tonight. I read the book when I was in the army and enjoyed the show. Scenes of Paris and Spain are welcome here. An R.C.A.F. officer arrived last week and made us members (the Boss and self) of the Ground Observer Corps. We are supposed to report aircraft flying overhead. Despite all the radar lines, planes can get through. Here's to the H-bomb.

## JEANNINE LAKE P.Q.
### (JUNE 26 1958)

Briefly, just in off the night shift. No lights so could not see what I was doing. Am now off to bed to avoid the boss who is ferocious at this hour. One of the lads is off to Seven Islands. Will get him to slip a Postal Note in with this note. Let's hope that he doesn't slip himself a bottle of whiskey instead. The beard is growing larger. Have not shaved since May 5th but must admit I've been tempted several times. Keep Mal at school. I'm tickled pink to think she is a boarder. How are her marks?

## JEANNINE LAKE P.Q.
### (JULY 1 1958)

Have your letter of June 20th. My worker returned sozzled from Seven Islands but says he posted a registered letter off to you last week. Today was very mild – I suppose it should be as we are into summer. Have had two nights away from work due to a bruised leg. The Boss was sure it was blood poisoning and wanted me to go into Seven Islands to the doctor. I knew the redness was not an infection but almost went anyway, just for the break. However rested it over in Jeannine Lake – all is fine now.

Of course I remember Uncle Rupert and the draughts and the Craven "A" cigarette tins. Only last week a set of games arrived and I was thinking how we used to play on the sitting room floor, Also Chinese checkers—I beat the cook and the Boss last night. Haven't played checkers for years. Now the table tennis has commenced so there will be little peace. The radio officer comes from Sunderland, North England above Newcastle. He's a little fresh off the boat but a few years should mellow him.

The airstrip is progressing very slowly. A few nights back, I had a bulldozer cutting when water began to gush from several holes. We had struck springs. This has rather ruined the schedule. The superintendent is mad on schedules and is always dispatching the great plans, full of dates and "completed" signs. He has not yet learnt the lesson I have taken after three summers up here – you cannot fight the weather and "Don't Panic." These new people come up to big jobs here bent on success and a quick name-making. The airstrip is their big test and I fear it will drag a few down.

The mud is treacherous – the D-8 (weighs 6 tons) was bogged down one evening. I am learning to drive it, also the 3-ton truck which is handy when the Boss has the Dodge. Clive, the English lead hand, sank to his knees and was slowly disappearing. I couldn't pull him out. The mud just sucks you down. Finally I called the enormous Cat over to drag the two of us out. We are trying to push the mud out but the water merely melts more of the frozen grey earth and ooze results.

Have been fortunate re keeping up with the news. Gail's mother is on the editorial staff of the Montreal Star. She apparently knocks off all the English reviews such as The New Statesman, the Economist, Times and Manchester Guardian supplements and sends them up. It's glorious not to have to worry about supplementals, well worth the additional work. I think I will go to Bain's. It will give me a lot more time and it's such a free house. The bus trip will be a pain after the proximity of the Themis but after three years I have had enough of serving drinks. Will still have to work a little somewhere, for a few hours each week but life wouldn't be quite natural without that. Must write to the manager re my decision.

JEANNINE LAKE P.Q.

(JULY 16 1958)

I have been sipping tea in the cook house, trying to begin this letter but the old French cook wants to talk. Every morn I drop in about 4 a.m. for the brew which takes me through to breakfast at six. He has just told me a joke but I didn't quite understand the punch line. The Canadiens have changed the French language as much as the Australians have changed English.

Tonight I had to call the work off at midnight—the rain has poured down and the airstrip, which really had been behaving marvelously, returned to its old mud-patch state. Have been working really hard at it to get the length built up so as the transport planes can land. The job has been given top priority over everything in the area and I remain the night foreman. Am fortunate in having some very capable people on heavy earth moving equipment. It does make the whole show a lot easier and I think, it is generally felt that the night shift acquits itself pretty well. Nearly every night I take a turn at the D-8 tractor. It will be a good trade to learn and this is the time to learn it. Maybe next year I shall return to Australia as a catskinner to work on the Snowy Mountains scheme for the summer.

Your letter from Mosman arrived. Very pleased the ten pounds arrived. The fool registered it. Yes, I receive and greatly enjoy your letters each week and trust that mine are filtering through alright. Heard from Tony last week – I was so surprised but had remembered his birthday.

Poor old Mal. I should write but she is just as tardy as the others. I wouldn't worry about her marks as I guess she is trying very hard and is under some pressure. The first thought I had on seeing nephew Christopher's photo was the likeness to his father in those old snaps in the black box in your clothes press at 67 Adams St.

I agree it must have been fun to be back in Sydney but where would you live if you moved there? I don't mean where you would exist in a room with a gas ring. Stick around Cootamundra for a few years where you have the house, friends, some independence and your relatives. Don't worry about later on – as soon as I have a bit of spare dough I'll set you up (after your world trip and a visit to your son in Canada). Very amused at the Skamp family break-up. It is eight or nine years since I quit boarding at their place in Young – don't really blame her for leaving him.

The mosquitoes and black flies are at their peak. They entangle themselves in the beard, ears and clothing and even here in the kitchen, they are hacking their way through my shirt. Have done an enormous wash tonight. It should rain more often.

A letter from Mrs. Bain. Mr. B. (he is head of boiler division of Dominion Bridge Company which is a big engineering and steel works construction company) has been to a convention at the Thousand Islands Club which is on the N.Y. State border. They went down to Rochester and returned via Niagara Falls and Hamilton Ont. Barbara has bought the Volkswagen which means a lift into McGill each morning and some driving in the city. Murray is married on Aug 23rd and Grandma is fit and has been visiting one of her daughters in Ottawa.

What is holding Uncle Bill's legacy up? Does Caroline get a share? If it comes through, I shall take a holiday in September. If not, then I will remain here until the last day as fees have increased by $150 to $600 per session.

JEANNINE LAKE P.Q.

(JULY 26 1958)

I was pleased to have your letter this week. It was again from Mosman and it was a coincidence my sending the money order and you receiving whilst on holiday in Sydney. Again I notice your enthusiasm for the big city but life in a lousy room or costly apartment isn't the same as two weeks and I am sure that taken all round, you would be best amongst those who like you and who like you. Sorry to hear of your fall – trust you will be a little more wary of the drinks with your youngest son. Am still annoyed that Ned didn't appear Jan 6 1954 at my farewell.

Well, the big news here is that we have had Douglas DC's in on the strip already today and it is only 8 a.m., two have descended. It is most satisfying to see the work we have done this summer—the grey ooze has been turned into a hard brown strip which the pilots claim is very good. The boss is a fool and I feel that a good share of the work has been done in the dark at night. I drive one of the tractors for 30 minutes each evening – am becoming the operator in case I need the trade. They earn much more than I do. It does annoy me at times to be classified as a student and to have to boss this gang of drunks on a low monthly salary. However it must be, and there is the parable of the labourers in the vineyard – "The last shall be first, and the first shall be last."

So Uncle Bill's legacy is delayed because Auntie Peg does not want to sell the M.L.C. shares. As Tony says "I always felt something would happen to block it." How long can she hold things up? At the rate the Australian pound turns into Canadian dollars, my portion will probably be worth three streetcar tickets by the time I receive it. Would you print the name and address of the legal birds who are handling things? They are too vague for my liking as they have never bothered to contact me.

Have not seen much of the summer. Really, am as white as a sheet. The boss is most annoying as he is generally loud-mouthed all day long and his room and office are next to my chamber. As I said previously, he is a fool and has to be tolerated until the end of the summer. Will return in mid-September to the Bains and then take a week off somewhere down south.

Am looking forward to the return to McGill—nearly three months on this patch of work and really it is quite long enough. All last night I had the tractors and trucks carting off muskeg from a new section of the strip which we are excavating. It was a bit of a risk as there was always the chance of the tractor sinking. Built a road right into the centre of it which should stun the Boss when he sees it but it worked out.

Tell Mick and Jeanette to send over more snaps of Christopher. David C. says his child is the most exquisite looking thing he has seen! He did very well again in his annual accountancy exams. Marriage has done him well. How old is Ned? Contemplating?

LAKE JEANNINE P.Q.

(AUG 11 1958)

1.30 a.m. Your letter arrived in five days which considering the possible delays between Cootamundra and here is miraculous. I have put the odd dent in my Dodge and lightly brushed the side of a truck in the darkness. But at the moment I am furious – there is no work due to the rain and instead of the quiet kitchen and the cook doing the juicy steak for me, the place is filled with card- playing truck drivers. I can't very well eat in front of them as the Boss has forbidden forays into the meat house. I will have to wait on and trust to my superior staying powers. Let it be enough to say that there are times when I find these people most trying.

The roads which join Janice and Jeannine Lakes has responded well to the dry month of July and provides a little innocent speeding.

I am looking forward to driving the Bains' Dodge. Barbara has a brand new Volkswagen which should be good practice material as she has to come into the hospital every morning. She works in blood research at the Royal Victoria Hospital which is the teaching hospital for McGill.

What a lot of rot this presentation to royalty is. It is ridiculous the way Australians follow and swallow –imagine the fraud of writing to our esteemed relative-M.P. John Brook Howse. And who is Sir Eric Harrison? – the Trade Commissioner? I note that our new immigration minister from South Australia is howling for more British immigrants – he was obviously not on the S.S. "Otranto" in 1954 to observe the types returning after the 10 pounds sterling free trip out to Sydney.

I am very well. The job is less interesting now that the object of constant air traffic has been achieved. Seven planes brought in five thousand gallons of gas yesterday. The night shift is extending and maintaining the airstrip. We have just a small patch of muskeg to remove but it is proving rather difficult. I station the caterpillar on dry land and tie a wire cable around the blade of the other Cat before sending it into the swamp. The two together push and drag the ooze through to one side where I have the shovel dragging for it like a fisherman casting. The shovel dumps it on the trucks which stagger through more slush before dumping it, several hundred yards away. I have the area illuminated with portable light plants. Such is the foreman's job, a command and all these giant machines spring into action. My own mechanical ignorance is pathetic but I am at least mastering the mighty D-8. I may yet return for a summer's work on the Snowy River scheme.

A movie tonight –something about the blue grass horse racing country in Kentucky. I enjoyed it which means I must be in the bush quite some time. It is over three months now and happily the summer is drawing to a close. I have no complaints; it being necessary but four months is a long time.

Had a very long and intelligent letter from Caroline. When she sits down and takes her time at writing, it is not difficult for me to note the increasing maturity. It will be fun to see you all again.

JEANNINE LAKE

(AUG 22 1958)

The drizzle which is known as Labrador Sunshine has continued for the past five hours. The shift was working on the strip but at midnight I changed them to roadwork. The machinery does less damage out there when the earth is wet although it is difficult beginning to build a road at one o'clock in the morning. When dawn breaks I am usually a little surprised at what the evening work has been –the nights are much longer now, darkness at nine o'clock and the light again about five. Really, the dawn is a beautiful scene – I look forward to it every morning because it provides the only color (other than the green trees). The northern lights hang down low over the strip – sometimes they fill the sky and spread from one horizon to the other. When it is mild, I go for long walks on the road. One night I walked from Jeanine Lake to Lake Jeannine in 2 and one-quarter hours. It is nine miles. On the way out I met two trucks whose drivers had just seen a "grand loup" or the big wolf. I remembered these stories from our school book "Tales of the Northern Lights" and imagined myself up the tree with the wolf pack below.

I crept up on a bear at the garbage dump—poor thing. They shot it an hour later. It was quite large and once it looked directly at me and almost sent me sprinting to the shack.

Mr. Tait who is the superintendent of area 16-D brought back the good news from Montreal that all the board I have paid since May 6$^{th}$ is to be refunded. This means a $50 per month raise which will be useful in view of the rise in McGill fees.

Also my holiday – I am supposed to be going to Dekle Beach down in Florida. Gail Mc. has friends there and they have asked us down. God knows how we'll get there. She is being best girl at a wedding in Montréal on Sept 13 and we have to be back for registration on Sept 23. Florida must be nearly 2,000 miles form Montreal i.e. The top of the state but I think Dekle Beach is up from Miami on the east side. I have "been" on so many trips to Mexico etc that I am somehow skeptical of this one but the sun and beach after this summer spent in the darkness would be enjoyable.

Tell Mal in your next letter to her that I gave a guy $5 to buy a money order, to be placed in an envelope with my letter. The Post Office at Seven Islands think Australia is a communist country or doubt its existence at all. They have sent it to Ottawa. I made no mention of it in my letter to Mal. Have you even cashed the ten pounds I sent you? On both occasions I have had Newfoundlanders do it for me – they don't speak French which adds perhaps to the confusion which is widespread throughout the postal service in Quebec.

More machinery arrives each week. A giant shovel which scoops up a cubic yard of rock crawled in yesterday. Am using it to dig ditches. Practice continues with the D-8. Must send you some photos of the machine age. I swiped a truck with the blade one night. Fortunately I am the foreman!

One of the truck drivers became rebellious last week – he told the General Foreman his troubles and returned saying "the General Foreman told me to do such and such." I said "Good, you're fired." He went to Jeannine Lake and the old general foreman, who is French-Canadian, just looked up at him from his desk and said: ""Your final pay cheque will be ready in the morning."

JEANNINE LAKE

(AUG 30 1958)

My final letter from here, a thought which pleases me, The planes have finally penetrated the fog and rain bringing me with them an overdue letter from you and sister Mal. I wrote her a few days ago—also sent her two pounds but this foolish Post Office (or Bureau de Poste as it is known up here)will undoubtedly delay forwarding it. I was pleased that the ten pounds arrived.

I met two Australian geologists over in Jeannine Lake. They were on a tour of iron ore areas in Canada and were surprised to find another local in town. After four years here, I have to admit that Australians seem pretty English. I felt a bit like the Woolloomooloo Yank in jeans and tartan shirt, white helmet and beard. We had a fine yarn – they thought Australian doctors were "on" themselves too much.

The night shift continues to flourish here although rain has fallen every day this week. No more work on the strip but have been out on the roads each evening. I let Clive the English guy (who we hope will have my job when I depart) build a section of the new road without any interference from the night foreman. I called out around two in the morning and found it had collapsed in the centre with the tractor in the hole. I'm still laughing about it.

The Dodge has been removed to Jeanine and in its place I have a jeep which is quite fun on the slippery roads. Last night the fog was so bad on the hills that I had to remove a tractor as the driver just couldn't see a foot in front of him. It is cold at night now – ice formed for the first time this week and white frost appeared. Sky is clear, the moon bright and white. Listening to the B.B.C. on Clive's short-wave radio. Often we have Radio Moscow and occasionally radio Australia.

Still waiting on that $50 raise. At present there is an agonizing delay – no one seems to have been told about it and my boss was fired last week for drinking. Also my room mate who was hitting himself with neat whiskey all day.

## MONTREAL
### (SEPT 24 1958)

A little late this week. Came down from the bush safely on Sept. 11.Settled in at the Bain's after Gail had helped me move all my junk from the Themis. We set out Saturday night. Mrs. McEachern took us to the airport and then we just settled back to the trip.

Descended at Burlington Vermont and New York City, arrived at Miami at 5.30 a.m. It was sweltering—the tropics indeed. An enormous black thundercloud hung over the airport and the grey suit felt decidedly uncomfortable as we were whisked into Miami Beach where all the tourist hotels line the beach. Our place, known as the "Shorecrest" had the private beach, pool and restaurant with the palm trees and rows of beach beds like toast racks. It was pleasant to surf once more. Luckily the heaviest sea for a few months came up so the surf was similar to Manly on an average day. I was a little disappointed because my light skin after four months of night shift couldn't take much more than an hour of sun.

This is shocking but since Sunday I have not stopped. Now at Gail's home after registering for a new session. It is still summer – the campus looks unreasonably green and cool. All the girls are back in their new fashions and I am striding about quite confidently in my new silver grey trousers .I did go a little bezerk in New York, bought the smart tweed suit, slightly greenish but a respectable mixture of Anglo-American styling. In Miami I got the corduroy green check for $30. Gail is a great shopper and spent hours buzzing around Miami's smart shops. She was in her element on 5th Avenue. I left her and went down town, Wall St., and the very old Bowery section. She kept saying "What will we buy your mother?" I didn't have a clue as to size. Why don't you send me your measurements etc because Gail does have a clothes sense and is the bargain hunter? Her prize this trip was the "Cecil Chapman" dress for $20, down from $80.

On Sat. afternoon we saw "Look Back in Anger" which is by John Osborne, an English writer who allegedly speaks for our beat generation. I don't feel at all beat—it was a very good drama. We had dinner at the "Karachi" restaurant which is Indian and serves good curries. In the evening, saw "The Visit," starring the Lunts (Mr. and Mrs.) or Lyn Fontaine. She is an old girl but everyone seemed affectionate towards them both. I was tired and consequently a little bored with the play.

We stayed at the Gramercy Park on 22$^{nd}$ Street. It is quite convenient and we thought cheap at $4 per room. Our horror when the bill turned up at $9 each per night was considerable.

Sunday it rained all day. Saw a movie, "La Parisienne," with Bridget Bardot. She is , as they say here, "very cute." Sunday night to the Jerome Robbins Ballet, an American group. The dancing involved the old classics in contemporary scores and was so much more enjoyable. I enjoy the yearly "Swan Lake" etc but it is great fun to be in the States and see dance with jazz arrangements. One very amusing act was a skit on a classic corps de ballet. One diminutive hand or dainty foot was always appearing out of line.

On Monday I diddled around shopping, Wall St and junk land as before. In the evening (Gail was exhausted after her 5$^{th}$ Avenue battles) we dined at a charming place, the French Shack – broiled trout in grape sauce, white wine, liquors etc. We had quiet a time and it was such an attractive place, on 55$^{th}$ St around 6$^{th}$ Avenue. At midnight we took the plane from La Guardia airport and were back in Montreal by 2.30 a.m. after a stop in Burlington Vt. The customs selected me out of everyone for a roasting. I did have more than the allowed $100 clothing etc as the wardrobe on my return from the bush was pretty empty. However, I survived, slept at her place and that afternoon resumed back at 4301 Benny. The Bains have been very nice and I am happy there and feel quite at home. Granny is as fit as a fiddle and helped me get myself off to Florida .Am going up to the cottage for the weekend so will write again for I have more to say as soon as the time for reflection comes.

LACHUTE P.Q.

(SEPT 27 1958)

Up at the cottage. Was pleased to have your letter before we departed. Mr. and Mrs. Bain and Barbara are up for the weekend. It is a grey day, rains all de time. The cottage is concealed in a mass of bush. The colors are beautiful – the maple leaf is at its Fall peak, red, brown, purple, fawn, even the mushrooms are bright red and light purple. Trees are maples, birch and a few spruces which is a delightful change after the pines of northern Quebec. The hill, across the lake, is just a wild splash of brightness, dotted by other wooden cottages. The Bains come up each weekend. It is sane living; the city scene of the week's battles is far to the rear. Granny is holding the fort and one of her other daughters is coming up from Ottawa to stay with her. She is really a very nice old woman and we have amusing conversations on odd topics.

We have a portable T.V. set up here with us. At present the Montreal and Hamilton teams are bashing one another to bits. I would like to see a decent Maher Cup match or play some cricket again.

I have spent the week settling back after the holiday. Have had some trouble arranging courses as times are conflicting on the courses I wish to take. I intend continuing with Zoology, in fact two courses – one in Physiology which will deal with the way mechanisms such as breathing, movement, nervous and gland secretions have changed from early animal life up to man; the other is the history of Biology which will begin with the Greeks, before Christ and finish with a study of the present ideas on the evolution of species or the work of Charles Darwin. I don't think I shall do any more Chemistry so my other courses will be in the Faculty of Arts. One I have already chosen is the History of Soviet Russia, rather a vital subject in this Space Age.

I take a lunch with me to McGill each day – one of Barbara's friends drives us in so four blood research girls and the student fill the car. At noon, I go to Gail's home and we have soup and what ever is around. Her brother John is 18 and is in his first year of Arts at McGill. He will probably go into medicine. He has quite a name to live up, to. Gail has gone to Memphremagog to stay with the Bruces for the weekend. She is a good friend of the daughter who I have not met. Mr. Bruce is one of the Canadian heads of the Aluminum Company and they have an attractive house on the lake. Last week I met the chief of the Macleod clan who is a student at McGill. He is John Macleod and a pleasant, rather young Scot with a high-class English accent. My Florida tan is fast disappearing. It was really one of the happiest few days I have spent anywhere.

Caroline should be able to do better in Geography. I can't blame her for the Mathematics marks. Sunday night I went to a cocktail party out at the Air Vice Marshal Ferrier's. David and Louse were there. Poor old David has some trouble with his back – arthritis due mainly, according to the specialist, to bad posture. I am still pretty straight and you might inform my big brother, the waist is 32. May play football this year.

MONTREAL

(OCT 1958)

It is a pleasantly warm day after a week of dull, uninteresting grey. In a few minutes I will have to stir myself sufficiently to rise and walk over to the Arts Building where the old Yugoslav, Professor Mlendovic, will lecture on the history of the Soviet Union. I enjoy being with him in such a small class. It is only this year that I have found myself in classes of ten or twelve people and the change from the mass lectures is most agreeable.

Last weekend was Thanksgiving – I had said that I would remain to keep an eye on Granny who is so fit and well but I know Mrs. Bain worries when she is alone. They have all departed for the country.

Saturday, David Cuthbertson called up and we took Sarah Ann (Sally) for a walk in her pram. She is looking very fine and six-monthish. I would really enjoy seeing nephew Chris at this stage. I imagine he is a second edition of Papa Michael. Louise is beginning an extension course at McGill on Thursday nights, something to do with buying and selecting homes. I am sitting with Sally for 30 minutes as it coincides with David's accountancy lectures. Whilst I was holding her on the street, an old lady appeared and said: "Doesn't she look like Daddy!."

Gail came out for supper. Granny entertained royally. They had met for Thanksgiving Dinner Thursday night when Mrs. Bain put on the enormous turkey dinner. Sat night I left Granny with the T.V. whilst we went to a movie in town. "God's Little Acre," one of Erskine Caldwell's stories of the southern states. It was very amusing. I enjoy these American authors especially now that I have seen a small part of the United States.

Sunday was Gail's 21st birthday. She came out all day, studied a little. I gave her a pair of silver earrings, Granny is in great form as she enjoys having something to do. We watched T.V. at night: the Ed Sullivan Show, the C.B.C. Theatre, a forum on foreign affairs and then the news. Monday, quiet in the morning but in the afternoon a picnic on the mountain with Gail and Murray Code who came out after lunch. He has the beard, Granny was quite impressed but I gladly cut my whiskers off two weeks before coming down. Caroline doesn't like them apparently as she has requested a "university" photo.

Yesterday I went to a lecture on the Soviet Union – a journalist (Ukrainian) who had been over there for two years discussed the 20th Party Congress. By coincidence my term paper has to be on the effects of this congress on Russian policy.

A great storm here in Quebec as the Housewives' Consumer Association starts to war against the 'trading stamps' racket which they say puts the price of food up. We are off Friday night to spend the weekend with the Bruce's on Lake Memphremagog (about 90 miles) amongst the eastern Townships. More from there.

## MONTREAL

## (OCT 27 1958)

I have established myself in the Municipal Library for the afternoon. It is situated in the East, on Sherbrooke St. and adjacent to Fontaine Park. The last three hours I have spent with Locke's "Essay on Human Understanding." I think that I have had sufficient for the day. In fine spirits – the weekend at Lake Memphremagog went off most enjoyably. Motored down the hundred-odd miles Friday night. The Bruce house is most attractive and some evidence of the association with the Aluminium Company. They had the huge fire which reminded me of those daily battles in the kitchen and sitting room at 67 Adams St. Sat around with the shepherd's pie which Mrs. Bruce had given daughter Barbara before leaving. Slept well under the electric blanket. They are really ideal with no weight and warm as toast.

Sunday was sunny and windy. The leaves across the lake – which runs for 30 miles into Vermont State—were colorful in the sunlight and the mountains blue. Such a relief from the city. These hills are the beginning of the Appalachian chain which includes the well-known Green Mountains of Vermont. We walked over to the neighboring houses occupied once by the McEacherns but sold on the Doctor's death. On the other side are the Fergusons – he is the chief editor of the Montreal Star, that afternoon English paper here. Their house is quite luxurious –wood panels, gardens, patio and winterized for use during the snow months. We strolled over some land which the McEacherns still own and then returned to have the enormous steak dinner with peas, salad, apple pie and red wine. I was in my element – the music etc.

Came back Sunday night after I had cooked a barbecue of chops etc. The Bains had been up to the cottage and Aunt Kay had come down from Ottawa. Have spent the week fairly quietly – on Tuesday Gail and I had dinner at Le Caveau (I had brains) and then on to the symphony concert. It was the first night and Montreal madames out in their furs and smart dresses. My seats are in the $3^{rd}$ row of the orchestra stalls so we certainly hear and see quite the works.

Wednesday, the brains put me off in the stomach but I rallied sufficiently to play David at squash—2-2 was the result with both too exhausted to play the deciding game. Thursday, I guarded the baby whilst Louise and D. were at their respective lectures. She is sweet now and has a tooth or two; I eat there when I baby-sit. Friday to the movie society and then to Gail's for dinner. Her mother was in good form and had the inside story on the Social Register which has recently been published in Canada and which is a colossal joke to everybody but the fools who have promised to purchase it at $125, and especially the ones who aren't included. Johnny, the brother arrived in with another of his prep-school friends and they entertained with folk songs and guitar music.

I see a lot of Murray Code, the mill engineer from the bush. He is down working on the design of the big plant but plans to sneak off to Europe very soon. Could you dig up Meg's address in Los Angeles? I may hitch out to the west after the exams – have plenty of addresses of the Bains in Manitoba and more in B.C.

MONTREAL

(NOV 3 1958)

Just four days from your birthday so a happy birthday, Mum, from your third son. I had the examination last Saturday so will miss out by a day or two. Thank you for the cheque from Uncle Bill's legacy. It was the most pleasant surprise imaginable and it will be useful when the reality of the medical years begin presenting themselves. My first year will cost about $1,200 not including board which I don't have to worry about at Bains. The summers shorten to about two months which doesn't permit the roll to be collected in the bush. Fees are up to $750.00.

I have written off the J.P. declaration and now have to see if I can gain permission to have the money sent out to me. The 300 pounds I will try and save – as soon as I get things fixed up, I will send you 10 pounds for your birthday and another ten for any bills which you may have around the house. Am going to get a Xmas parcel off to you and the family this week and hope it gets to you O.K.

Gail and I were at David's last Sat night. Their baby is very sweet, of course most of them are. Sundays we spend the afternoon at the Municipal Library. Last Saturday Mrs. McEachern had me to dinner to meet a Dr. Beelings who was born in Tasmania but had studied medicine at Edinburgh. He later became professor of Physiology at McGill from which position he retired five yeas ago. They spent those years in Europe and last Xmas went off to Tasmania and saw quite a lot of Australia although they spent only two days in Sydney. Molly B. is a very good friend of Mrs. McEachern and is really a charmingly bright person. She thought Mr. Menzies "a delightful person' after meeting him at a party. I said he was a "swine."

The Bains are all hale and hearty—Granny often asks of Nanna and yourself. She and I hold the fort at the weekend. Last night she invited me to the church meeting where they presented the minister with $2,500 after 25 years. I declined. Have not done too much recently.

To the Montreal Symphony for an all-Mozart concert which included a Mass. Drove Barbara around the block in her new car. It is strange after the rattling freedom I had in the bush with the powerful Dodge wagon. Am going to get a Learner's Permit and practise on Mr. Bain's Dodge. The license would be handy. We have the McE. car whenever we really want it. Gail is the good city driver. She drove the rental Chev all day on our trip down to Key West.

Squash with David tonight and baby sitting for them tomorrow. It is the greatest of joys not to have the Themis Club hanging over me.

The week has begin to rush headlong away. Last night I met Patricia Chapman from Cootamundra down at Windsor Station and she gave me the cravate and news of you. The cravate is very smart – I have never worn one except in the bush, for fun one day when I turned up, at a foremen's meeting with one of the radio operator's, around my neck. I enjoyed seeing Patricia – sorry she didn't see the rest of the family including my illustrious nephew but she seemed happy to be back home in Montreal.

I was down at the Australian Trade Office yesterday – the typiste greeted me like a long-lost brother and we conversed in French. The Commissioner (graciously) was able to see me for five minutes and I asked him about getting Uncle Bill's pounds out into Canadian dollars. At the end of the interview he asked me if I was Australian which was slightly annoying. I almost said: "Yes, you rabbit in your G.P.S. old school tie." I now have to write to the Commonwealth Bank for permission and in the meantime would you please discover whether or not I still have a bank account open in Australia. If so, what number and where? Ned might know. I nearly wrote for his birthday but as no one ever replies (excepting you), the incentive is lost. Give him my regards. Tony owes me a letter and I am writing Michael this week.

No news of Vod. Ask Ned to write exactly the position of my two insurance policies – the last I had about them was a mysterious letter from the A.M.P. Society asking me to permit borrowing on the policy by someone . ,I thought they had all lapsed but remember now that Ned was going to sell my golf sticks and thus keep things going. Just between us, if I can cash them, you can have whatever they are worth as I don't intend keeping them on. You deserve a medal for keeping Caroline's going. Just as soon as I can arrange Uncle Bill's legacy I will have the 20 pounds dispatched to you.

At the weekend I took Gail to an Italian movie "The Nights of Cabirea," a most amusing tale of a street-walker in Rome. Johnny, her brother, came too. He is 18 and a nice young fellow. Sunday to the library as usual and then a meal with Mrs. McE. and Gail, a quiet evening with photos and music. I will never forget the way Mick used to bring out the snap shots or how I used to methodically go through his drawer without leaving a trace of disorder.

Friday night I went around to David's and minded the child whilst they went to "The Reluctant Debutante," an amusing comedy from England which you would enjoy. We saw "Oliver Twist" at the McGill Film Society. Gail bought some food (I allowed her $1.35) in the supermart and we cooked it at David's. They are pretty broke but he gets his C.A. completed next September and should be out of the wilds for all time. His father has just taken over the new appointment in New York so that his parents will be living there and traveling all over South America. His mother is extremely nice and I will be meeting the old boy at Xmas.

Tonight we are seeing Ogden Nash at McGill. I have my doubts on his value but I'm off to see it. Friday dinner at the McEacherns and theatre party afterwards; Saturday, the Bain's dinner party for Pa Bain's birthday and Tuesday again at the McE's to meet the wife of one of the Australian delegation to the United Nations. It is fun not having the Themis and I am working like a demon all day in the library. My Physiology report was handed around the laboratory as an example of how to write a report on an experiment. The topic was: "Enzyme Activity (Amylase) in the Style of Mytilus, the Clam"!!!

MONTREAL

(DEC 6 1958)

Have just finished the meal with Gail and Mrs. McEachern and now settled in the living room with the Hi-Fi. It is cold and this morning wind and snow fouled up traffic and put a few day's work into the hands of Montréal's unemployed. I wrote a Philosophy examination this morning and found it difficult to expound in the manner required. Had lunch with Murray Code at his one-room flat in the student quarter which surrounds the University and then spent a few hours reading the English weekly magazines in the periodical section of the library. David phoned Gail with the message that he had gone off to look at a duplex house and that our scheduled game of squash was off. I went up and played with a Pakistani engineer. Also confronted the Jamaican who still owes me $25. He was happily listening to calypso when the debt-collector arrived. No $25 but a promise for next weekend. Thus an active day and now the peaceful evening. Gail is working on a botany exam.

Friday my Hong Kong physiology partner, Julia, and self work with crayfish trying to test the beat of their hearts with different solutions of chemicals. Not much success as the heart was so small and we had to pin it up to a needle to write on a smoked drum. We murdered five craybobs – two Panamanians from South America were equally unsuccessful and destroyed another four animals.

Mum, this cheque I want you to cash and give this enclosed letter to the bank, send me a draft in Canadian dollars registered to 4301-Benny Ave. I guess the approval came from Sydney last week. i.e. 300 pounds to me, 28 pounds to you and a ten pound note in an envelope to me.

The Bains are all well. I have my final exam in the History of Biology in 10 days but have time enough to prepare. Please send some snaps of you, Pop and the family from 1927 onwards.

MONTREAL
(DEC 17 1958)

This morning I wrote my final exam in a half-course on the history of biology. I wrote so much that my finger has a blister. Let us hope it was the right stuff and not just a load of bull as so often these papers are. The lectures are now through until Jan. 6 and the holidays begin tonight. Am taking Gail to a meal, then to T.S. Eliot's "Murder in the Cathedral." John Mailond is the archbishop and has given us two tickets for which he refuses payment.

My fifth Xmas this year. It's bitterly cold outside. George Gillies, my old camp radio operator, is down from Quebec Cartier Mining and is writing off his last minute post cards to the U.K. now. We are in the periodical room where the poor souls who still have examinations tomorrow are studying. I have a lot to do over the Xmas break since my new free status has meant much more social life.

Last Sat. played eleven games of squash with David and then went with Gail to a cocktail party. Had several sherries and talked a lot of rot for two hours in a smoke-filled apartment before we excavated ourselves to see, at the Orpheum, a French-Canadian play "The Time of the Lilacs." It was a simple enough story of an old couple who rent out rooms in the city and I have never seen such convincing and warm acting upon the stage. We were in Row C and both enjoyed it tremendously. Back to her place for a late supper and then out to Benny Ave, late in the sleet and the snow.

Sunday Gail came to supper. I went in and collected her and George Ferguson, editor-in-chief of the Montreal Star, drove us out. We had a big meal and then went off to church with Mrs. B. and Granny. It was full of singing children, a Xmas movie and lots of carolling. Last night, Stan Fisher, crime reporter for the Star, drove me home after seeing me waiting at the bus stop in a snow storm. He quit McGill without finishing and now is in his element. He was on his way to interview one of Canada's ex-most-wanted-men who was recently recaptured down in Halifax.

The cold spell continues with a minor blizzard today and below zero weather most of the week. The shops are ablaze with color and music. Everyone seems to be spending a fortune. I must go down and buy a few local presents. Do hope you received my little parcel and that you are all parading in different shades of lip stick. Gail assisted with the selections on descriptions from me. Must write Nanna before the library closes. A very Merry Xmas to you all and may I be with you one of these years before the grandchildren outnumber the children.

MONTREAL

(NEW YEAR'S DAY 1959)

A fairly mild January, the first here in Quebec with the temperature outside around 15 degrees above and plenty of snow accumulated off the sidewalks. I have really passed a very happy Xmas season. Pleased to have your cards (Mal, thank you for the photos) and I shall be looking forward to getting the Bulletin subscription. No news from you as to whether or not you have received the air mail package dispatched three weeks ago with blouse for you, jewelry bag for Mal and lipsticks for you and Jeanette. I will be annoyed if it has been delayed.

The last 10 days have been most social. Monday week we went to the coffee and liquor business with a friend of Gail's. She is the daughter of Dr. Starkey and both he and his wife were there and invited us to a wine-mull party at their place this afternoon at five. The doctor is a pathologist and bacteriologist at the War Veteran's Hospital and has had a lot of work in the Services and the organization of laboratories at the various veterans' hospitals. This gathering ended around 10.30 p.m. – on to a party given by two English guys from McGill. They had punch and mince pies, a fire, music, the dance (which I refuse to attempt, mainly because I hated having to go through all that stuff whilst the young bank officer in New South Wales).

George Gillis came down from the bush. Had him out to supper. Gail came too and we all went skating over at the local Benny rink. Returned home to hot chocolate and the late movie on TV. Wednesday, Xmas Eve, I went down town early and armed with my two charge cards, completed my Xmas shopping by five that afternoon. Bought Gail a rather nice silver bracelet, Mrs. Bain a silk scarf, the rest of the family books except for Granny who gained a box of specially-scented soap. Our first party was due to begin at 9.30 p.m. I arrived to collect Gail at 10 and found her still in the bath. I am always amused at this but they have the Hi-Fi and the library and neither of us is ever really in a hurry. Well, we finally arrived at 11 p.m. to find the party a complete flop and the host wandering around pretty drunk. Escaped at midnight and raced up to Westmount where we had been invited to the Kilpatricks. They have a beautiful home on the mountain which overlooks the city. Piles to eat and drink – paintings and rich furnishings and many phonies and frauds. An Australian, Tony Suche with his most attractive Canadian wife was there. His people have a place at Burradoo, near Bowral. I suspect he owes his affluence to his wife's people who are in clothing manufacture.

Xmas Day, the tree and opening presents. I received a dressing gown from the Bains. In the early afternoon I called in on the Cuthbertsons. Both his parents had arrived and they were doing the presents with Sarah Ann enclosed within the play pen. I took in a set of tins which fitted into one another and a doll, all made by Mrs. Bain. Called into the Themis Club and then on to the McEacherns where Mrs. had gone down with 'flu and was looking bad. She went off to bed and Gail and Johnny, the brother, carried on with dinner for 13 people. I stayed on for a sherry and looked after the arrivals. Gail gave me a black leather bag (brief case) which should be capable of holding the bulky texts in the future. It is one of the nicest presents I have ever had and most useful as my old bag died two weeks ago. Back to Benny Ave for Xmas dinner. Mrs. B is wonderful and I treat this place as though it was my own which is how they want me to regard it. I injected a bit of our old games tradition into proceedings and started the table tennis in the basement. George Berkeley and his wife and child came over also – he is a Scottish engineer.

After the Big Eat (we began around 6.30 p.m.) I went into collect Gail and we went off to a party given by Dr. Frank Scott and a Mr. and Mrs Parkins. The former is on the Law Faculty and the latter is in the investment branch of Sun Life Assurance. I met the son of the Solicitor-General from Australia –his name is Bailey and a graduate of Melbourne University and Oxford. Mrs. Scott is the painter and the place is filled with abstract art. The idea for food at most of these affairs is the great stack of different cheese with French bread and crackers. (Excuse the fat stains on this writing paper but I was just examining one of Barbara's cod-liver oil capsules and pressed it a little too hard.)

Boxing Day to the Bruce's (I mentioned before that he is president of Aluminum Company) for tea. She is a most attractive woman and a close friend of Mrs. McEachern. Their house is a three-storied affair in Westmount. Stayed on for a meal. Many people are becoming quite familiar as the social round increases. I get quite a kick out of telling David about it as he is quite socially conscious although broke at the moment. I kid him abut being one of the Montreal young set and dig up a few names to drop when I call in on him.

Last night to a party given by Linda McDougall who also had us around to egg-nogs the previous Sunday. It was a relaxed affair with, thank God, no nonsense at midnight, Gail looked her usual stunning self and I wore my light tweed suit. I am still a light drinker.

MONTREAL

(JAN 13 1959)

Your long letter was most welcome. Really pleased that the blouse fitted O.K. I thought the color was right for you and Gail assisted in styles etc. The lipsticks are of course different shades so I had to describe each of your respective colorings. Will take a guess at Ned's Jill. I think she is the same as Jeanette.

I am very well. The final party of the season concluded on New Year's Day. It has been a genuine relief not having to meet people and just getting back into the old routine of library etc.

On Monday night, after spending the day collecting equipment, Gail and I went up to St. Sauveur, in the Laurentians, on the bus. That night it was 35 degrees below and for the two days it blew and kept well below zero so we didn't get a chance to ski. The village is a most attractive little place, a cluster of brightly painted, neat houses, all covered with snow and warm looking. We stayed with a French-Canadian family and spoke French all the time. They had three children and the husband who said there was no work in winter. It didn't keep them from having an enormous TV set which was on all day.—"she never stopped" and Pa calmly sat at the kitchen table reading. On the main street there was "The Inn" and inside the big fireplace, bar and restaurant so we sat around and read, too. The change was pleasant but sorry there was no skiing as there are numerous hills just down from the village. I wore the late Dr. McEachern's skiing outfit, David's boots, Johnny's poles and my skis.

Lectures began Thursday, casually enough and with some complications as my professor of physiological zoology and limnology has decided to test a few of her teachings by having a baby in the next few months. Limnology is the study of fresh water life and is a seminar course which involves the students (only six of us) giving the lecture and doing most of the work ourselves in the library. After four years now of assorted courses, nothing surprises but I shall be contented as soon as I have the McGill medical acceptance. Have an interview early in h.

On Sat., squash with David and then to a meal at the McEachern's, followed by the French-Canadian movie "Tit-Coq" which I found very amusing because I know them fairly well after three summers in the bush. I had a letter from the University of California which may mean a job at the medical centre for the summer. Gail is trying to get into one of the hospital psychology departments.

Sunday, after a day in the library, had Gail to supper and TV which was lousy so we quit early. Barbara has just descended from upstairs and made a bowl of pop-corn. She is an excellent cook.

Your Xmas at "Makela" must have been fun, with young Christopher filling in the gap left by Caroline and Deirdre. I guess old Ned will be next presenting Uncle John with more relations. Sally is looking well and David is as proud as Punch. No news of Vod. It is strange that all I hear about him now is through you but contact will emerge at the ripe moment.

MONTREAL

(JAN 21 1959)

Am sitting in the Zoology library at noon. Light snow falls outside and the streets are a mess of sticky black. This winter has almost set the record for snow. Outside 4301 Benny Ave. there is a mound four feet high which we have shoveled off the path since late November. It is not really cold but blizzardly.

Read of your heat wave and of the sailor being eaten by a shark off H.M.A.S. Cootamundra. On Saturday I was at a reunion of medical students from the three P.Q. universities. Luncheon (avec du vin) followed by a tour of the University of Montreal which is beautifully equipped by the Province and is run by the Church to a great extent. McGill, of course, is privately endowed but needs funds. I told a Californian that sharks never worried surfers in Australia!

Viewed my first corpse – a delightful piece of preserved leather and as remote from life as the preserved cat I studied in past years.

Over then to St. Justin's Children's Hospital where we toured the new buildings, operating rooms, laboratories and wards. Saw some tiny premature babies and some rather pathetic little faces staring out from between cots and glass boxes. It was good to be there – it is rare enough, after the chaos of bush jobs and Themis, to feel at home in a place where you expect to work later on. As you can imagine, the tension at the University is widespread as the final acceptances should emerge around the end of February and from there to the end of June. It is an odd system and I feel they would have a more mature student body if things were started a little earlier so that we could settle down to serious work.

I am sending you and Mal a novel, "Twin Solitudes," by the Canadian author Hugh MacLennan. He is a friend of the McEacherns and much to her amusement has used Gail as a character is his new novel, "The Watch That Ends the Night," due to be published in Feb. "Twin Solitudes" is a fine study of French and English in the province. It should interest you and certainly provide a good look at the background of Montreal society. The top drawer here is the brewers, C.P.R. people and tobacco and sugar merchants. Saw two excellent movies at the Film Society – on the 2$^{nd}$ World War.

I am reading D.H. Lawrence's "Kangaroo" which is quite interesting. I find that five years is a long time to think back about Australia especially as the change has been more than geographical. At times I should like to return and do the tour of the country after you had tired of my stories of Canada. However the prospect of the approaching four years is itself pleasing. And yes, of course, you can tell my old friend Terry Meagher about my feelings re dancing – this is '59, not '29.

P.S. I was thrilled at the way my nephew Christopher is shaping up and have been showing off his photo like the proud uncle. Mr. Bain off tonight for a meeting at Niagara Falls. It is an overnight trip from here.

Your letter packed with the news of Aunt Peg's difficulties about getting back into her Kelsey Cottage at Newport. I have not felt well for this past week and spent Thurs. and Friday in bed. Am up today and feeling much better – the heaviest cold I have ever had! And God knows how long it is since I have spent two days in bed. I couldn't read much so saturated myself with the portable TV set and watched westerns, dramas etc, even the heavyweight fight from Madison Square Gardens.

Taken out to the Kon Tiki Restaurant. It is really unique –you walk in off the blizzard-swept Peel St. and enter a foyer lined with fabric walls and patterns of Polynesia. There are woodcarvings and totem poles. The bar is set in rocks or a cliff face. A waterfall runs down one side and the light reflected to put all the smartly-dressed ladies at their best. Lanterns and motives, a great outrigger canoe hangs from the ceiling off the eating rooms. We ate an enormous quantity of spare sweet ribs, beef cuts and rolled fish balls, before it was announced that these were merely the entrée. The main course was a mass of vegetables, rice, chicken and exotic sauces. Rum drinks were served – the first was "Lana Grog" – almost too much for my weak tolerance and cost to the host of $1.75, or a modest 16 Australian shillings. Gail received her cocktail complete with folding umbrella. During the meal a very smooth almost creamy drink was served in replicas of coconuts. Then ice cream belching blue smoke and a rum sauce of chopped peel completed things. Our hostess was Mrs. Landry, an old friend of the McEachern family.

Saturday we visited the Indian Independence Day celebration – hot curry and evening of "culture" including classical Indian music and dancing. We met a charming couple (in sari) who filled in a lot of background for us both. I find it difficult to understand just what Paddy Meagher is doing out there as a Jesuit.

On Sunday the family skied into the cottage, the woods very beautiful in winter but my cold had begun and I was sneezing, also very cold. My ski harness gave me quite a time, falling off in five feet of soft snow. The ice on the lake is thick and we crossed it without losing anybody.

Wednesday I had an interview with Dr. Alan Ross who is chief pediatrician at the Montreal Children's Hospital. An extremely nice man who was realistic about the difficulties of getting into Medicine but said he would do what he could. He is a good friend of the Mrs. McEachern and has been Gail's doctor all along. She is now his oldest patient.

I was interested to hear of Vod's doings. It does seem ironical to have to rely on Australia for news of Calgary. Very cold here today – two below zero. Mr. and Mrs. Bain have just returned from the supermarket loaded with food for the week's eating. Mrs. McEachern departed yesterday by air for ten days in New York. She has tickets to several plays including "My Fair Lady" and "West Side Story."

## MONTREAL
### (FEB 17 1959)

Came down town tonight to the library in order to work on a paper I am writing on the 20$^{th}$ Congress of the Soviet Union, The library has a digest of the Soviet press in English on their reference shelf. My cold has finally left me after three weeks! Still the sniffle but am feeling my usual self. Vic Murray, the Canadian who came over from England with me, turned up for skiing last weekend. I was too intent on losing the cold to go up to the Laurentians. One of the party/carload had driven up from Toronto broke a shoulder so the engagement for Saturday night was cancelled. I met Vic's fiancé later. She is a librarian and also from Winnipeg. Gail and I went out to a small bistro for the evening. Sunday brunch with the Winnipeg set in Montreal and then to Gail's place. Julia Tsao, who is my partner in Physiology, came over and cooked an enormous Chinese dinner. She and I contributed to the food (I am always having meals at Gail's) and Julia, who is from Hong King, took over the kitchen. We had dried Chinese vegetables, exotic sweet sauces, sweet beef, curried chicken, cabbage, and port – quite different to the standard restaurant offerings.

My social activities have 'quieted' down since the Xmas rush. Montreal is a peculiar city and it is a interesting one socially. At the top is the medical profession – Montreal is a city very proud of her Medicine and with the hospitals, McGill, the Neurological Institute, and the type of men practicing here, Medicine is at a high level. This is a major reason for the difficulty in getting into the faculty. I have mentioned meeting a Dr. Starkey – his daughter Susan, one of Gail's friends, told me yesterday that he would be pleased to write off a letter of reference if I wanted it.

No news on my summer plan. Have had a letter from an aunt of John Pigram, a Mrs. Morille, who says I can stay with them on the West Coast until I get things fixed up. No further news from the San Francisco Medical Center and of course no news from McGill or Vancouver. It is fortunate (perhaps it is unfortunate) that I have nothing else planned. All are well at the Bains with Mr. B., after Vancouver and Toronto, now off to New York. He left at 6.30 a.m. and will be back for supper tonight. NYC is just the hour and a bit by air. Quebec Cartier Mining is going ahead with their railway line. I see the contract for sleepers was given to an American firm. That is one aspect of American business – the Yankee firms get the gravy. There is more wood is Canada than there are sheep in Australia.

I did enjoy my first issue of the Bulletin and am looking forward to the next one. It will be irregular due to surface mail. I see that a Western Australian doctor is coming to do graduate work in anatomy at McGill in September. If I am in, then he will be one of the assistants in the dissecting laboratories.

MONTREAL

(MARCH 15 1959)

Spending a quiet Sunday arranging my scattered affairs for the annual push which is on me for the fourth time i.e. final examinations. Also completing medical application forms so that they will be ready in the event of McGill declining my decision to study here for a further four years. The big news is expected before the end of the month. Frankly I am fed up with all this waiting. A decision either way will at least be definite. I also have been in touch with Sydney University re getting into second year med. Will have more on that when the present fiasco is settled.

Last night we saw Eugene O'Neill's play "Long Day's Journey into Night" down at the Orpheum. It was put on by the Theatre du Nouveau Monde which is mostly French-Canadian. It was very long and the scene involving the son and father dragged on. I had not noticed time when I saw the play in New York last February – the drama was too great but last night's effort, although generally well done, did slow up at points.

Tuesday night to the concert – good programme with the Americans – Fleicher (pianist) and Schippers (conductors). Met Barbara Bruce there and she drove us home. Enjoyed your news and also had a letter from Nanna on Saturday, She seems the same as always and is good to remember me each birthday.

All thought winter had gone but eight inches of snow came down Wednesday – a blizzard just as bad as anything we had seen during January and February. Murray

Bain returned from Emerald, which is near Knob Lake and north-east of Jeannine Lake. He is with Bell Telephone Communications –they install radar units and micro-relay stations across Canada. Everybody else is in fine form including Granny. I get her books from the library. She is a keen fan of Philip Gibbs and Angela Thirkle. The girl at the desk gave me an acid look when I requested the last one. Am working well -- it is glorious being free to remain at the library at night, I usually have my supper when I return at 10.30 p.m. Gail invites me home often but I don't like to make too good a thing of it. Canadians are extremely generous once you know them.

Last Sunday night I went to supper at Patricia Chapman's. They have a most attractive apartment not far from Benny Ave. She is looking well and seems gay and pleased with everything. She gave me a fine photo of you and several others of hometown Cootamundra. I did enjoy hearing all the news as I have only seen her briefly to collect the scarf you sent. I was most amused at many of her tales – it is good to know that High Society still exists in Cootamundra and that our neighbors are remaining respectable. I mean the ones at the back of us. Will let you know immediately I have news.

P.S. Bulletins arrive regularly. Most welcome.


MONTREAL

(MARCH 25 1959)

Spring has arrived. The sun is streaming through the library window. I have just wandered down from my Physiology lab. Rang the house once again but no mail which means most likely that Easter will have to pass without my knowing whether or not I am in or out. Had hoped that this letter was to bear the tidings but just as soon as things are resolved I will let you know. At the moment I am thinking of little else and the exams are looming, beginning April 23. My system now is to remain in the library until ten o'clock each night and then have the big dinner (like Vod at Double Bay). This week I have taken an hour off each evening and played squash for an hour.

Thank you both for the birthday wishes. Twenty five is certainly a fine age to have reached. The decay sets in I expect within the next few years. Gail had me in to dinner on the Big Day. Mrs. McEachern made the big steak dinner and we had wine (German), hot grapefruits etc which made it very pleasant and the first birthday I have celebrated since I was at "67." She gave me two hand-woven ties; out at the Bains, Granny presented me with a box of writing materials and Barbara surprised me with Harvey's book on the Circulation of the Blood.

Apart from that we have done very little recently except a movie, "Streetcar Named Desire," which both enjoyed. David, Louise and Sally came out to tea Sunday afternoon. Sally distinguished herself by walking and charming the Bains. Mrs. Bain put on a royal tea. Really went all out with an enormous array of food etc. I called in on David and family for a cup of tea on my birthday and I think David had made Louise over-do it. The atmosphere was slightly chill, not to me very amusing. The child is a beauty and great fun to observe.

I will now return to the books. Have done nothing about the summer as I am unsure about how long I shall require a job. Am not keen to return to the bush as three years is enough but my practical side is usually strengthened when the dollars get down much closer to the level they are now approaching. Thanks very much for the present –will look forward to buying a book.

MONTREAL

(APRIL 4 1959)

Well, I did NOT make it into McGill. The letter arrived on Monday and Mrs. Bain phoned in the news. I was most disappointed but then with about 120 people to be selected from 1,200-odd applicants, it must be like the Navy Selection Board. You get so far then the slashing begins. I had hoped that with not working this year I would be able to impress them with a fair average in the mid 70's. My average last year was 65. However they have given me the axe without taking my 4$^{th}$ Year efforts into consideration. The library is full of rather dejected looking aspirants. I know only one or two who received acceptances.

My other application to the University of British Columbia in Vancouver B.C. still hangs in the balance. Four weeks back they promised me an answer within two weeks. I would enjoy going out to the coast although the financial situation would be difficult. Have no other plans at the moment, just the wait and see attitude. My head at the moment is full enough of examination material. The finals begin April 23$^{rd}$ and my last is May 5. No plans on the summer – the general idea, if Vancouver falls through, is to make some money and then off to do it in England as I see no point in trying anything else which does not at the moment interest me. Enough of the misery – I am lucky to have got this far and this is about the first disappointment I've had.

Granny is ill again, the same abdominal trouble which will have to be treated in hospital. At 83, and with one major operation plus the heart attack, we are not looking forward to this trip. I enjoy the regular Bulletins – showed Gail the report on Mrs. John Howse in the company of Prime Minister "Pig Iron" Bob Menzies and Governor-General Slim – she said she was most impressed with my social background. Have some photos which I will send off this week. The delay has been caused by the shambles which I have mentioned in paragraph one. I shall be leaving Montreal which at one point in my career I should have been quite excited about.

We saw the Ballets African last Friday, a troupe from the French Equatorial colonies. Very colorful and full of drum music, feathers, wild dances etc. Mrs. McE. and Johnny came too. Yesterday, lunch with John MacLeod. He has a wild time ahead as head of the MacLeod clan. I asked him if they weighed him in kippers on his birthday, like the Aga Khan is weighed in silver. His brother is the same age, 24 and one of Britain's youngest M.P.'s. John is one of the Dramatic Club's stars and says he is to flunk the year – a commerce student with not the slightest interest in banking, buying or business.

Spring beautifully in the air, the ice and drabness of the long winter gone. We eat our lunches on the McEachern terrace in their backyard and feel we have earned the warmth after the cold of Jan, Feb and March. I am working at the Themis tonight – they are having the cocktail party so I shall do my best to help things along with the drink dispensing.

MONTREAL

(APRIL 15 1959)

By this time you will have received Mrs. Bain's letter re my acceptance by U.B.C., the University of British Columbia Medical Faculty. I did mean to wire you; Gail kept telling me to but somehow in the excitement, three days slipped by, so it was hardly worth it. I am really very thrilled. Looking at this year's U.B.C. class list, I notice not one outsider (i.e. from abroad or the other provinces) so I really am fortunate. It is a comparatively new school, with a good standing over here.

The letter from U.B.C. coincided with one from McGill stating that I had been put on a list of deferred, and that a final decision would be made in June. I have not mentioned this to anyone else as it was due to Mrs. McEachern writing the letter to the dean of Medicine. She thought I should have got in here and with my finances being so desperate, sent off the note to the faculty without saying anything. It was really very good of her – there is a lot of "pull" used but I do think my rejection was fair enough and the act that I have made my second preference without assistance does please me. This way I have just myself to feel responsible for and I am looking forward to it all. So many rejections from U.B.C. this year including several guys who were either accepted here or put on the waiting list. You just don't realize the set-up over here. Perhaps in the four years ahead I shall discover the reasons behind a lot of the difficulties in getting into Med. School but here I am, with an acceptance after four years.

My main job now is to maintain my standing and graduate B.Sc. in May. Cartier Mining wrote, offering me a job which is a second astounding piece of news because jobs are scarce and out of the usual 30-40 students, they have taken about 2. I will go up again and work until Aug. 20th. The big move to the Pacific Coast will then follow – I'm so excited

About it all that it is most difficult to concentrate on the job presently in front of me. (I forgot to say in the first paragraph that I have to accept or reject the U.B.C. offer within two weeks. I don't want to sound too moral about the "pull" because it would be even then an outside chance. I am going up to see the Dean here this week to thank him for his consideration.)

The fees will be $450 and living around $500 for the session. Have to get a microscope ($200, instruments and books etc but providing my sum is O.K., I shall be alright. The expenses have never really bothered me because I am doing what I have looked forward to for a long time. Luckily the legacy is almost intact because I won't have time for work and the campus, reputedly the most beautiful in North America, stretching over acres and acres just outside of Vancouver and surrounded by the ocean. I will be a lot closer to Sydney – maybe with luck I shall pop down as sick-bay attendant on the Orient Line. More on Vancouver when I get there.

Have spent a passive week in the library and amongst the books except for the spots described above. We were out to dinner Friday night at a friend of Gail's. She is married to a mathematician who is a most interesting fellow from Belgium. He has worked in the Congo, the Arctic etc and now in the swing of the Montreal young business set. What an amusing group of Limeys, McGill graduates in commerce and arts and Canadians who work on St. James St. and like to think of it as someone in London thinks of "The City." I guess that's what it is though.

I'll get back to work now – my exam is on Thursday. Gail has four within three days but broken up by the weekend.

P.S. I have four years now of medicine. For the benefit of your suspicious friends, Ma, my programme is as follows:

First Year: Anatomy, Bio-Chemistry, Physiology, Clinical Sessions, Parasitology, General pathology, Introductory Pharmacology.

2nd Year: Anatomy, Medicine (Clinical Diagnosis), Microbiology, Intro. Obstetrics, Intro. To Psychiatry, Pharmacology and Toxicology, Public Health, Intro. To Surgery, Research Project.

If I survive all this in two years, then I shall divulge the contents of Years 3 and 4. Note that we have clinical sessions, Pathology, in First Year and have to complete a research project in 2nd Year. We are at the hospital part of the second year.

Add the four years at McGill, I should be qualified!


MONTREAL

(APRIL 27 1959)

I am writing from Gail's place prior to the chicken which sizzles under the oven and which should stifle the pangs. Your letter received yesterday. I hope by this date the disappointment at my not getting in here will have given way to your usual enthusiasm. It is such a business but I shall portray the whole story to you over the next four years. It feels good to know that with the usual energy and some additional luck. I shall be free to move off in four years. So many guys from Montreal were refused at U.B.C. and then given wait-and-see notices from McGill that I feel an enormous weight has been lifted. Yes, I get the B.Sc. providing I pass everything at the current examinations. I am slaving at them for the medical business is dependent on my completion intact of the B.Sc. course.

I guess you are right about the "pull" but then I can't say that it applied in my case although a guy I know with only a "60" average last year was definitely accepted whilst a lot of others have 'wait and see." He's from Westmount, the Potts Point or Adams St. of Montreal.

I am just so thrilled at the prospects of going out to the West Coast. I met an old Rugby Union friend yesterday who said Rugby Union is played a lot in B.C. and that the B.C. team beat the Australians. I may attempt a comeback. The University team plays against the college teams from California, Oregon and Washington. Just as close again to the border which is convenient for a look at the Golden West of the U.S. I must say that I am relieved to be starting there in September rather than remaining in the bush and wasting more time. As it stands, I shall be about 30 when I emerge but in the meantime I will seriously try to get down on a ship. Our summers are long enough. The lack of income would be the deciding factor. As I said before, I might get down as the Orient Line sick-bay attendant. What do people earn in winter in N.S.W.? I should make 46 Pounds per week this summer or $100 which is fair enough.

Played squash yesterday. Our final game after nearly five years of Saturday afternoons. I won 3-1. We were both so exhausted as we were both trying so hard to win the final game. David wants to play again but I said it will have to be unofficial as I want to take the title to Vancouver. The baby, Sally, is a most attractive child.

The Bains are in fine shape except for Granny who has her off days. She is not going to have the operation – for what reason we are not sure but at 83 the doctor probably made a sound decision. The weather is Spring at its best. We have our lunches on the terrace and sit out in the sun. No news yet when I go bush with Quebec Cartier Mining but the details should arrive any day. Will probably go down to Ottawa and get my expired passport attended to, before I go north. It will be a short summer this time, my 4th with Q.C.M. There are now 3,500 up there so it changes (for the worse) each year. George Gillies, the radio operator, is in town but I am too involved with the exams.

SHELTER BAY P.Q.

(MAY 13 1959)

I am beginning my fourth summer with Q.C.M. in the bush. Every August I vow not to return but each May I wake up to see pine trees and the camp. This time will be shorter and spiced with the anticipation of Vancouver and the Golden West. I finished the packing which was a nightmare of books, bush clothes and stuff to go out to the Coast by car. A friend is taking most of the heavy junk and I will take the remnants in mid-August. Gail leaves at the end of June. She is doing a summer course in Chemistry which will allow her to take her Organic Chem. when she returns for her fourth year. This completes her pre-medical requirements. Her subjects have been mainly English and Psychology. Her U.B.C. course ends about the time I get out there which isn't quite the coincidence it appears. I begin on Sept. 8th. I finished the exams on Tuesday and spent the week in relaxing, mainly on the McEachern back terrace where they have the deck chairs etc. Saturday Gail gave a luncheon – John MacLeod, Barbara Bruce and eight others.

I came up Monday on the four-engine Viscount T.C.A. The place in which I have spent the last three days is in a group of administration buildings, a staff lodge and cafeteria which is on the outskirts of the old village of Shelter Bay. The village is a paper manufacturing town – the Quebec North Shore Paper Company has a dock where the timber is loaded for the pulp mills. It is cut in the woods and floated down the rivers and collected in great jams. It is then loaded into an elevated trough which runs over two miles and floats the wood to the bark remover and from here to the dock area where it accumulates in an enormous mountain. It is quite astounding to see the amount of machinery used to transport the wood up to the top of the pile. Water is used on level ground but steel chains with grip-spikes cart it uphill. There are several waterfalls in the area – one is quite spectacular. Adjacent to the staff lodge (where I am sharing a room with an English engineer) is a trailer park where 15 gaily painted caravans form a small community on wheels. It must be a drab sort of existence but looking out my window I see the women gossiping and visiting one another just as they would do in any town. Children abound. Each unit has a large tank of oil for heating and a few silver bottles of gas for cooking. The road to Jeannine Lake begins here – also the railroad which will connect the port (which is being built) to the mine at Jeannine. It is certainly an enormous development and as it grows, the position of the individual diminishes. More on this in a few minutes as I am now going to see the Boss of Personnel – there has been a mix-up re my salary etc.

Just had your letter dated May 6th. Off to have the medical examination and am on the payroll as labourer! You can't trust a soul – the higher they go, the more slinky they get.

MONTREAL

(MAY 20 1959)

TELEGRAM: GRADUATED BACHELOR OF SCIENCE STOP EXCELLENT JOB WITH EXPLORATION TEAM FOR SUMMER. LOVE ALL.

I am behind in my writing due to the fiasco of the past week. I arrived back from Seven Islands on Sat. week last after quitting the labourer's job at $1.20 per hour which had replaced the promised $375 per month. The company has now agreed to pay me the week's salary in addition to my expenses. My return coincided with the holiday weekend but by Monday night I had my sights on a job and at 9.30 a.m. Tuesday morning I was on the payroll of Aurora Explorations Limited which is run by an old Québec Cartier Mining geologist for American interests yet to be named. My work this week has been to price the outfitting of our exploration unit of four men. When the money arrives, we go on the big buying spree and possibly at the end of the week, I shall be off by myself to Roberval on Lac St. Jean to check on the arrival of our purchases.

As soon as supplies are collected and the ice removes itself from the bush country 250 miles to the north, we shall visit the bush and maybe stake out a few claims on the iron ore. I am being paid more than I was scheduled to be from Quebec Cartier as I have no board deduction ($60 per month at QCM).

You should have my telegram re the B.Sc. I did better this year with four second classes and one first in a Zoology course. The latter was my one and only and I was second in the class with around 85 per cent. So the not having to appear at the Themis nightly has made a difference although I've been active on other directions. Gail managed to pass the Maths test. The amazing thing is that I was able to help her with it quite a lot which, if you remember my failures at High School, is surprising. She goes off to the Neurological Institute to be the ward aid and I usually manage to sun myself for two hours on the terrace over lunchtime. The weather is quite hot now but usually muggy and not the Cootamundra heat.

The Bains are all O.K. Mrs. B. is coming in for my graduation and Gail will have the day off. It is a pity that you won't be here because it is quite an attractive scene although much of the romance has worn off for me during the past four years of handing out the gowns and sorting them etc. Johnny is going to take pictures to send back to you. Maybe you and Mal will make it for my Vancouver bow, presumably four years hence. Mrs. McEachern gave me the present of a book of "Contributions to Science by Medical Students," written by a U.B.C. professor of neurology who was a friend of Dr. McEachern. His name is William Gibson.

Gail is spending the six weeks at U.B.C. at another friend's place, Dr. Ward Turvey whose daughter Elizabeth we recently took to dinner and theatre on her way back to B.C. from Europe.

I am off downtown now to go through a few war surplus stores and then out to the office –as it is now 10.15 a.m., I guess I should strike a blow.

MONTREAL

(JUNE 8 1959)

It is a very grey morning and I am awaiting the Nordair flight to Roberval. Do you remember? I began my bush career there three years ago with Q.C.M. The new job is really quite interesting – I have spent the last few days buying all the equipment for the exploration party. It has been an enormous task as I have to get everything from first aid supplies to motorboats. The chief geologist flew up from Cleveland Ohio and I discovered at lunch that I was working for the second largest steel corporation in the world. U.S. Steel, which owns Q.C.M., is of course the largest. The name of this company is Aurora Explorations Ltd, c/o Nordair, Roberval North P.Q. so start addressing my mail as you read it there. I have missed your letters recently but I suspect there has been some confusion over my location. The head of industrial relations immediately offered me a job when I returned to see the heads at Q.C.M. headquarters in Montreal but this job is a great improvement and I am now heading off to organize our base at Roberval.

Have been very busy since my return, socially and at work. Gail co-sponsored a party last Sat night with two others: the latter arrived from New York on Sat with a group of odd souls ranging from an antique dealer to an aircraft engineer. The party was held at the Richardsons – he is the top lawyer for the Aluminium Corp. and the two daughters, Martha (interior decorations) and Grace (Oxford) fling themselves about in the social world. The grounds of the house are most attractive – cool, hedge and walks on the mountain with an almost exciting view of Montreal. God, what a different life the rich lead. The party was a great success. I didn't have a summer suit so just wore the white shirt rather than boil. We had wine, goose liver, meats etc outside. I bought all the food as Gail was working at the Neurological Institute on the bed pans. Eight years ago her father was chief of neurology there. He is well-remembered here.

I have discussed the U.B.C. school of medicine with quite a few doctors and medical students. They all think it is a rising influence and agree that McGill depends mainly on her great past rather than on the last 15 years for her great name. We went to a party after Gail's supper finished at 9 p.m.

On Saturday, Mrs. McEachern gave us the car and we motored down to the States. Had a picnic lunch on the way at Plattsburgh, N.Y. State. I bought a "wash 'n wear" suit. Gail gave me two "smart" ties which go with it perfectly. She bought a blouse, sun suit etc for her mother. We then drove down the side of Lake Champlain through delightful hills and green valleys, mountains, and farms. Right on the lake we came to an old colonial mansion which had been converted into an inn. We stayed there Sat night and had the enormous steak diner. On Sunday morning, we crossed the lake on a ferry and drove on to New England soil in Vermont. Everything green and the houses white – came through customs with Gail wearing all the clothing she had bought for her mother and a dress packed in her bag. Officially you must be out of the country 48 hours but they don't seem to ask many questions. My accent still gives me away.

ROBERVAL P.Q.

(JUNE 16 1959)

It seems an extraordinary long time since I have heard from you. I trust Cartier Mining have been the cause of the delay and disruption of that vital pipeline of news which I look forward to receiving each week. I have not heard anything from you since I sent the telegram to say I had got the B.Sc., passed my finals in much better form than usual, and that I was off on an exploration job. I have been here a week and have finished the major part of the outfitting and supply arrangements. It does take a bit of activity to get six men into the bush. Today I have talked with Cleveland Ohio twice, Montreal three times, and have made a splendid trip down to Port Alfred which is a paper pulp and aluminium port at the junction of the Saguenay and St. Lawrence Rivers. I was driven the 90 miles by the local storekeeper who took me to an enormous delicious steak at the Hotel Champlain at Chicoutami and then on to the port where I had to see the Department of Transport about a license to operate our radio.

We will be working 230 odd miles north in the bush. The two geologists and prospectors, bushman and cook are already in but as I have been left with the logistics, I won't be out of here for a few days. It is far from unpleasant as I have a large room, with carpet, phone, desk, bath and twin beds. I have glasses of fresh orange juice in the morning and plenty of steaks go on the bill. Amidst all the business calls, I occasionally phone Gail who is looking forward to her trip out West. She is due to start the summer course at U.B.C. at the end of this month.

I did see quite a bit of Lake St. Jean today. At Avida is the largest aluminium plant in the world – it spreads over acres of ground and the company has its own town, police force. In fact, everything except a cemetery, according to my host, the Roberval storekeeper. We went up to the powerhouse at Shipshaw and the guides took us around the plant. The whole scheme is beautifully landscaped so that the iron power poles which straddle the countryside are almost in touch with the surroundings. It is really a most interesting project.

No news yet from Mrs. Bain. Granny was dying when I left and told me she wouldn't be around when I returned.

George Gillis returned from U.K. by B.O.A.C. and has now gone off to Vancouver where another old Cartier Mining friend, Clive Tanner, is working. We were all on the harassed night shift last summer at Janice airstrip. I am going to write a note off to Tony for his birthday – the Bulletins arrive regularly and I enjoy them.

P.S. Mum, let me know how you are re debts etc. My position a bit light due to the surge of expenses beginning September. The company behind Aurora is Republic Steel, second only to U.S.Steel – no worries at the end of the month!

ROBERVAL

(JUNE 28 1959)

It is Sunday and I am back once more in that familiar situation – the safari cot nailed to two pine trees, the big sleeping bag (another Woods Arctic ) and the butter box supporting a few books. Have three letters from you so everything can now return to normal. The rain is pelting down but we are all dry inside the 8 feet by 10 feet tents. The camp is well set up. At the moment we have two geologists, two prospectors, the cook, pilot and your son. The supply set-up has turned out fine – even the four chairs which I bought on sale, have been generally approved. The cook tent has a portable 3-burner kerosene stove as well as a wood burning stove and oven. The floor and walls are plywood and the roof of canvas. There is an office tent which contains all the maps and photos, rock specimens, geology reports. The three other tents are for sleeping. I hired the cook in Roberval. He is really good and is clean and cheerful.

Last night I had a choice of pork spare ribs, spaghetti and hot sauce or fried trout or all of them. Not bad but remember the people who refine the ore down in the States are making $3 per hour. The pilot of the Cessna speaks no English so I have to interpret for the Boss who speaks little French. My first day here was spent flying straight lines on a map and taking readings off a magnetometer which is a very sensitive and expensive instrument ($1,000) but is most effective in any iron exploration as the needle performs a song and dance whenever a large iron deposit is passed over. So far we haven't found anything but it is necessary to fly at 500 feet for this thing to be really effective. And due to the wind, this hasn't been possible yet.

Yesterday Albert, the 60-year-old prospector and myself were dropped off on a lake about 20 miles to the north of camp (The camp is only about 80 miles west of Jeanine Lake and 230 odd miles north of Lac St. Jean which is well-marked on any map of the province). We walked all day up fairly steep rocky hills; had to build ourselves a cat-walk tree bridge across a fast-flowing stream and after seven miles, emerged , thanks to Albert's use of the compass, on the lake we had arranged with the pilot to collect us. As it had rained and the bush was wet, I was sopping. Lit a good fire and made ourselves a brew. The weather had looked grim so we were half-expecting to be left out for the night. However it fined up and we were on the plane, heading for the warm kitchen at 5 p.m. Today is too wet to emerge from our canvas cocoons and I hear snores, a sound not often heard in a prospector's camp a 3 o'clock in the afternoon.

I am looking forward to having that photo of you from the Woman's Day magazine. Ensure that somebody sends it to me. I always enjoy the news in your letters – my three brothers and sister are so socially active that I feel quite static. However I am thinking of a few days in San Francisco before Vancouver. That is always one of my problems in the bush: I make plans for a holiday and then go through my expenses for the coming school years and somehow balance it out to include a short break although perhaps financially I overdid it last time on the Florida trip.

It does seem strange Caroline going off to parties at the Manning's. It sure doesn't take too many years for the youngest to catch up to the oldest in a family.

Did I give you the details of graduation? I guess so and will send photos as soon as they come through.

Zoology is the science of animal natural history. It involves the various habitats, the body forms, physiology and how they are classified into groups. The most interesting aspect of Zoology is in the study of change through evolution from very simple animals with one body cell, through the very complicated ones with millions of cells, different tissues and behaviour. I can understand you being puzzled by it – you can imagine what it was like at the beginning in First Year. Mal, why not trot down to the library and look at the Encyclopedia Britannica under Zoology. You will at least learn what your brother has taken four years to find out.

Gail at the moment intends to do Medicine. They live two minutes from the McGill Medical Building and she has the free fees. It will be a pity if they knock her back. Doctor Wilder Penfield, who is a family friend and the top brain surgeon, told Mrs. McEachern that Gail shouldn't apply unless she was at the top of the class. I'm just so relieved that the mad race to get in somewhere is all over and that I can settle into the four years with the knowledge that I'll have to use what I am learning as a definite tool.

Yes, we'll have to get you and Mal out to B.C. for graduation in 1963!!

No news of Vod. I'll take citizenship out in December s there's no point in not being a national of the country you are living in and as a Canadian, we don't have any rot getting into the States or returning to North America. In the long run, it's only paper. I forgot to ask Ned for a photo of Jill, my prospective sister-in-law. I was amused at him noticing the gin in your hand in that racing picture. It seems funny to admit it but the drink I like best is a gin and tonic. You will enjoy "Sporting Tables" – another one to see is "Some Come Running" with Frank Sinatra. Mrs. McEachern is usually critical of our movie selections but apologized after we had dragged her out to see the latter.

I needed a reference for my radio operator's license. Mrs. McEachern wrote it and had Mr. Ferguson, who is editor-in-chief of the "Montreal Star" sign it. It is a most generous document and will be useful for future summer jobs when I have to re-establish myself in the West. Mr. Fitzhugh, my boss here over Dan the geologist, is chief geologist for Republic Steel. He is also giving me some Vancouver contacts. He has returned to Cleveland and is off to Brazil but will be back here for July 20 to decide how much more we will need to be doing. So far the way the rock formations appear, there doesn't seem much iron in "dem dere hills." I cannot describe the flies – there are millions of buzzing, biting blackflies, deer flies and mosquitoes. My arms and face are a mass of nicks where the monsters have had a meal. We have a fine swimming beach on the other side of the Peninsula – water is not too cold but Canadians are soft when it comes to putting themselves out for sport. They are tough enough in the bush – it's just when everything is left up to them alone, they prefer the bed.

I saw "All for Mary" with my girl friend Mary in London. It's about a mix-up in a Swiss chalet over the ex-wife with an old nurse. I am very well. May be off on a "fly-camp" for four days – our mail is weekly at best so don't worry if longer between letters.

BUSH CAMP P.Q.

(JULY 10 1959)

Your long letter with the piece from the Herald on U.B.C. came yesterday. Very much pleased with all the news and trust that you now have me pinned down to the Roberval address although I am far from that pleasant little town. Yes, the Duke and Queen went through Seven Islands, Chicoutami and Port Alfred as well as Montreal. I was a week or so ahead of them for the last three places. The guests at the Royal Ball behaved like the pigs they are –it is very amusing to observe that the social tops of a large city are like a group of cretins whenever a Royal person appears on the scene. I am wholly with the Duke on his touchiness with the press who are like a mob of vultures.

Granny has her bad days and is declining gradually. I cannot quite get over the fact that Ned is getting married—100 guests!!Is the fellow at the Bank of New South Wales Barney Ebsworth? If so, I remember him as an extremely good chap. Give him my regards. I would like to see nephew Christopher – have one fine photo of him at 14 months which I show to everybody. "Il est un beau petit garcon." My French is getting worse but fluently worse and I rattle along, using shocking slang and the local expressions which I pick up easily. The cook, two prospectors and self have some amusing moments. There is a humour which after a few seasons in the bush seems to come very naturally among a group of people used to this type of life.

Albert and Joe have both spent years trapping, hunting and looking for the gold mine. I have been out with them in traverses. We talk all the time. Joe says he never gets as much work done when I am there. We light a big fire at noon and drink masses of tea. Tea is definitely the drink of the north. I can't face coffee and have the brew, no sugar no milk but with a piece of lemon. We make our fires smoky to keep the flies off whilst we eat our ham sandwiches. The flies are bad and thick – they are buzzing and biting all day and the insect repellants are only mildly effective.

Saw an otter in the lake whilst returning in the canoe. The beaver builds a mud house and lives in a hole with his tail resting barely in the water. When the level of the lake sinks, he is off to open up the dam which he and his friends have built across the inlet to the lake. I walked across the top of such a dam built up a foot or two of fallen trees which they slice down with their teeth. The dam's width was a foot and it was some 50 feet across. Also came across a spruce partridge which looks like a hen but can fly reasonably well. Heard some young squeaks and there was the brood – the old lady came towards me, so close we could have knocked her silly with our picks and geological hammers. Then she pretended to run attempting to lead us off from the young, but exposing herself to danger. Most impressive.

The rest of the working hours are spent in the plane, gazing at the map as we dash along at 500 feet elevation. The geologist got airsick yesterday so we don't fly in the wind any more. The radio came in today, $1,500 or so worth, and I am the operator. Have moved into a tent by myself which is excellent as I disturb no one by burning the midnight oil. Dan, one of the geologists called the Big Master in Cleveland last week and we are here at least until the end of July. It seems pretty certain that events will close down as nothing of any interest has been found but as we are here, we will be able to use the next three weeks to look around. I am hoping to remain on the payroll in Roberval and Montreal so that all should be well until mid-August at least.

Gail is tremendously enthusiastic over the West Coast and writes long letters about the University and the gay time she is having out there. She is at Dr.Turvey's, a neurologist friend of the family. They have four attractive daughters!

P.S. This letter goes out on the last plane for ten days.

Very pleased to have your letter this afternoon and to know that all is well. I came down Sunday after an exciting take-off which took us the length of our lake, across a narrow and shallow strait and half way across another, deeper part of the lake. The cursed plane refused to lift until the last moment and both pilot and self were happy to see the trees below us as we turned and slowly rose. The plane was the Husky, a lumbering bush craft put out by a Toronto firm but most reliable. Rest of the trip uneventful with Bert, the pilot, sitting bored and yawning and self gazing out the perspex at what could be my final glimpse of the Quebec woods. The lake was 2,600 feet above sea level and we had a gradual descent to Lac St. Jean which is 300 feet. A perfect flying day and we landed beautifully, skimming over the sun-bathers on the breakwater which protects the seaplane base from the waves, which at times are considerable and make it hard on the floats when a plane hits the wave and crashes on to several more whilst landing.

Installed at the Chateau Roberval in the usual comfort. I cannot rave about the food simply because our cook in the bush was unbeatable. Did I mention that he brought with him 45 small tins of spice – . His last bosses were the Cyrus Eaton exploration and drilling camps, further north of the Ungava Trough. Our camp is at the southern end. Eaton is the son of Cyrus Eaton Senior who was a founder of Republic Steel, the owners of Aurora exploration. They are trying to interest Herr Butcher Krupp in the iron reserves of northern Quebec.

Is it any wonder that we are all cold-footers when it comes to joining up when a Nazi millionaire has his factories restored and is treated like a king, on his visits to Québec and M. Duplessis. The latter is the aging tyrant premier of Quebec who feeds all the state monies into this own election campaigns and who denies dough to the universities such as McGill and L'Universite de Montreal because he prefers to keep the rural population solidly behind him and the only way to have them so, is to hold them off from the High Schools etc.

I am going to try and find a flat for myself when I get to B.C. It will have to be pretty small but I'm determined not to have the matchbox room and cheerless landlady. It is really so long since I have paid board myself that the thought of parting with the monthly rent is staggering but I am hoping to do a small amount of tutoring or work in the library which may bring in a few dollars. At the moment

I feel I cannot come back to this long summer business – the money, of course, is vital but these final four years demand continuity and it will be a lot better for me in the long run to get lab or hospital experience during the holidays. More later when I get the job as assistant to the Head Male nurse on the Orient Line summer cruise to Sydney. That would be fun.

What a difference it makes having the home to go to in Montreal It is the first place I have felt free to come and go as I please since leaving 67. I am actually as lazy about the Bain's house as I was at 67 and happily watch the lawn grow until I am prodded into action. Gail is tremendously enthusiastic about life in the West or as they say, life on the Coast. She has sent me photo-cards of the University which I will send you once I am seated there. Her Chemistry is not going too well – she claims she is terribly confused by it all and just can't follow it. The exam is on Aug 15. It is a complete University course condensed into six weeks i.e. she does as much Chemistry in six weeks as I did in one year at McGill. I plan to arrive there about mid-August but if a good job turns up in Montreal for a month, I shall have to take it. There is a chap leaving in a few days with some of my luggage. If I can reach Montreal before he departs, I shall give him the rest of my junk and then hitch out, using the saved-fare for expenses on route and visiting cousin Vod in Calgary.

The final plane load brings out the cook and Indian Joe, the prospector tomorrow. I have an inventory, storage and insurance plus a few bills to pay and then I will be off to Montreal. Am not due at the office until Monday the 27th so July should be a full month.

P.S. Are you still against the typewritten letter? It must be easier to read.


VANCOUVER BRITISH COLUMBIA

(AUG 6 1959)

Seated at my new home in the U.B.C. library and attempting to collect the numerous impressions of the past week. The trip has been the most wonderful experience. Five of us set out in the 1956 Chev. Two English girls (Sally Horner and Jill Fawcett), both extremely nice and enthusiastic, Gino – the Dutch investment man who was the organizer, and another Englishman, made up the five. The latter was older than the rest of us and was so bloody English at times that he ended up giving us all the horrors. He ate roast beef the entire trip – all we could afford were hamburgers and the specials of the day. Left Friday night with the luggage rack piled high and the trunk packed. Came down through Ottawa and at three in the morning were wandering around Parliament House much to the amusement of the Mounties and the attendants who seemed pleased with the activity, seldom seen on the night shift.

Across the Province of Ontario to North Bay on the Great Lakes. Swam in Lake Huron with waves and tingling fresh water and then crossed into the United States by ferry at Sault St. Marie (pronounced Soo – the origin is French for ":jump," the jump being the rise in the lock which joins up the Great Lakes into the inland transportation system for the grain exports to Europe and the manufactures of the American mid-west.) On across Michigan and Wisconsin, similar country to the rolling hills of Ontario. We slept when we felt like it, either on the move or by pulling up for a few hours. The trip really got exciting when we hit the state of North Dakota. We were driving along calmly when a town appeared from behind a pass. Valley City. Everywhere we stopped in the West, we talked with people. They are so different and friendly. After Bismarck N.D. we hit the Bad Lands of Dakota which must be familiar to you all via the movie westerns. There is a Theodore Roosevelt Memorial Park and here at 3.30 a.m. we watched the sun rise over the eroded hills and canyons. We drove about, climbed up hills for vistas of the gullies – the geology or structure of the rocks is the most interesting side of the area and I almost wished that Dan, my old bush boss, could have appeared to talk on the formations and the history. Much of what we have seen is a little too big for me to describe. We saw deer, prairie dogs, chipmunks, elk, an enormous bear, skunks (they stink when you run over them) and many unidentifiable furred animals.

I began driving in Montana. The whole state is a fabulous mixture of mountains and valleys, of parched hills and on the western side the foothills of the Rockies. We called in at Miles City for a swim and then went into an old swinging-door bar with the long wooden bar, the tables and the cowboys drinking neat whiskey. Again we talked easily – the heat is dry and the wide streets and easy pace of the people reminded me very much of the Riverina district. Bought large straw cowboy hats – the girls thought I fitted into the western pattern very easily. Stopped at Butte, famous for its copper and silver, In Montana and Dakota the silver dollar is currency so that when you pay with a $10 bill, you receive your change in these enormous silver dollars. They are tough on the pockets and you feel pretty wealthy with the weight. Crossed Idaho at night and then into Washington early Tues morning. I drove from Spokane to the Grand Coulee Dam which is enormously impressive, not just the Dam itself but the whole ancient river valley system surrounded by worn, rusty rocks. We had to cross a series of ranges – the Rockies or Continental Divide which separates the drainage systems of North America: on the West side, the Columbia River and on the east, the Missouri.

It was fun creeping over the hills and rolling down incredible views of snow-topped peaks, jagged mountains, salmon streams. We had plenty of stops and swims but finally the Canadian border loomed and we realized that things were coming to an end. It was Wednesday night and when we called Elizabeth and Gail, they had just finished the dinner party to welcome us! We were late and pretty tired but had a fine greeting. The Turveys are quite wealthy and live in a two-storied place with spacious lawns ad gardens He is a neurologist and they have four daughters, Liz works for the C.B.C. and is a graduate of U.B.C. Jocelyn is in nursing and Kim begins her first university year next month. Andrea, who is 14, remains at high school and is full of beans. I have been staying in this house dominated by women but will move out tonight or tomorrow and find a room.

Gail is looking extremely well. She is tanned and very fair. She lives across from the Turveys – her chemistry has turned into a shambles and provided I can concentrate sufficiently, I shall be giving her a hand with it for the exam is on Sept. 13. I don't start for another month so am looking around for part-time work. The location of the university is ideal – it had a government grant of land, an entire point which is surrounded by sea and the mountains in the background. More on the university as soon as I settle down.

P.S. Tonight we dine with an advertising executive and wife from New York.

## VANCOUVER

(AUG 24 1959)

You will think me quite insane when I tell you that tomorrow morning, Gail and I are off to San Francisco. Joan Ross and her brother are driving down in the new Buick to a dance, 100 miles south of S.F. and must be there Sat night. Thus we have three days to do the 1,000 miles which is less hectic than our 3,200 miles in five days, coming across from Montreal.

Great excitement in the house for we decided to go only at dinner this evening. I called Joan as I get on well with her. They live near the Turveys and we all swim in their pool which is set in an enormous garden. Gail has a photo of it which I will send on. Last Sunday we were there and Joan served tea in the silver service with the guests reclining in plush lawn chairs. Everything rather different to the entry into Montreal in December 1954.

Dr. Turvey has given me the letter of introduction to a doctor in S.F. and mentioned that I am "like all medical students, short of folding lettuce." Last Saturday we went around the Vancouver General Hospital – met several doctors and was introduced to the patients and nurses as "Dr. Howse" which made me feel quite important. The General is the largest hospital in Canada and I will be there quite a lot during the next few years. Dr. T. seems to enjoy having a few men around the house, Gino is still here, wooing the eldest daughter Elizabeth. She is a script writer at the C.B.C. and quite attractive. She and Gail are pals. The Vancouver beau, I think, will win the day as soon as Gino returns to Montreal. Jocelyn, 21, has just completed her Registered Nurse course in 4 years and now returns for another year at U.B.C. to get her B.Sc. (Nursing). Kim, 18, is away for the summer at some resort as waitress; Andrea, 14 and a cutie, is busily packing for camp. She sails a 100 miles up the Coast and will be away two weeks. Mrs. Turvey is really a most wonderful person –she and Dr. T. were away in Europe for eight weeks whilst he went to several congresses and medical meetings and she is always happy and talkative, and so thrilled at the way Gail and I decided on the trip that she is providing us with the dough for a night out at a very famous spot – more later when we get there.

Have been to several parties and met many of the Beat Generation for which the West Coast is so famous. I think they are mainly people who find things a little too involved so retire behind a screen of "nothing is any good."— hopeless types and fakes. A night at the Fogel's – he is a big advertising man who plays polo and she is pleasant but suffers from being too far from New York City and she gets a bit monotonous moaning about Vancouver. Both were in the paper last week – he flinging his stick from a horse and she watching the match. Yesterday we were at Uncle Jack's – he is Doctor T's brother and rather a dynamic type of businessman. They have a pool. I did a running spring from their 6-foot board and flopped into the water – no spring in the board much to my horror. Have your letter of Aug. 6.

SAN FRANCISCO

(AUG 26 1959)

I hope that the postcard and letter have brought you as far as Crater Lake, Oregon. It is one of the most beautiful national parks in the States. We motored on Friday afternoon through the high timber country of Oregon, along the inland road which lets down gradually into the sagebrush country of California. Just across the state line we went through a fruit inspection – California protects her enormous citrus industry by banning food imports from other states. Immediately you cross into "Cal" you sense the difference. The roads are better and the traffic races along, well over the 55 m.p.h. speed limit which is ignored by everyone.

Drove into San Francisco Sat morning via the S.F.-Oakland Bay Bridge and the elevated highway which places you in the downtown area quickly and without the fuss of getting lost. Murray and Joan Ross have gone to their dance in Salena and as yet have not shown up. We are at the Hotel Crane, 245 Powell St, across from Union Square Park. It is wonderfully convenient since Union Square is the focal point of the city. On Sunday we went to the Zoo and had supper at a little French restaurant before going to the "Red Garter," a rollicking beer joint, run along the lines of the old-time places with piano, ukuleles, guitars ad everybody singing, eating peanuts and tossing the shells on the floor. On Saturday we ate an Indian curry at an exotic place with rugs, bead curtains, and bearded servants and later took the cable car from Powell where it turns about on a turntable and rattles off for Fisherman's Wharf. The cable cars date from 1873 and help the locals and tourists over the steep hill, upon which the city is built.

Went over and through Nob Hill where the old mining and railroad magnates built their lavish houses. They were destroyed in the fires following the earthquake of 1906 and have been replaced by luxury hotels and apartment houses (expensive). Fisherman's Wharf is the home of the local fishing fleet but has been jazzed up for the tourists with costly restaurants. There are open-air markets where you can buy lobster, crab, prawns and fish. Out by the Zoo is Ocean Beach where the Pacific comes in on the long beach which reminded me very much of Sydney or more, of the south coast at Eden. Something was missing and it was the lack of any swimmers. It is prohibited to surf due to the 'undertow' and as there is no lifesaving outfit, there aren't too many game enough to try it. Many beach fishermen were there with long rods and trailing lines. Monday Gail went off on a shopping spree, using I don't know what for money. The shops are most chic as S.F. is the swishiest city in the States. The women are all so well dressed especially here in the heart of downtown.

Have been to the movies – an excellent Russian film "The House I Live In" and "Triumph of the Will," made by Hitler to help him convince Germany that his ideas were going to create a super nation. The Civic Centre is a group of large municipal buildings including the Memorial to War Dead, Town Hall, Library and Museum. Looked at the Museum of Modern Art – I remain rather unresponsive to most of it. S.F. is very conscious culturally and is the birthplace of what they call the "Beat." We have been to a few places and listed to poetry set to a jazz background and appreciated in a sorry sort of way by the patrons who are mostly young and Bohemian. As everywhere, there is a genuine core but it is obscured.

Great fun at the Curran Theatre where we saw "West Side Story" with the original New York cast. Music by Leonard Bernstein who is famous in the States as a conductor and someone who really pushes music and tries to make it more than a rehash of the European classics to which we have been slaves. The dancing and dances were excellent, the voices and story also.

More from Vancouver. My permanent address will be: 1640 Alma St. Vancouver. Will tell you what it is in my next letter. Have been having a really tremendous time.

VANCOUVER

(SEPT 4 1959)

We have returned to Vancouver and the first wet weather appeared on the Canadian border. I had your letter of Aug. 31 this morning, and I expect to move into Alma St. tonight and collect anything you have sent there. The trip up was immensely enjoyable. Left Monday morning after some last minute shopping by the girls. I have a small present for you both, rather tiny but a reminder of San Francisco. It is such a chic city and I liked it more than any other pace I have been. We drove up via the coast road, coming out of the city on the Golden Gate Bridge and winding our way along the bare, hilly Californian coast with the Pacific, blue and clear, for there was no fog. Took a complete motel unit which was cheap and comfortable for four people. California has areas which are very like Australia especially as they have planted many gum trees (they may even be growing naturally for I doubt if there would be the numbers if all were planted). They are certainly a relief after all the pine trees in the north. On to Oregon and the long, sandy beaches, rocks and windy points. Stayed in a motel right on the sea and explored the caves. My Zoology has opened up my interests quite a bit. Wednesday we looked at the sea lion caves – you walk down 300 feet from the road into an enormous cave where the sea lions live out the winter and stormy periods. They were honking and the bulls roaring. Others were sunning themselves on the ledges outside. The owners have kept everything natural for the sea lions would blow if they started caging etc. The sea washes into the caves and you watch from a gloomy ledge and railing. They smell pretty high but are quite fascinating. Left the coast and through Portland which is an important port. Seattle is apparently more attractive than the brief impression I have had of it. The drive from S. to V. was quite mechanical on the new superway.

The Ross's Vancouver home is big; double storied and just a block from the Turvey's. He is head of the Royal Bank out here and on arrival we all had a drink. It amused me how normal and casual I was with somebody I would have been all out to impress had I remained a bank clerk. It was their 27$^{th}$ wedding anniversary and they had as guest one of the Canada Trust Company men. They went out to dinner and we had the splendid meal served by the Swedish maid in the fine-looking dining room. Mrs. Ross comes from Victoria B.C. and has been to Australia several times but not recently. She remembers Eden in 1929 and I told her it doesn't seemed to have changed much.

Odd that you should mention Charles Howse. When I was down at the General with Doctor Turvey, a doctor asked me if I knew of a Dr. Howse who had died out here. I said I didn't. The Head Nurse told Dr. T. that there just couldn't be two Howses unrelated from Australia. So that, when I read him what you had mentioned, we were all most interested. Dr. T. remembers him now and how he died of tuberculosis of the membranes around the brain inside the skull, whilst interning here. More of this later when I investigate.

One great evening in S.F.: we were dining at Koe's, a place usually frequented by the locals. Next to us were four people who finally invited us to drinks at their apartment because they felt sure that we were foreigners from our haircuts and antics with the knife and fork. Quite a party, two architects, three women and the four of us. One of the girls spoke French; one of the architects was an amateur geologist so there was plenty of common ground. Finished up with the Irish coffee at the Buena Vista which was like an open cocktail party – everyone talking to strangers etc. The barmaid shouted me an extra Irish coffee!

Writing from the Library. Your birthday Mal and have just this morning sent a wire off to Ned and Jill, for the wedding. Medicine began Tuesday with registration and welcoming addresses by the Dean and Assistant Dean. Wednesday we began lectures – a fairly heavy programme with every day except Wednesday packed with laboratories; 8.30 a.m. to 5.30 p.m. Thus this year appears to be no holiday, not that I need one after San Francisco (you don't say "Frisco!") Our trip back was most scenic but have written you all that and go on to describe my room which is quite large and has a sun porch and tiny kitchenette and two clever cupboards in which I can store my junk. Alma St. is not far from U.B.C., only 10 or 15 minutes by bus. Gordon Petersen, a Yale graduate, collects me and brings me back every day so that is one problem out of the way. I can walk to the beach although don't picture up anything like Bondi. There is sand and sea but no real surf as Vancouver lies in a bay, well protected from the open Pacific. The cooking has been O.K. so far but I have an idea I will beefed up with it in eight months, when the session ends.

Gail went back Tuesday morning. She helped me get the place in shape and did the enormous wash and ironing. On Sunday we swam at the Ross's and then Joan, after tea, drove us through Stanley Park and over the bridge to North Vancouver and some of the scenic coastline. Different to Oregon but still attractive and there are many islands just off the coast. We are off to the medical picnic on one of those islands tomorrow. Dr. T. has given me four shirts and seems pleased to have found someone with a size 16 neck. Have to go off to anatomy now. Our introduction to the bodies so will have some lunch before .

## AUTHOR'S NOTE

This letter concludes five years of letters from a young traveler who thought for several years he was en route home to Australia. He is beginning to think of Canada as home. His Great Adventure has taken him around Europe and deep into the Canadian woods on construction jobs. He has learned to love Montreal and gained a degree from McGill University, whilst working nights as a barman-dishwasher at a downtown ladies club. The beginning of the long sought medical studies seems a good place to end this initial salvo of letters. They resume with the Volume of Medical Days and help chronicle the setbacks and changes that were ahead.

# GLOSSARY

**barbie:** not the doll but BBQ

**barrow boys :** mobile fruits stall sellers

**baths:** public swimming pool (Cootamundra's olympic-sized outdoor pool)

**beaut:** tops

**berserk:** crazy

**big spit:** vomit/seasickness

**Big Smoke:** Sydney

**billy:** traditional tin can for boiling tea water

**blew through:** left scene, disappeared quickly

**blood house:** pub/bar with fights, heavy drinking

**bludger:** loafer

**bob:** shilling, small bit of money in old Imperial currency

**bodgie:** young person with a special haircut e.g. Mohawk

**boob:** mistake, error

**bottler:** fine person, fine situation

**brew:** tea

**Bulletin:** National newsmagazine

**bum boats:** small boats selling souvenirs

**burl:** a try

**Caldwell:** Clive Caldwell was a leading Royal Australian Air Force ace during WW II, a family friend.

**chooks:** hens

**cockies:** sheep farmers

**cold-footed:** someone reluctant to join wartime army

**colossal:** great, awesome

**Cootamundra N.S.W.:** hometown of the Howse family

**crook:** ill

**crooked on:** critical of

**dear:** expensive

**Digger:** soldier, veteran or Australian

**DJ's:** department store
(David Jones)

**Domain:** Sydney free speech park

**drones:** idle, bums

**drum:** information

**dunny:** outdoor toilet

**fair dinkum:** for sure, genuine

**Family:** Mum is Mary Howse, Mal or Caroline (sister), Michael, Tony, Denis
(Ned) are the three brothers; nephew Christopher is Michael's son, Jill is
Ned's wife; Vod is Cousin Michael.

**fettling:** railway work

**Fisher Park:** park opposite family home on Adams St., Cootamundra

**flutter:** small bet

**full:** drunk

**galah:** idiot

**gay:** happy

**grid:** bicycle

**Gunga:** good friend, mate, from Gunga Din's loyal character.

**have it on:** fight over

**horrors:** shivers

**jumper:** sweater

**KRT :** Kappa Rho Tau fraternity house , Peel St. Montreal

**Ken Gee:** famous English Rugby League footballer

**Kiwi:** New Zealander, from NZ national bird

**Lord Montague types:** homosexuals, gays

**Luna Park:** iconic Sydney amusement fair

**mad on:** keen on

**mattock:** pick

**mighty:** excellent , awesome

**mis:** miserly, cheap

**Mt. Kosciusko:** peak in N.S.W, ski country

**Murrumbidgee:** River N.S.W. near hometown

**Nineteen O Five:** Calgary home at 1905 10th St S.W. in Calgary

**on:** fight

**on themselves:** overly aware of themsleves

**pal:** friend (from the Romany gypsy)

**Peddah:** native market

**Pelaco:** brand of shirt

**perk:** to vomit

**pictures:** movies

**Polly Perkins:** from a popular song

**pommy:** Englishman

**pound:** currency unit before dollar

**quid:** pound, (see above)

**Riverina:** sheep-raising country area in N.S..W.

**rort:** a con, mere scheme to make money;

**rugby:** Rugby Union was the amateur version of football whereas Rugby League was the professional sport and a more rugged game. Union had more social cachet, was played in the Great Public Schools (GPS) and allegedly was more gentlemanly. We all played Rugby League.

**sheddies:** glasses of sherry

**shout:** pay for round of drinks

**sixes:** in cricket, a six (6) is scored when the batter hits the ball out of the field

**Sixty Seven (67):** Australian home on Adams St., Cootamundra N.S.W.

**skiting:** boasting

**slick:** very pleasant

**smoker:** get together

**snags:** sausages

**spin:** five pounds

**squatter:** farmer, sheep or cattle rancher

**station:** sheep farm

**stonkered:** filled up

**stoushed:** beaten

**'strine:** Australian English

**sweets:** candies

**take a shot:** needle someone

**talent:** attractive girls

**togs:** swimming suits

**Tommie:** British soldier

**toms:** tomatoes

**toss the voice:** vomit

**try:** score (touchdown) in rugby

**tykes:** Catholics

**Wallendbeen:** small village near Cootamundra N.S.W.

**wheels:** those in charge i.e.bosses

**wig-wam:** tepi

**windy:** scared

**Wirrilla:** Uncle Angus's sheep station on Murrumbidgee River,

**WOG:** Worthy Oriental Gentlemanl

**wog:** disease

**Woolloomooloo Yank:** Australian aping American

**Yarmouth Bloaters:** smoked herring

**yarned:** chatted

9 781525 543852